Send Some King's Ships

U.S. Navy, Royal Naval Patrol Service, and Royal Canadian Navy Ships Combating German U-boats off North America's Eastern Seaboard, and RNPS and South African Naval Forces Vessels in African Waters as well, 1942–1945

In January 1942, following the United States' entry into WWII, German U-boats began a reign of terror off America's Eastern Seaboard; over the next several months, sinking hundreds of ships almost at will. With the combatant ships of the then-small U.S. Navy, spread thin in distant theaters, Vice Admiral Andrews desperately sought vessels to protect the coast. Those available consisted of Navy remnants of World War I, private yachts and fishing vessels hastily obtained and armed, and a few small Coast Guard cutters. This force was insufficient to protect major ports, let alone escort merchantmen. Andrews needed help, and got it when Great Britain sent twenty-four King's ships to America to operate under his command. Eventually, with a gradual increase in the numbers of aircraft and ships available to search for and find U-boats, the enemy moved on to South African waters where the hunting was easier. The eighteen remaining King's ships followed, and began anew, to assist a small, unprepared Navy to combat the deadly menace. One hundred, thirty-two photographs, maps and diagrams; appendices; a bibliography; and an index to full names, places, and subjects add value to this work.

Send Some King's Ships

U.S. Navy, Royal Naval Patrol Service, and Royal Canadian Navy Ships Combating German U-boats off North America's Eastern Seaboard, and RNPS and South African Naval Forces Vessels in African Waters as well, 1942–1945

Cdr. David D. Bruhn, USN (Retired)
and
Lt. Cdr. Rob Hoole, RN (Retired)

HERITAGE BOOKS
2022

HERITAGE BOOKS
AN IMPRINT OF HERITAGE BOOKS, INC.

Books, CDs, and more—Worldwide

For our listing of thousands of titles see our website
at
www.HeritageBooks.com

Published 2022 by
HERITAGE BOOKS, INC.
Publishing Division
5810 Ruatan Street
Berwyn Heights, Md. 20740

International Standard Book Number
Paperbound: 978-0-7884-4080-9

Heritage Books by Cdr. David D. Bruhn, USN (Retired)

Battle Stars for the "Cactus Navy":
America's Fishing Vessels and Yachts in World War II

Enemy Waters:
Royal Navy, Royal Canadian Navy, Royal Norwegian Navy,
U.S. Navy, and Other Allied Mine Forces Battling the
Germans and Italians in World War II
Cdr. David D. Bruhn, USN (Retired) and Lt. Cdr. Rob Hoole, RN (Retired)

Eyes of the Fleet:
The U.S. Navy's Seaplane Tenders and Patrol Aircraft in World War II

Gators Offshore and Upriver:
The U.S. Navy's Amphibious Ships and Underwater Demolition Teams,
and Royal Australian Navy Clearance Divers in Vietnam

Guns Up, Depth Charges Readied:
U.S. Navy, Commonwealth, and Other Allied Escort Ships
Shepherding Convoys, and Battling German and Italian Air
and Naval Forces in the Mediterranean in World War II

Guns Up:
Naval Action in the Yellow Sea off Korea, 1950–1953

Home Waters:
Royal Navy, Royal Canadian Navy, and U.S. Navy
Mine Forces Battling U-Boats in World War I
Cdr. David D. Bruhn, USN (Retired) and Lt. Cdr. Rob Hoole, RN (Retired)

Ingram's Fourth Fleet:
U.S. and Royal Navy Operations Against German Runners,
Raiders, and Submarines in the South Atlantic in World War II

MacArthur and Halsey's "Pacific Island Hoppers":
The Forgotten Fleet of World War II

Nightraiders:
U.S. Navy, Royal Navy, Royal Australian Navy, and
Royal Netherlands Navy Mine Forces Battling the
Japanese in the Pacific in World War II
Cdr. David D. Bruhn, USN (Retired) and Lt. Cdr. Rob Hoole, RN (Retired)

On the Gunline:
U.S. Navy and Royal Australian Navy Warships off Vietnam, 1965–1973
Cdr. David D. Bruhn, USN (Retired) and
STGCS Richard S. Mathews, USN (Retired)

Ready to Haul, Ready to Fight:
U.S. Navy, Royal Australian Navy, and
British Merchant Navy Cargo Ships
in the Pacific in World War II

Salvation from the Sky: U.S. Navy, Royal Australian Air Force, and
Royal New Zealand Air Force Heroic Air-Sea Rescue in the Pacific in World War II
Cdr. David D. Bruhn, USN (Retired) and Stephen Ekholm

Send Some King's Ships:
U.S. Navy, Royal Naval Patrol Service, and Royal Canadian Navy Ships Combating German U-boats off North America's Eastern Seaboard, and RNPS and South African Naval Forces Vessels in African Waters as well, 1942–1945
Cdr. David D. Bruhn, USN (Retired) and Lt. Cdr. Rob Hoole, RN (Retired)

Support for the Fleet:
U.S. Navy and Royal Australian Navy Service Force Ships That Served in Vietnam, 1965–1973

We Are Sinking, Send Help!:
The U.S. Navy's Tugs and Salvage Ships in the African, European, and Mediterranean Theaters in World War II

Turn into the Wind:
Volume I: US Navy and Royal Navy Light Fleet Aircraft Carriers in World War II, and Contributions of the British Pacific Fleet

Turn into the Wind:
Volume II: US Navy, Royal Navy, Royal Australian Navy, and Royal Canadian Navy Light Fleet Aircraft Carriers in the Korean War and through End of Service, 1950–1982

Wooden Ships and Iron Men:
The U.S. Navy's Ocean Minesweepers, 1953–1994

Wooden Ships and Iron Men:
The U.S. Navy's Coastal and Motor Minesweepers, 1941–1953

Wooden Ships and Iron Men:
The U.S. Navy's Coastal and Inshore Minesweepers, and the Minecraft that Served in Vietnam, 1953–1976

To the Merchant mariners who plied their trade in dangerous waters, and to Navymen serving aboard escorts, which shepherded merchant vessels and sought to find and destroy marauders beneath the sea.

Contents

Photos and Illustrations

Maps and Diagrams

Foreword

Send Some King's Ships is an interesting and engrossing read. It tells an unusually complete story of how in WWII, far from principal combat theaters, vital shipping lanes through traditionally safe routes close to coasts were attacked by enemy submarines. The expansive coastlines of maritime countries at war, the shipping operating along them, and their relatively unprotected ports, were easy prey for these submarines. They posed immediate and serious threats that were difficult to deal with early in the war. This was particularly true of nations with insufficient anti-submarine forces (like the United States) who found it difficult to combat the well-armed and well-led boats that could attack shipping at times and places of their choosing.

As highlighted in the book's preface, Admiral Karl Doenitz, commander of the German submarines, famously stated that the primary objective regarding the use of his U-boats was to "destroy more enemy tonnage than can be replaced by all Germany's enemies put together." In pursuit of this objective, he sent groups of U-boats, often in sequential waves, to poorly protected waters, offering Allied shipping as easy targets. These were weapons that could hide by day, and surface at night to employ their torpedoes, guns, and sometimes mines to send merchantmen and their vital cargos to the bottom, often in sight of the still well-lighted coastal cities.

In this book, David Bruhn and Rob Hoole take readers to two of the most dangerous areas for shipping during the war. First, the Eastern Seaboard of North America during the first half of 1942. The U.S. Atlantic coastline stretches over 2,000 miles from Maine to Florida. Northward lie Canadian waters. After a disastrous six months during which hundreds of ships were lost—and with them many lives of crewmembers, passengers, and Naval Armed Guardsmen—the United States and Canada, with help from Britain, finally prevailed in limiting losses to U-boats. To be accurate, effective countermeasures induced Doenitz to move-on where the cost/benefit ratio of his valuable assets could achieve better results.

Second, the herculean task shouldered by the small South African naval forces in trying to counter the onslaught of U-boats mirrored the earlier challenges in North American waters, and is recounted and analyzed. A theme that runs through the book, and the basis for its title, is the assistance that the Royal Navy first provided the U.S. Atlantic

Fleet, and subsequently the South African Naval Forces. This assistance took the form of twenty-four trawlers and whalers converted to desperately needed anti-submarine vessels. Taken up by the British Admiralty for war duty as units of the Royal Naval Patrol Service, these modest, coal-burning vessels were fitted with ASDIC (sonar), a single deck gun, smaller anti-aircraft weapons, and depth charges.

Built for service in the North Sea fishing grounds, these ships could hold the sea in dirty weather and, equally important, were crewed by tough ex-fishermen and merchant seamen. They turned the tide. With such meager assets, wars are won.

Most especially, *Send Some King's Ships* hammers home the great devastation wrought by the German submarines off Canada and America during the first half of 1942. There have been many books and articles written about the U-boat onslaught on the Eastern Seaboard, a majority of which have a regional emphasis (New England, Hatteras area of North Carolina, etc.), or have focused on the expansive U.S. Eastern Sea Frontier, without including the other components of the larger Eastern Seaboard: Canadian east coast waters, and the east coast waters of Florida, which were a part of the U.S. Gulf Sea Frontier. Additionally, war diary references to shipping losses generally only concern themselves with the originator's area of responsibility. However, a ship sunk one mile or farther seaward of a Sea Frontier boundary was still sunk, and still a victim of a U-boat. This book endeavors to encompass a fuller picture by chronicling operations in the wider area.

Bruhn and Hoole are to be commended for providing readers a comprehensive description of the uphill battle faced by the naval "home guard" in North American and South African waters in 1942-1943. The men aboard the small vessels and the aircrews of planes patrolling overhead which finally brought the U-boats to heel, have never gotten full recognition for their vital contributions to the war effort. They get that recognition here.

Send Some King's Ships also reminds us of the steadfast leadership of such tireless professionals as Vice Admiral Adolphus Andrews, USN and the role of the ships Britain sent to America to work directly for him. This action, a sort of reverse to the "Lend-Lease" aid then being provided by the United States to Britain, paid great dividends and helped put the Allies on the road to ultimate victory.

Rear Adm. Christopher Weaver, USN (Retired)

Foreword

This book tells the remarkable story of the little known and largely unsung but vital contribution made by the small, converted, anti-submarine trawlers and whalers that operated off the East Coast of the United States and around the Cape of Good Hope to counter Axis submarines during the Second World War.

In South African waters, the Admiralty's war plan, based on experience gained during World War I, was to requisition trawlers and whalers for use as anti-submarine vessels and port minesweepers. These vessels would be principally manned by the South African Division of the Royal Navy Volunteer Reserve (RNVR(SA) which had come into being in 1913 following the unification of the four British colonies in South Africa three years earlier to form the Union of South Africa. While it was constitutionally part of the Union Defence Force (UDF), and funded by the South African Parliament, the part-time Division's peacetime training, organization, administration, and discipline was the responsibility of the British Commander-in-Chief at Simon's Town. And in time of war, the Division would be mobilised and placed at the disposal of the Admiralty which remained responsible for the seaward defence of South Africa and the protection of its trade on the high seas.

With the war still in its infancy, the South African Government under the leadership of General Jan Smuts decided that, for sovereignty reasons, the UDF should be responsible for the seaward defence of South Africa. As a result, Smuts approached Rear Admiral Guy Hallifax, a recently retired Royal Navy officer living in South Africa, to establish and lead the new service, which would be known as the Seaward Defence Force (SDF).

The first task facing Hallifax was to acquire ships and to train men as quickly as possible to meet the new force's commitments. A large measure of assistance was rendered by the Royal Navy during the formation of the SDF, and the force took over the vessels that had already been requisitioned locally by the Admiralty. The Royal Navy also agreed to release some Royal Naval Reserve (RNR) and retired Royal Navy (RN) personnel living in South Africa as well as some members of the RNVR(SA) to serve in the new force.

The SDF was the successor to the small South African Naval Service (SANS) which had come into being in 1922 and all but shut down in 1934 when the last of its three ships, two minesweeping trawlers which had been used to train the RNVR(SA), were returned to the Royal Navy. The service's other ship, which had been returned a year earlier, had been a hydrographic survey vessel. The demise of the tiny SANS was mainly the result of budgetary cuts following the Great Depression. But the situation had not been helped by the lack of interest shown by the army and air force officers making up the senior leadership of the UDF at the time. But, despite this retrograde step, the RNVR(SA) had continued to thrive. This had produced a ready pool of officers and men immediately available for war service in 1939.

With the formation of the wartime SDF, existing members of the RNVR(SA) were given the option of volunteering to transfer to the new force, while men volunteering for wartime naval service in South Africa could either join the SDF, or the RNVR(SA) and serve in the Royal Navy. Later, the much-expanded wartime RNVR(SA) was amalgamated with the rapidly growing SDF, and from 1 August 1942—just before the first U-boat offensive began in South African waters—the amalgamated force became the South African Naval Forces (SANF). From that date, all members of the RNVR(SA) on loan to the SDF became members of the new SANF, while those serving around the globe with the Royal Navy became seconded members of the SANF for the period of hostilities. In addition, many South Africans had long made a career in the Royal Navy or served in the RNR and had reached the highest levels.

South Africans consequently served in just about every type of ship from the greatest battleships to small motor torpedo boats and took part in nearly every major naval operation of the war. Besides serving at home and abroad in SANF ships, they served with the Royal Navy in the Atlantic, including in the King's ships sent to the US eastern seaboard, the Mediterranean, the Pacific and Indian Ocean, as well as in the famous Arctic convoys. They commanded British ships and submarines, took part in the X-craft attack on the German battleship *Tirpitz* and many also served in the Fleet Air Arm. Significant South African losses were sustained when the *Neptune* and *Gloucester* were lost in the Mediterranean and the *Dorsetshire*, *Cornwall* and *Hermes* were sunk by the Japanese in the Indian Ocean.

Meanwhile, under the leadership of Rear Admiral Hallifax, the SDF had quickly assumed responsibility for anti-submarine patrols and minesweeping duties in the approaches to South Africa's major ports and had taken over the port war signal stations and merchant ship examination services at these ports. When it formally came into existence on 15 January 1940, the SDF comprised 15 converted minesweepers, a few shore establishments, and a total personnel strength of 74 officers and 358 ratings. Of these, 36 officers and 182 men were volunteers on loan from the RNVR(SA).

By April 1940 two of the initial fifteen trawlers and whalers had been fitted out with Asdic (sonar) for detecting submarines, and a month later, the new SDF was engaged in the arduous task of clearing mines laid by the German commerce raider *Atlantis* in the main shipping route near Cape Agulhas, at the southernmost extremity of the African continent. Early operations were also undertaken with the Royal Navy in local waters, including the successful high-seas interception of a Vichy French convoy off the South African coast in November 1941.

In mid-1940, two more anti-submarine whalers had been added to the growing SDF and five large Southern-class whale catchers, the best equipped and most modern in the Antarctic whaling fleet had been requisitioned. Four of these were converted to anti-submarine vessels, while one was fitted out as senior officers' ship for the Mine Clearance Flotilla. By December 1940 there were eight anti-submarine vessels and 24 minesweepers in commission. Over the course of the next two years, a further 12 anti-submarine vessels and 13 minesweepers would be brought into service.

The activities of the SDF were not confined to South African waters, and less than a year after its formation, the new Service extended its operations far beyond the borders of South Africa. In response to an urgent request from the Admiralty in November 1940, a flotilla consisting of the four Southern-class anti-submarine vessels, and a flotilla of minesweepers were dispatched to the Eastern Mediterranean to join the hard-pressed British Mediterranean Fleet under Admiral Cunningham.

In local waters, the situation facing British and South African naval forces upon the onslaught of U-boat attacks in October 1942, while like that experienced earlier in the US Eastern Sea Frontier, was even more acute. With patrol duties off Cape Town, nearby Saldanha Bay, and Durban occupying much of the efforts of the fourteen SANF anti-submarine whalers and trawlers, additional vessels were desperately needed to augment these ships and the handful of RN escorts at the Cape to shepherd vessels between South African ports. Fortunately, help began to appear in late 1942, with the arrival of the first four British anti-submarine trawlers at the Cape on 24 December, vanguard of a group of eighteen Royal Navy anti-submarine trawlers and whalers previously employed in American waters. These vessels would remain in South African waters for the remainder of the war.

Although South Africa had no navy of her own at the outbreak of World War II, the establishment of an efficient seagoing force, and the rapid expansion of the SANF during the conflict, was remarkable. South Africa's 'little ships,' which were awarded 129 battle honours, earned an enviable reputation in local waters and overseas, and South African sailors established a proud fighting tradition. At the peak of hostilities in 1944, the South African fleet consisted of 78 vessels, and by the end of the conflict in 1945, the SANF, was operating modern anti-submarine frigates which would form the backbone of the permanent navy established immediately post-war for the protection of the vital Cape route during the ensuing Cold War.

Dr Allan du Toit, AM
Rear Admiral, RAN (Rtd)
University of New South Wales, Canberra
20 September 2021

Foreword

Shortly after the USA entered World War II, Germany launched a devastating U-boat campaign against merchant marine traffic along the eastern seaboard of America. As a result, the Eastern Sea Frontier, the stretch of the Atlantic between Nova Scotia and Florida, had the unhappy distinction of being the most dangerous area for shipping in the world. This frontier was the responsibility of Vice Admiral Adolphus Andrews, USN who in the first months of 1942 had inadequate forces to combat this threat.

In *Send Some King's Ships* David Bruhn and Rob Hoole focus on the assistance provided by the Royal Navy (RN) in deploying to the USA in March 1942, 24 anti-submarine vessels: 22 converted fishing trawlers and 2 whalers from the Royal Navy Patrol Service (RNPS). Manned by RN Reserve officers and sailors, many who had much experience combating U-boats in British waters, these rugged little coal burners provided valuable assistance to Andrews.

The book follows the fortunes and tribulations of these King's ships and their subsequent deployment in October 1942, to counter the U-boat threat off South Africa. By this time six of the 22 trawlers had been lost; three to U-boat actions and three to collisions at sea. The King's ships remained in South Africa until war's end.

Whilst the Royal Australian Navy (RAN) was not involved with the RNPS, it did provide qualified anti-submarine warfare (ASW) personnel to the RN many of whom served in ASW trawlers. The background to this support was an Imperial Conference held in London in 1937 where the various categories of naval training required to provide manpower for the outbreak of a major war were analysed and Australia agreed to provide trained Reserve personnel, both officers and sailors, for anti-submarine operations.

The RAN Reserve Depot at Rushcutters Bay in Sydney's eastern suburbs was selected as the site for a specialised school and the RAN's anti-submarine school, HMAS Rushcutter, was commissioned on 13 February 1939. By the outbreak of war in September 1939, 62 officers had qualified as Anti-submarine Control Officers (A/SCO) and 32 sailors had qualified as Submarine Detectors (SD). The RN was offered a supply of 12 A/SCOs and 12 SD Sailors every two months but responded by asking for as many A/SCOs as possible and for 20 SDs each month. To meet this requirement, there was an immediate increase in the training output to 72 officers and 240 sailors per year. RAN requirements also had to be met but these were relatively small at this stage.

The A/SCO course was a well-rounded training course of five months duration consisting of four modules:

- One month at HMAS Cerberus with instruction in gunnery, torpedo and signals,
- One month sea time in the tender HMAS *Kybra*, studying seamanship, navigation and electrics,
- Two months ASW instruction at Rushcutter,
- One month at sea in the sloop HMAS *Moresby* gaining ASW experience as well as seamanship and navigation, and
- One week at Rushcutter – examination.

The sailor's SD course was five weeks, involving three weeks instruction at Rushcutter and two weeks practical experience at sea.

The first of what was to be a steady stream of officers and men soon set off for the United Kingdom. The 'Phoney War' ended with the German invasion of Norway in April 1940. Eight large trawlers of the grandly named 15th and 16th Anti-Submarine Striking Forces, each with an Australian A/SCO, were soon in action in Norwegian waters, operating close to enemy-held airfields. Given the intensity of the air attacks, it was remarkable that only three of the trawlers were lost. All eight Australians survived, winning between them a Distinguished Service Order (DSO), a Distinguished Service Cross (DSC) and two Mentions in Despatches.

The conquest of France, Belgium and Holland brought Germany to the sea and confrontation with the RN. A second struggle with U-boats began and the transfer to the UK of qualified Australian officers was stepped up. At first, the officers went to trawlers and the new corvettes, while sailors were usually allocated to destroyers. By the end of 1943, some 1,119 RAN officers and sailors were serving in British ships and by the War's end, twenty percent of the specialist ASW officers and sailors in the Battle of the Atlantic had been trained in Rushcutter.

A few of the more experienced officers were given their own commands in ASW trawlers. One of these officers, Lieutenant Commander Arthur Callaway, RANVR, took command of HMS *Lady Shirley*, in March 1941. *Lady Shirley* became the first RN vessel commanded by an Australian to destroy a U-boat. On 4 October 1941, the trawler encountered *U-111* southwest of the Canary Islands and engaged her with depth charges and gunfire. Callaway was awarded the DSO, 'For great daring and skill in a brilliant action against a U-boat.' Two DSCs, six Distinguished Service Medals, a Conspicuous Gallantry Medal and five Mentioned in Despatches were awarded to the members of the crew.

Tragically, Callaway and *Lady Shirley*'s crew of 33 later lost their lives when she was attacked by *U-374* in the Strait of Gibraltar on 11 December 1941. *U-374* was sunk on 12 January 1942 off the coast of Cape Spartivento, Sardinia, by torpedoes from the submarine HMS *Unbeaten*; there was one survivor.

At least another six enemy submarines were sunk by ships commanded by Australian officers. Among them, perhaps the most distinguished graduate of Rushcutter, Lieutenant Commander (later Captain) Stanley Darling, RANR.

Stanley Darling was born in Hobart, Tasmania, on 17 August 1907. He joined the RANR as a Midshipman in July 1925, was promoted Sub Lieutenant in April 1927 and Lieutenant in April 1929. He undertook annual RAN Reserve training periods of 30 days in various ships and was noted as having 'above average ability, initiative and zeal.' He was promoted to Lieutenant Commander in April 1937 and commenced anti-submarine training at Rushcutter in early 1940 and on completion, was loaned to the RN.

On arrival in Britain in October 1940, he was given command of the ASW trawler HMS *Loch Oskaig*. He was also given tactical command of a group of four ASW trawlers operating off the British east coast escorting convoys through the dangerous waters of 'E-Boat Alley.' In December 1941 he commanded another trawler, HMS *Inchmarnock*, doing months of hard sea time from Gibraltar to the Faeroes. In August 1942, Darling went to North America to command the Flower-class corvette HMS *Clarkia*, which was loaned to the USN in early 1942. He saw service as a convoy escort in the Atlantic, West Indies and the run from Britain to Gibraltar. In November 1943, he was appointed command of the first of a new class of frigates, HMS *Loch Killin*. She was fitted with the latest ahead-throwing weapon, Squid, and state-of-the-art electronics, some experimental. All much appreciated by Darling who was an audio engineer by profession.

In June 1944, *Loch Killin* was attached to the Second Escort Group under Captain 'Johnny' Walker, which was guarding the western flank of the Normandy invasion. He was to receive a DSC and two bars for sinking three submarines during his period in command. Darling's first victim was *U-333* which was sunk west of the Scilly Isles on 31 July 1944. A few days later in the Bay of Biscay, on 6 August, *Loch Killin* detected and sunk *U-736*. With the war in Europe drawing to a close, Darling accounted for his third U-boat, *U-1063*, in the English Channel off Start Point Devon, on 15 April 1945. Stanley Darling continued in the RAN Reserve after the War, retiring as a Captain, with an Order of the British Empire (OBE) to add to his three DSCs.

Another RANVR officer who served in the King's ships in both the US Eastern Sea Frontier and South African waters was Lieutenant Commander Stuart Fell. He commanded four ships during his loan service in the RN. Stuart Faithful Fell was born in Ballarat in the Central Highlands of Victoria on 26 February 1916. He enlisted in the RANVR in September 1939 and completed the anti-submarine course at Rushcutter in November 1940 after which, he took passage to the UK.

Fell joined the ASW trawler HMS *Wellard* in Londonderry Northern Ireland on 14 February 1941 as A/SCO and for watchkeeping duties. On 2 May he was promoted to Lieutenant and on 12 August 1942 became the 1st Lieutenant (Executive officer) and A/SCO. During his period in *Wellard*, he served in the Eastern Sea Frontier and in South Africa. He joined the ASW trawler HMS *Northern Dawn* in command on 12 August 1943, again in South Africa. On 30 October 1944, he assumed command of the ASW trawler HMS *Blackfly* which was in Home Waters. In February 1945 he undertook a tank landing ship (LST) familiarization training at HMS St Clement in Essex, England, one of the many Combined Operations Training Establishments. Fell then briefly commanded the escort patrol craft HMS *Kilmore* from 20 March 1945, before taking command of *LST-3014* on 26 July 1945 as an Acting Lieutenant Commander. He returned to Australia in January 1946 and demobilized in May.

Send Some King's Ships describes a brutal episode in the campaign against the German U-boats in World War II. As well as highlighting the very positive contribution of the ASW trawlers lent by the RN to assist the USN, the book provides an excellent insight into the anti-submarine operations in US and subsequently South African waters. It also reminds the reader of the difficulties in engaging a relentless and capable foe and the fact that many casualties occurred.

Commodore Hector Donohue AM RAN (Rtd)

Foreword

David Bruhn and Rob Hoole have in this book produced a compelling and very detailed account of the World War II activities of often unsung, small, naval forces off the East Coast of the United States and off South Africa. Supported by a wealth of facts and quotations, their eloquent descriptions of many anti-submarine warfare (ASW) and mine warfare events in these theatres must be seen as a significant contribution to the body of history which details the defeat of Kriegsmarine U-boat forces.

The actions by packs of German U-boats off the US eastern seaboard and their escapades even further afield off South Africa are two of the lesser reported campaigns within World War II. The concurrent and rather effective German submarine mining of Chesapeake Bay and various ports along the US East Coast is equally under-investigated, despite such mining constituting a direct attack on the US homeland. This excellent book addresses these literary shortfalls through highlighting some of the innovative, resourceful and strategically vital Allied responses to these Axis forays.

Whilst the ships assigned to address these specific Axis threats were, in the most part, from the less-capable end of the warship spectrum, this does not diminish the vital part they played in enabling eventual Allied victory. In particular, the deterrent effect of the presence of such small warships, even if only lightly armed, must not be lost to history and is ably highlighted in this work. Wars are not only won during direct confrontation between high-end warfighting units; the contributions of a wide variety of often smaller and cheaper vessels—such as sonar-fitted armed trawlers, wooden minesweepers, and Q-ships—can aggregate quickly to enable an overall decisive edge.

The contribution of lessons to modern warfare from this period in history remains significant. Attacks on the East Coast by U-boats in the period immediately after US entry into the war saw the defensive forces allocated being those immediately available from within the peacetime US Navy. The requirement for reinforcement by the King's Ships ably highlights that such peacetime navies must be able to sustain a viable defence until wartime shipbuilding programmes can catch up with an emergent threat, holding the line until shipyards eventually build sufficient new assets to allow defence to morph into offence and then into victory. That the enemy gets a vote in such activities is then reiterated in this book by the excellent description of the Axis operational shift away from the US East Coast, once the US Navy had built sufficient organic defensive forces, to new hunting grounds off South Africa where the King's Ships were then redeployed to bolster that navy.

The deployment of Royal Navy ASW assets to aid our Allies, as told in this fact-packed book, has become one of the UK's enduring tasks. Throughout the Cold War the Royal Navy maintained its pre-eminence in Atlantic ASW, and continues to do so today. That this sphere of warfare remains an area of very close cooperation between the Royal Navy and the United States Navy is a subject with which I am especially familiar and particularly proud.

During my early naval career, I was honoured to have Rob Hoole as one of my mentors. In this book he has continued that lasting relationship between us and I feel privileged to have been asked to write this foreword to his latest work. In Chapter 9, Rob, along with David Bruhn, notes that by that point in their book "many readers…will appreciate the great burden shouldered by Eastern Sea Frontier naval forces in the first half of 1942." I will go further, by highlighting that this work will allow a great many people to fully appreciate the unglamorous yet vital contribution of a fleet of oft-forgotten small ships and under-resourced commanders as they defended Allied shipping, eventually going on to defeat fascism. For researching and scripting this excellent addition to the historical record, both authors should be very proud.

I thoroughly recommend this detailed description of the activities of the King's Ships, and those of our Allies, to naval historians, to maritime warriors and also to the many military strategists who occasionally need factual detail and evidence to remind them that the early stages of conflict can be highly burdensome and require contingencies to be developed and resourced long before the formal declaration of hostilities.

Chris O'Flaherty
Captain, Royal Navy

Acknowledgements

Photo Acknowledgements-1

Maritime and aviation artist Richard DeRosset working in his studio on a painting depicting the attacks by North Korean air and sea forces on the USS *Pueblo* (AGER-2) on 23 January 1968.

I am deeply grateful to Richard DeRosset for his masterful painting used as the cover art for this book. The brilliant rendering depicts a little-known event, the sinking of the German submarine *U-215*, on 3 July 1942, by the British anti-submarine vessel HMT *Le Tigre*. Sent from Germany to mine Boston Harbor, the undersea boat had just torpedoed and sunk the American Liberty ship SS *Alexander Macomb* 175 miles east of Cape Cod, Massachusetts, when the small, converted trawler found and dispatched her with depth charges.

In his foreword, Rear Adm. Christopher Weaver offers the outlook of a U.S. Navy flag officer, and of a seagoing officer who spent the bulk of his career with the Atlantic Fleet. As such, he knows the Eastern Seaboard well, along which much of the action in the book took place. He graduated from the U.S. Naval Academy with the Class of 1971, majoring in International Affairs. He served aboard the frigates USS *Marvin Shields*, *Capodanno*, and *Samuel Eliot Morison*, and the tank landing ship USS *Boulder*. He subsequently commanded the oceangoing minesweeper USS *Exultant* and destroyer USS *Spruance*. Tours on the Navy staff in Washington D.C., included head, Surface Combatant Ship Branch of the Surface Warfare Division, and head, Mine Warfare and Explosive Ordnance Disposal Branch of the Expeditionary Warfare Division.

Photo Acknowledgements-2

Rear Adm. Christopher Weaver, USN (Ret.)

Weaver later commanded U.S. Naval Station, Norfolk, Virginia; the Naval District of Washington; and the Navy Installations Command. He holds a Master of Public Administration from The George Washington University and is a distinguished graduate of the Eisenhower School for National Security and Resource Strategy, of the National Defense University.

Rear Adm. Allan du Toit graciously took the South African portion of this book in hand, reworked it, and added much information from his own books and PhD dissertation, and that of other notable South African authors and scholars. This resulted in a very comprehensive account of the efforts of both South African Naval Forces and Royal Navy anti-submarine vessels in combating enemy U-boats in South African waters, and their role in ultimate Allied victory in the war.

Photo Acknowledgements-3

Rear Adm. Allan du Toit, AM RAN (Retired)

Du Toit retired from naval service in 2016 after forty years combined service in two Commonwealth navies (South Africa and Australia). Born and reared in South Africa, he entered the South African Navy in 1975 and joined the Royal Australian Navy in early 1987. As a Warfare Officer at sea, du Toit served in mine counter measures vessels, submarines, frigates, destroyers and amphibious ships, commanding at each rank from Lieutenant to Rear Admiral. Flag officer assignments included two Middle East coalition command appointments. His final appointment was as Australia's Military Representative to NATO in Brussels.

Admiral du Toit authored two books, *Ships of the South African Navy* and *South Africa's Fighting Ships - Past and Present* during his operationally-focused career, and over the years he has also contributed to various other books, journals and naval history conferences. Keenly interested in academics, he was recently a visiting fellow and adjunct lecturer at the University of New South Wales (UNSW) Canberra, while completing all requirements for his doctorate degree, the focus of his research being the defence of the Cape Sea Route during the Cold War.

I am also grateful to South African Evert Kleynhans, who is a Senior Lecturer in the Department of Military History at Stellenbosch University, South Africa. Information found in his PhD dissertation—The Axis and Allied Maritime Operations Around Southern Africa, 1939-1945—was of great value to *Send Some King's Ships*, and he graciously reviewed applicable parts of the manuscript.

Commodore Hector Donohue AM RAN (Rtd.) has generously provided much assistance for previous books and has done so again. In his foreword, he details anti-submarine warfare training provided to officers and men of the Royal Australian Navy in Australia, before many of them set off for Britain to join and serve aboard Royal Navy anti-submarine vessels. This information, and his identification of a few particularly noteworthy events involving heroic actions by members of the RAN, add color and greater breadth to the book.

Photo Acknowledgements-4

Commodore Hector Donohue, AM RAN (Rtd.)

Donohue began his career in the RAN in 1955 as a seaman officer and subsequently sub-specialized as a clearance diver and torpedo and anti-submarine officer. His service in the RAN included command of the destroyer escort HMAS *Yarra* and the guided missile frigate HMAS *Darwin*. Ashore, he held a number of senior positions in Defence policy and force development prior to retirement in mid-1991.

Photo Acknowledgements-5

Capt. Chris O'Flaherty, RN

Captain Chris O'Flaherty offers in his foreword, the perspective of a serving officer of the Royal Navy, who joined the Service in 1987. Deploying for much of his early career in the navy's smallest ships, he served as a diving and underwater bomb disposal officer in three different classes of minehunter and sweeper. After serving in frigates and aircraft carriers in both the North Atlantic and the Middle East, and later commanding the Fleet Diving Squadron, in 2017 he was elected as the Royal Navy's Hudson Fellow at St. Antony's College, University of Oxford. Having completing his fellowship studying 'Naval Mines as an Instrument of Statecraft,' he commanded the Royal Navy's Maritime Warfare Centre before taking up his present assignment researching International Relations at the UK Defence Academy.

George Duddy, a retired Canadian professional engineer, has willingly served as content editor for a number of my books, and has done so again, for which I am very grateful. Duddy's family linage stretches back to the time of British sail, and tragic loss of Midshipman Percival George Duddy of HMS *Maidstone*, who died off the Cape of Good Hope on 26 April 1828, occasioned by a fall from the Mizzen top of the 36-gun frigate. Duddy has a deep interest and expertise in maritime matters associated with western Canada and the arctic, and is currently working on a book about this subject.

Photo Acknowledgements-6

George Duddy in front of an old U.S. Army Miki type tug, 2015.

I am also very appreciative of the assistance coauthor Rob Hoole provided with *Send Some King's Ships.* Rob and I previously coauthored the *Home Waters/Enemy Waters/Nightraiders* trilogy on Allied mine forces. Once again, he has lent his British Royal Navy perspective and expertise to a joint project for which he is uniquely suited, having a foot, so to speak, on each side of "the pond." A British citizen, Rob was raised in the Seattle area of America's Pacific Northwest before returning to England to serve Queen and Country in the Royal Navy. His biography and photograph may be found at the book's end.

Lieutenant Commander Mike Coombes, RN, also contributed to the book, via compilation of an online Navy List archive, a particularly rich resource for those researching the movements of British and other Commonwealth naval officers during the Second World War.

Finally, a tip of the hat to Lynn Marie Tosello. As final editor, her concentrated thought and suggested improvements add eloquence and readability to my manuscripts. Moreover, it is both interesting and a pleasure to work with her.

Preface

To destroy more enemy tonnage than can be replaced by all Germany's enemies put together.

—German Admiral Karl Doenitz's—Befehlshaber der Unterseeboote (commander of the submarines)—primary objective regarding the utilization of his U-boats; from a press interview intercepted and translated by the Allies during the war.[1]

Photo Preface-1

Drawing by Charles Dixon of the sinking of RMS *Lusitania* on 15 May 1915 by a German submarine, from *The London Graphic*, 16 November 1918. The caption asserts, "The greatest sea crime on record: the sinking by a Hun U-boat without warning of the great liner *LUSITANIA*, with the loss of 1400 lives."
Naval History and Heritage Command photograph #NH 892

Following Japan's unprovoked attack on Pearl Harbor on 7 December 1941, the Congress of the United States declared war on Japan at 1610 the following day. On 11 December, Hitler declared war on the United States, Mussolini obediently followed suit and, in response at 1530 that same day, Congress declared war on Germany and Italy.[2]

Attacks by U-boats on U.S. coastal shipping were expected since, in addition to those carried out in the European Theater, Germany had also conducted submarine attacks, off America's Eastern Seaboard in

World War I. The first attack of the second war occurred on 12 January 1942, when *U-123* torpedoed and sank the British freighter SS *Cyclops* in Canadian waters, 300 miles east of Cape Cod. The submarine was under the command of Kptlt. Reinhard Hardegen, who would become one of Germany's top U-boat Aces during the war. He was credited with 21 merchant ships sunk, and another 4 ships damaged, and also sinking the U.S. Navy "Q-ship" USS *Atik* (AK 101) and also damaging the British armed merchant cruiser HMS *Aurania* (F28).[3]

An account of the action with *Atik* (serving as a "wolf in sheep's clothing") may be found in in Chapter 6. Q-ships were rusty, "clapped out," seemingly-defenseless merchant vessels but with concealed weaponry, designed to lure submarines into carrying out surface attacks employing their deck guns. If successful in decoying a U-boat commander to surface (interested in conserving his torpedoes for "bigger game"), a Q-ship could, in theory, rapidly bring her hidden weapons into action, and sink her powerful, but then more vulnerable, adversary.

MOST DANGEROUS WATERS IN THE WORLD

Photo Preface-2

American freighter SS *Carolyn*, circa 1917-1918. During World War II, she became USS *Atik* (AK-101), a Q-ship lost with "all hands" on 27 March 1942, as a result of combat action with the German submarine *U-123*.
U.S. Naval History and Heritage Command Photograph #NH 102438

The use of Q-ships as "staked goats," instead of employing capable warships to hunt enemy submarines, gives hint of the dire straits the U.S. Navy found itself in at war's commencement in lack of adequate warships. The Navy was wholly too small – it had too few ships to fight the two-ocean war in which it found itself. Until America's industrial might, and particularly her shipyards, could begin to meet dramatically increased requirements for ships of all types, at-sea commanders did not have the necessary resources to adequately carry out all their wartime duties and responsibilities.

One of the commands with the greater dearth of naval vessels was the Eastern Sea Frontier which, during the first four months of 1942, had the unhappy distinction of being the most dangerous area for shipping in the whole world. This frontier, formerly named the North Atlantic Naval Coastal Frontier until 6 February 1942, was the responsibility of Vice Adm. Adolphus Andrews, U.S. Navy. He had taken command on 10 March 1941, and would continue until 1 November 1943. In this capacity, he had the daunting task of sweeping free of enemy submarines the entire stretch of the Atlantic between Nova Scotia and Florida.[4]

Photo Preface-3

Vice Adm. Adolphus Andrews, USN.
Naval History and Heritage Command photograph #NH 56042

Admiral Andrews' challenges were particularly dauting, given the U.S. Navy was woefully unprepared for the U-boat blitz on the Atlantic Coast that began in January 1942. He suffered from a lack of air power (a result of pre-war agreements with the Army) and adequate numbers of suitable naval vessels. He had very little to work with initially, only 100 or so aircraft along the entire coast, and an assortment of District craft and some U.S. Coast Guard cutters brought under Navy command. The latter shortfall was largely the Navy's fault, particularly regarding a lack of small warships or patrol craft necessary to carry out anti-submarine patrols and coastal convoy escort duties along America's vast eastern coastline.[5]

Map Preface-1

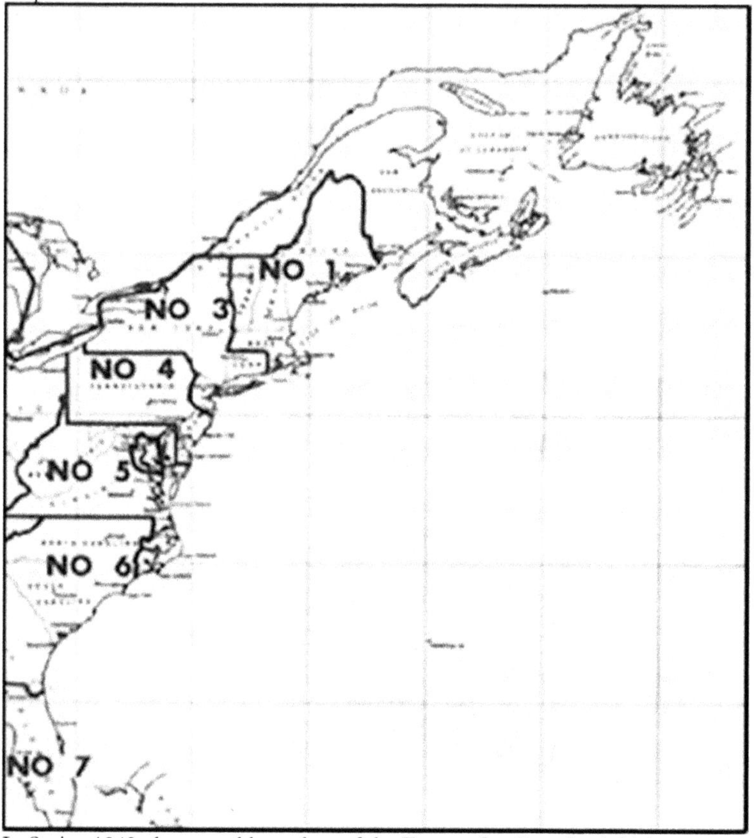

In Spring 1942, the coastal boundary of the Eastern Sea Frontier (which encompassed Naval Districts No. 1, and 3 through 6) stretched from northern-most Maine, which shared a border with Canada, down America's East Coast to the Georgia/Florida border. (For some reason, unknown to the authors, there was no District No. 2)
Julius Augustus Furer, *Administration of the Navy Department in World War II*, 1959

Recognizing this weakness, President Franklin D. Roosevelt, a former Assistant Secretary of the Navy (17 March 1913 to 26 August 1920), had previously intervened. On sundry occasions before the war, he prompted the Bureau of Ships and the General Board of the Navy to adopt a small-craft program; but, later sardonically observed, "The Navy couldn't see any vessel under a thousand tons."[6]

Photo Preface-4

Assistant Secretary of the Navy Franklin D. Roosevelt in WWI (left-center, wearing light coat) in France, viewing a German big gun emplacement near Chateau-Thierry. It was occupied for a few days by a gun intended to fire on Paris, France.
Naval History and Heritage Command photograph #NH 288

Given the lessons taught by World War I, the Navy's failure to immediately implement a convoy system along the U.S. East Coast was criticized. This was no doubt the result of the limited Atlantic Fleet destroyer force which was heavily tasked and generally in very short supply. Most destroyers (DDs) were committed to escorting transatlantic convoys providing troops and critical war materials to the British war effort, and others to escorting U.S. Navy ships operating in the Atlantic to guard against possible offensive operations by the German surface navy.[7]

What the U.S. Navy sorely lacked was a large number of small anti-submarine craft ("sub-chasers") like the hundreds that had been hastily built in World War I, then discarded or sold-off. Andrews had an insufficient number of these types of escorts to form and escort convoys; the few vessels that he did have were carrying out anti-submarine patrols off major ports, and in the sea lanes. Assigning these vessels to convoy escort duties would leave shipping entering and leaving ports unprotected. Ironically, massing numbers of coastal merchant ships into inadequately protected convoys would make the U-boats' job of sinking ships even easier and more effective.[8]

DESTRUCTION OF MERCHANT VESSELS BEGINS

The massacre of shipping along the Atlantic Coast by U-boats, initiated with the sinking of SS *Cyclops* on 12 January, began in earnest two days after she went down, when U-boats moved into the shipping bottleneck of Cape Hatteras. By month's end, twenty vessels had been sunk in what remained of that month, along the Eastern Seaboard.[9]

Date	Ship	Nationality	Date	Ship	Nationality
12 Jan 42	*Cyclops* steam merchant	British	21 Jan 42	*Alexandra Hoegh* motor tanker	Norwegian
13 Jan 42	*Frisco* steam merchant	Norwegian	22 Jan 42	*Olympic* steam tanker	Panamanian
13 Jan 42	*Friar Rock* steam merchant	Panamanian	23 Jan 42	*Thirlby* steam merchant	British
14 Jan 42	*Norness* motor tanker	Panamanian	23 Jan 42	*Empire Gem* motor tanker	British
15 Jan 42	*Coimbra* steam tanker	British	24 Jan 42	*Venore* cargo ship	American
18 Jan 42	*Allan Jackson* steam tanker	American	25 Jan 42	*Varanger* motor tanker	Norwegian
19 Jan 42	*Norvana* steam merchant	American	25 Jan 42	*Culebra* steam merchant	British
19 Jan 42	*Lady Hawkins* passenger ship	British	26 Jan 42	*West Ivis* steam merchant	American
19 Jan 42	*City of Atlantic* cargo ship	American	27 Jan 42	*Francis E. Powell* steam tanker	American
19 Jan 42	*Ciltvaira* cargo ship	Latvian	27 Jan 42	*Pan Norway* motor tanker	Norwegian

BRITAIN PROVIDES MUCH-NEEDED ASSISTANCE

Such protection as Andrews could furnish to shipping during this blitz, was painfully inadequate, but help from an Ally was forthcoming. The

Royal Navy lent the United States Navy 24 anti-submarine vessels (22 converted fishing trawlers and 2 whalers), each equipped with a deck gun, depth charges, and Asdic (sonar). Manned by aggressive, former merchant seamen and commercial fishermen, who had much experience combating U-boats in British waters, these rugged little coal burners, identified below, provided valuable assistance in the Eastern Sea Frontier, and later the adjacent Gulf Frontier as well. (Appendix A provides summary information about the characteristics of these vessels, and Appendix B, a list of the officers who served aboard them from their arrival in American waters through war's end.)[10]

Twenty-four Royal Naval Patrol Service Vessels

HMT *Arctic Explorer*	HMT *Lady Rosemary*	HMT *Pentland Firth*
HMT *Bedfordshire*	HMT *Le Tigre*	HMT *Senateur Duhamel*
HMS *Buttermere*	HMT *Northern Chief*	HMT *St. Cathan*
HMT *Cape Warwick*	HMT *Northern Dawn*	HMT *St. Loman*
HMT *Coventry City*	HMT *Northern Duke*	HMT *St. Zero*
HMT *Hertfordshire*	HMT *Northern Isles*	HMT *Stella Polaris*
HMT *Kingston Ceylonite*	HMT *Northern Princess*	HMS *Wastwater*
HMT *Lady Elsa*	HMT *Norwich City*	HMT *Wellard*

ROYAL NAVAL PATROL SERVICE (RNPS)

Unique silver badge awarded to those who served six months or more in the RNPS, worn on the sleeve of the recipient's uniform. Because a majority of RNPS members were Reservists, it became a "Navy within a Navy," one commonly referred to as "Harry Tate's Navy," "Churchill's pirates," and "Sparrows."

Because of her expansive coastlines, and realizing that there would be German mining and U-boat attacks in adjacent waters, Britain recognized and provided in World War II, as she had in the First World War, hundreds of minesweepers and anti-submarine patrol vessels to allow the Royal Navy some freedom of movement and to keep her ports open to merchant shipping.

At the outbreak of war, the Royal Navy commandeered the Sparrow's Nest at Lowestoft, a private estate in Suffolk, to set up the headquarters for the Royal Naval Patrol Service. The Sparrow's Nest had been built as Cliff Cottage in the 19th century, a summer retreat for Robert Sparrow, the owner of a luxurious country house in nearby

Worlingham. The estate became known as HMS Europa. (Unlike the names of vessels, the names of Royal Navy shore establishments preceded by HMS are not italicised because the 'ships' in question are 'stone frigates' to which shipboard terminology and customs still apply.) Located at the most easterly point of Great Britain on the North Sea, Lowestoft was then the closest military establishment to the enemy.[11]

Out of necessity, the Royal Naval Patrol Service utilised outdated and poorly armed vessels, mostly requisitioned coal-burning trawlers crewed by ex-fishermen. The RNPS also helped man Royal Navy MMS (Motor Minesweepers otherwise known as "Mickey Mouse") and BYMS (British Yard Minesweepers). Many of the former were built in Canadian yards while the latter were the British-procured version of the famous U.S. Navy YMS minesweeper.

The RNPS came to bear several unofficial titles that poked fun at it by others. One that gained prominence was "Harry Tate's Navy." This reference dated back to the First World War; it was jargon for anything clumsy and amateurish. It originated from an old music hall entertainer who portrayed a clumsy comic who couldn't come to grips with various contraptions, and whose act included a car that gradually fell apart.[12]

In WWII, regulars in the Royal Navy used this reference to scorn the trawlers and drifters of the Royal Naval Patrol Service. Nonplused, the members of the RNPS proudly adopted the title "Harry Tate's Navy" which, as the war went on, became a worthy synonym for courage. Because the peacetime crews of fishing vessels evolved into Royal Naval Reserve seamen in the minesweeping and anti-submarine fraternity, they quickly acquired a special camaraderie with one another. This amity continued throughout the war, though by its end, with the expansion of the service, most RNPS members were Royal Navy Volunteer Service "hostilities only" members with little previous connection to the sea. (An explanation about the differences between the RN, RNR and RNVR follows in a few pages).[13]

The officers and men of the RNPS fought in all theatres of the war, earning over 850 gallantry awards as well as over 200 Mention in Despatches. A Victoria Cross (VC) was won during the Norwegian Campaign by Lt. Richard Been Stannard RNR, the only one awarded to the unit. Stannard was commanding officer of HM trawler *Arab* (FY202) of the 15th Anti-Submarine Striking Force. He received his VC for gallantry under air attack during operations off Namsos, Norway.[14]

Today, some of the few remaining original buildings of HMS Europa in Sparrow's Nest, Lowestoft, house the Royal Naval Patrol

Service Museum and the War Memorial Museum. There is also a memorial in Belle Vue Park, in the north end of Lowestoft, to commemorate members of the RNPS who died during 1939-1946 and who have no known grave other than the sea, as well as a few who died on shore and who, too, have no known grave.[15]

Photo Preface-5

Rob Hoole with RNPS veteran George Hunt, in February 2020. Hunt served aboard the unnamed motor minesweeper HMS *MMS 1084* and the anti-submarine whaler HMS *Sobkra* (FY331) in World War II. There is still a monthly gathering of RNPS veterans in Portsmouth, which he attends.
Courtesy of Rob Hoole

ROYAL NAVY SHIP NOMENCLATURE

Trawlers and whalers taken up by the Royal Navy and other Commonwealth navies, and converted to anti-submarine vessels or minesweeping vessels, were commonly identified by the designation A/S (for anti-submarine trawler or whaler) or M/S (minesweeping trawler or whaler). Commissioned ships in the Royal Navy were identified by HMS (meaning His or Her Majesty's Ship). Trawlers, some commissioned and some not, might have HMT (His or Her Majesty's Trawler) associated with their name in lieu of HMS. (This was unique to Royal Naval Patrol Service trawlers, apparently because of their large numbers; HMW was not used for whalers.)

It is important to note that different references might identify the same ship in slightly difference ways. For example, *Bedfordshire*, which was lost to a U-boat in American waters, might have been identified by all of the below, or perhaps even a different name variant:

- HMS *Bedfordshire*
- HMT *Bedfordshire*
- HM trawler *Bedfordshire*
- HM A/S trawler *Bedfordshire*

If this is not confusing enough, European nations commonly use "M/S" to denote motor ships; merchant vessels propelled by internal combustion engines, as opposed to those powered by steam, which are identified by "S/S", "S.S.," or "SS," meaning steam ship. The United States, UK and a few other countries, which also use S.S. for steamships, use M/V or MV to identify diesel-propelled ships as "motor vessels," which are identical to "motor ships."

To avoid, in a reference to a string of Royal Navy ships, having to place HMS before each one, the convention is to use "HM Ships" once (meaning Her or Her Majesty's Ships) with the names of the ships following this descriptor. The prefix HMS was used for all units of corvette and fleet minesweeper size and above. Only smaller vessels, e.g., motor minesweepers, trawlers, drifters, motor launches, submarines, etc., were sometimes named by type but could equally as well be named HMS. For security, sailors' cap tallies had 'H.M.S.' printed on them during wartime; not the complete name of the ship or submarine in which they were serving.

PROGRESS BEGINS TO BE MADE ON FRONTIER

Hunting the hornets all over the farm.

—Description by President Woodrow Wilson of the ill-advised use of destroyers for anti-submarine patrol duties in World War I.[16]

In March 1942, the RNPS vessels arrived in American waters to augment the efforts of a few old Navy ships including Henry Ford-built "Eagle Boats," Coast Guard cutters, and requisitioned yachts and smaller patrol craft, which had been doing their best to stem the tide of U-boat sinkings of shipping. The following month, some of the defensive measures enacted began to take effect.[17]

One of these measures involved the use of a "bucket brigade" system, as Admiral Andrews termed it. Because of the prevalence of night attacks by the U-boats—which remained hidden by day, resting on the bottom in shallow offshore waters—coastwide vessels were ordered to anchor overnight. These stays were in the Chesapeake or Delaware Bays, and a defensive-mined and protected anchorage was provided for them behind Cape Lookout; a 56-mile-long section of the Southern Outer Banks of North Carolina.[18]

By use of these lay-overs, a vessel could make Jacksonville, Florida, from New York in about four daylight runs. Eastbound shipping from New York bound for Europe, was routed via the sheltered Long Island Sound and Massachusetts Cape Cod Canal. This practice reduced the overall losses, but the coastline from Wilmington, North Carolina, northward to Norfolk, Virginia, continued to be the scene of numerous sinkings. Submarines operating off Diamond Shoals lay on the bottom in shoal water by day and hunted at night.[19]

At this site on 12 May 1942, the trawler HMT *Bedfordshire* fell victim to *U-558* with the loss of all hands aboard. (This tragedy, and a description of the resultant British Cemetery at Ocracoke Island, North Carolina, where four bodies that washed up on the beach at the island, are buried, is the subject of Chapter 1.)

One of the measures enacted to protect shipping was the use of destroyers for anti-submarine patrols. Woodrow Wilson recognized decades earlier that it did not work in World War I and, for the most part, it did not work at this later date. If visibility was even reasonably good, any alert U-boat commander at periscope depth could sight a destroyer well before its sound gear picked up his submarine, and could easily evade it. Assigning the few destroyers available to roving patrols proved of little practical use, and this action resulted in the loss of the antiquated, World War I vintage destroyer USS *Jacob Jones* (DD-130) on 28 February 1942. Her sinking with great loss of life is described in Chapter 4.[20]

Photo Preface-6

HMT *Bedfordshire* outfitted as an armed trawler.
Courtesy of the National Archives and Records Administration

Photo Preface-7

Destroyer USS *Roper* (DD-147) on convoy duty, in Hampton Roads, Virginia, 1942.
National Archives photograph #80-G-K-472

USS *ROPER* SINKS *U-85* OFF CAPE HATTERAS

> *Fire was begun by all the batteries that could be brought to bear. The No. 1 machine gun opened promptly and accurately to cut down the German sailors as they hurried to their guns. The No. 5 three-inch gun, under a gun captain who had never before been in charge of a gun during firing, got the range quickly and scored a hit on the conning tower. Damage must have been severe for soon after the submarine began to sink. Orders to fire a torpedo were immediately given aboard the* ROPER *but the U-boat disappeared before the order could be obeyed.*

—Commander, Eastern Sea Frontier's War Diary, April 1942, describing action by the destroyer USS *Roper* (DD-147) in sinking the *U-85* off Cape Hatteras, North Carolina.[21]

By early April 1942, the previous ineffective use of destroyers to randomly patrol sea lanes, had been refined to patrol and search of localized, endangered areas. The destroyers in the Frontier were then still too few to put a convoy system into effect, and provide adequate screens to escort merchantmen.[22]

The "stopgap" practice of assigning available destroyers and anti-submarine vessels to specific important sectors paid off on 14 April 1942, when USS *Roper* (DD-147) sank the *U-85* with naval gunfire. *Roper*, like her former sister ship *Jacob Jones* (now wreckage on the ocean floor) was a 314-foot Wickes-class destroyer. Well past her best days, having been commissioned on 15 February 1919, she still had a good turn of speed. Geared turbines producing 24,200 shaft horsepower could propel the 1,154 tons displacement trim DD to a top speed of 35 knots. (At least with a clean hull and well-maintained machinery; better yet, new machinery.) Despite, some likely shaking and vibration at speed, *Roper* was able to run down a recently-built German U-boat, less than a year old, trying to outdistance her on the surface to escape.[23]

Lt. Comdr. Hamilton Wilcox Howe, USN, her commanding officer (and of the first American ship to sink an enemy submarine in the waters of the Frontier), was awarded the Navy Cross for this action. Details about this combat action may be found in Chapter 7.

Photo Preface-8

Navy Cross Medal

Lt. Comdr. Hamilton Wilcox Howe, USS *Roper*'s commanding officer, being presented the Navy Cross by Vice Adm. Adolphus Andrews, commander, Eastern Sea Frontier, at his headquarters on 7 July 1942, for the destruction of the enemy submarine *U- 85*.
U.S. Navy photograph

As shown in the following table, sinkings by Allied forces of U-boats off the Eastern Seaboard continued at a modest pace of one per month until July when, with numbers and proficiency of defensive forces much improved, four were destroyed. Of the seven submarines sunk by aircraft and surface vessels in 1942, three were in the Cape Hatteras area, a favorite U-boat "hunting ground."

U-boats sunk by Allied Forces off America's Eastern Seaboard in 1942

Date	U-boat	Description
14 Apr 42	*U-85*	Sunk off Cape Hatteras, by gunfire from the destroyer USS *Roper* (DD-147)
9 May 42	*U-352*	Sunk south of Cape Hatteras, by depth charges from the USCG cutter *Icarus* (WPC-110)
30 Jun 42	*U-158*	Sunk west of Bermuda, by depth charges from a USN Mariner aircraft (VP-74/*P-1*)
3 Jul 42	*U-215*	Sunk east of Boston, by depth charges from the British trawler HMT *Le Tigre* (FY243)
7 Jul 42	*U-701*	Sunk off Cape Hatteras by depth charges from a U.S. Army A-29 Hudson (Bomber Squadron 396)
15 Jul 42	*U-576*	Sunk off Cape Hatteras, by depth charges from two USN Kingfisher aircraft (VS-9), and gunfire from the Naval Armed Guard of the motor vessel MV *Unicoi*
31 Jul 42	*U-754*	Sunk south of Nova Scotia, by depth charges from a RCAF Hudson aircraft (113 Squadron/*P-625*)[24]

EASTERN SEA FRONTIER CONVOYS, AND OTHER DEFENSIVE MEASURES, SPUR MOVEMENT OF U-BOATS SOUTHWARD, AND OFFENSIVE MINING

As soon as strengthened Allied forces in one area brought diminishing returns to the enemy, Admiral Doenitz generally reassigned U-boat wolfpacks to more promising locations, leaving one or two submarines to patrol former convoyed areas, seek targets of opportunity, and to attempt to pin down naval vessels and planes assigned to the defense of shipping to those areas.[25]

The southern movements of most of the U-boats in the western Atlantic, resulted in increased sinkings in the Gulf Sea Frontier and Caribbean waters, specifically 73 in May 1942. In June, the Gulf, the Caribbean, and the eastern approaches to them became the most dangerous areas for shipping in the World. Particularly, three vulnerable areas: off the Passes of the Mississippi (at the river's mouth in the Gulf of Mexico), the East Coast of Florida, and the Yucatan Channel (a strait between Mexico and Cuba).[26]

A new type of U-boat activity, which began off Newfoundland in May and which was extended into the Eastern, Gulf, and Caribbean Frontiers, was the sowing of mines off seaports, in the hope of catching ships entering or leaving. On 15 June, mines laid by *U-701* three days earlier in the ship channel to the Chesapeake Capes, sank the tanker SS *Robert C. Tuttle*, and the British trawler HMT *Kingston Ceylonite*, and damaged the destroyer USS *Bainbridge* (DD-246). A second tanker, the SS *Esso Augusta*, was also slightly damaged.[27]

Kingston Ceylonite was the third of the twenty-two RNPS trawlers to be sunk in East Coast waters as a result of enemy action. (The other two RNPS vessels sent to America were the whalers *Buttermere* and *Wastwater*.) The first, *Northern Princess*, had been sunk by *U-587* on 8 March off the Grand Banks, Newfoundland, even before the trawlers she was voyaging with from Britain made their first port in North America. The second was *Bedfordshire* which, as previously discussed, was torpedoed off North Carolina.

HMT *Le Tigre* partially avenged *Kingston Ceylonite*'s loss when, on 3 July she used depth charges to sink the minelaying submarine *U-215*, whose task was to sow mines in Boston Harbor. Chapter 10 is devoted to *Le Tigre*, which would become renowned within the Royal Naval Patrol Service as, "the U-boat killer in American waters."

RCN AND RN CORVETTES REPORT FOR DUTY

The sudden drop in sinkings in the Eastern Sea Frontier from twenty-three in April 1942, to five in May, to three in August, following the coastal convoy set-up, meant little more than driving the submarines from one area to another.

—Samuel Eliot Morison, *The Battle of the Atlantic 1939-1943*.[28]

The losses by submarines off our Atlantic seaboard and in the Caribbean now threaten our entire war effort. The following statistics bearing on the subject have been brought to my attention.

Of the 74 ships allocated to the Army for July by the War Shipping Administration, 17 have already been sunk. Twenty-two percent of the Bauxite fleet has already been destroyed. Twenty percent of the Puerto Rican fleet has been lost. Tanker sinkings have been 3.5 percent per month of tonnage in use.

We are all aware of the limited number of escort craft available, but has every conceivable improvised means been brought to bear on this situation? I am fearful that another month or two of this will so cripple our means of transport that we will be unable to bring sufficient men and planes to bear against the enemy in critical theatres to exercise a determining influence on the war.

—Gen. George C. Marshall, U.S. Army chief of staff, communicating to Adm. Ernest King, commander in chief, U.S. Fleet and chief of Naval Operations, on 10 June 1942, his concerns regarding the loss of vital shipping in the Atlantic and Caribbean Sea.[29]

The coastal convoys operating between Key West, Florida, and Norfolk, Virginia from May until September, were dependent primarily on the British trawlers, and eleven Atlantic Fleet destroyers:

- USS *Bainbridge* (DD-246)
- USS *Broome* (DD-210)
- USS *Decatur* (DD-341)
- USS *Dickerson* (DD-157)
- USS *Du Pont* (DD-152)
- USS *Ellis* (DD-154)[30]
- USS *Herbert* (DD-160)
- USS *MacLeish* (DD-220)
- USS *McCormick* (DD-223)
- USS *Roper* (DD-147)
- USS *Simpson* (DD-221)

In August 1942, plans were made to create an interlocking convoy system. Unfortunately, the British trawlers did not have "the legs" (fuel endurance) for assignment to lengthy convoys between New York and Guantanamo Bay, Cuba. This shortcoming resulted in commander, Eastern Sea Frontier being lent twelve Royal Canadian Navy and Royal Navy Flower-class corvettes, supplemented by three RN destroyers. The newly assigned corvettes reported under Admiral Andrews' command between 27 August and 3 September; many of them were detached from their existing, temporary escort and patrol assignments in the Gulf and the Caribbean.[31]

The trawlers continued to be used by the Naval Districts for local escort work and patrol.[32]

RCN and RN Corvettes assigned under commander, Eastern Sea Frontier's control, as escorts to New York-Guantanamo convoys

- HMCS *Fredericton* (K245)
- HMCS *Halifax* (K237)
- HMCS *Oakville* (K178)
- HMS *Buttercup* (K193)
- HMS *Columbine* (K94)
- HMS *Godetia* (K226)
- HMCS *Snowberry* (K166)
- HMCS *Sudbury* (K162)
- HMCS *The Pas* (K168)
- HMS *Lavender* (K60)
- HMS *Pimpernel* (K71)
- HMS *Saxifrage* (K04)

Supplemental RN Destroyers for New York-Guantanamo convoys

- HMS *Churchill* (I45)
- HMS *Havelock* (H88)[33]
- HMS *Warwick* (D25)

SUB-KILLING RCN CORVETTE AND HER CAPTAIN

Since Andrews' Frontier suffered the loss of only three ships "sunk in convoy" between mid-May and year's end in 1942 (including the New York to Guantanamo runs), there is no coverage of these operations, owing to space limitations. Instead, several pages in Chapter 12 are devoted to the Flower-class corvette HMCS *Oakville*, a part of the escort force of a Trinidad-Aruba-Key West convoy immediately prior to her assignment to Andrews' command. *Oakville* sank *U-94*, during an attack by the German submarine on the convoy. For this action, the corvette's commanding officer, Lt. Comdr. Clarence A. King, DSC, RCNR, was awarded a Distinguished Service Order and the U.S. Legion of Merit (the first American decoration to be awarded to a Canadian in World War II).

 DSO	Distinguished Service Order Established by: Queen Victoria, 6 September 1886 For meritorious or distinguished service by officers during war	Distinguished Service Cross Established by: King Edward VII, 28 June 1901 For meritorious or distinguished service before the enemy 'by men of His Majesty's Fleet'	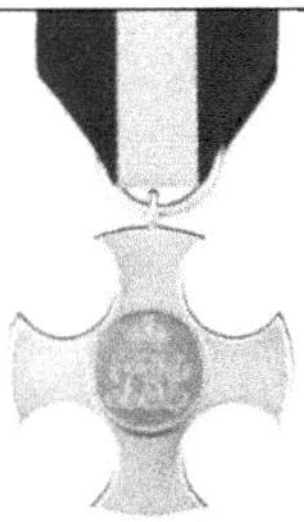 DSC
 LOM	United States Legion of Merit Established by President Franklin D. Roosevelt, 20 July 1942 For exceptionally meritorious conduct in the performance of outstanding services and achievements	To be mentioned in despatches describes a member of the armed forces whose name appears in an official report in which their gallant or meritorious action in the face of the enemy is described.	 War Medal

King, one of Canada's finest naval officers, retired with the rank of Captain in 1946. From the time he was 13 years old, in 1899, until the end of World War II, King spent most of his life at sea. He was 53 years old when World War II broke out, and was decorated in both the First and Second World Wars for destroying German U-boats.

In World War I, while serving in 'Q' ships as navigator, first lieutenant and captain successively, King was credited with one kill and two probable submarine sinkings, and was awarded his first

Distinguished Service Cross (DSC). In WWII, in addition to *U-94*, he was credited (while in command of other ships) with participating in the sinking of *U-845*, *U-448*, and *U-247*. During his distinguished naval service, King was awarded the DSO, DSC & Bar, U.S. Legion of Merit, and was twice Mentioned in Despatches. It is noted that Commonwealth servicemembers who are mentioned in despatches (MiD) do not receive a medal for their actions, but are authorized to wear an oak leaf device on the ribbon of an appropriate campaign medal.

ROYAL NAVY TRAWLERS / WHALERS ORDERED TO SOUTH AFRICAN WATERS

As previously noted, German U-boats began moving southward, when they found operating along the Eastern Sea Frontier had become increasingly difficult, to concentrate their efforts in the Caribbean Sea and the Gulf of Mexico where hunting was easier. May through September 1942 was the most dangerous period for shipping in these southern waters. Navy "top brass," in the early innocent days of the war, had believed that narrow passages, swift currents, and island barriers would offer protection from submarine attack. But in those waters, in five months, enemy submarines sank an average of 1 ½ ships per day. (Coverage of action in the Gulf and Caribbean Sea Frontiers is not within the scope of this book.)[34]

Finally with the Eastern Sea Frontier relatively peaceful in October 1942, and the Royal Naval Patrol Service trawlers and whalers lent to Andrews in receipt of new orders from the British Admiralty, *Send Some King's Ships* departs American waters and follows these intrepid anti-submarine vessels to South African waters.

Of the twenty-two trawlers and two whalers which left Britain in February 1942 for American waters, six trawlers had been lost; three to U-boat actions and three to collisions at sea. The trawlers and whalers (as well as many other small vessels) were not fitted with radar. In peacetime, during low visibility conditions, such as when "socked in by fog," they would likely have remained in port. However, wartime patrol and/or escort duties now existed. Steaming in low visibility conditions (when rain and overcast blocked the sun, or in prevailing fog, or darkness at night) with navigation lights extinguished to help avoid detection by enemy submarines, was risky business.

RNPS Trawlers lost to U-boats and Ship Collisions

Date	Trawler/Cause	Date	Trawler/Other Ship
8 Mar 42	HMT *Northern Princess* *U-587*	11 Apr 42	HMT *St. Cathan* Dutch merchant ship *Hebe*
12 May 42	HMT *Bedfordshire* *U-558*	6 May 42	HMT *Senateur Duhamel* USS *Semmes* (AG-24)
15 Jun 42	HMT *Kingstone Ceylonite* *U-701*	19 Sep 42	HMT *Pentland Firth* USS *Chaffinch* (AM-81)

CONDITIONS IN SOUTH AFRICAN WATERS MIRROR THOSE INITIALLY IN THE EASTERN SEA FRONTIER

As was the case in northern waters, once strengthened Allied anti-submarine measures in the Gulf and Caribbean Sea Frontiers began to accrue unacceptable U-boat losses to his forces, Admiral Doenitz shifted emphasis to a new area of vulnerability. This was across the Atlantic in South Africa, through whose water's large numbers of Allied merchant and naval vessels passed daily.

Similar to the U-boat blitz launched in American waters in January 1942, the commencement of sustained U-boat operations ten months later in South African waters, abruptly awakened there an immediate awareness of the need for dedicated anti-submarine warfare measures.

Large numbers of ship sinkings off the southern African coast, compelled South African and British naval authorities to adopt a series of anti-submarine measures, which succeeded in stemming the horrific losses of merchant vessels, cargos, and crews. This was accomplished by August 1943.

These measures, like those enacted in the Eastern Sea Frontier, included the following:

- employment of patrol aircraft, with the Royal Air Force greatly assisting the modest South African air forces
- ordering the "King's Ships" in American waters to South Africa, to bolster the South African naval forces' whalers and trawlers
- utilization of a coastal convoy system, once sufficient escorts were available to shepherd merchant vessels[35]

These measures, and procedures including the centralized control of naval and air forces, and of escort operations, resulted in the sinking of three U-boats between 1942 and 1944.

DESTROYER HMS *ACTIVE* SINKS *U-179*

In addition to its own modest force of converted whalers and trawlers, the South African Naval Force benefited greatly from the presence of a long-established Royal Navy base at Simon's Town, South Africa. Located in the Cape Area through which all shipping proceeding east or west "round the tip of Africa" must pass, warships operating from there were of great value in those waters.

Photo Preface-9

Simon's Town, South Africa with, in the foreground, the cruiser HMS *Shropshire* prior to her transfer to the Royal Australian Navy, November 1942.

On 8 October 1942, HMS *Active* (H14) was dispatched with the destroyers HMAS *Nizam* (G38) and HMS *Foxhound* (H69), to help collect survivors from the British merchant vessel SS *City of Athens.* Shortly before midnight, HMS *Active* (Lt. Comdr. Michael Tomkinson, RN) obtained a radar contact at a distance of 2,500 yards. Then, an Asdic (sonar) contact ahead at a range of 1,600 yards was gained and a large submarine sighted on the surface. She was the *U-179* (that earlier had sunk the Greek SS *Pantelis*), which appeared to be stopped, seemingly charging her batteries.[36]

Active increased speed to 25 knots and altered course slightly to starboard to bring the enemy broader on her beam, so that more guns could bear. At 800 yards, the target was illuminated by searchlight, and B gun opened fire. No hits were scored and, as the range closed to 500 yards, the submarine dove. *Active* altered course, and steadied up with the submarine's conning tower slightly off her bow. As the U-boat passed down the port side of the destroyer at close range on a converging course, *Active* attacked with a 10-depth charge pattern, set to depths of 50 and 150 feet. The explosives burst all around the U-boat, and the depth-charge party reported that the submarine was blown to the surface as a result of the attack and then sank.[37]

Lt. Comdr. Michael Wilfred Tomkinson, who had previously been Mentioned in Despatches (MiD) on 4 October 1940, and later awarded the Distinguished Service Cross on 25 August 1942, received a Bar to his DSC (signifying a second award of the medal) on 9 February 1943 for this action.[38]

U-179 was the first of three German submarines sunk by Allied forces in South African waters in World War II.

Date	U-boat	Description
8 Oct 43	*U-179*	Sunk near Cape Town, South Africa, by depth charges from the destroyer HMS *Active*
20 Aug 43	*U-197*	Sunk south of Madagascar, by depth charges from two British Catalina aircraft (Squadron 259/C & 265/N)
11 Mar 44	*UIT-22*	Sunk south of the Cape of Good Hope, by South African Catalina aircraft (SAAF Squadron 262)

ROYAL NAVY / SANF TRAWLERS AND WHALERS

Map Preface-2

Coastline of South Africa

As previously mentioned, in autumn 1942, groups of Royal Naval Patrol Service trawlers detached from their U.S. Naval District commands, proceeded southward and traversed the Caribbean Sea to Trinidad, then on to the Brazilian port of Pernambuco (today Recife). There, they "coaled" ship for passage to West Africa across the narrows of the Atlantic. Following arrival at Freetown, Sierra Leone, they made their way down the West Coast of Africa to South African waters.

Eighteen Surviving Royal Naval Patrol Service Trawlers and Whalers

A/S Trawlers	A/S Trawlers	A/S Trawlers
HMT *Arctic Explorer*	HMT *Le Tigre*	HMT *St. Loman*
HMT *Cape Warwick*	HMT *Northern Chief*	HMT *St. Zeno*
HMT *Coventry City*	HMT *Northern Dawn*	HMT *Stella Polaris*
HMT *Hertfordshire*	HMT *Northern Duke*	HMT *Wellard*
HMT *Lady Elsa*	HMT *Northern Isles*	**A/S Whalers**
HMT *Lady Rosemary*	HMT *Norwich City*	HMS *Buttermere*
		HMS *Wastwater*

All of the RNPS trawlers took up their new duties by year's end; the whalers HMS *Buttermere* and *Wastwater* arrived later, in March 1943. The chapters about these vessels' deployment in African waters include some interesting tidbits. Among the many rough, hardfisted ex-merchant seamen and fishermen aboard the King's anti-submarine vessels, was a poet of rare talent. When war broke out, Rhodes scholar Australian Michael Thwaites, who had just left Oxford, joined the Royal Naval Volunteer Reserve. He had previously won the Newdigate Prize in 1938 for his long poem "Milton Blind," and he was later to receive the King's Medal for poetry.[39]

Thwaites served aboard HMS *Wastwater* as her "Jimmy" or First Lieutenant (ship's executive officer to USN readers). Following the war, in 1950, after a stint as a Lecturer of English at the University of Melbourne, he was appointed to the Australian Security Intelligence Organisation, as Director of Counter-Espionage. Additional details about this captivating individual may be found in the body of the book.[40]

The arrival of the RNPS vessels to augment the SANF whalers and trawlers identified in the table, enabled the commencement of merchant ship convoy operations. The SANF vessels, which were too few to perform both harbor protection and to serve as credible convoy escort forces, had previously been limited to anti-submarine patrols only.

Cape Town Anti-Submarine Flotilla		Durban Anti-Submarine Flotilla	
Ship	**Type**	**Ship**	**Type**
HMSAS *Blomvlei*	trawler	HMSAS *Rondevlei*	whaler
HMSAS *Mooivlei*	trawler	HMSAS *Smalvlei*	whaler
HMSAS *Sonneblom*	whaler	HMSAS *Blaauwberg*	whaler
HMSAS *Immortelle*	whaler	HMSAS *Sydostlandet* (lost)	whaler
HMSAS *Pretoria*	whaler	HMSAS *Cedarberg*	whaler
HMSAS *Vereeniging*	whaler	HMSAS *Odberg*	whaler
HMSAS *Turffontein*	whaler	HMSAS *Tordonn*	whaler
HMSAS *Standerton*	whaler		

The African Naval Forces boasted fourteen (excluding HMSAS *Sydostlandet*) A/S whalers and trawlers, assigned to either the Cape Town or Durban Anti-Submarine flotillas, for duties in the Southern Cape and Eastern Cape areas, respectively. HMSAS *Sydostlandet*, previously a unit of the Durban A/S Flotilla, had been lost in April 1942, when she ran aground near the Umgeni River mouth during rough weather. She is listed in the table, but was no longer a unit of the SANF. (A list of the officers who served aboard the South African whalers and trawlers may be found in Appendix C.)

The final four chapters of the book are devoted to the ceaseless efforts of the RNPS and SANF trawlers and whalers, and a few other Allied escort vessels, to safeguard merchantmen in South African waters. These waters then had the unhappy distinction, following preceding similar periods in the Eastern Sea Frontier, thence the Gulf and Caribbean Frontiers, of being the most dangerous waters for shipping in the world.

The King's Ships (trawlers and whalers) remained in South Africa until war's end. After returning home to Britain, the vessels were paid off by the Royal Navy in 1945, and disposed of. They were returned to their original owners—if requisitioned (taken) by the Admiralty for naval service—or placed on the Disposal List for sale to merchantile (commercial interests)—if instead purchased for naval service. Most, if not all, took up working the North Sea fishing grounds, and continued their service into the early- to mid-1960s.

ROYAL NAVY

The RNVR (classic, wartime reservists known as 'Saturday night sailors') were gentlemen trying to be sailors.

The RNR (professional seamen and part-time Navy officers) were sailors trying to be gentlemen.

and The RN (regular Navy officers) were neither trying to be both.
—Old saying in the Royal Navy, courtesy of Rob Hoole

The Naval Reserve Act of 1859 established the Royal Naval Reserve (RNR) as a reserve of professional seamen from the British Merchant Navy and fishing fleets, who could be called upon during times of war to serve in the regular Royal Navy. In 1862, the RNR was extended to include the recruitment and training of reserve officers, who wore on their uniforms a unique and distinctive lace consisting of stripes of interwoven chain. The Royal Naval Volunteer Reserve (RNVR) was created in 1903.

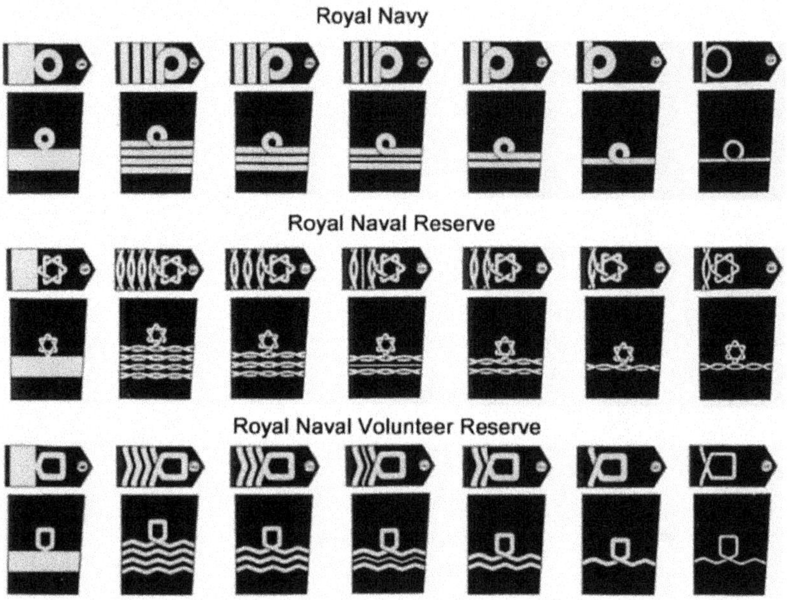

World War II British Naval Officer shoulder boards and sleeve insignia

While the Royal Naval Reserve was composed of personnel from the merchant marine and fishing communities, members of the Royal Naval Volunteer Reserve came from other civilian backgrounds. Another difference was the gold braid officers wore on their sleeves to denote rank. Those of the RNR were in intersecting waved pairs, while the pattern of RNVR braid was single waved lines—thus the RN moniker "wavy Navy" when referring to the latter officers.

The Royal Naval Patrol Service was mostly populated by RNR and RNVR members, and the same held true for the Dominion navies. At the onset of war, some regulars serving in the Royal Navy made fun of RNR and RNVR personnel, whom they termed amateurs. However, the amateurs soon became professionals in anti-submarine patrol, escort, and mine clearance duties. In particular, dealing with sea mines (not covered in this book), was a warfare area generally underappreciated by Navy "top brass" who'd gained promotion aboard battleships, cruisers and destroyers.

Having completed this comprehensive introduction, it's now time for readers to (vicariously) stand out to sea with the crews of "minor warships" sent in harm's way to combat formidable enemy submarines, because they were among the few naval forces available to do so.

World War II-American Theater 1941-1946

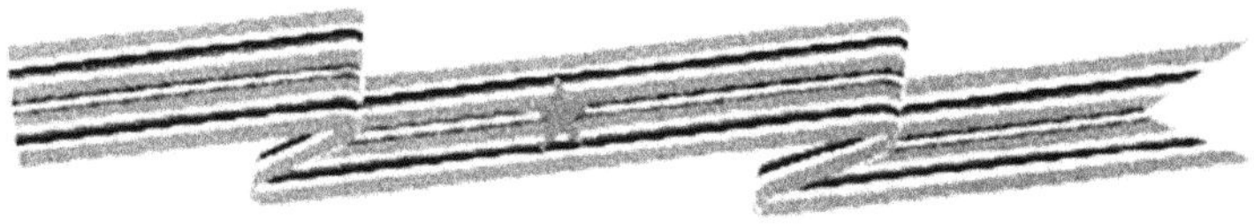

Escort, antisubmarine, armed guard and special operations banner with 1 Bronze Star

1

Loss of HMT *Bedfordshire*

The Bedfordshire *was one of twenty-four that was sent over to the States. We sailed down to Norfolk, Virginia, then down to Morehead City, which was our base, and we worked from there convoying, escorting and then patrolling.*

I think they were a dam good crowd, we lost a good bunch of lads. You can always easily replace a ship but not 35 men. Why I kind of missed that boat is another story only him up there can answer I presume?"

—Royal Naval Patrol Service Stoker Samuel Nutt, one of four surviving crewmen of HMT *Bedfordshire*, recalling decades later, the A/S (anti-submarine) trawler operating from Morehead City, North Carolina, in 1942, and the loss of his shipmates.[1]

Photo 1-1

Cemetery at Ocracoke, Hyde County, North Carolina (since 1977, a Commonwealth War Cemetery), where four bodies that washed up on the beach of Okracoke Island are buried. Two were identified as Telegraphist Stanley R. Craig, and Sub Lieutenant Tom Cunningham. The other two seamen were not identified but both were presumed to have come from the *Bedfordshire*, as they were wearing Royal Navy uniforms.

Map 1-1

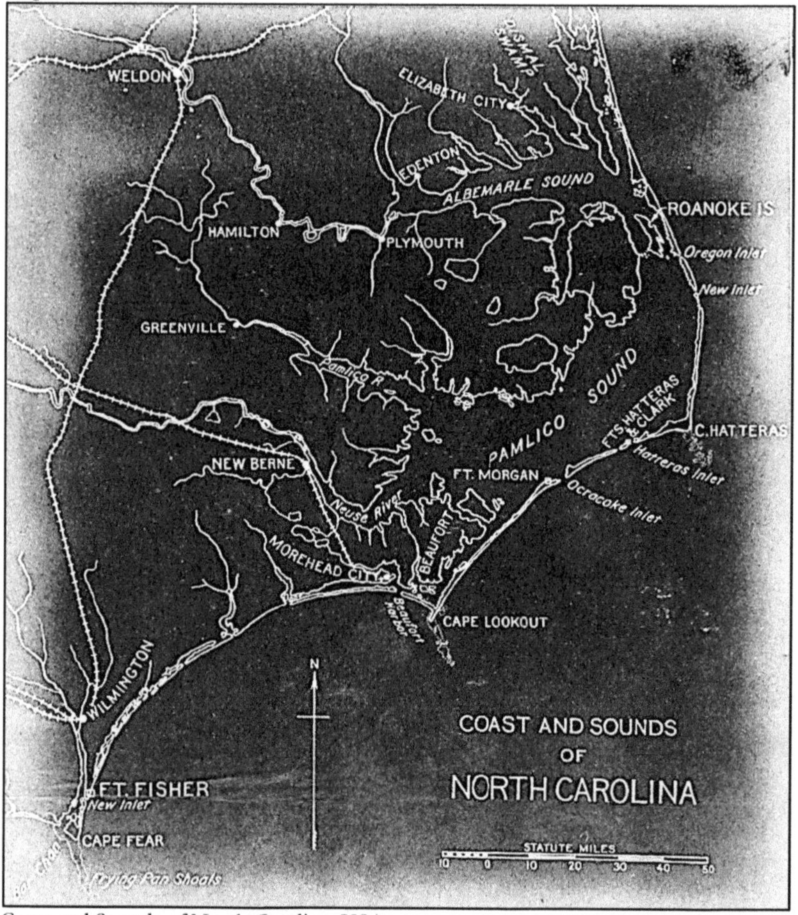

Coast and Sounds of North Carolina, USA
National Archives #USN 901634

On 10 May 1942, the British anti-submarine trawlers HMT *Bedfordshire* and HMT *St. Zeno* left Morehead City, North Carolina, to rendezvous with, and then escort, a coastal convoy from Cape Lookout to Cape Hatteras. The vessels joined the convoy in the afternoon and proceeded northeast. Typically, a pair of escorts, the convoy's sole protectors, would sail with one vessel ahead of it and the other positioned seaward on its flank. Sometime that evening, the anti-submarine trawlers changed positions, before successfully delivering the convoy to Cape Hatteras around midnight.[2]

Before continuing with this story, a diversion is made to provide background information about how it came to be that British trawlers were operating under U.S. Navy command in American coastal waters.

TWENTY-FOUR BRITISH A/S VESSELS BOLSTER UNITED STATES EASTERN SEA FRONTIER FORCES

The Japanese attack on Pearl Harbor on 7 December 1941, came as a complete surprise to Germany's political and military leaders. But, seizing the opportunity and acting quickly, Hitler declared war on the United States on 11 December. The U.S., although still technically a neutral country, had been assisting Britain via a variety of actions, increasing an existing strain between itself and Germany. This assistance included: (1) the Destroyers for Bases Agreement, (2) Lend-Lease, (3) the Atlantic Charter, (4) the hand-over of military control of Iceland from the United Kingdom to the United States, and (6) the extension of the Pan-American Security Zone. Following Germany's declaration of war, the United States Congress followed suit, declaring war on the Deutschland hours later.[3]

With the two countries now in a state of war, the Kriegsmarine (German Navy) U-boat command equipped the first six submarines that were to operate in American waters as near to the coast as possible. Five actually deployed. Their planned U-boat offensive against shipping along the Eastern Seaboard was designed to cut off the vital flow of resources to Allied nations, particularly Britain. Germany believed that England, as an island nation, would be crippled without a continuous flow of maritime supply.[4]

The total number of U-boats ready for service was still small at that point, but a larger monthly rate of increase was expected in the spring of 1942. The success of the first five German submarines in American waters was considerable. Admiral Karl Doenitz, Befehlshaber der Unterseeboote (commander of the submarines), explained the reasons for this success in his essay, *The Conduct of War at Sea*:

> The American defense was inexperienced; on the other hand, the U-boat commanders were exceptionally experienced. It was possible to operate very near to the coast and on the surface. Traffic was heavy here; consequently, the results were great. The U-boat command, therefore, sent every boat available for operations in American waters to this area in order to profit by the favorable situation.[5]

Doenitz's U-boats arrived in American waters in January 1942 and began attacking merchant freighters and tankers with relative impunity. Heavy merchant losses within sight of shore along the East Coast, were a shock to U.S. and other military leaders. Britain, who was relying on the cargos carried by those merchant vessels to continue its war efforts and supply its populace with food and essential commodities, was especially alarmed. The U.S. Navy and Coast Guard were in desperate need of anti-submarine vessels. In a permitted reversal of the flow of military aid to Britain made possible through the United States Lend-Lease Act, the Royal Navy sent HMT *Bedfordshire* and twenty-one other militarized British trawlers, and two whalers to the United States in early 1942.[6]

When purpose-built and requisitioned trawlers were commissioned for service in the Royal Navy, they gained the prefix HMT before their name to indicate His Majesty's Trawler. However, it is also common to find in references to them, the use of HMS for His Majesty's Ship.

TRAWLER CHARACTERISTICS / CONVERSION

Representative of the other trawlers, HMT *Befordshire* was a 443-gross ton, single-screw, steel-hulled steam commercial fishing trawler, 162.3 feet in length, with a 15.3-foot draft, and a 26.6-foot beam. This single deck, masted vessel was fitted with a single triple-expansion, reciprocating-steam engine, capable of propelling her at about 12 knots. Launched on 17 July 1935, she had been built by Smith's Dock Company (of South Bank-on-Tees at Middleborough, England) for the Bedfordshire Fishing Company.[7]

Photo 1-2

HMT *Bedfordshire* outfitted as an armed trawler.
(Courtesy of the National Archives and Records Administration)

Her layout was typical of a steel-hulled British steam trawler of the middle 1930s. Deck gear occupying the main deck included a large double-drum trawl winch just forward of the raised wheelhouse, two gallows-frames used for towing the trawl net, and a smaller hand windlass, and steam anchor windlass on the foc's'le. Five square hatches forward of the trawl winch provided access to the fish hold. Ten round hatches on either side of the deck house were used for filling the side bunkers with coal. There was also a small stern house containing a head (water closet), and a liver boiler house used for rendering down livers for fish oil. A single lifeboat hung from stern davits.[8]

The most prominent feature topside was the deckhouse, which housed the wheelhouse, chart room, and captain's cabin. Space below decks was taken up mostly by the engine and boiler rooms, crew berthing, and fish holds. The pantry, mess decks, saloon and officer accommodations occupied the vessel's stern compartments. A skylight above the area's passage provided light and fresh air. Amidships was taken up by the engine and boiler spaces; as well as side, cross, and reserve coal bunkers; and two fresh water storage tanks. The fish holds dominated a third of the vessel's length forward of the engineering spaces. The forward area, accessed from the foc's'le via a companion way, contained storage space, the chain locker, crew quarters including their own stove for warmth, and the forepeak (the forwardmost interior part of the ship, within the angle made by her bow).[9]

Bedfordshire was completed by August 1935 and turned over to the Bedfordshire Fishing Company in Grimsby, England. (Grimsby, located on the south bank of the Humber Estuary where it connects to the North Sea, would become by the 1950s the largest fishing port in the world owing to its close proximity to the North Sea fishing grounds.) As war became imminent in summer 1939, the British government realized it lacked sufficient vessels to defend its shores and merchant shipping. The Admiralty acquired *Bedfordshire* in August 1939, just prior to Germany's invasion of Poland on 1 September, and England's formal declaration of war against Germany on 3 September.[10]

The Admiralty also acquired 21 other trawlers from Grimsby and 35 from Kingston upon Hull (a port city in Yorkshire, England) at the same time as *Bedfordshire.* Over the course of the war, it would purchase 250 Grimsby type trawlers to supplement those trawlers of its purpose-built naval fleet. *Bedfordshire*'s conversion to a naval vessel was completed in December 1939, which included fitting her with Asdic (sonar) and anti-submarine weapons including depth charge racks. Conversions completed, she joined the 17th A/S (anti-submarine) Group based at Swansea, located on the south coast of Wales, for patrol in the British Channel which separates Wales from Devon and Somerset in southwest England.[11]

Bedfordshire's conversion was similar to that of other trawlers. She received a raised steel platform on her foc's'le to support a World War I era 4-inch quick-firing deck gun. Enemy aircraft were to be engaged with a similar vintage .303 Lewis machine gun located at the stern. Since she was intended for anti-submarine warfare, her primary weapons were depth charges jettisoned overboard by throwers and rails. Storage racks for the charges were located below the bridge and at the stern. This type of vessel's ability to carry out a sustained depth charge attack was limited by her ability to reload. Replacing expended depth charges was laborious, requiring much manhandling and hauling of ropes and pulleys from below.[12]

By December 1940, twin .50-caliber machine guns were added, as well as a steam-powered Holman Projector that fired explosive projectiles at enemy aircraft. While ineffective against bombing attacks from higher altitudes, the weapon (pictured below) was far cheaper, and easier to procure and install in large numbers than conventional anti-aircraft artillery.[13]

Photo 1-3

British steam-powered Holman Projector anti-aircraft weapon. Photo by Lt. Louis Klemantaski, RN, March 1940, taken before trials at Porthtowan, Cornwall.

Below decks, the fish hold was converted to crew quarters and anti-submarine gear storage. The ship's hull, bulkheads and frames were strengthened to bear the weight of the guns. Any previously installed minesweeping and all fishing gear, including some of the trawl winch parts were removed to provide room for stores. Regarding the armament of converted vessels, as noted by *The Canberry Times*, 25 March 1941:

> Rarely were any two trawlers alike in armament as a hotchpotch of weapons were 'won' by an ever-eager ship's company to add to their firepower; particularly in respect to AA [anti-aircraft] weapons.[14]

VOYAGE TO AMERICA / DUTIES ASSIGNED

> In the middle of the month aid was promised from an unexpected quarter. On the 13th [of February], Cominch [Commander in Chief, United States Fleet] informed Commander, Eastern Sea Fronter that 24 trawlers were being sailed from England for St. John's [Newfoundland Island] "in the course of the next few days." They were "being lent to C in C U.S. Fleet for A/S operations under Command on East Coast North America."
>
> —Entry by Vice Admiral Adolphus Andrews, USN, Commander, Eastern Sea Frontier in his February 1942 War Diary.

In February 1942, HMT *Bedfordshire*'s crew, along with those of the other twenty-three anti-submarine vessels, were notified that they would be deployed across the Atlantic for service in American waters where U-boats were sinking merchant ships at alarming rates. The ocean crossing was dangerous and rough. During the transit, *Bedfordshire* lost her small boat, and her ash chute in heavy seas. (Such chutes were used to discharge ash from the furnace bottoms overboard at regular intervals to keep the stoke-hold clear of ash while at sea.)[15]

The British trawlers made the voyage in groups and arrived throughout the last weeks in March. Near the end of her transit, HMT *Northern Princess* (Lt. Dryden Byrne Phillipson, RNR) was torpedoed and sunk by *U-587* (KptLt Ulrich Borcherdt) on 8 March off the Grand Banks, Newfoundland. Tragically all hands were presumed lost, as no wreckage or bodies were recovered. Following a period of overhaul at the U.S. Navy Yard at Brooklyn, New York, the trawlers were put into service.[16]

Fourteen of the remaining twenty-three vessels were ready for duty at month's end, when *Bedfordshire*, under the command of Lt. Russell Bransby Davis, RNR, and four other trawlers proceeded south. *Bedfordshire* was assigned duties as a convoy escort off the U.S. East Coast and Canada. Her specific assignment was to the Fifth Naval District, sections two and three. This role placed the trawler on duty off North Carolina's outer banks.[17]

LOSS OF HMT *BEDFORDSHIRE* TO *U-558*

Returning to the account of *Bedfordshire* operating from Morehead City, North Carolina, it is believed that after delivery of the convoy to Cape Hatteras, around midnight on 10 May, she headed southwest toward Cape Lookout. Her orders for the night of 11 May, were to patrol between No. 4 buoy (34°53'N, 75°31' W) and No. 14 buoy (34°18'N, 76°24'W).[18]

On the afternoon of 11 May, *Bedfordshire* sent a routine message at 1512, reporting that she was at sea on patrol. Unbeknownst to her crew, the trawler's movements would place them in the direct path of the German submarine *U-558*, commanded by KptLt Gunther Krech. While en route to the Gulf of Mexico, Krech halted in the waters off Cape Lookout to practice "crash dives," an evasive maneuver from the surface to escape attacking aircraft or naval vessels. As *U-558* surfaced from one of these dives, Krech sighted two patrol vessels in the distance and dove again to hide. One of them was HMT *Bedfordshire*.[19]

One of these vessels had in turn sighted the submarine and, after racing to the spot where it had disappeared, began a four-to-six-hour unsuccessful sonar search. As search activities by the patrol vessels diminished, *U-558* came up to periscope depth; finding the patrol vessels nearby, she remained submerged for around another hour. About 2000, Krech decided to make a run for it on the surface, believing that *U-558* could evade the slower patrol vessels.[20]

The sub surfaced and while in the process of attempting its escape, a lookout stationed topside in the conning tower, reported a flashing white light astern that was almost immediately extinguished. *Bedfordshire* was in pursuit, and after two hours was gaining ground on her prey. In the early morning hours of 12 May, Krech, realizing that his adversary was alone and relatively small, turned to fight. After identifying the pursuing vessel as a British anti-submarine trawler, he fired two torpedoes, which both missed. Krech then fired a third torpedo. The trawler was then making an evasive turn, and it hit her squarely amidships, port side.[21]

The resultant explosion nearly lifted *Bedfordshire* out of the water; the trawler was up on her bow, with her stern also jerking upward. Krech recorded in his log that he saw a secondary explosion before she sank. *Bedfordshire* plunged to the bottom so abruptly that no distress signal could be sent. Of the thirty-seven crewmembers aboard her, all perished. For several days, the U.S. Navy was unaware of the trawler's loss, there being no witnesses, radio signals, or survivors. The initial indication that she had been lost was when the first of four bodies of deceased crewmembers washed up on North Carolina beaches. The Navy launched a search for survivors, employing aircraft and surface vessels, but found no cause or evidence of her disappearance.[22]

The German submarine, continuing her journey south after sinking *Bedfordshire*, encountered HMT *St. Loman* south of Cape Lookout. *St. Loman* reported a torpedo being fired at her at 0226 on 12 May, while at position 34°11'N, 76°27' W. Krech, having missed his target, continued on to the Gulf of Mexico, to hunt wary merchant shipping plying waters along the Gulf Coast.[23]

On 16 May, the U.S. Navy acknowledged HMT *Bedfordshire* was missing in action, and likely sunk. By 8 June, the British Admiralty had officially announced the loss of the trawler and notified the next of kin. Four members of *Bedfordshire*'s crew, who had been ashore and missed the trawler's departure from port on 10 May, survived. Stoker Samuel Nutt and Leading Cook Richard Salmon were on shore leave. Leaving a Morehead City bar, they were arrested and thrown in jail. Upon their release the following day, they went down to the waterfront and found their vessel had already sailed. Ordinary Seaman Richard Steadman had hurt his knee and been transferred to another ship. It is unknown why John D. Steward missed the ship.[24]

LEST THEY BE FORGOTTEN

HMT *Bedfordshire*'s Crew Casualties

Lt. R. B. Davis, RNR (In Command)	G. H. Fisher, Stoker 2nd. Class
Temp. Sub. Lt. H. Clutterbuck, RNVR	H. Ford, Seaman
Temp. Sub. Lt. B. Hall, RNVR	J. Kelly, Seaman
Temp. Sub. Lt. T. Cunningham, RNVR	W. Lee, Leading Seaman, RNR
F. W. Barnes, Engineman	E. W. Lukins, Act. Stoker Petty Officer
S. Bennett, Ordinary Seaman	A. A. McCrindle, Seaman
L. P. Bickford, Seaman	A. McKenzie, Stoker
E. S. Carruthers, Ordinary Seaman	F. F. Maltby, Leading Seaman, RNR
G. W. Cerrino, Leading Seaman, RNR	E. N. Morton, Ordinary Seaman
W. F. Clemence, Ordinary Seaman	W. J. Myers, Stoker
F. Cragg, Ordinary Seaman	S. W. Smitten, Ordinary Seaman
S. R. Craig, Ordinary Telegraphist	P. E. Stone, Seaman

J. R. Dick, Seaman
T. M. Dicks, Ordinary Seaman
A. Dryden, Seaman
A. W. Duncan, Chief Engineman, RNR
G. Featherstone, Ordinary Telegraphist
C. T. Travell, Ordinary Signalman
C. W. White, Ordinary Telegraphist
L. J. Williams, Stoker, 2nd. Class
R. Davis, Ordinary Seaman, RCNVR
J. L. McCauley, Ordinary Seaman RCNVR[25]

Two of the deceased sailors were members of the Royal Canadian Naval Volunteer Reserve—Ordinary Seaman Russell Samuel Davis, and Ordinary Seaman James Lorne McCauley. They were apparently temporarily assigned to the ship, referred to in Commonwealth navies as being seconded.[26]

THREE HM TRAWLERS LOST TO ENEMY SUBS

HMT *Bedfordshire* was the only one of the twenty-four British trawlers that served off the United States to be directly attacked and sunk by a German U-boat near the U.S. East Coast. Her wreck site is seventeen miles southeast of Beaufort Inlet, North Carolina, in 105 feet of water.[27]

The earlier loss of HMT *Northern Princess* on 8 March 1942 to U-587, occurred off Newfoundland. HMT *Kingston Ceylonite* was sunk on 15 June 1942, in a minefield laid off Virginia Beach by *U-701*. One of her eighteen casualties (of a 32-man crew) was a Canadian serving in the Royal Navy, Ordinary Seaman Frederick Munden, RN.[28]

2

U.S. Navy Unprepared for War

An examination of the foregoing list shows vessels varying in speed from 9 knots to a possible 15 knots for the Eagle boats and the Dione *of 16 ½ knots. The Coast Guard Cutters are the best fitted for anti-submarine work, but are small and are mostly fully occupied in their regular Coast Guard duties. There is not a vessel available that an enemy submarine could not outdistance when operating on the surface. In most cases the guns of these vessels would be outranged by those of the submarine. The limited capabilities of these vessels are apparent.*

—Commander, North Atlantic Naval Coastal Frontier describing, in a letter to the Chief of Naval Operations on 22 December 1941, the capabilities of the twenty-surface craft then at his disposal.[1]

In the early afternoon of 7 December 1941, word went out over New York radios that all officers attached to the North Atlantic Naval Coastal Frontier should report immediately for duty. The headquarters for the frontier was in the Federal Building, 90 Church Street, New York City. On its fifteenth floor was the office of then Rear Adm. Adolphus Andrews, USN.[2]

Photo 2-1

Vice Admiral Adolphus Andrews, USN.
Naval History and Heritage Command photograph #NH 56042

Ten months earlier on 10 March 1941, Andrews, the commandant of the Third Naval District, had assumed additional duties as the first commander, North Atlantic Naval Coastal Frontier. This frontier encompassed all the territorial waters of the United States from the Canadian-U.S. boundary to the north, southward to the southern boundary of Onslow County in North Carolina. The shape of the frontier, and the distance that it extended offshore is shown in the map.[3]

Map 2-1

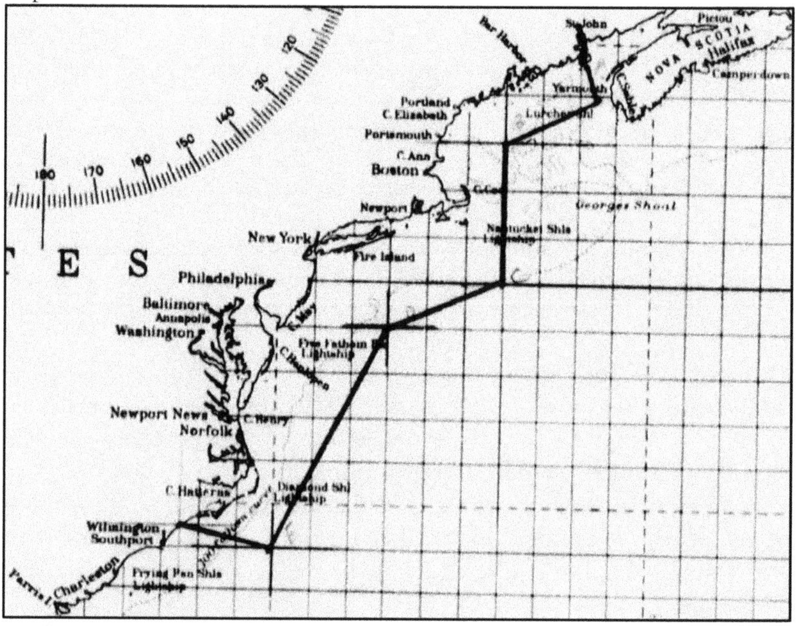

North Atlantic Naval Coastal Frontier boundaries
Commander, North Atlantic Naval Coastal Frontier War Diary, December 1941

Within the limits of the Frontier, Andrews was charged with:

- The defense of the North Atlantic Naval Coastal Frontier
- The protection and routing of shipping
- The support of the United States Fleet
- The support of the Army and associated forces[4]

It was well enough to have plans for the defense of the Frontier, but it was imperative to have forces and material to carry them out. A short time after war broke out, Andrews had at his disposal only twenty, mostly antiquated craft of World War I or earlier vintage:

- Four patrol yachts: USS *Coral* (PY-15), *Siren* (PY-13), *Sylph* (PY-12), and *Tourmaline* (PY-20)
- Four 110-foot submarine-chasers: USS *SC-102*, *SC-330*, *SC-412*, and *SC-437*
- The 165-foot Coast Guard cutter USCG *Dione* (WPC-107)
- Six 125-foot *Active*-class Coast Guard cutters: USCG *Active* (WSC-125), *Antietam* (WSC-128), *Dix* (WSC-136), *Frederick Lee* (WSC-139), *Jackson* (WSC-142), and *Rush* (WSC-151)
- Two 200-foot patrol gunboats: USS *Dubuque* (PG-17), and *Paducah* (PG-18)
- Three Eagle boats: USS *PE-19*, *PE-27*, and *PE-56*[5]

USN Patrol Yachts	**Built**	**USN Sub-chasers**	**Built**
USS *Coral* (PY-15)	1914	USS *SC-102*	1918
USS *Siren* (PY-13)	1929	USS *SC-330*	1918
USS *Sylph* (PY-12)	1929	USS *SC-412*	1918
USS *Tourmaline* (PY-20)	1930	USS *SC-437*	1918
USCG Cutters	**Built**	**USCG Cutters**	**Built**
USCG *Dione* (WPC-107)	1934	USCG *Frederick Lee* (WSC-139)	1927
USCG *Active* (WSC-125)	1926	USCG *Jackson* (WSC-142)	1927
USCG *Antietam* (WSC-128)	1927	USCG *Rush* (WSC-151)	1927
USCG *Dix* (WSC-136)	1927		
USN Eagle Boats	**Built**	**USN Gunboats**	**Built**
USS *PE-19*	1919	USS *Dubuque* (PG-17)	1904
USS *PE-27*	1919	USS *Paducah* (PG-18)	1905
USS *PE-56*	1919		

United States Coast Guard
Established: 4 August 1790

Executive Order 8929 of 1 November 1941 transferred the Coast Guard to the Navy. On 1 January 1946, the service reverted from Navy control to its previous place within the Treasury Department.

As indicated in the quoted material at the chapter's head, the most capable anti-submarine vessels among this small group were the U.S. Coast Guard cutters. With the exception of the patrol yachts USS *Siren*, *Sylph*, and *Tourmaline*, they were the only relatively modern vessels.

FRONTIER NAVAL VESSELS

Patrol gunboats

The patrol gunboats USS *Dubuque* and *Paducah* were assigned duties concomitant with their advanced ages. *Dubuque* taken from her most recent duty as a Naval Reserve mine training ship, was returned to full commission on 1 July 1941, after which she patrolled on the New England coast until 14 October. She arrived at Little Creek, Virginia, on the 16th to serve as gunnery practice ship for the U.S. Navy Armed Guard School located there. For the duration of the war, *Dubuque* trained merchant ship armed guard crews in Chesapeake Bay. These gunners, all USN personnel, were assigned and served aboard merchant vessels to operate the armaments installed on them[6]

Paducah was similarly ordered from duty training Naval Reservists in the 9th Naval District at Duluth on Lake Superior in Minnesota, to the East Coast. Through World War II, she also trained Armed Guard gunners in Chesapeake Bay, thus giving vital service to the Merchant Marine's crucial World War II assignment.[7]

Photo 2-2

Patrol gunboat USS *Dubuque* (PG-17), location and date unknown.
Naval History and Heritage Command photograph #NH 54576

Sub-chasers

USS *SC-102*, *SC-330*, *SC-412*, and *SC-437* were wooden-hulled subchasers. At least two of them, perhaps all four, were serving as Naval Reserve training vessels when the U.S. entered World War II. They were remnants of 120 submarine chasers which, designed to counter German U-boats during the First World War, had served on the East Coast of the U.S. and in Europe. The first chasers had arrived in Ireland in May 1918. Others also were based out of the Azores; Plymouth, England; Brest, France; Gibraltar; and at Corfu, Greece. The vessels were small, roughly 110 feet in length and with 85 tons displacement.[8]

Photo 2-3

Sub-chaser USS *SC-330* crossing the Atlantic, circa September-October 1918.
Naval History and Heritage Command photograph #NH 91189

Eagle Boats

Late in 1917, the Navy realized that it needed steel ships smaller than destroyers, but with greater ranges than the 110-foot submarine chasers developed earlier in the year. The submarine chasers were limited to a range of about 900 miles at a cruising speed of 10 knots, owing to their high consumption of gasoline and limited fuel storage although they were capable of speeds up to 18 knots.[9]

Faced with a deficit in suitable vessels, attention turned to building steel patrol vessels with the involvement of auto-builder Henry Ford. Informed of the need for anti-submarine vessels to combat the U-boat menace, Ford asserted: "What we want is one type of ship in large numbers." On 7 November, Ford accepted membership on the U.S. Shipping Board, whose task was to increase the number of U.S. ships supporting the World War I efforts, in an active advisory role. Examining the Navy's plans for the projected steel patrol ships, he urged that all hull plates be flat so that they could be produced quickly in quantity; and he persuaded the Navy to accept steam turbines instead of reciprocating steam engines.[10]

Ford established a new plant on the Rouge River on the outskirts of Detroit, and began building suitable vessels that were dubbed "Eagle Boats," 200-foot sub-chaser vessels produced using mass production techniques, and employing factory workers. The first keel was laid in May 1918. The machinery and fittings for these boats were largely fabricated at Ford's Highland Park plant in Detroit, then assembled on the 1,700-foot line at the Rouge River facility. The process replaced conventional shipyard launching of sliding down slideways, by employing a floating dry dock. The hulls moved slowly from the assembly line on enormous, tractor-drawn flatcars. and then were placed on a 225-foot steel dock alongside the river's edge, which was then sunk 20 feet into the water to float the vessel. The first Eagle boat was launched on 11 July. As completed, the boats were sent by the Great Lakes and the St. Lawrence River to the Atlantic coast.[11]

Photo 2-4

Eagle Boat 27 (*PE-27*) and 48 (*PE-48*) at the Boston Navy Yard, November 1940. U.S. Navy photograph NY2-1371-40, Boston National Historical Park Collection, NPS Cat. No. BOSTS-11005

The term "Eagle Boat" stemmed from a *Washington Post* editorial which called for ". . . an eagle to scour the seas and pounce upon and destroy every German submarine." However, the Eagle Boats never saw service in World War I, largely as a result of Ford's excessive initial optimism and the inexperience of his labor and supervisory personnel in shipbuilding. Upon the signing of the Armistice in November 1918, the number of boats under contract, standing at 112, was cut to 60. Of these, seven were commissioned in 1918, and the remaining 53 were commissioned in 1919.[12]

In WWII one of the three assigned to the Frontier met a sorry fate. On 23 April 1945, Eagle boat 56 (which had been reclassified *PE-56*) was torpedoed and sunk by the German submarine *U-853* (Oblt. Helmut Fromsdorf) three nautical miles south-southeast of Cape Elizabeth, Maine. The vessel broke in two and sank after a heavy explosion amidships, with the loss of her commanding officer, Lt. James Early, four officers and 44 men. The destroyer USS *Selfridge* (DD-357) picked up one officer and twelve men about 30 minutes later. As indicated by a plaque at Cape Elizabeth, Maine, her loss marked the greatest single incident of the loss of Navy personnel in New England waters (the northern portion of the U.S. East Coast) in World War II.[13]

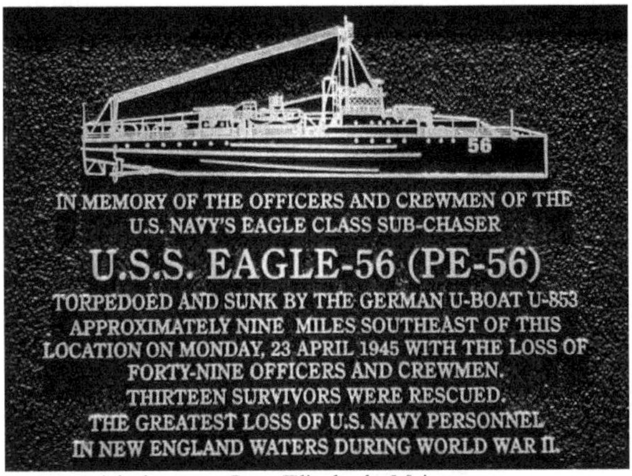

A memorial plaque at Cape Elizabeth, Maine.
Courtesy of NavSource and Bob Canchola

Patrol Yachts

The oldest of the District's four patrol yachts that ultimately became the USS *Coral* (PY-15), was built in 1914 by Pusey and Jones, Wilmington, Delaware, for John K. Stewart, a partner in the Stewart-Warner Speedometer Company. He sold the 207-foot steam yacht then named *Sialia* to Henry Ford on 20 January 1917 for $250,000. Less than six months later, the Navy purchased her for World War I service. She was delivered to the Navy on 10 June, and commissioned on 30 June 1917 as USS *Sialia* (SP-543).[14]

Photo 2-5

Steam yacht *Sialia* under way prior to her World War I Navy service.
Naval History and Heritage Command photograph #NH 102217

The war service of the stately yacht was tranquil. After initial duty as a patrol vessel in the Philadelphia area, in April 1918 she was sent to Hampton Roads, Virginia, where she served for a year as flagship for commander, Cruiser and Transportation Forces. Following the war, she was loaned to the U.S. Coast and Geodetic Survey from 10 June 1919 to 15 March 1920. A few months after being returned to the Navy, *Sialia* was sold back to Henry Ford on 12 April 1920.[15]

Photo 2-6

Patrol yacht USS *Coral* (PY-15) in port, location and date unknown.
Naval History and Heritage Command #NH 81384

Ford renamed her *Yankee Clipper* and, in 1925, had her rebuilt and lengthened seven-and-a-half feet. He sold the yacht in 1927, and she went through a series of private owners before the Navy reacquired her on 25 November 1940. She was recommissioned as a patrol yacht USS *Coral* (PY 15) on 27 February 1941.[16]

YACHTS AND WORKHORSES PRESSED INTO DUTY

Following the Japanese attack on Pearl Harbor, the U.S. Navy acquired approximately 700 vessels from private owners, which they designated as patrol yachts (PY), coastal patrol yachts (PYc), or patrol craft (YP). After arming them they sent them to sea as inshore or offshore patrol vessels. The vessels spanned the spectrum from luxurious yacht to waterfront workhorse—fishing vessel, whaler, tug, and freighter. Their collective service is the subject of author Bruhn's book *Battle Stars for the "Cactus Navy."* Cactus was the code name for Guadalcanal, where some of the most seaworthy vessels—tuna clippers from San Diego, and fishing vessels from New England—were sent to support the First Marine Division. Employed as small supply vessels, their duties involved plying Japanese-patrolled, reef-infested waters to provide U.S. Marine and Army combat troops desperately needed food, fuel, ammunition, and other materiel.

The main differences between the patrol yachts (PY) and coastal patrol yachts (PYc) were size and age. The patrol yachts—spanning 154 to 245 feet, and displacing 500 to 1,220 tons—were larger than their coastal patrol cousins and generally older, built between 1906 and 1931. Almost all were of steel, which along with their size, allowed for the installation of heavier armament than was possible in the svelte wooden coastal patrol yachts.[17]

Some of the yachts obtained by the Navy were sold for a nominal fee, loaned, or donated to the Service. While their previous owners probably winced as they watched hand-rubbed mahogany, scoured teak, and gleaming bright-work disappear under thick coats of gray paint, many of these same individuals also donned a Navy uniform and traded their luxurious offices for a pitching deck.[18]

Photo 2-7

Gunner's Mate First Ernest Borgnine, U.S. Navy.
Naval History and Heritage Command photograph

Most of the men who served in the patrol yacht force came from more modest backgrounds than previous yachtsmen owners; some achieved considerable acclaim and notoriety after the war. Ernest Borgnine, a crewmember aboard the *Sylph* (PY-12), became a famous actor, with roles in dozens of acclaimed films as well as television shows to his credit, most notably the popular series *McHale's Navy* (1962-66). During his service in the Navy, Borgnine rose from seaman to gunner's mate first class.[19]

PAUCITY OF FRONTIER AIRCRAFT, AS WELL

Aircraft would have been a vital resource in the protection of the area, but a similar shortfall existed in both the USN and USA air forces available within the North Atlantic Naval Coastal Frontier. In all, in December, there was a total of 103 planes within the Frontier, divided into the following categories:

Trainer – 51	Patrol (P or PB) – 6
Scout (OS or OB) – 18	Torpedo (TB) – 3
Utility – 14	Fighter – 3
Transport – 7	Bomber – 1

On 7 December 1941, the defense of the Frontier was undertaken with these forces: 20 vessels, and 103 planes, of which about three-quarters were unsuited to the task assigned.[20]

FRONTIER DEFENSE THROUGH YEAR'S END

Three important measures were implemented to protect the coast and defend Frontier waters as soon as war broke out. All available air and surface craft took up patrol of the areas that had been assigned to them by war plans. An existing inshore patrol off important harbors was maintained, and an offshore patrol established (soon after 7 December). The latter task was undertaken by U.S. Army aircraft, because the Frontier possessed no planes capable of conducting searches so far out to sea.[21]

SMALL CRAFT AND DEFENSIVE MINING

> *It is requested that small vessels be equipped with radio for transmitting voice or telegraph as may be required for reception by Army warning net ashore, be stationed fifty or more miles offshore to report approaching enemy aircraft, surface vessels, and submarines to Army Aircraft Warning Service. If available, crews should be made up of Naval Personnel, otherwise of undoubtedly loyal civilians.*

—Chief of Naval Operations dispatch of 15 December 1941 to the commandants of all Naval Districts within the Frontier.[22]

Requiring small craft to supplement the patrol work of aircraft and surface vessels, the Chief of Naval Operations (CNO) solicited assistance from the commandants of Naval Districts. Specifically, that civilian craft be fitted with radios to report enemy sightings. This action followed an important measure already being undertaken. The use of defensive mines against a possible enemy submarine offensive was announced on 10 December in a dispatch that read as follows:

> A mined area covering the approaches to New York Harbor has been established. Incoming vessels will secure directions for safe navigation from patrol vessels stationed off Ambrose Channel Entrance.[23]

Photo 2-8

Fleet at anchor in New York Harbor, circa 1939.
Naval History and Heritage Command photograph #NH 923

All merchant shipping bound to and from New York Harbor used the Ambrose Channel. Considered to be part of lower New York Bay, the channel lay several miles off the coasts of Sandy Hook in New Jersey and Breezy Point, Queens in New York. It terminated at Ambrose Anchorage, just south of the Verrazano Narrows Bridge, the gateway to New York Harbor.

Throughout December, a system of mines, booms, and nets that were designed to augment controlled minefields already put in place by the Army, was extended and strengthened in areas along the East Coast.

Special Warning No. 140 advised all ships and stations on 19 December, that "A mined area covering the approaches to Chesapeake Bay has been established. All vessels are required to take pilots before entering the bay." The Chesapeake Bay covers parts of six states and is the largest estuary in the United States. Its mouth is about twelve miles wide between its northern point near Cape Charles, Virginia, and its southern point close to Cape Henry, Virginia.[24]

Map 2-2

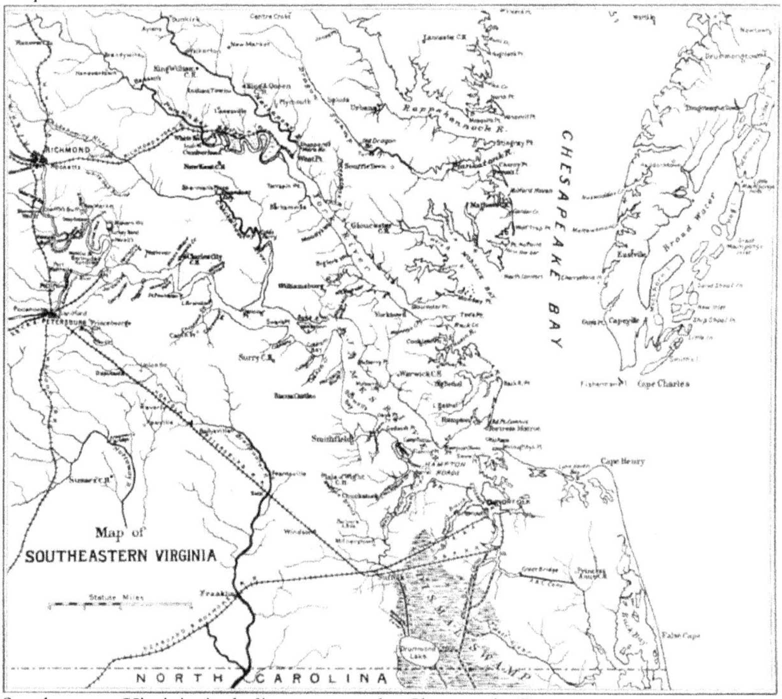

Southeastern Virginia, including entry to the Chesapeake Bay
National Archives photograph USN 901626

The following day, the CNO expressed his desire to increase the protection in this area by laying a field of moored, contact mines at the entrance to the Chesapeake. Similar fields were sowed in the approaches to the Boston, Massachusetts, and Portland, Maine, harbors by 23 December. Up and down the coast, nets, booms, and minefields were laid to increase protection in vital areas.[25]

3

German Submarines Arrive

History is repeating itself and, as in 1914-1918, so in 1939-1942, although we shall not win the war by defeating the U-boats, we shall assuredly lose the war if we do not defeat them.

—British Admiralty Report.[1]

At 0130 EWT [North American Eastern War Time Zone], January 14th [1942], the Panamanian tanker NORNESS *was hit by three torpedoes and went down…sixty miles southeast of Montauk Point [the eastern tip of the south shore of Long Island, New York].*

—The sinking of the Panamanian-flagged Norwegian motor tanker MT *Norness* by *U-123*, marked the opening of unprecedented German submarine attacks upon merchant shipping in North Atlantic Naval Coastal Frontier waters.[2]

Photo 3-1

German type IX, 750-ton class submarine, 1940.
Naval History and Heritage Command photograph #NH 111282

Following Germany's declaration of war on the United States on 11 December 1941, Admiral Doenitz initiated plans for a devastatingly swift blow on America's Eastern Seaboard. Operation PAUKENSCHLAG (Drumbeat) involved the employment of the five type IX U-boats and their commanders listed in the table. Also identified are the dates the U-boats (units of the 2nd Flotilla) sailed from Lorient, France, and the number of ships that each sank or damaged between 14 January and 6 February 1942.[3]

Photo 3-2

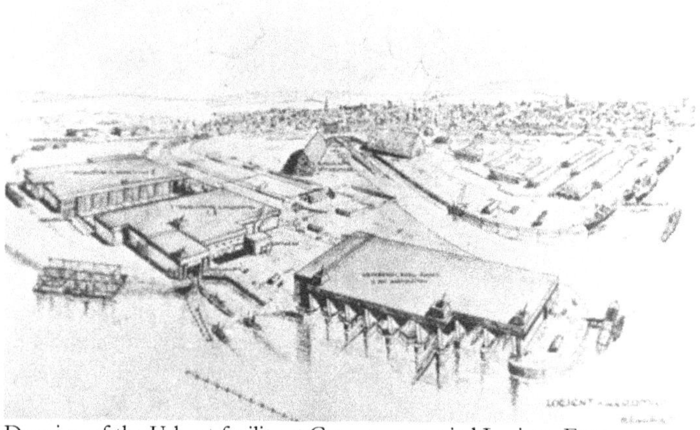

Drawing of the U-boat facility at German-occupied Lorient, France.
Naval History and Heritage Command photograph #NH 111304

2nd Flotilla
(2. Unterseebootsflottille)
Based at Lorient, France
June 1941-August 1944

During this dreadful 24-day period, the submarines sent twenty-three vessels to the bottom and damaged two others. Kptlt. Reinhard Hardegen's *U-123* singularly accounted for the loss of eight ships and torpedoing of another which, fortunately, survived to sail another day.

Operation PAUKENSCHLAG Type IX U-boats

Date	**U-boat/Type**	**Commander**	**Ships hit**
18 Dec 41	*U-125* / IXC	Kptlt. Ulrich Folkers	1 S
23 Dec 41	*U-123* / IXB	Kptlt. Reinhard Hardegen	8 S, 1 D
24 Dec 41	*U-66* / IXC	KrvKpt. Richard Zapp	5 S
27 Dec 41	*U-130* / IXC	KrvKpt. Ernst Kals	5 S, 1 D
27 Dec 41	*U-109* / IXB	Kptlt. Heinrich Bleichrodt	4 S
S: Sunk	D: Damaged		23 S, 2 D[4]

Before delving into representative U-boat attacks against merchant shipping along the East Coast, and the resultant losses of vessels and crewmembers, a description of the fearsome submarines that Andrews' paucity of antiquated forces faced, is appropriate.

TYPE IX SUBMARINE WEAPONS LOAD

Diagram 3-1

German submarine T-1 torpedo variant
National Security Agency OP-20-G publication, *Battle of the Atlantic Volume IV Technical Intelligence from Allied Communications Intelligence*

The armament of Type IX U-boats included: a quantity of torpedoes (their principal weapon), mines when carried in lieu of some of their torpedoes, a single large deck gun, and a smaller anti-aircraft gun.

At this point in the war, submarine commanders had available for their use, a 21-inch compressed air torpedo (T-1) with three settings:

- 44 knots to a range of 6,500 yards
- 40 knots to 8,700 yards
- 30 knots to 15,300 yards[5]

As noted, higher weapon speed resulted in shorter ranges. The air-propulsion torpedo had the disadvantage of leaving a visible trail of bubbles on the surface on its way to the target, and was accordingly mostly used in night attacks. Because the T-1 required less inspection and maintenance than the subsequently-developed T-2 and T-3 electric torpedo, it was generally employed by U-boats conducting lengthy patrols, as were the five Operation PAUKENSCHLAG submarines.[6]

The type IX long-range boats were fitted with 6 torpedo tubes below the waterline (4 at the bow and 2 at the stern), and carried 22 torpedoes inside the submarine. Functioning as minelayers, the boats could carry 44 TMA or 66 TMB mines. The boats were fitted with one large 10.5cm deck gun with about 110 rounds; anti-aircraft armament and related ammunition capacity varied throughout the war.[7]

German TMA and TMB mines were laid from the torpedo tubes of submarines. The TMA was a moored influence mine. When deployed, its buoyant mine body (manufactured with an aluminum alloy shell and a 507-lb explosive charge) floated near the surface, tethered to a heavy anchor by either a 492- or 888-foot cable. The TMB was a ground-influence mine. Its cylindrical shell, also aluminum alloy, enclosed a charge which varied between 926 and 1,235 lbs. Because the mine rested on the seafloor, and needed to be near enough target ships to do them harm, it was normally laid in shallow, 72 to 90-foot water. The term "influence" means that these type mines were detonated by the magnetic or acoustic signature of a passing ship—created by ferrous (magnetic) metals used in their construction, or the noise their engines and propellers produced.[8]

The deck gun of German submarines was intended as a defensive weapon against small surface vessels, for which the torpedo was not a suitable weapon, or against vessels posing little threat, and thereby saving valuable torpedoes for more fruitful targets. The U-boat however, was a poor gun platform since it was tender (rolled a lot), and waves frequently make the deck slippery and hazardous. To prevent the possibility of gun crew members being washed over the side under the lifelines, they were fastened to them with safety lines. A gunner, layer and loader, usually under the supervision of the second watch officer, operated the gun.[9]

Deck guns had no range finders, so engagements had to take place at close range. A chain of sailors was required to hand-retrieve ammunition shells from below control room deckplates, then pass them up the conning tower, and onto the upper deck. A small watertight locker near the gun held a few "ready rounds." A good crew could get off 15 to 18 rounds per minute. However, use of its gun made a U-boat very vulnerable. Before diving after deploying the gun, it and its ammunition had to be secured, and the gun crew returned inside the submarine, resulting in delayed submersion.[10]

From 1941, the 3.7cm SK C/30U gun was the standard anti-aircraft weapon fitted in type IX boats.[11]

CHARACTERISTICS / PERFORMANCE / TACTICS

The type IX U-boat was designed in 1935-1936 as a large ocean-going submarine. The Type IXB variant was an improved version of this submarine with the range increased by 1,500 nautical miles and, owing to carrying additional fuel, slightly heavier. The design was improved again in successor type IXC boats from 1939 onward. The *U-123* under Kptlt. Reinhard Hardegen would become perhaps the most famous IXB boat. Between 20 June 1941 and 17 April 1942, she sank twenty-two vessels and damaged five others.[12]

A review of the characteristics of the IXB and IXC boats, coupled with performance of the T-1 torpedo, gives an inkling of practices and tactics of the five submarines participating in Operation DRUMBEAT. They sailed from Brittany in northwestern France, between 18 and 27 December 1941, each carrying sealed orders to be opened after passing 20 degrees west longitude, which directed them to different destinations. All the boats were to be in position by 13 January 1942 for a fast, surprise attack on the Eastern Seaboard of the United States.[13]

German Submarine Type IXB and IXC Characteristics

Characteristics	IXB	IXC
Length	251 feet	252 feet
Beam	22 feet	22 feet
Displacement surf/sub/total (tons)	1,051/1,178/1,430	1,120/1,232/1,549
Draft	15 feet 5 inches	15 feet 5 inches
Power surfaced/submerged (hp)	4,400/1,000	4,400/1,000
Speed surfaced/submerged (kts)	18.2/7.3	18.3/7.3
Range surfaced/submerged (miles)	12,000 (10 kts)/ 64 (4 kts)	13,450 (10 kts)/ 63 (4 kts)
Max depth	755 feet	755 feet
Crew complement	48-56 men	48-56 men[14]

In this area, the submarines had operating advantages, other than density of shipping, based on geography and practices of urban populations ashore. If patrolling aircraft or surface vessels posed a threat, by day the submarines could rest on the seafloor of the gently-slopping continental shelf (see map on next page), and shut down their engines. Once nightfall came, they could surface, run their engines to recharge batteries, "air out the boat," then move into position to prey on silhouetted coastal shipping targets until an effective "dim-out" was inaugurated to eliminate urban glow.

Map 3-2

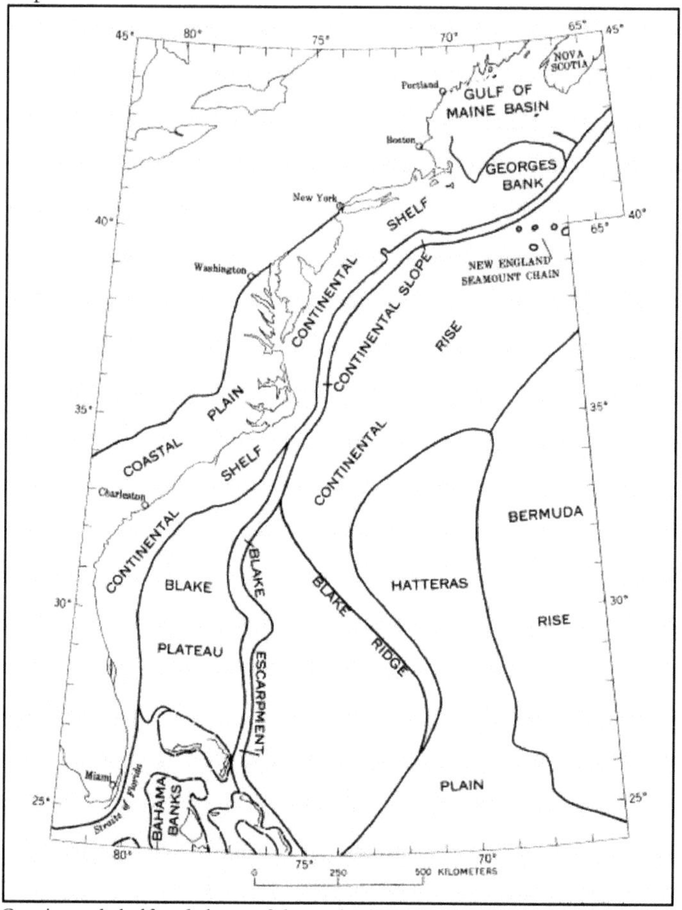

Continental shelf and slope of the United States Atlantic Seaboard
Atlantic Continental Shelf and Slope of The United States Geologic Background, 1966

One of the most significant advantages was the neglect of local communities to dim their waterfront lights, and of military authorities to require them to do so, until well after the submarine offensive began. Although in a location outside the operating area of this book, German submariner Reinhard Hardegen recalled the following at age 85, the night of 9 April 1942 off Jacksonville, on Florida's northeast coast, when *U-123* sank the SS *Gulfamerica* in full view of people on shore:

> There was moonshine, how you say, moonlight. There were lights on the shore. And many people. Bars were open. People were on the beaches.[16]

Hardegen could see a roller coaster, all lit up, and streams of car headlights heading toward the shore. To avoid hitting civilians near the shore with gun rounds, which were often used to finish off torpedoed vessels, he positioned the *U-123* between the coast and the tanker so that he could shoot in the direction of the sea. That humanitarian gesture could have cost him and his crew their lives, as an American destroyer soon gave chase and almost successfully attacked his sub.[17]

COMMENCEMENT OF OPERATION PAUKENSCHLAG

> *The heart of the problem of anti-submarine warfare can perhaps best be stated in terms of mathematics. Effective application of the methods and efficient use of weapons depend directly upon the numerical strength of the forces involved.... Changes in principle or redesign of instruments will accomplish little if it is impossible to increase the numerical strength of ships and planes to the amount required.*
>
> —Commander, North Atlantic Naval Coastal Frontier
> War Diary, January 1942.

On 11 January 1942, Andrews received word that the British cargo ship SS *Cyclops* had been torpedoed and sunk about 300 miles due east of Cape Cod, Massachusetts. Although her loss occurred further out in the Atlantic than the area for which he was responsible to defend, enemy intentions, and associated impending threat to North Atlantic Naval Coastal Frontier waters, were now clear.[18]

The arrival of submarines in waters off the East Coast was not unexpected. It was reasonable to assume that what the Germans had achieved with huge success in WWI, with less capable submarines (spring and summer 1918), would be attempted again. (A chapter of Rob Hoole's and my book, *Home Waters: Royal Navy, Royal Canadian Navy, and U.S. Navy Mine Forces Battling U-boats in World War I*, is devoted to this submarine offensive.)[19]

In every respect, the coastal waters of North America offered an attractive hunting ground for submarines. The great length of the sea lanes running down the Eastern Seaboard and into the Caribbean, placed imposing burdens upon any forces trying to protect them. At all times, these lanes were crowded with merchant vessels proceeding, ordinarily, alone.[20]

Such ships offered easy, frequent, and valuable targets. Most valuable of all were the numerous tankers running from northern U.S.

East Coast ports to the oil refineries in South America and the Gulf of Mexico. (Of particular importance were the Dutch islands of Curaçao and Aruba, off the coast of Venezuela, where over half a million barrels of gasoline and oil derivatives were produced daily.) At the southern extremity, these lanes flowed into the confined waters of the Caribbean. There, shipping compressed into narrow channels presented an alluring opportunity to a resourceful enemy looking for hunting grounds far from European waters but of ultimate impact on them. The target area dictated long submarine patrol durations, greater fuel consumption in transit, and meant less time on station in areas of interest.[21]

On 12 January, the day after the sinking of *Cyclops*, at least four U-boats were known by the Allies to be about 300 miles east of Nantucket Light (a lighthouse on Nantucket Island off southeastern Massachusetts), and believed to be proceeding westward. The following day, Andrews was informed that commandant, First Naval District had closed the ports of Boston, Massachusetts; Portland, Maine; and Portsmouth, New Hampshire, to ship departures.[22]

NAVAL DISTRICTS

The defense of shorelines and inland waterways of the United States and its territories and island possessions were divided into sixteen naval districts and two river commands. The vessels and craft assigned to each district were allocated to either the local defense force or the adjacent naval coastal force. Larger escort and patrol vessels best equipped and armed to deal with the enemy submarine threat in naval coastal frontiers were assigned to commanders of these areas.[23]

United States Eastern Seaboard Naval Districts

District	Area	Headquarters
No. 1	Maine, New Hampshire, Vermont, Massachusetts, Rhode Island (including Block Island)	Boston, Massachusetts
No. 3	Connecticut, New York, northern part of New Jersey (including counties of Mercer, Monmouth, and all counties north thereof), also the Nantucket Shoals Lightship	New York, New York
No. 4	Pennsylvania, southern part of New Jersey (including counties of Burlington, Ocean, and all counties south thereof), Delaware (including Winter Quarter Shoal Light Vessel)	Philadelphia, Pennsylvania
No. 5	Maryland less Anne Arundel, Prince Georges, Montgomery, St. Mary's, Calvert, and Charles counties; West Virginia; Virginia less Arlington, Fairfax, Stafford, King George, Prince William, and Westmoreland counties; and the counties of	Naval Operating Base, Norfolk, Virginia

	Currituck, Camden, Pasquotank, Gates, Perquimans, Chowan, Tyrrell, Washington, Hyde, Beaufort, Pamlico, Craven, Jones, Carteret, Onslow, and Dare in North Carolina; also, the Diamond Shoal Lightship	
Potomac River Naval Command	The Potomac River Area, including the District of Columbia, and certain bordering counties in Maryland and Virginia	Navy Yard, Washington, D.C.
Severn River Naval Command	Anne Arundel County, Maryland	United States Naval Academy, Annapolis, Maryland
No. 6	South Carolina, Georgia, and North Carolina, except counties of Currituck, Camden, Pasquotank, Gates, Perquimans, Chowan, Tyrrell, Washington, Hyde, Beaufort, Pamlico, Craven, Jones, Carteret, Onslow, and Dare; and the counties of Nassau and Duval in Florida	Charleston, South Carolina
No. 7	Florida, except the counties of Nassau, Duval, and those west of Apalachicola River	Miami, Florida[24]

Map 3-3

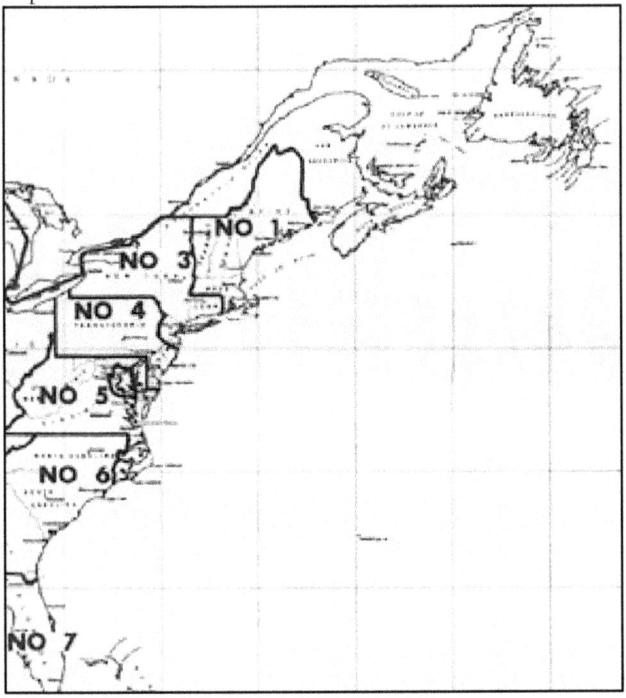

Naval Districts No. 1 and 3 through No. 7; western portions of 6 and 7 are not shown
Julius Augustus Furer, *Administration of the Navy Department in World War II*, 1959

ESTABLISHMENT OF SEA FRONTIERS

In recognition that the existing coastal frontiers overlapped the boundaries of naval districts, and that associated naval operations took place in coastal zones in which both the Army and Navy exercised control, new commands called "sea frontiers" were established on 6 February 1942. The designated areas, which included the existing coastal zones as well as the land areas of the coastal frontiers, were created by a joint Army and Navy agreement, the former charged with the defense of the land areas while the latter maintained inshore and offshore patrols. The newly created sea frontiers were commanded by a vice or rear admiral who might or might not also be the commander of a naval district.[25]

As part of this Navy restructuring, the North Atlantic Naval Coastal Frontier would become the Eastern Sea Frontier, and Vice Adm. Adolphus Andrews, commander, Eastern Sea Frontier.

LOSS OF TANKER *NORNESS* TO SUBMARINE *U-123*

Photo 3-3

Panamanian-flagged Norwegian motor tanker MT *Norness*.
Coast Guard photograph taken the day before she was lost to *U-123*

About an hour and a half after the ports of Boston, Portland, and Portsmouth were closed, the first ship within the limits of the North Atlantic Naval Coastal Frontier was attacked. At 0130 on 14 January, the Norwegian motor tanker *Norness* was sunk sixty miles southeast of Montauk Point on Long Island, New York, by three torpedoes fired by Kptlt. Reinhard Hardegen's *U-123*.[26]

Norness had left New York, loaded with 12,222 tons of crude oil, en route to Halifax, where she was to join a convoy bound for the UK.

The tanker had earlier been fitted with a gun while in Robinson Drydock at Newark, and was to receive ammunition for it at Halifax. Following installation of the gun, she had gone to the Esso Refinery at Constable Hook, New Jersey, and taken on board the fuel oil for England.[27]

In early morning darkness on 14 January, Able Seaman Peder Andersen was awakened by a powerful explosion, causing the ship to list heavily to port. He made it up on deck, practically naked, and was met by a "rain of black oil." He saw the port lifeboat hanging upside down, and ran over to the starboard side to help launch the boat there, which the heavy list made extremely difficult. The 3rd Mate was in charge of this boat. When 20 men had gotten into it, he called up to the remaining survivors on deck that it couldn't hold any more.[28]

Andersen and others then saw a black shadow gliding slowly very close to the stricken *Norness*, coming all the way up to her stern, "as if he knew we had no ammunition for the gun," before firing a second torpedo which hit the pumproom and caused a giant "sea of flames." Andersen tried to protect himself against flying debris as best he could. *Norness* righted herself somewhat, enabling the remaining men to launch another boat. They rowed away as fast as they could, and cleared her side before she was then hit by another torpedo and sank.[29]

A strong, northwesterly wind was blowing and it was freezing cold. Andersen found a raincoat in the boat, as well as some sweaters which he used as pants, but oddly being covered in oil was what kept him warm and probably saved his life. One of the other survivors, an able seaman named Sande had been retrieved from the water after falling out of the other lifeboat, and his clothes froze to his body. Fortunately, there were more sweaters and raincoats in the boat so that he was able to change his clothes.[30]

That afternoon they were spotted by a blimp and a couple of hours later, the destroyer USS *Ellyson* (DD-454) picked up two dozen surviving officers and men and took them to Newport, Rhode Island, where they were admitted to the Navy hospital. The Coast Guard cutter *Argo* (WPC-100) rescued six men, and nine were picked up by the fishing vessel *Malvina* and also taken to Newport. Two crewmen had been lost—Oiler Karl Egil Bremseth and Stoker Kare Johan Reinertsen—when the tackle broke while trying to launch the port lifeboat.[31]

NEARLY TWO DOZEN SHIPS SUNK, TWO DAMAGED

Between 12 January and 6 February 1942, the five submarines engaged in Operation PAUKENSCHLAG—*U-66*, *U-109*, *U-123*, *U-125*, and *U-130*—collectively sank twenty-three ships off the Eastern Seaboard and damaged two others. Fuel expended, they then returned to Lorient, France. (All 25 victim ships are identified in a subsequent table.)

The first three ships to fall victim to German submarines were sent to the bottom off Nova Scotia and Newfoundland:

- *Cyclops*: 125 miles southeast of Cape Sable, Nova Scotia
- *Frisco*: off Nova Scotia
- *Friar Rock*: 110 miles southwest of Cape Race, Newfoundland

Photo 3-4

Aft end of the conning tower of *U-85*, circa 1941-42.
Naval History and Heritage Command photograph #NH 85259

Following these sinkings, *U-123* (*Cyclops* and *Friar Rock*) and *U-130* (*Frisco*) moved southward to join the other submarine in attacking merchant shipping in American coastal waters. The worst day for merchantmen came on 19 January when three ships went down off Cape Hatteras, North Carolina. This area, where the continental shelf reached out almost to the 100-fathom curve (water depth of 600 feet), proved to be a favorite hunting ground for the U-boats.[32]

Ships Sunk off the Eastern Seaboard, 12 January – 6 February 1942

Date	Ship/Sub	Registry	Type	Tons	Location
12 Jan 42	*Cyclops* *U-123*	British	steam merchant	9,076	41°51'N, 63°48'W
13 Jan 42	*Frisco* *U-130*	Norwegian	steam merchant	1,582	44°50'N, 60°20'W
13 Jan 42	*Friar Rock* *U-130*	Panamanian	steam merchant	5,427	45°30'N, 50°40'W
14 Jan 42	*Norness* *U-123*	Panamanian	motor tanker	9,577	40°28'N, 70°50'W
15 Jan 42	*Coimbra* *U-123*	British	steam tanker	6,768	40°25'N, 72°21'W
18 Jan 42	*Allan Jackson* *U-66*	American	steam tanker	6,635	35°57'N, 74°20'W
19 Jan 42	*Norvana* *U-123*	American	steam merchant	2,677	36°07'N, 75°23'W
19 Jan 42	*Lady Hawkins* *U-66*	British	passenger ship	7,988	35°00'N, 72°30'W
19 Jan 42	*City of Atlantic* *U-123*	American	cargo ship	5,269	35°42'N, 75°21'W
19 Jan 42	*Ciltvaira* *U-123*	Latvian	cargo ship	3,779	35°25'N, 75°23'W
21 Jan 42	*Alexandra Hoegh* *U-130*	Norwegian	motor tanker	8,248	40°53'N, 65°56'W
22 Jan 42	*Olympic* *U-66*	Panamanian	steam tanker	5,335	34°03'N, 75°18'W
23 Jan 42	*Thirlby* *U-109*	British	steam merchant	4,887	43°20'N, 66°15'W
23 Jan 42	*Empire Gem* *U-66*	British	motor tanker	8,139	35°06'N, 74°58'W
24 Jan 42	*Venore* *U-66*	American	cargo ship	8,016	34°50'N, 75°20'W
25 Jan 42	*Varanger* *U-130*	Norwegian	motor tanker	9,305	38°58'N, 74°06'W
25 Jan 42	*Culebra* *U-123*	British	steam merchant	3,044	35°30'N, 53°25'W
26 Jan 42	*West Ivis* *U-125*	American	steam merchant	5,666	35°03'N, 73°10'W
27 Jan 42	*Francis E. Powell* *U-130*	American	steam tanker	7,096	38°05'N, 74°53'W
27 Jan 42	*Pan Norway* *U-123*	Norwegian	motor tanker	9,231	35°56'N, 50°27'W
1 Feb 42	*Tacoma Star* *U-109*	British	steam merchant	7,924	38°46'N, 64°17'W
5 Feb 42	*Montrolite* *U-109*	Canadian	motor tanker	11,309	35°14'N, 60°05'W
6 Feb 42	*Halcyon* *U-109*	Panamanian	steam merchant	3,531	34°20'N, 59°16'W[33]

19 Jan 42	*Malay* *U-123*	American	steam merchant	8,206	35°25'N, 75°23'W[34]

By the end of January, a pattern for enemy attacks on merchant shipping was clearly discernable. Ordinarily, the submarines hunted at night, on the surface and alone. As many torpedoes were fired as necessary to sink a vessel or to prevent its successful salvage. During one attack, four were sent into a ship over a 5-hour period. The use of torpedoes was supplemented when possible, by gunfire. Three of the ships sunk had been silhouetted against the lights from the shore; a fourth had been proceeding with dimmed navigation lights.[35]

ONE THAT GOT AWAY

Photo 3-5

Captain John M. Dodge, Master of the American tanker SS *Malay*, which was attacked by the German submarine *U-123* off North Carolina on 19 January, 1942.
Naval History and Heritage Command photograph #NH 44608

At around 0400 in early morning darkness on 19 January, the unarmed tanker SS *Malay* was shelled by *U-123* off Oregon Inlet, a passage from the Atlantic through North Carolina's Outer Banks to the Pamlico Sound. *Malay* was the leading ship in an unescorted convoy of five vessels with dim navigational lights set.[36]

Kptlt. Reinhard Hardegen had underestimated the size of the 8,206-ton tanker and decided to take her under fire with his deck gun to save torpedoes. From about 700 yards astern her, the U-boat fired ten rounds at the *Malay*. Five or six struck her, fatally wounding one man, destroying two lifeboats, damaging the bridge and crew quarters, and starting a fire on board.[37]

U-123 left *Malay* aflame to pursue another ship of the group and, eventually, torpedoed the Latvian cargo ship *Ciltvaira.* While thus engaged, Hardegen heard radio messages from *Malay*, reporting that she had been attacked by a submarine, and was on fire, about ten miles south of Wimple Shoals buoy (35 miles north of Cape Hatteras). Realizing the size and importance of *Malay*, he then returned to the tanker. In the interim, the passing Swedish merchant vessel *Scania* had helped the crew of *Malay* by passing firefighting equipment to them. Subsequently using these gifts, the tanker's eight officers and 26 crewmen had controlled the fire and managed to get the ship under way again.[38]

When Hardegen relocated the *Malay*, the British merchant ship SS *City of Delhi* was stopped nearby to recover one of her lifeboats. Having only one torpedo left, he decided to use it against the tanker instead of attacking the easy target because the former was more valuable. At 0600, *Malay* was again shelled; hit by that last torpedo starboard side, just aft of amidships; and was reported sinking. The crew abandoned ship in three lifeboats, but reboarded about an hour later. (Sadly, one of the lifeboats had capsized and four men drowned.) *Malay* reached Hampton Roads, Virginia under own power that same day, and was later repaired and returned to service.[39]

EFFORTS OF SHIP'S MASTER RECOGNIZED

Merchant Marine Distinguished Service Medal

Awarded to any seaman in the U.S. Merchant Marine who, on or after September 3, 1939, distinguished him or herself during the war by outstanding conduct or service in the line of duty. Not more than one medal shall be issued to any one seaman. For each subsequent instance sufficient to justify the award, additional insignia will be awarded and worn with the medal.

The ship's master, Captain John M. Dodge, was awarded the Merchant Marine Distinguished Service Medal in recognition of the successful efforts by him and his crew to save the damaged tanker. The associated medal citation reads:

The President of the United States takes Pleasure in Presenting the Merchant Marine Distinguished Service Medal to

John M. Dodge
Master of SS Malay 01/19/42

For meritorious service in the line of duty.

In the early morning hours, his ship was attacked by shell fire doing heavy damage to the bridge and port quarter. The wheel was ordered hard right at the first shot and the ship maneuvered inshore in an effort to elude the submarine. Two hours later a torpedo hit amidship. As a result of this explosion, a tremendous hole was torn in the starboard side; another burst through the deck; the telemotor steering gear was put out of commission; and she took a heavy list to starboard. A quick inspection of the damage indicated that the ship might be capable of proceeding under her own power, and the Master determined to bring her into the nearest port. The hand steering gear was put into commission, and emergency repairs were made to broken steam lines and control gear in the engine room. Then, while under way, the equalizing valves were opened to put her on an even keel and the ship was brought safely into an American port.

His courage, leadership, and exemplary seamanship, so largely contributory to the salvage of his ship, are in keeping with the highest traditions of the United States Merchant Marine.

For the President
Admiral Emory Scott Land[40]

4

More U-boats Arrive off East Coast

Those [ships lost] at the beginning [of February 1942] were apparently sunk by submarines that were just about to return home. The comparative calm that followed can be attributed to the fact that most of the U-boats that arrived in January, left this coast before others from Germany took their place.

How many submarines there are within the Frontier at the present time is uncertain—the best estimates are between four and seven—but it is clear, as the month ends, that submarines in groups of unknown number are operating off the Eastern coast from Newfoundland to the Caribbean.

—Commander, Eastern Sea Frontier War Diary, February 1942.

The five U-boats of 2nd Flotilla—*U-66*, *U-109*, *U-123*, *U-125*, and *U-130*—deployed from Lorient, France, to carry out PAUKENSCHLAG ("Drumbeat"), ended operations on 6 February and headed for home. Paukenschlag was meant to be a fast and surprise attack on the Canadian and U.S. Eastern Seaboard, and it succeeded as such. However, its conclusion provided only brief respite.[1]

By the time the Paukenschlag U-boats were returning to their French base in February, the next wave had already hit hard. Its seven submarines would, in turn, be followed by other waves of U-boats sent to North American waters. In these successive waves were many of Germany's most experienced commanders, including Topp (*U-552*), Hardegen in *U-123* again, Witt (*U-129*), Degen (*U-701*), Schnee (*U-201*), Mohr (*U-124*), and Lassen (*U-160*).[2]

SECOND GROUP OF U-BOATS

In order to increase sinkings wherever possible, the U-boat command used the long approach route and sailed in a group the boats of which were to operate in North American waters. They followed roughly on a great circle course in a wide rake-like formation. In this way convoy traffic was often unexpectedly encountered…. This great circle procedure continued throughout the whole summer and autumn of

> *1942, convoys being attacked again and again and dispersed by U-boat packs lying in wait. The 1939 building program developed in such a way that, by late autumn [1942], 42 boats were available for American waters, for operations against Cape Town, for three convoy-attacking groups in northern waters, in the North and Central Atlantic, and often an additional group to attack the Gibraltar-England traffic.*
>
> —From Adm. Karl Doenitz's essay *The Conduct of War at Sea.*[3]

Unlike the first group of German submarines deployed to the Atlantic Seaboard—all type IXB/C U-boats of a single flotilla based at Lorient—the second was a diverse group of under-sea vessels comprised of two different types, from three separate flotillas, based at various ports in France. These U-boats and their parent commands are identified below, also when the submarines left on patrol, their commanders, and the number of ships each was credited with sinking between 24 January and 12 March 1942. Thirty-one vessels were sunk; one other remained afloat, but was a total loss owing to extensive damage suffered:

2nd Flotilla
2. Unterseebootsflottille
Lorient, France

U-103 **(IXB)**
U-106 **(IXB)**
U-108 **(IXB)**
U-504 **(IXC)**

7th Flotilla
7. Unterseebootsflottille
St. Nazaire, France

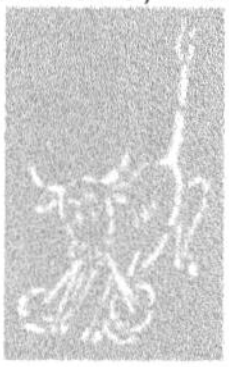

U-96 **(VIIC)**
U-578 **(VIIC)**

3rd Flotilla
3. Unterseebootsflottille
La Rochelle, France

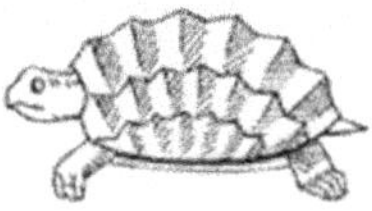

U-432 **(VIIC)**

Type IXB/C and VIIC U-boats

Date Left	U-boat/ Type	Commander	Ships hit
3 Jan 42	*U-103*/IXB	Kptlt. Werner Winter	4 S
3 Jan 42	*U-106*/IXB	Oblt. zur See Hermann Rasch	5 S
8 Jan 42	*U-108*/IXB	KrvKpt. Klaus Scholtz	5 S
21 Jan 42	*U-432*/VIIC	Kptlt. Heinz-Otto Schultze	5 S
25 Jan 42	*U-504*/IXC	KrvKpt. Hans-Georg Friedrich Poske	4 S
31 Jan 42	*U-96*/VIIC	Kptlt. Heinrich Lehmann-Willenbrock	5 S, 1 T
3 Feb 42	*U-578*/VIIC	FrgKpt. Ernst-August Rehwinkel	3 S
S: Sunk	T: Total loss		31 S, 1 T[4]

TYPE VIIC U-BOATS ("THE WORK HORSES")

The characteristics and armament of the type IXB/C variants of the long-range 251-foot U-boats (called "1,200-tonners" in reference to their displacement) were described in the preceding chapter. Before continuing with the activities of boats of the second wave, a description of the VIIC type is in order, as is an overview of "Milch Cows" used to supply type IX and VII attack submarines with fuel, torpedoes, and other supplies and services.

Although their range was not as great as that of the larger IX types, the VIIC was the workhorse of the German U-boat force, with 568 commissioned during the war. The VIIC was an effective fighting boat, one employed in almost all areas where the U-boat force operated, but was considered an "Atlantic boat." The boats were generally popular with their crews because of their fast crash dive speed, which was thought to give them more protection from enemy attacks than bigger, more sluggish types that took longer to submerge.[5]

All but eleven of the boats had five torpedo tubes, four at the bow, and one at the stern. The *U-72*, *U-78*, *U-80*, *U-554* and *U-555* had only two bow tubes, and the *U-203*, *U-331*, *U-351*, *U-401*, *U-431* and *U-651*, no stern tube. The VIIC carried 14 torpedoes, could carry 26 TMA mines, and was fitted with one 8.8cm (3.5 inch) quick-firing deck gun for which it had about 220 rounds.[6]

German Submarine Type VIIC Characteristics

Characteristics	VIIC
Length	220 feet
Beam	20 feet 4 inches
Displacement surf/sub/total (tons)	769/871/1,070
Draft	15 feet 6 inches
Power surfaced/submerged (hp)	3,200/750
Speed surfaced/submerged (kts)	17.7/7.6
Range surfaced/submerged (miles)	8,500 at 10 kts/80 at 4 kts
Max depth	722 feet
Crew complement	44-52 officers and men[7]

"MILCH COW" (SUPPLY SUBMARINE) SUPPORT

In order to make the Atlantic crossing to North America, some of the smaller VII boats sacrificed a large portion of their fresh drinking water and put diesel fuel in the tanks instead. Beginning in May 1942, specially-built large U-tankers were available to provide support. The so-called Milch (Milk) Cows were type XIV submarines, of which only ten were built during the war. These were the *U-459*, *U-460*, *U-461*, *U-462*, *U-463*, *U-464*, *U-487*, *U-488*, *U-489*, and *U-490*.[8]

The role of the Milch Cows was to support the VII and IX fighting U-boats with fuel, supplies, and ammunition. Supply submarines were initially successful operating a safe distance out to sea off the U.S. East Coast. Their presence permitted the smaller VIIC U-boats to operate in American waters, and in the Caribbean during 1942 but vastly improved Allied radar and better air coverage of the Atlantic lead to their elimination during 1943. Once the Allies learned of the existence and role of the Milch Cows, they were a priority target for all Allied forces.[9]

U-459 was the initial Milch Cow built and the first to make an operational deployment. She departed Heligoland (a small archipelago in German Bay, northwestern Germany, in the North Sea) on 29 March 1942, and ended her deployment forty-eight days later at St. Nazaire, France. In early May, she refueled fifteen U-boats northwest of Bermuda, extending the range and patrol time of type IX U-boats by 8 weeks and type VII by 4 weeks. This also afforded Admiral Doenitz the option of attacking much farther south than previously possible.[10]

Photo 4-1

German "Milch Cow" *U-464* in port, location and date unknown.
Naval History and Heritage Command #NH 111262

Germany had learned much about U-boat warfare in World War I. One of the most important lessons was the need to keep submarines at sea as long as possible to optimize the sinking of Allied ships. Yet the most critical aspect of pursuing a U-boat campaign off North America was the lack of supply bases either afloat or ashore from which to easily resupply its boats. The most obvious answer lay in acquiring island bases. However, mid-North Atlantic islands were scarce, and none were under German control.[11]

The most desirable potential island base was the Portuguese Azores archipelago. German U-boats operated freely in neighboring waters to these islands. While ashore, their spies, and sympathizers were not molested until mid-1943, when Antonio Salazar, Portugal's fascist dictator, finally allowed the British to establish a base in the Azores. From there, patrol aircraft, aided by U.S. Navy hunter-killer groups (destroyer-escorts built around an escort carrier), were finally able to eliminate the U-boat threat in the "Azores gap." Portugal was a neutral country, and this action occurred after Salazar decided to hedge his bets in favor of the Allied side, as Germany's military advantage began to wane.[12]

Map 4-1

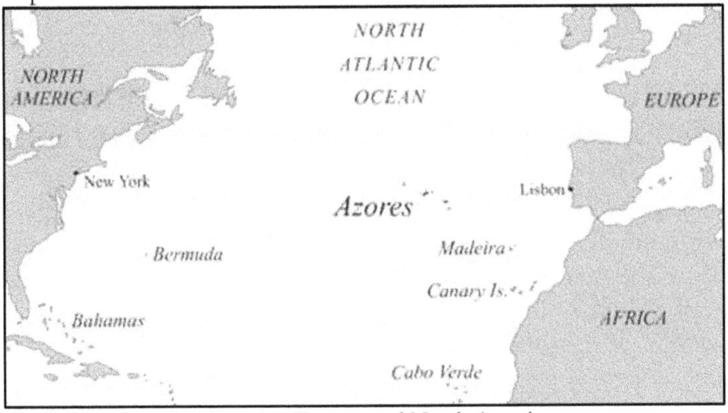

North Atlantic region between Europe and North America

MILCH COWS HUNTED AND DESTROYED

Get the Milk Cows at any cost!

—Order from British Prime Minister Winston Churchill to the Allied Naval Headquarters in London.[13]

Jumping well ahead in the narrative of U-boat operations off the U.S. East Coast in February 1942, a diversion is made to explain the threat posed to the Milch Cows. After their employment began in spring 1942, their destruction became the highest priority in the Atlantic War.

The reason was simple; a single U-tanker—carrying 636 tons of fuel and up to twelve torpedoes stowed internally and externally—could keep a dozen U-boats at sea for weeks.[14]

In order to maximize storage space, the designers of the type XIV tankers had eliminated all torpedo tubes, and only two light caliber 37mm and a single 20mm AA gun was provided for self-defense. Possessing only light weapons, and unable to dive quickly, the ponderous Milch Cows were at high risk during replenishment operations on the surface. However, what really spelled their doom (nine of the 10 tankers were sunk, and one scuttled by her crew after being damaged by aircraft-dropped depth charges) was the fortuitous capture by the Allies of the "Enigma" decoding machine. To arrange a rendezvous for resupply, it was necessary for the U-tankers to communicate with the U-boats via high-frequency long-range radio communications. Once the Allies broke the German Navy's top secret "Ultra" code, and knew exactly where the tankers were, their situation was like "lambs led to the slaughter."[15]

NORTH ATLANTIC NAVAL COASTAL FRONTIER IS ENLARGED, THEN RE-DESIGNATED THE EASTERN SEA FRONTIER

On 4 February 1942, the boundaries of the North Atlantic Naval Coastal Frontier were enlarged via the transfer of the Sixth Naval District from the Southern Coastal Frontier to it. Three days later, the Secretary of the Navy in a dispatch of 6 February, as part of a larger reorganization, re-designated the combined Frontier the Eastern Sea Frontier.[16]

During this period of administrative change and through February, U-boat habits did not change significantly. Attacks continued to be made, largely at night, by submarines operating on the surface. Gunfire, remarkable for its accuracy (given that surfaced, rolling submarines made poor gun platforms), was frequently employed to supplement the work of torpedoes. Toward the end of the month, a slight, though discernible shift of activity southward took place, indicating that perhaps March would bring increased intensity of warfare in the South Atlantic.[17]

FORCES AVAILABLE / DESTROYER PATROL

> *The search for forces went on throughout February. If the results were not very gratifying, it was less because the forces were well hidden than because they were not in existence.*
>
> —Commander, Eastern Sea Frontier War Diary, February 1942.

Little improvement was made in naval strength required to defend merchant shipping, because additional forces in large number did not exist. Partial alleviation of this situation came on 7 February in a dispatch from commander in chief, U.S. Fleet, Adm. Ernest King, authorizing Andrews to:

> Employ at sea anywhere within your Frontier at your discretion, any or all of the 70 ft. and 80 ft. cutters of the Coast Guard which normally are assigned to local defense forces.... By attack combined with escort and patrol operations, the primary task is to protect shipping in the Frontier lanes.[18]

Four days later, in a dispatch to all Naval Districts of the Frontier and Naval Operating Base, Newport, Rhode Island, Andrews directed commanders to:

> Arm, equip, and provide with depth charges, all 70 to 75 foot and 80 to 83 foot Coast Guard cutters immediately. As many depth charges as practicable should be carried. Gun should be one pounder and machine guns 50 caliber. If available, with three inch, 23 caliber on the 83 foot cutters if practicable. Listening gear to be installed as it becomes available. This to be given the highest priority. These vessels are to be used on coastal sea lane patrol. Expedite action and report immediately action taken.[19]

The general tenor of replies to this order was that material to implement plans in place would not be available until sometime in the future.[20]

NOTIFICATION OF TRAWLER DEPLOYMENT

Mid-month, a promise of aid came from an unexpected quarter. On 13 February, King informed Andrews that twenty-four trawlers were being sailed from England for St. John's, Newfoundland, "in the course of the next few days." They were being lent to commander in chief, U.S. Fleet

(King) for anti-submarine operations under "Command on East Coast North America [Andrews]."[21]

Andrews, who wanted destroyers to patrol the sea lanes, was doubtful about the capabilities of the trawlers, as expressed in correspondence to the commanders of the naval districts and naval operating base:

> They are not equipped to operate in southern climates, they contain not so much as a small pipe threading tool with which to make repairs, and, with two exceptions, they are coal burners requiring a very high grade of coal. Of needed assistance, they certainly will be, but it is not considered that these vessels would be satisfactory escort units.[22]

DESTROYERS SOUGHT

Another source of assistance emerged in February, when destroyers from the Fleet were assigned to commander, Eastern Sea Frontier. On 23 January, Andrews had strongly recommended that at least one destroyer, equipped with listening gear, be based at Hampton Roads to assist in meeting the enemy threat at the point of greatest danger. Located in southeastern Virginia, Hampton Roads was a large natural harbor where the James, Nansemond and Elizabeth Rivers poured into the mouth of the Chesapeake Bay. "Roads" in nautical terminology means "a place less sheltered than a harbor where ships may ride at anchor."[23]

In the last week of January, USS *Roe* (DD-418)—a new destroyer commissioned on 5 January 1940—had been assigned for ten days on temporary duty to the commandant of the Fifth Naval District (Com 5), whose headquarters was at Naval Operating Base, Norfolk, Virginia.[24]

Photo 4-2

USS *Roe* (DD-418) under way when first completed, circa 1940.
Naval History and Heritage Command photograph #NH 103525

On 3 February, when submarine activity around Cape Hatteras was reaching its full fury, another request was made for the immediate assignment of two destroyers to Com 5, for temporary duty owing to the critical situation in the vicinity of the Virginia Capes. The Virginia Capes lay directly northward of Cape Hatteras. Seven destroyers—*Hilary P. Jones* (DD-427), *Roe* (DD-418), *Ludlow* (DD-438), *Wainwright* (DD-419), *Mayrant* (DD-402), *Trippe* (DD-403), and *Rowan* (DD-405)—were made available to Andrews.[25]

Three of these destroyers were assigned to the Norfolk area, and one sent to Naval District Four, which encompassed the states of Pennsylvania, the southern part of New Jersey, and Delaware. Disappointingly only days later, all seven were detached from duty under Andrews, and were on their way to Ireland on a new assignment. Substitutions were made on 19 February, when the *Dallas* (DD-199), *Upshur* (DD-144), and *Jacob Jones* (DD-130) were ordered to duty under commander, Eastern Sea Frontier. Two of these destroyers went to the Norfolk area, while the *Jacob Jones* remained in New York. She was joined on 27 February by the *Dickerson* (DD-157).[26]

Unlike the modern destroyers that had been assigned temporarily until dispatched to a distant theater of war, the latter four were all old, World War I vintage "four pipers." Adding to this disadvantage, and what all eleven had in common, was that none remained long enough in any one place to perform with complete effectiveness. In a letter to Andrews, the commander of the inshore patrol of the Fifth Naval District accurately summed up the situation:

> A very unsatisfactory condition exists, resulting from frequent changes in destroyers assigned for temporary duty with the Local Defense Forces of this district.
>
> Upon arrival it is usually found that vessels need fuel, provisions, stores, and repairs. Each time a change is made, there is considerable loss of time occasioned by supplying the needs of the vessel. Also frequent confusion in orders; new vessels have to get local orders, communication plans, special information, and indoctrination.
>
> The result is that there is a great deal of lost motion and considerable loss in effectiveness of anti-submarine patrols.[27]

The most obvious solution to this unsatisfactory condition was the permanent assignment of destroyers to duty with the Frontier. Andrews believed, and had communicated to higher command that fifteen such destroyers were "absolutely essential" for defense of shipping within the Frontier. However, only a limited number of them were then available to the U.S. Navy, which believed that more on coastal sea lanes meant less on the trade routes to Britain which to them was the priority need.[28]

This reality of limited escort availability left Andrews with two unsatisfactory alternatives. These were concentrating forces at one point, thus leaving other areas open to submarine attack; or dispersing forces throughout endangered areas, but not in sufficient numbers to guarantee absolute protection of any particular sector. The principle of dispersion was chosen, but it was recognized that additional assistance would be necessary if the Frontier was to combat the activities of the submarines with good success. Therefore, destroyers in the Fleet were assigned to temporary duty under Andrews whenever they happened to be on the East Coast for repairs and overhaul. However, this stopgap solution resulted in a reduction in overall efficiency, as any particular destroyer only operated for a limited number of days within the Frontier.[29]

CONVOY SYSTEM CONSIDERED

> *Conditions along the overseas trade routes on which convoys have been principally used, differ materially from conditions along coastal sea lanes. Ships plying between England and America cannot time their voyages to seek the protection that daylight affords, nor can they break their passage by lying over in sheltered harbors at night. In addition, vessels far at sea are deprived of the air coverage afforded by planes operating from shore bases. Advantage of all these defensive measures can be taken by coastwise merchant vessels.*
>
> —Commander, Eastern Sea Frontier War Diary, February 1942.

The First World War had demonstrated that ships, men, and weapons could be brought into the most successful combination against U-boats through use of the convoy system. British experience in the early years of World War II had confirmed this lesson of the past. However, experience had also shown that the effectiveness of a convoy depended directly upon the strength of the forces engaged in protecting it. Unless convoys were adequately defended, the hazards to merchant vessels formed together in large and insufficiently protected concentrations were increased, rather than diminished.[30]

On 12 February, Admiral King had directed Vice Admiral Andrews to submit a plan for a convoy system to protect coastal shipping in the

Eastern Sea Frontier. Andrews presented his views on the subject in a letter dated 26 February. Included were some figures on the volume of merchant shipping within the Frontier. Every day, the following average numbers of vessels were in transit southward, and an equal number plying northward:

- 15 from the west end of the Massachusetts Cape Cod Canal to New York, via the Long Island Sound
- 16 from New York to the Delaware Capes
- 20 from the Delaware Capes to Cape Henry, Virginia
- 15 from Cape Henry to south of Charleston, South Carolina[31]

Each day, there were, in all, between 120 and 130 ships requiring protection within the boundaries of the Frontier. Andrews had only 28 surface vessels that could be employed for convoy work, and should all of these ships be used on such duty, the harbor entrances and coastwise (coastal) lanes would be practically stripped of protection. He described the untenable situation thus:

> At the present time there are available in the Frontier but 9 vessels, exclusive of the EAGLES which are unreliable, that have a speed of fourteen knots or better. There are also but 19 vessels with a speed between 12 and 14 knots. This latter grouping includes 10 125-foot Coast Guard cutters, 5 EAGLE boats, 3 PY's, and 1 165-foot slow Coast Guard cutter. The foregoing takes in all vessels of the Frontier that have any possible qualifications for the duty in question.[32]

In view of the large number of merchant vessels that would require convoy protection, and the limited number of ships and planes available to provide such protection, Andrews replied to King with the recommendation "that no attempt be made to protect coastwise shipping by a convoy system until an adequate number of suitable escort vessels is available."[33]

It was apparent, however, that something had to be done to increase the safe passage of cargo vessels. Accordingly, Andrews suggested several steps that might be taken to deal with the existing situation before convoy use was adopted:

- Every possible use be made of inland waters and canals
- Ships be routed as close inshore as safe navigation permitted with schedules so arranged that particular danger points would be passed during daylight

- Coastwise lanes be given every possible protection with every type of available plane and craft
- If the enemy abandoned his present method of offshore sinkings to operate against inshore lanes, daylight runs between such points as New York and Delaware Capes, and Hampton Roads be instituted with concentration of patrol around Hatteras
- All shipping, including overseas shipping to and from the West Indies, South America and Cape Town be routed along the coastal lanes since escort vessels were not available for ships routed offshore
- Coastal convoy from Cape Cod to Halifax be instituted[34]

JACOB JONES SUNK WITH GREAT LOSS OF LIFE

Photo 4-3

Destroyer USS *Jacob Jones* (DD-130), circa the 1930s.
Naval History and Heritage Command photograph #NH67838

One of the destroyers assigned to temporary duty with commander, Eastern Sea Frontier, was the USS *Jacob Jones* commissioned on 20 October 1919. Throughout January 1942, she had been on patrol and escort duty in the North Atlantic protecting shipping on the sea lanes between America and England. Immediately preceding her duty with the Eastern Sea Frontier, she had undergone a brief overhaul and repairs at the Boston Navy Yard.[35]

On the morning of 27 February, her commanding officer, Lt. Comdr. Hugh Black, went to the headquarters of Eastern Sea Frontier, in New York City, to report his ship ready for sea. There he met with Capt. John T. G. Stapler, USN (Retired), the staff operations officer. (Stapler had been awarded the Navy Cross during World War I for his performance while Commander of Division EIGHT, Submarines, operating on the Atlantic coast.)[36]

In conference with Captain Stapler, Black's new duty was discussed. The *Jacob Jones* was to patrol and search the area between Barnegat, New Jersey, and the Five Fathom Bank Lighted Buoy off the entrance to Delaware Bay. By day, she was to keep some 40 miles offshore, running along the 100-fathom curve (a contour line on a chart connecting points of equal depth; in this case those of 600 feet). At night, the destroyer was to move shoreward to search approximately five miles off the line of lighted buoys between the north and south extremities of her patrol area. After these matters had been discussed and charts for the district reviewed, Black returned to his ship.[37]

Later that morning, 27 February, the *Jacob Jones* proceeded to sea. Shortly after her departure, the destroyer *Dickerson* became available, and word was sent to the *Jones* that the two ships would divide the patrol area between them at the line of 39°10' North latitude. On their way, they passed the burning hulk of the American tanker SS *R.P. Resor*, torpedoed earlier that day off Sea Girt, New Jersey. The *Jones* circled the ship for two hours, in an unsuccessful search for survivors, before returning to her course.[38]

Jacob Jones arrived in her patrol area that evening, and throughout the night, completely darkened without navigation lights showing, maintained a southwest course. A light wind was blowing, but the sea was calm and, overhead, clouds moved slowly across the hazy sky lit by a full moon. About 0500, as the moon began to fade and the first streaks of dawn were breaking over the eastern horizon, a torpedo hit the port side of the destroyer with a tremendous explosion. A second or two later, another one hit the after part of the ship.[39]

The two torpedoes striking almost simultaneously, resulted in the port side of the *Jones* sustaining almost unbelievable damage. The first may have exploded the ship's magazine, for it carried everything away forward of a point just aft of the bridge, including the chart house, the bridge itself, and the officers and petty officers' quarters. The second, striking about 40 feet forward of the fantail, carried away the after part of the destroyer above the keel plates and shafts. About all that was left was the center section, as described by surviving crewmembers:

> Everything forward was just a mass of tangled steel all torn away and everything. No bridge at all.
>
> Number 1 stack and the bridge were gone. Number 2 stack was laying over against the galley deck house, and the deck over Number 1 fireroom was rolled up against the galley deck house. The deck

> over the forward compartments was rolled up against the machine gun nest over the top of the engine room.[40]

It was obvious to the twenty-five or so men, who were able to get up on deck after the explosions, that the *Jacob Jones* would sink. All the officers had been killed, save one who was badly wounded, dazed, and practically incoherent. Under the direction of an enlisted man, "Dusty" Rhodes, the survivors set to work trying to hoist the boats out of their cradles, only to find them jammed in the skids. So, the men turned to the rafts. Four or five were launched before the ship went down.[41]

One raft was very close to the *Jones* when, at about 0600, the after part of the still floating middle section lifted high in the air, and slipped down into the ocean, forward part first. Seconds later, a sheet of flame rose out of the water, and "a little jar" ran across the face of the sea. Then a column of water shot skyward, falling a moment later over the raft below; the depth charges on the submerged hulk were going off. The fourteen survivors on the raft took the full force of the concussions, and some were killed, dying one at a time.[42]

Two hours later, the rafts were sighted by First Lieutenant L. R. Blackburn Jr. in an observation plane. He contacted the Eagle boat USS *PE-56*, which set a course for the location given. At 0907, she sighted an empty lifeboat. Fifteen minutes later, she came alongside a raft in which there were three men and four bodies. The survivors were recovered and, over the next three hours of searching a further nine were picked up (twelve in total), before the Eagle boat was ordered to proceed to Cape May, New Jersey, with the rescued men. Water Tender Carl Smith died on the way in. Search by plane and ship over the next two days failed to find any trace of additional survivors.[43]

USS *Jacob Jones* (DD-130) was the first man-of-war sunk within the limits of the Eastern Sea Frontier by enemy action. She fell victim to *U-578*, one of the smaller VIIC "Atlantic boats."[44]

SHIPS SUNK BY THE SECOND WAVE OF U-BOATS

Between 24 January and 12 March 1942, the second wave of German submarines sent to North America—*U-459*, *U-460*, *U-461*, *U-462*, *U-463*, *U-464*, *U-487*, *U-488*, *U-489*, and *U-490*—sank thirty-one ships off the Eastern Seaboard, and one in the Caribbean. A few of the ships identified in the table were sunk outside Eastern Sea Frontier waters, such as north of Bermuda, or in the Gulf Sea Frontier. Their inclusion reveals the full destruction of ships by these particular U-boats.

Ships Sunk off the Eastern Seaboard, 24 January – 12 March 1942

Date	Ship/Sub	Registry	Type	Tons	Location
24 Jan 42	*Empire Wildebeeste* *U-106*	British	steam merchant	5,631	39°30'N, 59°54'W
26 Jan 42	*Traveller* *U-106*	British	steam merchant	3,963	40°00'N, 61°45'W
30 Jan 42	*Rochester* *U-106*	American	steam tanker	6,836	37°10'N, 73°58'W
2 Feb 42	*W. L. Steed* *U-103*	American	steam tanker	6,182	38°25'N, 72°43'W
2 Feb 42	*Amerikaland* *U-106*	Swedish	cargo ship	15,355	36°36'N, 74°10'W
3 Feb 42	*San Gil* *U-103*	Panamanian	cargo ship	3,627	38°05'N, 74°40'W
5 Feb 42	*India Arrow* *U-103*	American	steam tanker	8,527	38°48'N, 72°43'W
5 Feb42	*China Arrow* *U-103*	American	steam tanker	8,403	37°44'N, 73°18'W
6 Feb 42	*Opawa* *U-106*	British	motor merchant	10,354	38°21'N, 61°13'W
8 Feb 42	*Ocean Venture* *U-108*	British	cargo ship	7,174	37°05'N, 74°46'W
9 Feb 42	*Tolosa* *U-108*	Norwegian	steam merchant	1,974	34°40'N, 73°50'W
11 Feb 42	*Blink* *U-108*	Norwegian	cargo ship	2,701	35°00'N, 72°27'W
15 Feb 42	*Buarque* *U-432*	Brazilian	cargo ship	5,152	35°10'N, 65°50'W
16 Feb 42	*Ramapo* *U-108*	Norwegian	steam merchant	2,968	35°10'N, 65°50'W
18 Feb 42	*Somme* *U-108*	British	steam merchant	5,265	35°30'N, 61°25'W
18 Feb 42	*Olinda* *U-432*	Brazilian	cargo ship	4,053	37°30'N, 75°00'W
19 Feb 42	*Empire Seal* *U-96*	British	motor merchant	7,965	43°14'N, 64°45'W
19 Feb 42	*Miraflores* *U-432*	British	steam merchant	2,158	39°21'N, 73°18'W
20 Feb 42	*Lake Osweya* *U-96*	American	motor merchant	2,398	43°14'N, 64°45'W
21 Feb 42	*Azalea City* *U-432*	American	steam merchant	5,529	38°00'N, 73°00'W
22 Feb 42	*Torungen* *U-96*	Norwegian	steam merchant	1,948	44°00'N, 63°30'W
22 Feb 42	*Kars* (total loss) *U-96*	British	motor tanker	8,888	44°15'N, 63°25'W
22 Feb 42	*Republic* *U-504*	American	steam tanker	5,287	27°05'N, 80°05'W

23 Feb 42	*W. D. Anderson* *U-504*	American	steam tanker	10,227	27°09'N, 79°56'W
26 Feb 42	*R. P. Resor* *U-578*	American	steam tanker	7,451	39°47'N, 73°26'W
26 Feb 42	*Mamura* *U-504*	Dutch	motor tanker	8,245	29°00'N, 76°20'W
27 Feb 42	*Marore* *U-432*	American	cargo ship	8,215	35°33'N, 74°58'W
28 Feb 42	*USS Jacob Jones* (DD-130) *U-578*	U.S. Navy	destroyer	1,090	38°37'N, 74°32'W
9 Mar 42	*Tyr* *U-96*	Norwegian	motor merchant	4,265	43°40'N, 61°10'W
12 Mar 42	*Ingerto* *U-578*	Norwegian	steam merchant	3,089	41°33'N, 51°02'W
16 Mar 42 Caribbean	*Stangarth* *U-504*	British	steam merchant	5,966	22°40'N, 65°20'W[45]

Readers desiring to corollate the latitude and longitude of a ship sinking to a rough geographic position may be aided by the map on the following page with its parallels of latitude and longitude.

Map 4-2

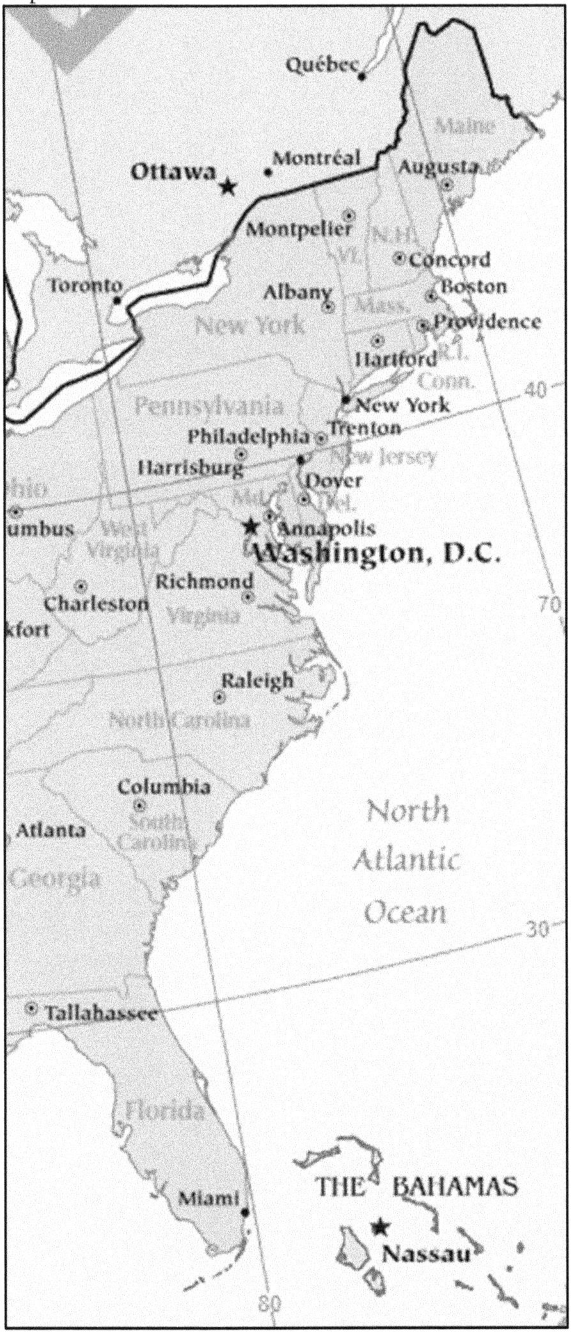

United States East Coast

5

The Trawlers and Whalers Arrive

Courage America, help is on the way!

—Comment by the gunner's mate aboard the anti-submarine whaler HMS *Wastwater*, as she and her sister ship HMS *Buttermere* proceed toward the glitter of New York City Harbor just weeks after the United States entered the war in December 1941.[1]

These vessels are of very sturdy construction, about 500 tons displacement, 180 to 200 feet in length, 12 knots speed, and of about 18 ft. draft. They are armed with one 4-inch gun, one .50 cal. twin mount, two depth charge racks and two depth charge projectors. They are all equipt with the British Asdic anti-submarine echo ranging apparatus. This gear indicates visually on a recorder the range to the object contacted and, on a magnetic compass, the bearing of the object contacted.

—Commandant, Sixth Naval District War Diary entry for 25 March 1942, recording the arrival of eight British trawlers—HMT *Cape Warwick*, *Lady Rosemary*, *Le Tiger* [*Le Tigre*], *Northern Chief*, *Northern Duke*, *Northern Isles*, *St. Cathan*, and *Welland*—for duty.[2]

In early March 1942, individual groups of Royal Naval Patrol Service anti-submarine vessels began arriving at the U.S. Naval Frontier Base, Tompkinsville, Staten Island, New York. In total, they comprised 21 trawlers and 2 whalers. Twenty-four ships sailed from Britain but, sadly, the trawler HMT *Northern Princess* (4.06) was sunk by *U-587* on 8 March off the Grand Bank, Canada, with the loss of all hands, before ever reaching her first American port.[3]

The arrival dates of the King's Ships, as well as the identities of their commanding officers, if known, are provided in the table.

Arrived at U.S. Naval Frontier Base, Tompkinsville

	4 March 1942
HMT *Le Tigre* (FY243)	T/Lt. Colin Arthur Hoodless, RNR
	7 March 1942
HMS *Buttermere* (FY205)	Sub Lt. George William Farrow, RNR
HMS *Wastwater* (FY239)	T/Lt. John Henry Louis May, OBE, RNVR

8 March 1942	
HMT *Senateur Duhamel* (FY327)	
HMT *St. Cathan* (FY234)	Lt. John Mackay, RNR
HMT *Wellard* (FY137)	Lt. Robert Fletcher Turnbull, RNVR.
10 March 1942	
HMT *Cape Warwick* (FY167)	T/Lt. William Edward Goggin, RNR
HMT *Lady Rosemary* (FY253)	T/Lt. Henry Brown, RNR
HMT *St. Zeno* (FY280)	T/Lt. John Kirke Craig, RNVR
11 March 1942	
HMT *Hertfordshire* (FY176)	
12 March 1942	
HMT *Norwich City* (FY229)	T/Lt. Leslie Hugh Stammers, RNVR
13 March 1942	
HMT *Northern Chief* (4.34)	T/Lt. George William Osborne Howe, RNR
HMT *Northern Duke* (4.11)	T/Lt. James Alfred Wright, RNR
HMT *Northern Isles* (4.25)	T/Lt. John Maurice Baldry, RNVR
26 March 1942	
HMT *Northern Dawn* (FY146)	Lt. Joseph Oswald Williams, RNR
29 March 1942	
HMT *Bedfordshire* (FY141)	Lt. Russell Bransby Davis, RNR
HMT *Coventry City* (FY267)	T/Lt. John Coade Grose, RNR
HMT *Kingston Ceylonite* (FY214)	A/Skipper Lt. William McKenzie Smith, RNR
HMT *Lady Elsa* (FY124)	T/Lt. Sidney George Phillips, RNVR
HMT *Stella Polaris* (4.258)	Skipper Thomas Normandale, RNR
Reported to American Command on Unknown Dates	
HMT *Arctic Explorer* (FY162)	T/Lt. Christopher Pawley, RNVR
HMT *Pentland Firth* (FY108)	Skipper Edward John Lockwood Davies, RNR
HMT *St. Loman* (FY276)	T/Sub Lt. Richard Colin Warwick, RNR[4]

ANTI-SUBMARINE WHALERS

Built in Britain in 1939 for the Norwegian whaling industry, she was one of a group commandeered and converted for anti-submarine escort service. Fortunately she had never killed a whale and so was free of the stench of whale-oil which, once it pervades a ship, never leaves her.

As an oil-burner she was easier to keep clean than the coal-burning trawlers. She had a couple of knots more speed, and a rudder like a barn-door which made her extremely manoeuverable. Against this was her low freeboard amidships, necessary for the towing of whale carcasses, two on each side. As a result, she was a semi-submarine in heavy weather, as I soon discovered.

—Michael Thwaites, who as a lieutenant, RNVR, was assigned as First Lieutenant aboard HMS *Wastwater*, describing in *Atlantic Odyssey*, his initial impressions of her.[5]

Of the twenty-three A/S vessels, listed above, all but two—the whalers HMS *Buttermere* and *Wastwater*—were trawlers. Published material about the Royal Naval Patrol Service ships that served in American waters often refer collectively to them all as "trawlers." Famed Australian poet Michael Thwaites served as first lieutenant (executive officer for USN readers) aboard HMS *Wastwater* during World War II, and later wrote *Atlantic Odyssey* describing his experiences aboard the whaler.

Wastwater, *Buttermere*, and their four sisters were named after the enchanting stretches of water of the English Lake District. Wastwater, remote and romantic, was the wildest and deepest lake in England. Of course, not everyone understood her pedigree. A USN sailor, standing on the quay, upon looking down and reading her name, exclaimed, "*Waste-water*! Gee, that's a hell of a name.[6]

Lake-class Anti-submarine Whalers

Ship	Comm.	Disposition
HMS *Buttermere* (FY205) ex-*Kos XXV*	18 Oct 39	sold in May 1946
HMS *Ellesmere* (FY 204) ex-*Kos XXIV*	12 Oct 39	torpedoed and sunk by *U-1203* west of Brest, France, on 24 February 1945
HMS *Thirlmere* (FY206) ex-*Kos XXVI*	27 Oct 39	sold on 24 May 1946
HMS *Ullswater* (FY252) ex-*Kos XXIX*	15 Nov 39	torpedoed and sunk by a German motor torpedo boat in the English Channel on 19 November 1942
HMS *Wastwater* (FY239) ex-*Kos XXVIII*	7 Nov 39	sold in May 1946
HMS *Windermere* (FY207) ex-*Suderoy VII*[7]	8 Nov 39	sold in 1947

After a period of overhaul, the British ships were put into service; the first fifteen (13 trawlers and 2 whalers) were ready for duty as the month of March ended. Their employment at sea could not come too soon for, as Admiral Andrews noted in a war diary entry:

> In this month [March 1942], shipping schedules were disrupted; the morale of merchant crews steadily deteriorated; insurance companies ceased writing policies on cargo vessels. In this month, when the total losses equaled the sum of the losses for January and February, all hope that the Germans would be unable to carry out a sustained attack along this coast vanished.[8]

CHALLENGES OF ANTI-SUBMARINE WARFARE

Off America's East Coast in early 1942, the initiative resided with the U-boats. Enemy submarines could, with relative freedom, determine the time, location, and method of attack—thereby shaping the conflict. At this point in the war, anti-submarine warfare (ASW) forces were at a constant disadvantage with, inevitably, a time lag between the action of the attacker and the response of the defender. Success in anti-submarine warfare depended greatly on the rapidity with which ASW forces could close the gap of this time lag. In other words, sufficient forces needed to be present in the area of an attack, or be able to arrive there rapidly, in order to locate and destroy a submarine before it could escape.[9]

Map 5-1

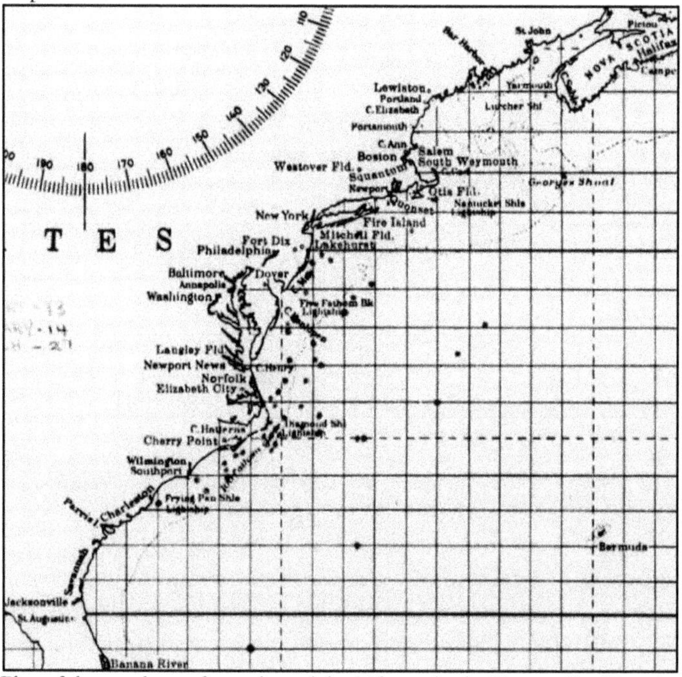

Plot of the numbers of vessels sunk by U-boats in the Eastern Sea Frontier in the first three months of 1942; a total of 13 ships in January, 14 in February, and 27 in March. (Note: Additional ships were sunk or damaged in other areas of the Canadian and U.S. Eastern Seaboard—of which the Eastern Sea Frontier comprised the largest portion.) Commander, Eastern Sea Frontier War Diary, March 1942

STILL TOO FEW DESTROYERS

Different measures had been enacted in an effort to meet the threat against merchant shipping. These included the sending of ships along the most sheltered routes, daylight sailing, and various methods of search and patrol. However, from the beginning it had been understood that the danger from the submarines could only be eliminated through the action of superior forces. There was a shortage of every type of ship and plane that could be used effectively against the U-boat, but there was especially an insufficient number of destroyers. This type of ship, with its speed, maneuverability, superior sound gear, and ability to keep the sea in conditions that forced smaller craft into port, was the deadly and traditional enemy of the submarine.[10]

Unfortunately within the Atlantic Fleet there were then, not enough destroyers to meet even basic needs; adequate protection of one area could only be given at the expense of some other. On 8 March, the availability of destroyers for use in anti-submarine work in the Eastern Sea Frontier was somewhat increased by the following guidance from commander in chief, Atlantic Fleet (Cinclant), Vice Adm. Royal E. Ingersoll, USN:

> When such employment is practicable and does not interfere with escort fleet vessels, tasks, and fleet operations, destroyers and other suitable escort ships making passage through the Sea Frontier Zones incident to scheduled movements should be utilized to fullest extent in the protection of merchant shipping. So that plans may be made to employ them as above in such cases Commander Sea Frontiers concerned and CincLant should be informed.[11]

The fourteen destroyers identified in the table performed one or more days on patrol (DP) in the Frontier in March. Their combined 63 days equaled, on average, about two destroyers per day in the Frontier. *Herbert*, *Roper*, and *Dickerson* were the backbone of this destroyer strength, totaling together, 34 days on patrol. All of the destroyers but two— *Macomb* and *Emmons*—were of WWI vintage.

DP	Ship	Comm	DP	Ship	Comm
18	USS *Herbert* (DD-160)	21 Nov 19	3	USS *Greer* (DD-145)	31 Dec 18
8	USS *Roper* (DD-147)	15 Feb 19	2	USS *Ellis* (DD-154)	7 Jun 19
8	USS *Dickerson* (DD-157)	3 Sep 19	2	USS *Du Pont* (DD-152)	30 Apr 19
5	USS *Dallas* (DD-199)	29 Oct 20	2	USS *Cole* (DD-155)	19 Jun 19
4	USS *Upsur* (DD-144)	23 Dec 18	1	USS *Hamilton* (DMS-18)	7 Nov 19
4	USS *Tarbell* (DD-142)	27 Nov 18	1	USS *Macomb* (DD-458)	26 Jan 42
4	USS *Dahlgren* (DD-187)	6 Jan 20	1	USS *Emmons* (DD-457)[12]	5 Dec 41

Vice Admiral Ingersoll, who would be promoted to the rank of admiral on 1 July 1942, noted the following about the loss of shipping to U-boats along the U.S. East Coast:

> The fabric of shipping is closely interwoven; no single strand can be broken or snarled without destroying the basic pattern of the commerce of the world. What is happening on the east coast of this country directly affects the fortunes of our allies across the sea.[13]

The hunt for additional forces, begun in December 1941, continued throughout March 1942 with some success. Additions of all kinds were welcomed, although reinforcements were primarily in the less-effective type of anti-submarine vessels—few new destroyers, patrol craft, or sub-chasers came into the Eastern Sea Frontier. Andrews, however, remained anxious to obtain any vessel he could lay his hands on. On 15 March, he sent a dispatch to all leaders of activities under his command, which revealed the pressing need for almost anything that could float, "Vessels in your district that can be purchased and are capable of carrying depth charges and guns and are fit for patrol report at once."[14]

Some success in this endeavor was achieved. Five yachts, varying in length from 75 to 175 feet, were obtained and immediately converted for service, but another possibility proved untenable. Investigation into the potential use of Menhaden fishing boats from the Fifth and Sixth Naval Districts, previously used in World War I, revealed that their low speed, about 8 knots, would severely restrict their service as anti-submarine vessels.[15]

Photo 5-1

USS *Menhaden* (SP-847), commissioned in the Navy on 21 May 1917, for service in WWI as a minesweeper, and later returned to her owner on 12 March 1919.
Naval History and Heritage Command photograph #NH 102027

Photo 5-2

"Menhaden Fisherman" type of converted minesweepers at Lorient, France, in 1918. The ship in the foreground is USS *Anderton* (SP-530), which was originally named *Raymond J. Anderton.* Minesweeping gear on the sterns of the two ships includes minesweeping floats and davits. A rack, holding two depth charges, is mounted on the stern of the more distant minesweeper.
Naval History and Heritage Command photograph #NH 45099

In spite of the difficulty of supply, by the end of March, there were a total of 95 vessels, exclusive of destroyers, operating under commander, Eastern Sea Frontier:

- 3 patrol craft
- 5 patrol escorts
- 7 patrol yachts
- 5 sub-chasers
- 60 Coast Guard cutters of varying size
- 13 RNPS trawlers and 2 RNPS whalers[16]

RNPS TRAWLERS REPORT TO NAVAL DISTRICTS

On the evening of 21 March, the eight trawlers identified in the table, left Tompkinsville, New York, at 2100, and proceeded southward, bound for Charleston, South Carolina, headquarters of the U.S. Sixth Naval District. They were followed three days later by HMT *Norwich City*, *Senateur Duhamel*, and *Hertfordshire*, which sailed for Norfolk, Virginia on the 24th. These three trawlers and *St. Zeno* reported to Commander, Inshore Patrol, Fifth Naval District, on 27 and 28 March 1942, respectively. The whalers HMS *Buttermere* and HMS *Wastwater* reported to the Ambrose, New York, Section Inshore Patrol of the

Third Naval District sometime in March, and were joined there by the trawler HMT *Northern Dawn* on 26 March.

U.S. Sixth Naval District, Charleston, South Carolina	
HMT *Cape Warwick* (FY167)	HMT *Northern Duke* (4.11)
HMT *Lady Rosemary* (FY253)	HMT *Northern Isles* (4.25)
HMT *Le Tigre* (FY243)	HMT *St. Cathan* (FY234)
HMT *Northern Chief* (4.34)	HMT *Wellard* (FY137)

U.S. Fifth Naval District, Norfolk, Virginia	
HMT *Hertfordshire* (FY176)	HMT *Senateur Duhamel* (FY327)
HMT *Norwich City* (FY229)	HMT *St. Zeno* (FY280)

U.S. Third Naval District, Ambrose Section Inshore Patrol, New York	
HMS *Buttermere* (FY205)	HMT *Northern Dawn* (FY146)
HMS *Wastwater* (FY239)[17]	

ARRIVAL IN NEW YORK

In the morning, off Nantucket Shoals [Massachusetts], there is fog about and visibility is down to a quarter of a mile. "Close to 1 cable," winks the lamp from Buttermere's bridge, but even so it is difficult to keep station on her, a pale ghost retreating ever into the fog.

—Michael Thwaites describing *Wastwater* and *Buttermere* proceeding shoreward to New York, following passage from their base at Reykjavik, Iceland. The admiral there, in briefing Lt. John Henry Louis May, OBE, RNVR, on his orders to take *Wastwater* to North America, had advised him that he'd been told to send his two best ships.[18]

The "rusty British trawlers," as the American press described them, arrived in March and, by the beginning of April, Admiral Andrews instituted a "Bucket Brigade" of daylight convoys with Royal Naval Patrol Service anti-submarine escorts. For their part, following a few preliminary patrols, *Wastwater* and *Buttermere* settled into a regular routine of escorting convoys between the Hudson and Delaware rivers. In darkness, they would slip from silent piers between 0400 and 0500; feel their way down the harbor, past buoys flashing red, white or green; and out the long channel to the sea, where their convoy of merchant ships would be forming up at first light.[19]

Photo 5-3

Fleet at anchor in New York Harbor, circa 1939.
Naval History and Heritage Command photograph #NH 923

Upon reaching the area where the convoy they were to escort was forming up, the whalers would find a number of smaller vessels; mostly unnamed District yard patrol craft (YPs or "Yippies) awaiting their arrival, as explained by Michael Thwaites as well as challenges associated with shepherding groups of merchant vessels:

> Immediately we would be hailed by a swarm of small US boats and launches, known generally as Yippies. We were the Senior Officer Escorts, the Big Ships, as we stationed our group of Yippies according to their number, equipment, etc., like a Fleet Admiral deploying his destroyer flotillas and cruiser squadrons.
>
> Besides keeping an eye on the escorts, we had to watch the merchant ships, spurring on the laggards and restraining individuals who steamed away regardless of the convoy speed, and who at first understood neither flag signals nor our Loud Hailer.[20]

In southern transits, as a convoy made its way down the flat, sandy coastline—broken only by rows of houses, high water towers, and the tall buildings of Atlantic City, New Jersey—*Wastwater* and *Buttermere* navigated by buoys and by wrecks. Of the wrecks, some of the victims of U-boats showed the tops of their masts, while whole bows of others, more recently sunk, were still above the water. Reaching the mouth of the Delaware about dusk, the whalers would supervise the entry of the convoy, then anchor or take up patrol, before picking up a northbound convoy at dawn the next morning.[21]

Photo 5-4

Yard patrol craft *YP-9* comes alongside the gate vessel *YNg-3*, off Tompkinsville on 4 April 1942. Lightship *Ambrose* (LV-87)—which served as the sentinel beacon marking Ambrose Channel, New York Harbor's main shipping channel—is in the background. U.S. Navy photograph 80-G-360238

Wastwater and *Buttermere* were so employed for five months, spending four or five days at a time at sea, with sometimes little more than 24 hours in harbor for fueling and taking on stores, getting any defects repaired, and enjoying liberty ashore in New York City. It was a busy schedule, but one which was the envy of the trawlers, as the two whalers were the only ships lucky enough to be based in New York. (*Northern Dawn* was assigned to the Third Naval District for a short time, then joined the other trawlers ordered to the Sixth Naval District for duty with its Offshore Patrol Force.)[22]

Before leaving the story of *Wastwater* for a time, it is worthwhile devoting a couple of pages to the other two officers, besides Thwaites, comprising her wardroom, who epitomized the mettle and experience of many Royal Navy personnel. The commanding officer, Lt. John Henry Louis May, RNVR, was 42 years old, senior to Thwaits 26 and Jones 25. Before the war, May spent eight years in the Merchant Navy, acquiring a Second Mate's ticket, following which he was hired by a publishing firm.[23]

Joining the Royal Navy Volunteer Reserve at the start of hostilities, he initially served as a boarding officer aboard the trawler HMT *Northern Sun* on the notoriously grueling assignment known as the Northern Patrol, for which he was appointed an OBE (Officer of the Order of the British Empire). The mission of the Northern Patrol was to search the vast areas north of Scotland and Ireland, between the north of Scotland and Norway, around the Shetland and Faeroe islands and Iceland, and the Denmark Strait between Iceland and Greenland. Royal Navy ships on such patrols searched for German vessels involved in blockade running (breaking out of ports blockaded by Allied naval vessels) and commerce raiding (once at sea, unencumbered, attacking Allied merchant shipping). This involved boarding suspect ships in cold and hazardous weather conditions.

Temporary Lieutenant John Henry Louis May, RNVR, HMS *Northern Sun*, was "gazetted" for his appointment as an OBE on 11 July 1940 "in recognition of distinguished services during the War." (This term refers to the official notice of promotions and honors awarded by the Crown, published in *The London Gazette*). May's next appointment was as First Lieutenant of *Buttermere*, and this was followed by command of *Wastwater*. He served as commanding officer of the whaler from August 1941 to April 1943, then commanded the frigate HMS *Tobago* (K585) from 3 November 1943 to mid-1945.[24]

Sub. Lieutenant Geoffrey Holder Jones, RNVR, carried out the functions of gunnery officer, navigating officer, and wardroom secretary aboard *Wastwater*. The typical wardroom secretary was responsible for organising wardroom mess social events, running the beer & wine accounts, keeping the bar stocked and calculating and presenting officers' mess bills.[25]

Following school, Jones, a former rating, had joined the "weekend sailors" of the Mersey division of the RNVR, and first went to sea in 1933. He was a signalman aboard the cruiser-minelayer HMS *Adventure* (M23) when, on 13 November 1939, she was mined near the Tongue Light Vessel in the Thames Estuary. The blast (of almost certainly a magnetic mine laid by one of four German destroyers only hours previously) threw Jones from his bunk into total darkness but he was saved. He was more fortunate than many of his shipmates; the ship was badly damaged, and 23 of her crew were killed or fatally injured.[26]

In April 1940, Jones was a signal rating in the minesweeping trawler HMT *Tritonia* (a Lowestoft drifter which had been taken up from trade for minesweeping duties) when the captured German "Q-ship" trawler *Julius Pickenpack* (Schiff 26) was brought into the harbor at Scapa Flow, Scotland. Disguised as a Dutch ship called *Polares*, she was carrying arms to the German Army, which had invaded Norway, when she was captured by a boarding party from the British destroyer HMS *Griffin* (H31). Sent aboard her, Jones later recalled his delight at finding extra food and drink in the enemy ship, but he became uneasy when he realized that Schiff 26's armament included five magnetic mines of a novel type (lashed on deck under a fish trawl), as well as one 4.1-inch ship's gun (camouflaged as a boat), two field guns, several light and heavy machine guns, large quantities of ammunition, twelve depth charges, and two 21-inch torpedoes fitted in concealed bow tubes.[27]

The German vessel was evacuated, but when Lt. Comdr. (later Capt.) John Edward Maxwell Glenny DSO, DSC RN, an RMS (Render Mines Safe) officer and his assistant arrived from HMS Vernon, the torpedo and mine warfare school at Portsmouth, Jones volunteered to accompany them back to the ship and act as their signalman, relaying updates on their efforts to render the mines safe. Once, he had to summon *Tritonia*'s engineer, who advised that threads on the mines worked left-handed, rather than the usual right-handed, but did not remain and left Jones alone with the experts dismantling the mines.[28]

Later, Signalman Geoffrey Holder Jones, RNVR was gazetted for the award of the DSM (Distinguished Service Medal), in recognition of his valor, in the New Year Honours list published on 1 January 1941. He was then serving in the minesweeping trawler HMT *Daniel Clowden* (FY531). Soon after Jones received a commission and was appointed to *Wastwater*. A modest individual, when asked about the blue and white medal ribbon he was authorized to wear on his uniform blouse, Jones claimed to have joined the party in error, having heard some remark about "free beer," but this disclaimer fooled no one.[29]

Following his service aboard *Wastwater*, Jones was promoted to command his own ship, the minesweeping trawler HMT *Baffin* (T275). After joining her as commanding officer on 21 August 1942, he travelled to the West Indies and Canada; then suddenly was ordered back to England. During the frantic period before D-Day (the Normandy invasion) Jones served as a pilot for Portsmouth Harbour. Later, as commanding officer of the anti-submarine trawler HMS *Guardsman* (T393), Jones accepted the surrender of a U-boat. He had joined the trawler as commanding officer on 26 March 1945.[30]

Lt. Comdr. Geoffrey Jones died at age 95. In 1980, there was a service at St Andrew's School, Hove, in Sussex, to mark the retirement of Mr. Geoffrey Holder Jones, headmaster, once a boy signalman.[31]

EASTERN SEABOARD SHIP LOSSES IN MARCH 1942

Admiral Doenitz, after achieving much success in sinking shipping off the Eastern Seaboard between 12 January-12 March 1942, dispatched even greater numbers of U-boats to American waters, as the earlier ones sent there returned home from their successful patrols.

Vessels Sunk and Damaged by U-boats off the Eastern Seaboard

Period	Sunk	Damaged	Period	Sunk	Damaged
24 Jan-12 Mar 42	29	1	13-31 Mar 42	34	4

Expanded numbers of submarines, operating against unescorted merchant vessels, resulted in ever increasing losses of Allied shipping, as a comparison of the table in the previous chapter (24 January-12 March 42), and the one below (13-31 March 42) clearly demonstrate. Summary totals are provided above.

Ships Sunk off the Eastern Seaboard between 13 and 31 March 1942

Date	Ship/Sub	Registry	Type	Tons	Location
13 Mar 42	*John D. Gill* *U-158*	American	steam tanker	11,641	33°55'N, 77°39'W
13 Mar 42	*Albert F. Paul* *U-332*	American	sailing ship	735	36°00'N, 72°00'W
13 Mar 42	*Trepca* *U-332*	Yugoslavian	steam merchant	5,042	37°00'N, 73°25'W
13 Mar 42	*Tolten* *U-404*	Chilean	steam merchant	1,858	40°10'N, 73°50'W
14 Mar 42	*British Resource* *U-124*	British	motor tanker	7,209	36°04'N, 65°38'W
14 Mar 42	*Lemuel Burrows* *U-404*	American	steam merchant	7,610	39°21'N, 74°13'W
15 Mar 42	*Ario* *U-158*	American	steam tanker	6,952	34°37'N, 76°20'W
15 Mar 42	*Olean* (D) *U-158*	American	steam tanker	7,118	34°22'N, 76°29'W
16 Mar 42	*Australia* *U-332*	American	motor tanker	11,628	35°07'N, 75°22'W
17 Mar 42	*Acme* (D) *U-124*	American	steam tanker	6,878	35°06'N, 75°23'W
17 Mar 42	*Ceiba* *U-124*	Honduran	steam merchant	1,698	35°43'N, 73°49'W
17 Mar 42	*Mount Lycabettus* *U-373*	Greek	steam merchant	4,292	40°51'N, 59°18'W
17 Mar 42	*San Demetrio* *U-404*	British	motor tanker	8,073	37°03'N, 73°50'W
17 Mar 42	*Ranja* *U-71*	Norwegian	motor tanker	6,355	38°00'N, 65°20'W
18 Mar 42	*E. M. Clark* *U-124*	American	steam tanker	9,647	34°50'N, 75°35'W
18 Mar 42	*Kassandra Louloudis* *U-124*	Greek	steam merchant	5,106	35°05'N, 75°25'W
19 Mar 42	*Papoose* *U-124*	American	steam tanker	5,939	34°17'N, 76°39'W

19 Mar 42	*W. E. Hutton* *U-124*	American	steam tanker	7,076	34°25'N, 76°50'W
19 Mar 42	*Liberator* *U-332*	American	steam merchant	7,720	35°05'N, 75°30'W
20 Mar 42	*Oakmar* *U-71*	American	steam merchant	5,766	36°22'N, 68°50'W
21 Mar 42	*Esso Nashville* (D) *U-124*	American	steam tanker	7,934	33°35'N, 77°22'W
22 Mar 42	*Thursobank* *U-373*	British	motor merchant	5,575	38°05'N, 68°30'W
23 Mar 42	*Naeco* *U-124*	American	steam tanker	5,373	33°59'N, 76°40'W
24 Mar 42	*Empire Steel* *U-123*	British	motor tanker	8,138	37°45'N, 63°17'W
25 Mar 42	*Narragansett* *U-105*	British	motor tanker	10,389	34°46'N, 67°40'W
25 Mar 42	*Ocana* *U-552*	Dutch	motor tanker	6,256	42°36'N, 64°30'W
26 Mar 42	*Dixie Arrow* *U-71*	American	steam tanker	8,046	34°55'N, 75°02'W
27 Mar 42	*Svenør* *U-105*	Norwegian	motor tanker	7,616	35°55'N, 69°20'W
27 Mar 42	*USS Atik* (AK 101) *U-123*	American	USN "Q-ship"	3,209	35°38'N, 70°14'W
27 Mar 42	*Equipoise* *U-160*	Panamanian	steam merchant	6,210	36°36'N, 74°45'W
29 Mar 42	*City of New York* *U-160*	American	motor passenger ship	8,272	35°16'N, 74°25'W
29 Mar 42	*Hertford* *U-571*	British	steam merchant	10,923	40°50'N, 63°31'W
31 Mar 42	*San Gerardo* *U-71*	British	steam tanker	12,915	37°33'N, 68°22'W
31 Mar 42	*Menominee* *U-754*	American	steam tug w/barges	441	37°34'N, 75°25'W
31 Mar 42	*Allegheny* *U-754*	American	barge	914	37°34'N, 75°25'W
31 Mar 42	*Barnegat* *U-754*	American	barge	914	37°34'N, 75°25'W
31 Mar 42	*Ontario* (D) *U-754*	American	barge	490	37°34'N, 75°25'W[32]

The following chapter describes the loss of one of the above listed vessels, the "Q-ship" USS *Atik* (AK 101), to famed Kptlt. Reinhard Hardegen's *U-123*.

■ 6

USS *Atik* falls Victim to U-boat Prey – a Failed Experiment

The high command said today that a Q-boat—a heavily armed ship disguised as an unarmed vessel—was among 13 vessels sunk off the American Atlantic Coast and that it was sent to the bottom by a submarine only after a 'bitter battle.'

The Q-boat was of 3,000 tons and was sunk by a torpedo after a battle 'fought partly on the surface with artillery and partly beneath the water with bombs and torpedoes.'

—Radio broadcast from Berlin, Germany, on 9 April 1942, regarding the loss of the USS *Atik*, recorded by the Associated Press and printed in the *New York Times* on 10 April. During the period, 12 January-9 April, *U-123*, sank twelve vessels (including the "Q-ship" USS *Atik*), and damaged four others.[1]

In early afternoon on 23 March 1942, the USS *Atik* (ex-SS *Carolyn*) departed Norfolk, Virginia, on a "shakedown cruise." Three days later, at 2053 on the night of 26 March, two Navy radio stations received a distress message from a vessel using the call letters of SS *Carolyn*. The message reported that the *Carolyn* was burning forward, but that the fire did not appear to be serious. A second message, received two minutes later reported that the ship had been torpedoed and required assistance. Her position was 300 miles southeast of Norfolk.[2]

A second Q-ship, USS *Asterion* (AK-100), operating 240 miles south of the position of the *Atik*, received the distress message, and proceeded at best speed to reach her. Arriving hours later, she found no trace of the ship. In early morning the following day, 27 March, an Army bomber was sent to search for the still missing ship, while the destroyer USS *Noa* (DD-343) and ocean tug USS *Sagamore* (AT-20) were dispatched to her last reported position. En route, they encountered extremely heavy seas, and as a consequence the 156-foot tug was recalled the next day.[3]

Persistent search by Army and Navy planes to find the ship or evidence of her loss was unsuccessful until 30 March, when wreckage and five empty rafts was sighted at 34°52'N, 69°58'W, about ten miles south of *Atik*'s reported position. Twelve days later, commander, Eastern Sea Frontier concluded in a report, "… it is believed that there is very little chance that any of her officers and crew will be recovered. It is therefore recommended that if no further information is received by April 27, they be considered lost and that next of kin be notified."[4]

Additional efforts to locate survivors proved fruitless. All hands were presumed lost, either killed after being torpedoed by a U-boat, and an ensuing explosion that sank her, or were victims of a gale that hit the area shortly afterwards.[5]

Photo 6-1

SS *Carolyn*, location and date unknown. Newport News Shipbuilding & Dry Dock Co. photograph, *Atik* (AK-101). Ship History File, History and Archives Division. Naval History and Heritage Command

The idea for and use of Q-ships had been originated by the British Admiralty in World War I, during a period when U-boat attacks against shipping were at their worst. Following approval of a thought-out plan, nondescript procured merchant vessels were converted to heavily-armed ships, with their guns disguised or concealed in such a way as to encourage U-boats to attack them as seemingly defenseless prey. The idea was that, provided a decoy ship was given sufficient buoyancy, one or two torpedoes would be unable to sink her, then the disguise could be thrown off, her guns brought to bear, and the enemy submarine sunk. The effectiveness of the enterprise depended on the successful use and prolongment of surprise, so as to not prematurely make the U-boats aware of the ruse. If this was not played skillfully, the chances of success were greatly reduced. Further, as was demonstrated, a botched attempt left the Q-ship as a "sitting duck" for counter-attack by the attacked sub. Only a few ingenious commanding officers were able to conduct such operations through the remainder World War I with any distinction.[6]

The U.S. Navy's use of Q-ships in World War II, was related to the sudden appearance of U-boats in Atlantic coastal waters. One of the possible means considered to meet the emergency, the Q-ship scheme, was adopted. On 20 January 1942, Adm. Ernest King, commander in chief, United States Fleet, had sent Admiral Andrews a coded dispatch, which Andrews paraphrased in a war diary entry as follows:

> Immediate consideration is requested as to the manning and fitting-out of Queen repeat Queen ships to be operated as an anti-submarine measure. This has been passed by hand to OpNav [Chief of Naval Operations] for action.[7]

In response, Andrews wrote a lengthy letter, dated 29 January, highlighting that the most prevalent method of U-boat attacks had been at night, on the surface from close range, and that the submarines were concentrating on tankers. For this reason, a tanker would best answer the purpose of inviting an attack. He also suggested consideration of another type of Q-ship, a vessel "of such relative insignificant appearance that upon sighting it a submarine would not submerge." A small schooner might serve this purpose.[8]

On 20 February 1942, the chief of Naval Operations, Adm. Harold Stark, USN, informed commander, Eastern Sea Frontier, that his proposals had been approved, and that hereafter the matter would be known as "Project LQ." All communications on the matter would be made by word of mouth, insofar as practicable; a responsible officer would be placed in charge of the work; and on completion of ship conversions, "Project LQ" would be assigned to the commander, Eastern Sea Frontier.[9]

Photo 6-2

Adm. Harold R. Stark, Chief of Naval Operations, 1 April 1940.
Naval History and Heritage Command photograph NH 49967

Prior to the inception of this project, Admiral King had arranged for the selection of three vessels considered suitable for the intended purpose: a beam trawler, and two small cargo ships of the three-island type. The beam trawler MS *Wave* (which formerly operated out of Boston) had previously been acquired for conversion to an auxiliary minesweeper by the commandant, First Naval District, and had, in fact, been commissioned USS *Eagle* (AM-132) on 5 March 1942 at Portsmouth, New Hampshire.[10]

The two sister cargo ships *Carolyn* and *Evelyn* were built at Newport News, Virginia in 1912. For their new assignment, they were taken over from the A.H. Bull Steamship Company in New York City, by Huntington Morse and S. H. Helmbold of the U.S. Maritime Commission. Following their conversion in the Navy Yard at Portsmouth, New Hampshire, the commissioning of USS *Atik* and USS *Asterion* was recorded in the Log of that Yard, but not made a matter of record in the Navy Department.[11]

	USS *Eagle* (AM-132) ex-MS *Wave*	**USS *Atik* (AP-100) ex-*Carolyn***	**USS *Asterion* (AP-101) ex-*Evelyn***
Year built	1938	1912	1912
Length	133 feet	318 feet	318 feet
Beam	26 feet	46 feet	46 feet
Displ.	520 tons	3,209 tons	3,209 tons
Max speed	12.5 knots	10 knots	10 knots
Armament	One 4"/50 mount, two .50 cal. machine guns, four depth-charge throwers, five sawed-off shotguns, five Colt .45 automatic pistols, and 25 hand grenades	Four 4"/50 mount, four .50 cal. machine guns, six depth-charge throwers, miscellaneous collection of small arms similar to those aboard *Captor*	Four 4"/50 mount, four .50 cal. machine guns, six depth-charge throwers, miscellaneous collection of small arms similar to those aboard *Captor*
Complement	47 (5 O, 42 E)	141 (6 O, 135 E)	141 (6 O, 135 E)[12]

O: officers E: enlisted men

Photo 6-3

USS *Captor* (PYc-40) under way at sea, location unknown, circa August 1944. *Captor* was the ex-USS *Eagle* (AM-132), reclassified as a coastal patrol yacht on 18 April 1942. Archives photograph 80-G-245463

On 11 March, the commanding officers of the *Eagle* (Lt. Comdr. Lester Francis Rogers, USNR), *Asterion* (Lt. Comdr. Glen Walker Legwen Jr., USN), and *Atik* (Lt. Comdr. Harry Lynnwood Hicks, USN) were given personal and written instructions at the headquarters of commander, Eastern Sea Frontier. They also received a preliminary Operation Order covering a brief post-conversion "shakedown period," which would commence about 24 March.[13]

Since the three vessels would be departing from Portsmouth, New Hampshire, their commanding officers were to report to commander,

Submarine Division 101 when ready for sea; then proceed independently on widely divergent courses for shakedown in areas where enemy activity had not been reported. *Atik* and *Asterion* were to proceed such that, one would be approximately 480 miles southward of the other after five days at sea.[14]

The three Q-ships were to leave the Navy Yard, Portsmouth, in such a manner that they would appear to observers as armed vessels regularly commissioned in the Navy. At first opportunity, guns and depth charge throwers were to be concealed, identifying numbers removed from their bows, commissioning pennants hauled down, and other steps taken for *Atik* and *Asterion* to present the appearance of merchantmen, and *Eagle*, a beam trawler fishing out of Boston.[15]

Photo 6-4

Aerial view of Portsmouth Navy Yard, New Hampshire, on 21 July 1941.
Naval History and Heritage Command photograph #L39-13.09.01

If friendly ships or aircraft challenged the *Atik* or *Asterion* (requested their identity), they were instructed to respond using their former names and callsigns, which would indicate they were SS *Carolyn* and SS *Evelyn*, respectively. If enemy ships were to challenge, they were to use the false identification and callsigns as follows:

Q-Ship	False Name	False Registry	Callsign
USS *Atik* (AP-100)	SS *Vill Franca*	Portuguese	CSBT
USS *Asterion* (AP-101)	SS *Generalife*	Spanish	EAOQ[16]

In early afternoon on 23 March, the three Q-ships put to sea. In the gathering darkness three days later, *Atik* attracted the attention of Kapitänleutnant Reinhard Hardegen's *U-123*, on her second war patrol off the Eastern Seaboard. At 2200, on the surface, the submarine began stalking *Atik*. Shortly after midnight (at 0037 on 27 March), Hardegen fired one torpedo at a range of 700 yards, which struck the ship on her port side, under the bridge. Fire broke out immediately and, as the "freighter" assumed a slight list, she transmitted a terse SOS, "S.S. *Carolyn*, torpedo attack, burning forward, not bad."[17]

As *U-123* proceeded under her victim's stern, inspecting the aflame vessel, Hardegen observed one boat being lowered on the starboard side and men abandoning ship. After *U-123* turned away to starboard to pull clear of her, "*Carolyn*" gathered steerageway; turned to starboard as well, to steer a parallel course; dropped her concealment; and opened fire from her main and secondary batteries. The first 4-inch shell was short of the U-boat; as she bent on (increased) speed to escape, presenting a small target. The shots that followed were off in deflection. (This term refers to the offset, to the right or left, needed to hit the target.) Heavy .50-caliber machine gun fire, though, struck *U-123*'s decks as she sought to escape the trap into which Hardegen "like a callow beginner [his own words]" had fallen. One bullet mortally wounded Fähnrich zur See Rudi Holzer, on the submarine's bridge.[18]

After *U-123* had gotten well clear of *Atik*, behind the cover of the smoke emitted by her straining diesels, Hardegen assessed the damage. It proved minimal, and he recorded later, "We had been incredibly lucky." The submarine then submerged to carry out a second attack on her adversary, this time unseen. At 0229, *U-123* fired a torpedo into *Atik*'s machinery spaces. Satisfied that it would be the coup de grace, Hardegen stood off to await developments as the freighter settled by the bow, with her single screw clear of the water.[19]

Once again, *Atik* crewmembers embarked in boats. *U-123* surfaced at 0327, to finish off the stubborn Q-ship. Suddenly, at 0350, a devastating explosion blew *Atik* to pieces. Ten minutes later, Hardegen buried Holzer, who had died of his wounds, at sea; the only German casualty. *Atik*'s entire crew perished, either as a result of the two torpedo strikes, the blast that destroyed the ship, or during the severe gale that lashed the area soon after the ruined ship slipped into the deep.[20]

THE FOURTH AND FIFTH Q-SHIPS

It may be noted that during the period from 27 November to 1 December [1943], this Task Group was in the midst of a group of from 10 to 15 U-boats. Nine contacts, sightings or attacks on U-boats took place in our immediate vicinity, so that it is most unlikely that we were not seen by some U-boats. Evidently the U-boats are wary of attacking an independent tanker. If the Q-ship program has contributed to this wariness, as is suggested in several prisoner-of-war statements, many independent merchant ships may thereby have escaped attack, and the Q-ship program has thus been of value.

—Comdr. Louis Calott Farley, USN, commanding officer of the USS *Big Horn*, summarizing her last cruise as a Q-ship. She subsequently joined *Asterion* in a new assignment, North Atlantic Weather patrol duty, under the supervision at the U.S. Coast Guard and manned by Coast Guard officers and crew.[21]

On 14 October 1943, nineteen and one-half months after the sinking of USS *Atik*, commander in chief, United States Fleet (Cominch) directed the commander, Eastern Sea Frontier, to decommission the *Irene Forsyte* upon her return from Bermuda. Other steps were to be taken to lead to the conclusion of all anti-submarine patrols by Eastern Sea Frontier vessels disguised as merchant vessels. This decision resulted from the failure of the Q-ships to accomplish their intended mission—lure to the surface and sink enemy submarines.[22]

The last Q-ships to be put into service were the tanker USS *Big Horn* (ex-SS *Gulf Dawn*), and the schooner USS *Irene Forsyte* (ex-Canadian three-masted schooner *Irene Myrtle*). They were commissioned on 16 April 1942 and 26 August 1943, respectively.

	USS *Big Horn* (AO-45)	**USS *Irene Forsyte* (IX-93)**
Commanding Officer	Comdr. James A. Gainard, USNR	Lt. Comdr. Richard Parmenter
Year built	1936	1920
Length	441 feet 8 inches	144 feet
Beam	64 feet	27 feet 7 inches
Max speed	12.5 knots	13 knots
Armament	Five 4-inch .50 caliber single purpose guns, two .50 caliber machine guns, five "Tommy" guns, five sawed-off shotguns	One single 4-inch gun mount, one single 40mm gun mount, two single 20mm gun mounts, one anti-submarine rocket
Complement	239 (15 O, 224 E)[23]	unknown

Photo 6-5

USS *Big Horn* (AO-45) beginning conversion, 2 April 1942, at the Bethlehem Steel 56th Street yard, Brooklyn, New York.
U.S. Coast Guard Historian's Office photograph #19-N-29138

Photo 6-6

USS *Irene Forsyte* (IX-93) under way.
National Archives photograph #80-G-86383

7

Planning, Formative Stage of Coastal Convoys; USS *Roper* sinks *U-85*

Photo 7-1

American steam tanker *Harry F. Sinclair Jr.* burning, south of Cape Lookout, North Carolina, after being torpedoed by German submarine *U-203* on 11 April 1942. Though her casualties were heavy, the ship was not sunk. On 15 April, the burned-out vessel was towed into Morehead City by the British trawler HMT *Senateur Duhamel* (FY327).
National Archives photograph #80-G-464858

The numbers and results of U-boat attacks in the Eastern Sea Frontier in April 1942 were almost an exact repetition of the preceding month. The submarines still preferring to operate at night, frequently supplementing torpedoes with gunfire. The favorite area of activity continued to be Hatteras, though toward the end of the month, it was apparent that a slow shift to the south was taking place.[1]

On 31 March, the destroyers USS *Hambleton* (DD-455), *Hamilton* (DMS-18), *Emmons* (DD-457), *Ellis* (DD-154), and *Manley* (APD-1) were ordered to temporary duty in the Frontier. The *Roper* (DD-147), *Noa* (DD-343), and *Herbert* (DD-160) were already there, so April began with a total of eight destroyers in the area. In the week that followed, this number was gradually reduced and, on 9 April, only *Herbert* and *Noa* remained. For the next five days, there were, on average, only two destroyers per day in the Frontier. During this period, eight vessels were sunk by enemy action. The 9th, when four ships went down, marked the worst day of the month. The following day, commander, Eastern Sea Frontier strongly urged that an additional destroyer division be dispatched to reinforce the two destroyers then patrolling the area.[2]

That afternoon, 10 April, Admiral Andrews was informed that no destroyers could be made available "now or in the near future without taking them away from essential [transatlantic] escort of convoys or naval ships." On 16 April, commander in chief, United States Fleet (Admiral King) directed commander in chief, Atlantic Fleet (Admiral Ingersoll) to assign three ships to Admiral Andrews at once and "others to bring destroyer strength Eastern Sea Frontier to total of nine as soon as may be." Ingersoll immediately sent three destroyers and ordered three others to report upon completion of their current tasks. On the last day of April, there were nine destroyers operating in the waters of the Frontier. Throughout the last week, there were, normally, six destroyers on duty.[3]

During April, the destroyers available, being too few in number to support commencement of a desired convoy system, were assigned instead to the patrol and search of localized, endangered areas. This method, necessarily imposed by the exigency of limited strength, was in violation of two great principles of war: the conservation of energy, and the concentration of force. As discussed previously, after the nature of the task assigned to vessels on patrol and search in WWI had been graphically described to Woodrow Wilson, he stated that he "despaired of hunting the hornets all over the farm."[4]

EXTENT OF ANTI-SUBMARINE OPERATIONS

Earlier on 31 March, the destroyers *Hamilton* and *Emmons* had received orders to discontinue their training at Casco Bay, Maine, and report for duty with commander, Eastern Sea Frontier. (Commander Destroyer Force, Atlantic was based at Casco Bay during World War II because it offered protected anchorage close to North Atlantic convoy routes.) The first three paragraphs of the orders given to the two destroyers on 1 April, summarize the efforts then possible in the Frontier:

1. Enemy submarine activity exists off the Atlantic Coast. *GREER*, *ROPER*, *HAMILTON* and *MANLEY* operating singly in vicinity Cape Henry to Cape Lookout. *HERBERT* and *NOA* operating Winter Quarter to Cape Charles.
   Several 125 foot Coast Guard cutters and [patrol yacht] PY *TOURMALINE* operating same area.
   Some H.M.S. Trawlers in same area.
   Navy and Army planes patrol this area daily.
2. This force will search for and destroy enemy submarines.
3. When ready for sea proceed to vicinity Wimble Shoal Buoy searching en route.
   Search area from Wimble Shoal Buoy to Cape Lookout as circumstances may indicate, in general following to seaward of the coastal shipping lanes.
   Destroy enemy submarines.[5]

Hamilton and *Emmons* were to proceed from Casco Maine, down the East Coast to the Wimble Shoal Buoy in North Carolina waters. From there, they were to continue southward to Cape Lookout, North Carolina, searching the Hatteras area (bordered by Wimble Shoal to the north, and Cape Lookout to the south) for enemy submarines.

Northward off Virginia, the other destroyers and British trawlers were operating near the entrance to Chesapeake Bay (Cape Henry to Cape Lookout), or between Wimble Shoals (marking the beginning of the approach to the Chesapeake Bay from the north) and Cape Charles.

The most dangerous area for shipping continued to be the waters around Hatteras, where the narrowness of the continental shelf enabled U-boats to operate in deep water close inshore with great effectiveness and comparative impunity. Andrews had earlier taken steps in March to curtail the success of the U-boats, by directing northbound merchant vessels to proceed from Cape Lookout to the Chesapeake in daylight. At night, these ships were to lay in protected anchorages that had been established at each of the terminal ports.[6]

PLANNING FOR COASTAL CONVOY OPERATIONS

In mid-April, Andrews proposed further actions to increase the protection of ships sailing through this dangerous area. In a letter to Rear Adm. Manley H. Simons, USN, commandant of the Fifth Naval District, he suggested that all ships then sailing independently between Cape Lookout and the Chesapeake should be formed into convoys. Merchant vessels would put into Lookout at night, seeking refuge in the anchorage which was guarded by ships equipped with listening gear, depth charges, and guns. In early morning, the ships would form up together, four ships to a column. Vessels unable to maintain nine knots or capable of more than thirteen would sail independently.[7]

Map 7-1

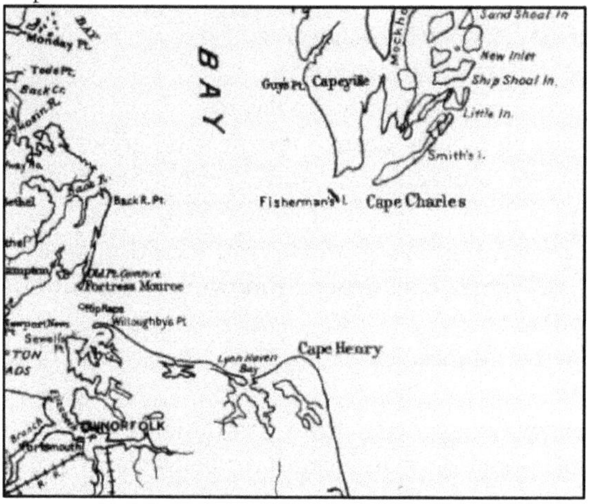

Entry to the Chesapeake Bay in southeastern Virginia
National Archives photograph USN 901626

Photo 7-2

Harbor Entrance Control Post, Cape Henry, Virginia. Personnel manning this post at the entrance of Hampton Roads, served as "eyes" for the intelligence nerve center in Joint Operations, Naval Operating Base, Norfolk, 23 May 1943.
Naval History and Heritage Command photograph #NH 96586

For each convoy, escort would be provided by one slow ship, which would lead the group, and by three fast ones able to patrol to seaward and to the rear of it. Whenever a destroyer was available from other duties, it would augment the escort force. Forty smaller craft, including twenty 83-foot Coast Guard cutters attached to the Fifth Naval District, would form a pool from which the escorting force would be obtained. In his letter to Simons, Andrews noted, "that the foregoing plan utilizes practically all available patrol vessels of the Fifth Naval District" and provided his rationale for this arrangement, "at the same time, by concentrating our shipping and patrol vessels as escorts, the best possible protection will be gained."[8]

On 22 April, Rear Admiral Simons replied that the proposed system was "practically in effect now," since all northbound ships were escorted from Cape Lookout, and all southbound shipping was provided with air coverage. In spite of the assuring statements by Simons, it was, however, impossible to introduce the convoy system envisioned by Andrews, because neither ships, nor men, were available in sufficient numbers to implement the plan.[9]

Meanwhile, Andrews was working on ways to improvise methods for the protection of shipping in the northern as well as the southern extremity of the Frontier. Devising a plan for convoying ships from Boston to Halifax and Sydney was complicated. Such a convoy would serve as the middle link in a chain of shipping extending from America's southern coastal waters to the open seas of the North Atlantic where at the northern end, control would have to pass from USN hands into those of the British. It was therefore necessary to devise a system that would integrate the activities of two different navies (actually three, because the Royal Canadian Navy was also deeply involved) and fit together the sailing schedules of yet-to-be-fully-developed USN coastal convoys with those of the North Atlantic.[10]

EASTERN SEA FRONTIER SURFACE FORCES

On 11 April, Eastern Sea Frontier vessels numbered only forty-eight, not counting destroyers that came and went within it. At the time, the three remaining British trawlers ordered to America—HMT *Arctic Explorer*, HMT *Pentland Firth*, and HMT *Northern Dawn*—were yet to report to commander, Eastern Sea Frontier for duty.[11]

The table on the following page, dramatically lacking numbers and sizes of appropriate anti-submarine vessels such as destroyers, vividly illustrates the scarcity of naval forces, in both quantity and warfare capabilities, then available to Admiral Andrews to combat the ongoing U-boat threat. Fortunately, U.S. Coast Guard cutters and the British anti-submarine vessels were available to shoulder much of the work on the Frontier. The latter, converted fishing trawlers and whalers built for challenging conditions in the North Sea held the sea well, and their crews had previous combat experience battling German submarines in European waters.

Surface Forces Assigned to Commander, Eastern Sea Frontier, not including temporarily-assigned destroyers, on 11 April 1942

US Naval Vessels	British Vessels	USCG Cutters
Gunboat	**A/S Trawlers**	USCGC *Tallapoosa*
USS *St. Augustine* (PG-54)	HMT *Bedfordshire*	**165-foot Cutters**
Patrol Yachts	HMT *Cape Warwick*	USCGC *Argo*
USS *Sylph* (PY-12)	HMT *Coventry City*	USCGC *Icarus*
USS *Siren* (PY-13)	HMT *Hertfordshire*	USCGC *Dione*
USS *Zircon* (PY-16)	HMT *Kingston Ceylonite*	USCGC *Calypso*
USS *Tourmaline* (PY-20)	HMT *Lady Elsa*	**125-foot Cutters**
USS *Ruby* (PY-21)	HMT *Lady Rosemary*	USCGC *Cartigan*
Patrol Vessels (173 foot)	HMT *Le Tigre*	USCGC *Dix*
USS *PC-471*	HMT *Northern Chief*	USCGC *General Greene*
USS *PC-472*	HMT *Northern Duke*	USCGC *Antietam*
USS *PC-473*	HMT *Northern Isles*	USCGC *Cuyahoga*
Patrol Vessel (110 foot)	HMT *Norwich City*	USCGC *Jackson*
USS *PC-507*	HMT *Senateur Duhamel*	USCGC *Rush*
Eagle Boats	HMT *St. Cathan*	USCGC *Agassiz*
PE-19	HMT *St. Loman*	
PE-27	HMT *St. Zeno*	
PE-48	HMT *Stella Polaris*	
PE-55	HMT *Wellard*	
PE-56	**A/S Whalers**	
	HMS *Buttermere*	
	HMS *Wastwater*[12]	

LOSS OF HMT *ST. CATHAN* TO COLLISION AT SEA

SOS DE PEOT (HEBE) AT 33.18 N 77.57 W.

SHIP SINKING POSN 33.13 78.11 AT 0639 GMT.

—Distress reports from the Dutch steamship *Hebe*, received by the commandant, Sixth Naval District at 0220 and 0252 local time, respectively, on 11 April 1942.[13]

HMT *St. Cathan* was lost on 11 April 1942, as a result of being rammed at about 0215, south-southeast of Little River, South Carolina, by the Dutch freighter SS *Hebe.* Both ships were under "blackout orders," meaning they were operating with their running lights extinguished. Hit on her starboard quarter, *St. Cathan* sank quickly in about five minutes, and the *Hebe* in thirty minutes. The entire crew of thirty-one of the *Hebe* survived but, sadly, only nine of the thirty-nine officers and ratings aboard the *St. Cathan* were saved. One of the nine was Lt. John Mackay, RNR, who had commanded the British trawler since 12 June 1941.[14]

Arriving on the scene, the patrol yacht USS *Beryl* (PY-23) found USS *Azurlite* (PY-22) and the Norwegian whale factory ship SS *Kosmos* lying-to and searching for survivors from the *St. Cathan.* The patrol vessel *YP-22* rescued seven sailors from *St. Cathan* and 31 from *Hebe*, and transferred them to *Azurlite* and *Kosmos. Beryl* embarked eight men from *Kosmos* and, in company with *Azurlite*, headed for Charleston, South Carolina. Between them, the two patrol yachts landed *Hebe*'s entire crew and the nine survivors of *St. Cathan.*[15]

LEST THEY BE FORGOTTEN

The following names of *St. Cathan* personnel are listed on bronze panels of the RNPS Memorial in Belle Vue Park, Lowestoft, England. The memorial is solely for those serving RNPS personnel who died 1939-46, and who have no known grave. Those who died, and whose bodies were recovered are not included on the memorial.

HMT *St. Cathan* Personnel whose bodies were not recovered

Sub-Lieut. George Patton Allwork	Ord. Seaman William George Mair
Ord. Seaman Ronald Charles Baker	Seaman James McKenna
Seaman Lawrence Burns	Chief Engineman Alexander Reid
Assistant Cook Frederick John Buxton	Petty Officer James Beatty Russell
Ord. Seaman David Snowdon Coulthard	Seaman Alec Arthur Skarratt
Ord. Seaman Russage Evans	Assistant Steward Joseph Taylor
Seaman John Findlay	Seaman William Rees Thomas
Seaman George William Glenton	Stoker Arnold Robert Watson
Leading Seaman Albert Robert Harris	Seaman John Webster
Sub-Lieut. Henry Bleby Hodgshon	Cook Douglas Frederick White
Ord. Seaman William Hughes	Seaman James Wylie
Stoker 2nd Class Christopher Hynes[16]	

The ballad "The *St. Cathan*" by Lawrie Burns pays tribute to, and serves as a remembrance of the men lost aboard the British trawler.[17]

DESTRUCTION OF *U-85*

In the first minutes of a new day, 0006 on 14 April, the destroyer USS *Roper* was near Wimble Shoal, North Carolina, proceeding south-southeast on course 166° at 18 knots, while patrolling her assigned area. The surface of a calm sea gleamed with phosphorescent light; overhead in the clear sky, many stars shone brightly; and off to starboard, the light on Bodie Island was clearly visible. Nearby, on the ocean's surface off Cape Hatteras, was the *U-85* under Oblt. Eberhard Greger.[18]

The German submarine had left St. Nazaire, France, on her fourth war patrol on 21 March. Two weeks later, she arrived off the Grand Bank of Newfoundland, where the warm Gulf Stream slams into the cold Labrador Current. On 10 April, still in transit to her operational area off the New Jersey coast, *U-85* found her first victim. It was the Norwegian freighter MS *Christina Knudsen* outbound from New York to Cape Town. Greger sank her with two torpedoes and then proceeded directly for his station off Cape Hatteras. On 13 April 1942, the submarine was sitting on the bottom in shallow water off the Bodie Island lighthouse waiting for targets. Late that night, she surfaced and, soon after, *Roper* gained radar contact on her.[19]

The contact was off the destroyer's starboard bow, bearing 190° true, at a range of 2,700 yards. *Roper*'s sound man, echo ranging a sector ahead of the ship, heard rapidly turning propellers at a range and bearing that correlated with that obtained by the radar operator. Then, almost dead ahead, the lookout sighted what appeared to be the wake of a small vessel running away at high speed. Range to the contact decreased very slowly as *Roper* increased her speed to 20 knots.[20]

The vessel ahead visually appeared to be a small Coast Guard cutter, but her speed made it possible that she was a submarine. Accordingly, *Roper*'s crew was called to General Quarters; and orders were given to prepare the machine guns, the 3-inch battery, the torpedoes, and the depth charges for action. Ahead of her, the unknown vessel continued to come left (to course 175°, 155°, 135°, and finally 115°), while *Roper* maintained a position very slightly on her starboard quarter, so as to avoid a possible torpedo fired from her stern tube. When *Roper* closed the vessel to 700 yards, the wake of a torpedo was observed passing close aboard her port side.[21]

As *Roper* closed to a distance of 300 yards, the pursued vessel suddenly made a sharp turn to starboard. Switched-on, the 24-inch searchlight of the destroyer illuminated a large enemy submarine. The

U-boat continued to turn to starboard, inside the turning circle of the destroyer, who maintained the searchlight on her adversary. All gun batteries that could be brought to bear opened fire. *Roper*'s No. 1 machine gun promptly and accurately cut down German sailors hurrying out of the conning tower hatch to man their guns. The number five 3-inch gun, found the range quickly and scored a hit on the conning tower. Soon after, the submarine began to sink. An order to fire a torpedo was given, but the U-boat disappeared below the ocean's surface before it could be carried out.[22]

About forty German crewmembers were in the water, but the destroyer was more immediately concerned with the certain destruction of the submarine, than with rescue of the personnel. Eleven depth charges were laid down on an estimated position, based on an excellent sound contact. The *Roper* stood by in the area until dawn broke. Rescue operations were not undertaken because it was feared that a destroyer, operating at slow speed or stopped to launch and retrieve boats, would be easy prey for any other U-boat that might be nearby.[23]

When day broke, a PBY Catalina arrived to assist in the work. The patrol plane dropped a depth charge over an oil slick and a mass of debris floating in the water; *Roper* added two more. Two more planes arrived at 0700 and, six minutes later, dropped smoke floats in the water. The destroyer, upon investigation, found that the floats marked the position of dead bodies of German sailors. Boats were launched to pick up the dead and any articles that could be found. An airship arrived at 0727 to cover the *Roper* while the search progressed, and to direct the search by the boats with blinker light and megaphone.[24]

During the next hour, the number of aircraft increased to seven and, just before *Roper* departed the scene, a British trawler arrived. At 0900, as bodies of the deceased were being taken aboard the destroyer, the recovery work was interrupted for a time, after the sound operator gained a sharp, stationary contact. Four depth charges were dropped, and the position was marked with an orange buoy. Large air bubbles rising steadily to the surface, suggested that the buoy marked the location of the sunken submarine. (The twenty-nine deceased ultimately recovered were later interred in Hampton Roads, Virginia.)[25]

DIVING OPERATIONS ON SUNKEN SUBMARINE

The wreck of the *U-85*, one of only 24 Type VII-B German submarines built, rested on the bottom in approximately 100-110 feet of water, about 14 miles east of Oregon Inlet, North Carolina. Since she lay in relatively shallow water, Navy "top brass" had hopes of salvaging the vessel and acquiring a great deal of valuable intelligence from her. On

15 April, only a day after the sub's sinking, a party of hard-hat divers was sent to the scene of *Roper*'s contact, based on and supported by the fleet tug USS *Kewaydin* (AT-24) and protected by the British trawler HMT *Bedfordshire.* The latter vessel was tasked with providing anti-submarine protection to *Kewaydin* and the divers.[26]

Photo 7-3

Fleet tug USS *Kewaydin* (AT-24) near the Norfolk Navy Yard, 17 November 1941. National Archives photograph #19-N-25935

Photo 7-4

Patrol yacht *Tourmaline* off the New York Navy Yard, in Brooklyn, August 1941. National Archives photograph 19-N-25372

On 16 and 17 April, the patrol yacht USS *Tourmaline* (PY-20) and one British trawler was assigned to further support the diving operations. On 18 April, HMT *Bedfordshire* and HMT *Lady Elsa* were at the scene, guarding the diving party aboard *Tourmaline. Bedfordshire* was the only trawler assigned on 19 April. Three days later, both the

Kewaydin and *Tourmaline* were engaged in "sub salvage," supported by *Bedfordshire.*[27]

War diary entries by commander, Inshore Patrol Fifth Naval District are somewhat sketchy, but on 27 April there is an entry "Submarine salvage operations continuing" in the Remarks section.[28]

U.S. Navy leadership had hoped to recover a four-rotor Enigma (M4) machine from the *U-85.* The Germans had recently added a fourth rotor to this encrypting device, which prevented Allied forces from breaking naval code using a previously captured Enigma machine. The divers did not locate the desired cipher device, but were able to recover several items from the wreck site. These included the 20mm bridge gun, the 88mm deck gun, the IZO torpedo aimer, the gyro-compass, and an unexploded depth charge.[29]

Photo 7-5

Photograph taken on board *U-85*, recovered from her wreckage.
Naval History and Heritage Command photograph #NH 96589

Photo 7-6

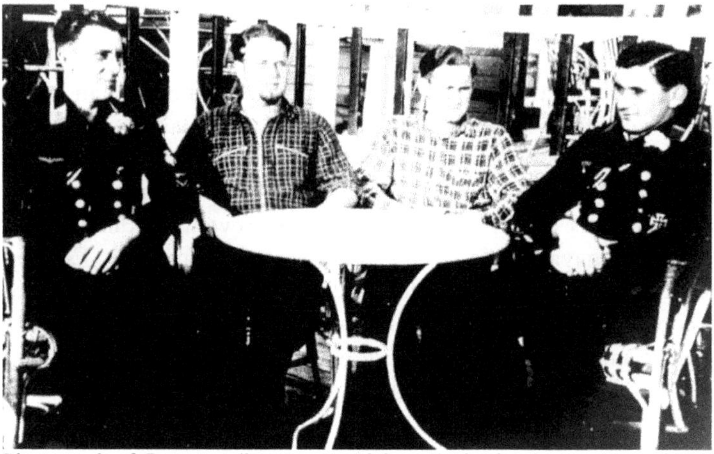

Photograph of German sailors recovered from the body of a crewman of *U-85* after she was sunk by the destroyer USS *Roper* off Cape Hatteras on 14 April 1942. Naval History and Heritage Command photograph #NH 96588

SHIPPING LOSSES

As shown in the table, dozens of ships were sunk, and a few damaged (D), by U-boats off the Eastern Seaboard in April 1942. Only a handful were under escort at the time of their demise.

Ships Sunk or Damaged off the Eastern Seaboard in April 1942

Date	Ship/Sub	Registry	Type	Tons	Location
1 Apr 42 unescorted	*Rio Blanco* *U-160*	British	steam merchant	4,086	35°16'N, 74°18'W
1 Apr 82 unescorted	*Loch Don* *U-202*	British	steam merchant	5,249	37°05'N, 61°40'W
1 Apr 42 unescorted	*Eastmoor* *U-71*	British	steam merchant	5,812	37°33'N, 68°18'W
1 Apr 42 unescorted	*Tiger* *U-754*	American	steam tanker	5,992	36°50'N, 75°49'W
2 Apr 42 unescorted	*Liebre* (D) *U-123*	American	steam tanker	7,057	34°11'N, 76°08'W
3 Apr 42 unescorted	*David H. Atwater* *U-552*	American	steam merchant	2,438	37°57'N, 75°10'W
3 Apr 42 unescorted	*Otho* *U-754*	American	steam merchant	4,839	36°25'N, 72°22'W
5 Apr 42 escorted	*Byron D. Benson* *U-552*	American	steam tanker	7,953	36°08'N, 75°32'W
6 Apr 42 unescorted	*Bidwell* (D) *U-160*	American	motor tanker	6,837	34°25'N, 75°57'W
6 Apr 42 unescorted	*Koll* *U-571*	Norwegian	motor tanker	10,044	34°39'N, 68°25'W

6 Apr 42 unescorted	*Kollskegg* *U-754*	Norwegian	motor tanker	9,858	34°58'N, 68°38'W
7 Apr 42 escorted	*British Splendour* *U-552*	British	motor tanker	7,138	35°07'N, 75°19'W
7 Apr 42 unescorted	*Lancing* *U-552*	Norwegian	whale factory ship	7,866	35°08'N, 75°22'W
8 Apr 42 unescorted	*Oklahoma* (D) *U-123*	American	steam tanker	9,264	31°18'N, 80°59'W
8 Apr 42 unescorted	*Nemanja* *U-84*	Yugoslavian	steam merchant	5,226	40°30'N, 64°50'W
9 Apr 42 unescorted	*Esparta* *U-123*	American	steam merchant	3,365	30°46'N, 81°11'W
9 Apr 42 unescorted	*Malchace* *U-160*	American	steam merchant	3,516	34°28'N, 75°56'W
9 Apr 42 unescorted	*Atlas* *U-552*	American	steam tanker	7,137	34°27'N, 76°16'W
10 Apr 42 unescorted	*San Delfino* *U-203*	British	motor tanker	8,072	35°35'N, 75°06'W
10 Apr 42 unescorted	*Tamaulipas* *U-552*	American	steam tanker	6,943	34°25'N, 76°00'W
10 Apr 42 unescorted	*Empire Prairie* *U-654*	British	steam merchant	7,010	37°33'N, 60°06'W
10 Apr 42 unescorted	*Christina Knudsen* *U-85*	Norwegian	motor merchant	4,904	39°00'N, 73°00'W
11 Apr 42 unescorted	*Gulfamerica* *U-123*	American	steam tanker	8,081	30°14'N, 81°18'W
11 Apr 42 unescorted	*Ulysses* *U-160*	British	steam passenger ship	14,647	34°23'N, 75°35'W
11 Apr 42 escorted	*Harry F. Sinclair Jr.* (D) *U-203*	American	steam tanker	6,151	34°25'N, 76°30'W
13 Apr 42 unescorted	*Korsholm* *U-123*	Swedish	motor merchant	2,647	28°21'N, 80°22'W
13 Apr 42 unescorted	*Leslie* *U-123*	American	steam merchant	2,609	28°35'N, 80°19'W
13 Apr 42 ON-80	*Empire Progress* *U-402*	British	steam merchant	5,249	40°29'N, 52°35'W
14 Apr 42 unescorted	*Empire Thrush* *U-203*	British	steam merchant	6,160	35°08'N, 75°18'W
14 Apr 42 unescorted	*Margaret* *U-571*	American	steam merchant	3,352	35°15'N, 74°38'W
16 Apr 42 unescorted	*Desert Light* *U-572*	Panamanian	steam merchant	2,368	35°35'N, 72°48'W
16 Apr 42 unescorted	*Robin Hood* *U-575*	American	steam merchant	6,887	38°45'N, 66°45'W
17 Apr 42 unescorted	*Alcoa Guide* *U-123*	American	steam merchant	4,834	35°34'N, 70°08'W
18 Apr 42 unescorted	*Victoria* (D) U-201	Argentinian	motor tanker	7,417	36°41'N, 68°48'W

19 Apr 42 escorted	*Axtell J. Byles* (D) *U-136*	American	steam tanker	8,955	35°32'N, 75°19'W
20 Apr 42 unescorted	*Harpagon* *U-109*	British	steam merchant	5,719	34°35'N, 65°50'W
20 Apr 42 unescorted	*Empire Dryden* *U-572*	British	steam merchant	7,164	34°21'N, 69°00'W
20 Apr 42 unescorted	*Agra* *U-654*	Swedish	motor merchant	4,569	34°40'N, 69°35'W
20 Apr 42 unescorted	*Steel Maker* *U-654*	American	steam merchant	6,176	33°48'N, 70°36'W
21 Apr 42 unescorted	*Bris* *U-201*	Norwegian	steam merchant	2,027	33°35'N, 69°38'W
21 Apr 42 unescorted	*Pipestone County* *U-576*	American	steam merchant	5,102	37°43'N, 66°16'W
21 Apr 42 unescorted	*West Imboden* *U-752*	American	steam merchant	5,751	41°14'N, 65°55'W
21 Apr 42 unescorted	*Chenango* *U-84*	Panamanian	steam merchant	3,014	35°25'N, 74°55'W
22 Apr 42 unescorted	*Derryheen* *U-201*	British	steam merchant	7,217	31°20'N, 70°35'W
22 Apr 42 unescorted	*San Jacinto* *U-201*	American	steam passenger ship	6,069	31°10'N, 70°45'W
23 Apr 42 unescorted	*Reinholt (D)* *U-752*	Norwegian	motor merchant	4,799	39°10'N, 72°00'W
24 Apr 42 unescorted	*Empire Drum* *U-136*	British	motor merchant	7,244	37°00'N, 69°15'W
25 Apr 42 unescorted	*Modesta* *U-108*	British	steam merchant		33°40'N, 63°10'W
28 Apr 42 unescorted	*Arundo* *U-136*	Dutch	steam merchant	5,163	40°10'N, 73°44'W
30 Apr 42 escorted	*Ashkhabad* *U-402*	Soviet	steam merchant	5,284	34°19'N, 76°31'W
30 Apr 42 unescorted	*Taborfjell* *U-576*	Norwegian	steam merchant		41°52'N, 67°43'W[30]

EXPANDED EASTERN SEA FRONTIER DUTIES

On 28 April, Admiral King informed Admiral Andrews that control of all tankers from the Panama, Caribbean, and Gulf Sea Frontiers to the Eastern Sea Frontier were vested in his hands "with the necessary authority to direct their sailings as required by the existing situation."[31]

8

The Tide Turns

Luck, which until this month, seemed to run against us on this coast, may well have entered to assist us in upsetting the calculations of an enemy who had sent more submarines to the Frontier in May than he ever had before.

The fact remains, however, that the addition of planes and surface craft and the constant training of air and surface personnel resulting in more efficient and constant attacks against submarines along the coast was beginning to have effect and enemy submarines began seeking less dangerous areas.

—Commander, Eastern Sea Frontier War Diary, May 1942.

In May 1942, there was an extraordinary change in the fortunes of the war beneath the sea in the Eastern Sea Frontier. April, when ships had gone down at a rate of almost one a day, was the worst month within the Frontier since submarines first invaded the coast in January 1942. As it had drawn to a close, there was no indication, and no hope, that the severe shipping losses could be appreciably reduced in the foreseeable future. Then, things began to change; in the first seventeen days in May, not a single ship was lost in the Eastern Sea Frontier. In the fourteen days that remained, only four vessels were sunk in these waters.[1]

The dramatically decreased ship losses cited by commander, Eastern Sea Frontier in his war diary for May 1942, were significant. However, losses off the North American Eastern Seaboard as a whole, which included Canadian waters, and the portion of the Gulf Sea Frontier off the east coast of Florida, as well as the Eastern Sea Frontier, were still of great concern. The following two tables identify ships sunk, damaged (D), or judged a total loss (T) as a result of enemy submarine action off the Eastern Seaboard.

Ever since U-boats arrived off the East Coast in January, there had been a gradual, but discernible shift southward in the scene of their operations. This pattern continued into the month of May, when U-boats struck in the Caribbean and the Gulf of Mexico with devastating effect. However, while the bulk of German attacks were concentrated in waters south of the Eastern Sea Frontier, it did not mean that the bulk of U-boats had left the Frontier to concentrate in the southern waters.[2]

Actually, there were more enemy submarines in the Frontier than ever before, but operations were not limited to the areas of Hatteras and the South; U-boats operated all up and down the coast, and in the Gulf of Maine and Canadian waters. To assist readers in identifying the general geographical locations in which these ships were lost, a map, also used in a previous chapter, follows the tables.[3]

Ships Sunk off the Eastern Seaboard in May 1942
(Canadian and U.S. East Coast, excluding Florida)

Date	Ship/Sub	Registry	Type	Tons	Location
1 May 42 unescorted	*Bidevind* *U-752*	Norwegian	motor merchant	4,956	39°35'N, 72°42'W
2 May 42	USS *Cythera* (PY-26) *U-402*	American	patrol yacht	602	33°15'N, 75°26'W
5 May 42 unescorted	*Lady Drake* *U-106*	Canadian	steam passenger ship	7,985	35°43'N, 64°43'W
5 May 42 unescorted	*Delisle* (D) *U-564*	American	steam merchant	3,478	47°19'N, 52°27'W
8 May 42	*Mildred Pauline* *U-136*	Canadian	sailing ship	300	39°45'N, 55°26'W
10 May 42 unescorted	*Clan Skene* *U-333*	British	steam merchant	5,214	31°43'N, 70°43'W
10 May 42 unescorted	*Kitty's Brook* *U-588*	British	steam merchant	4,031	42°56'N, 63°59'W
12 May 42 unescorted	*Leto* *U-553*	Dutch	steam merchant	4,712	49°32'N, 65°19'W
12 May 42 unescorted	*Nicoya* *U-553*	British	steam merchant	5,364	49°19'N, 64°51'W
12 May 42	HMT *Bedfordshire* *U-558*	British	RNPS A/S trawler	913	34°10'N, 76°41'W
14 May 42 unescorted	*Stavros* (D) *U-593*	Greek	steam merchant	4,853	39°45'N, 72°35'W
17 May 42 unescorted	*Fort Qu'Appelle* *U-135*	British	steam merchant	7,127	39°50'N, 63°30'W
17 May 42 unescorted	*Foam* *U-432*	American	steam trawler	324	43°20'N, 63°08'W
17 May 42 unescorted	*Skottland* *U-588*	Norwegian	steam merchant	2,117	43°07'N, 67°18'W
17 May 42 unescorted	*Peisander* *U-653*	British	motor merchant	6,225	37°24'N, 65°38'W
18 May 42 unescorted	*Fort Binger* (D) *U-588*	British	steam merchant	5,671	43°01'N, 67°02'W

22 May 42 unescorted	*Plow City* *U-588*	American	steam merchant	3,282	38°53'N, 69°57'W
23 May 42 unescorted	*Zurichmoor* *U-432*	British	steam merchant	4,455	39°30'N, 66°00'W
23 May 42 unescorted	*Margot* *U-588*	British	steam merchant	4,545	39°00'N, 68°00'W
25 May 42 in convoy	*Persephone* (T) *U-593*	Panamanian	motor tanker	8,426	39°44'N, 73°53'W
27 May 42 unescorted	*Polyphemus* *U-578*	Dutch	motor merchant	6,269	38°12'N, 63°22'W
30 May 42 unescorted	*Alcoa Shipper* *U-404*	American	steam merchant	5,491	37°49'N, 65°15'W
31 May 42 unescorted	*Liverpool Packet* *U-432*	Canadian	steam merchant	1,188	43°20'N, 66°20'W[4]

Ships Sunk off the Eastern Seaboard in May 1942
(East Coast of Florida portion of Gulf Sea Frontier)

Date	Ship/Sub	Registry	Type	Tons	Location
1 May 42 unescorted	*La Paz* (D) *U-109*	British	motor merchant	6,548	28°15'N, 80°20'W
3 May 42 unescorted	*Laertes* *U-109*	Dutch	steam merchant	5,825	28°21'N, 80°23'W
3 May 42 unescorted	*Sama* *U-506*	Nicaraguan	motor merchant	567	25°04'N, 79°45'W
3 May 42 unescorted	*Ocean Venus* *U-564*	British	steam merchant	7,174	28°21'N, 80°23'W
4 May 42 unescorted	*Eclipse* (D) *U-564*	British	steam tanker	9,767	26°30'N, 80°00'W
6 May 42 unescorted	*Amazone* *U-333*	Dutch	steam merchant	1,294	27°21'N, 80°04'W
6 May 42 unescorted	*Halsey* *U-333*	American	steam tanker	7,088	27°14'N, 80°03'W
6 May 42 unescorted	*Java Arrow* (D) *U-333*	American	steam tanker	8,327	27°35'N, 80°08'W
8 May 42 unescorted	*Ohioan* *U-564*	American	steam merchant	6,078	26°31'N, 79°59'W
9 May 42 unescorted	*Lubrafol* *U-564*	Panamanian	motor tanker	7,138	26°26'N, 80°00'W
14 May 42 unescorted	*Potrero del Llano* *U-564*	Mexican	steam tanker	4,000	25°35'N, 80°06'W
28 May 42 unescorted	*Yorkmoor* *U-506*	British	steam merchant	4,457	29°30'N, 72°29'W[5]

Map 8-1

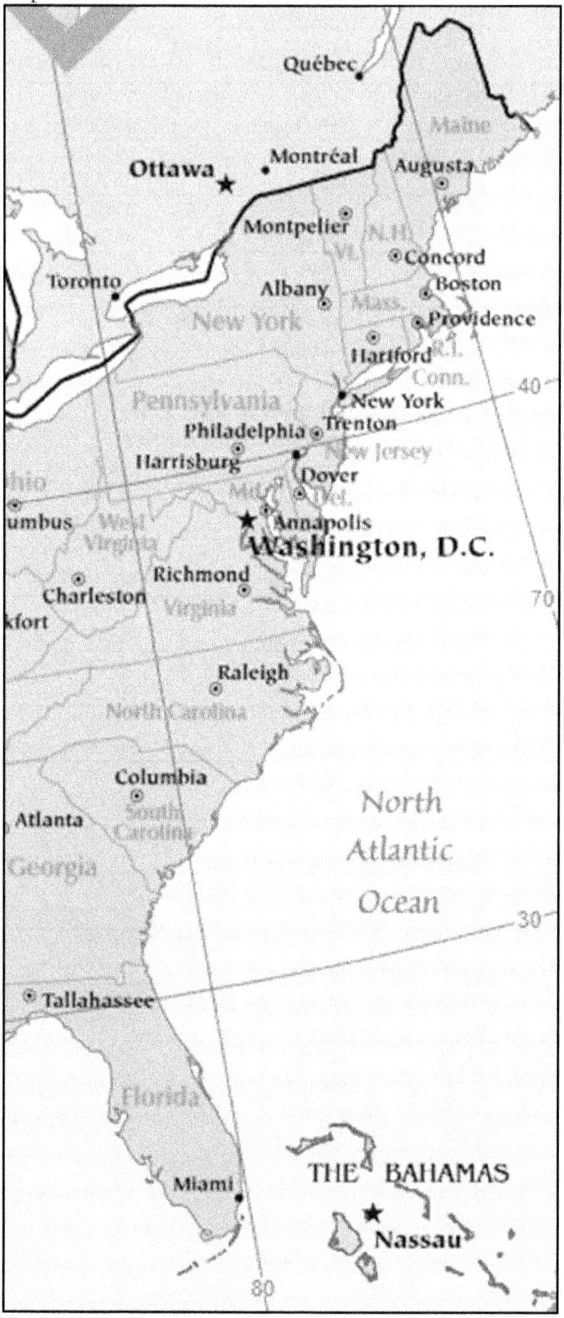

United States East Coast

Included in the ship casualties were the patrol yacht USS *Cythera* (PY-26) and trawler HMT *Bedfordshire.* Details about their losses to German U-boats, and the trawler HMT *Senateur Duhamel* to an accident at sea, involving the USS *Semmes* (AG-24), follow later in the chapter.

FACTORS CONTRIBUTING TO FEWER SHIP LOSSES

Several factors were involved in the radically altered situation in the theater of the Eastern Sea Frontier. These included, as previously noted, a shift in U-boat operations southward. Particular areas were exploited until operations began yielding diminishing returns. The submarines then began concentrating on new hunting grounds farther south.[6]

Contributing to the above phenomenon was an increase in May in the fighting forces available to commander, Eastern Sea Frontier. One hundred additional destroyer days were added to April's total, and there was about a 20 percent increase in larger patrol boats and aircraft.[7]

Another very important factor was the rapid progress the Eastern Sea Frontier made in organizing a training program for officers and men engaged in anti-submarine warfare aboard surface vessels assigned to the Frontier, or to subordinate naval districts. During the first few months of the war, a study was made by the U.S. Navy of British methods and practices, which had been developed since September 1939. Over the early years of the war, the Royal Navy had organized an elaborate program of anti-submarine training in order to provide specialized instruction for officers and crews.[8]

This training began with preliminary instruction at ASW (anti-submarine warfare) schools and working up bases, designed to achieve a reasonable standard of efficiency aboard newly commissioned ships before they began their first combat operations. Particularly important, the British ASW policy in regard to the use of Asdic (sonar) was carefully standardized in one manual, CB-4127. Additionally, submarine hunting tactics were standardized in necessarily broad outlines in another manual, CB-4097. The result of these procedures, and the training of personnel in them, was that any shipboard newly joined operators were able to perform their duties satisfactorily under the stress of combat.[9]

To provide training facilities and refresher training for combatant ships, the Royal Navy installed mechanical Attack Trainers at all important overseas bases. The attack trainers at Halifax, Canada; Iceland; Londonderry, Northern Ireland; and Greenock, Scotland, were made available to U.S. Navy personnel shortly after USN destroyers began North Atlantic convoy duty.[10]

To correct deficiencies in U.S. Navy training, Admiral King directed that an Atlantic Fleet ASW unit be established under Capt.

Wilder DuPuy Baker, USN, as commanding officer. On 7 February 1942, Vice Admiral Ingersoll reported that such a unit had been set up, with headquarters at Boston, Massachusetts. In a short time, the U.S. Navy awarded contracts to General Electric, Sangamo, and the Submarine Signal company for the manufacture of complicated attack training machines, based on those used by the British. Before they were ready, the ASW unit undertook the writing and compilation of an ASW manual, based on the study and analysis of all action reports submitted by surface vessels and aircraft of the Atlantic Fleet. On 12 April, Admiral King announced that he had set up a coordinated ASW unit at his headquarters in Washington, D.C., and that its commanding officer would be Captain Baker. The vacancy thus created in the ASW unit at Boston was then filled by Comdr. Thomas L. Lewis.[11]

On 28 April, representatives of these two units met to discuss plans for the enlargement of the ASW training program. It was agreed that support should be given for the development of a third ASW unit in the headquarters of commander, Eastern Sea Frontier in New York. The intended functions of their third unit were:

- Analysis and study
- Education
- Inspection
- As a result of the above, making recommended actions[12]

In May, Comdr. R. W. Hungerford, USN, recently returned from an extended tour of destroyer duty in the North Atlantic was designated officer in charge of the third unit. To assist him with scientific and technical issues, Lt. Richard Parmenter, USNR, was transferred from the ASW unit in Boston. Additionally, because some squadrons of the Army First Bomber Command came under the operational control of commander, Eastern Sea Frontier, a request was made for the appointment of an experienced Army pilot who might assist in analyzing reports of attacks on enemy submarines by both Army and Navy aircraft. From this nucleus, the ASW unit grew.[13]

ATTACKS AGAINST U-BOATS GREATLY INCREASE

Throughout the month of May the number of attacks by our surface craft against the enemy invaders greatly increased. There was evidence, as the weeks passed, that our crews were becoming more familiar with the various instruments used for tracking and locating the submarines, and more skillful in the handling of ships and weapons.

A reading of the [Eastern Sea Frontier] Enemy Action Diary will reveal how, on almost every day of the month, sights or contacts with the enemy were made and how vigilant were our forces in following up these contacts.

—Commander, Eastern Sea Frontier War Diary, May 1942.

As indicated in the quoted material, attacks against enemy submarines by Eastern Sea Frontier forces dramatically increased in May 1942. Three of the most successful attacks illustrate the significantly improved anti-submarine prowess of air and surface forces.

Photo 8-1

Destroyer USS *Broome* (DD-210), location and date unknown.
National Archives photograph 80-G-1024923002

SUB HUNT / ATTACKS BY DESTROYER *BROOME*

On the morning of 2 May, USS *Broome* (DD-210), a *Clemson*-class destroyer commissioned on 31 October 1919, was patrolling areas "F" and "W" of the Sixth Naval District, about 100 miles off Cape Fear, North Carolina. It was a beautiful day; gentle southwest winds rippled over the smooth sea, and the sun shone in the sky. At 1023, while proceeding on course 223°T at 22 knots, she made a sound contact, bearing 160° (forward of her port beam) at a distance of 2,300 yards. Two minutes later, she slowed to 15 knots when the target bearing was 154°, and the range 1,400 yards.[14]

Lt. Comdr. Karl Frederick Poehlmann called his crew to General Quarters but, three minutes later, when the range had decreased to 180 yards, contact was lost. Then, the destroyer dropped a smoke float over the estimated position of the submarine, and set up for an attack. The first of several was delivered fifteen minute later; a full pattern of nine depth charges fired from *Broome*'s K-gun depth charge projectors. As oil and air bubbles breeched the surface, propeller noises were heard by the sound operator. At 1102, after a second attack was made, a track of air bubbles and oil appeared once again, assisting the destroyer in tracking movements of the submarine.[15]

The submarine, moving continually and employing evasive tactics was turning inside *Broome*'s turning circle. At 1134, a periscope pierced the surface on the starboard beam of the destroyer, and fire was opened by her with 20mm and 3-inch gun batteries. Nine minutes later the sub tried to surface, but failed to do so. As propeller noises continued, the wake of the submarine was clearly visible, but moving slower with increased oil discharge emitted from her.[16]

Broome continued with her attacks but, while doing so, suffered a crack in the steam line to main generators (unrelated to the action at hand, she was an old ship). This resulted in both generators being temporarily out of service. At 1346, the destroyer fired her last two remaining depth charges at the target.[17]

Less than an hour later at 1435, the trawlers HMT *Le Tigre* and HMT *Cape Warwick*, which were on patrol in Area W, arrived on scene to continue the attack. That evening, *Broome* engineers inspected fire boxes, and found damage to the brickwork crowns of No. 3 and 4. After the associated boilers were secured, boilers No. 1 and 2 were cut in to supply the necessary steam. At 2014, *Broome* took station over the believed site of the wrecked enemy submarine. Alas, it had not been as grievously damaged as believed; may well have been purposely discharging air and oil to give that impression; and at some point, had slipped away.[18]

AIRCRAFT ATTACK ON BELIEVED ITALIAN SUB

At 0937 on the morning of 15 May, a Coast Guard OS2U Kingfisher patrol aircraft (*5771*) left Elizabeth City, North Carolina, on patrol. Sunlight obstructed by broken cloud formations created great patches of shadow on the water, but visibility was good. A brisk wind was blowing from the southeast, creating heavy seas. At 1230, about 30 miles east of Coast Guard Station No. 170 (at Caffey's Inlet, North Carolina), the pilot, sighted through binoculars, a "feather of wake" twelve miles distant off the starboard side of the plane.[19]

He turned toward the wake, and when approximately five miles from it, was able to identify its source as a surfaced submarine moving through the water. By throttling the plane down to one-quarter speed to reduce the sound of its engines, he was able to close to a mile and a half of the contact before it became aware of his presence.[20]

Photo 8-2

U.S. Navy OS2U Kingfisher floatplane, with a depth charge under each wing, in a hangar at a Naval Air Station, circa January-May 1942. National Archives photograph #80-G-K-2640

There were twelve men on the deck of what appeared to be an *Enrico-Tazzoli* type submarine, when the Kingfisher began its dive at the target. The sub immediately began a crash dive, and submerged before all the men on deck were able to get below. Of the two crewmen left stranded topside, one crouched alongside the conning tower, while the other scrambled toward the stern on his hands and knees. The little figure of the latter man could still be seen clinging to the sharply angled stern, as the plane leveled off fifty feet above the submarine to carry out her depth-charge attack.[21]

It was delivered at 1240, when two depth bombs set for 50 feet were dropped 150 feet ahead of the conning tower. No evidence of damage to the sub was immediately forthcoming. But then, dark grey pieces of wood rose to the surface and, a quarter of a mile off, an oil slick appeared winding in a great curve from the point of attack, until it came full circle. Ten minutes later, oil in large quantities appeared on the surface.[22]

The Kingfisher remained in the area until 1330, when two other Coast Guard planes arrived to relieve it. Post-analysis of the attack cast doubt on its success. The depth charges, after hitting the surface, would have advanced 50 feet in the water because of the speed of the plane, and would have exploded 5 seconds after entering the water since they were set at 50 feet. In that interval, a submarine moving at 8 knots would advance 70 feet. In short, this meant that the explosions would have occurred 150 feet ahead of the conning tower, or about 30 feet ahead of the bow of the submarine.[23]

Typically, this would not be close enough to kill a submarine, and the only debris to be found were six-by-six timber. Once again, a hunted, attacked, and possibly damaged enemy had apparently discharged oil to suggest its demise, then crept away.[24]

U.S. COAST GUARD CUTTER DESTROYS U-BOAT

Thirty meters of water… what could I do?

—Kapitanleutnant Hellmut Rathke, commanding officer of *U-352* and prisoner of war, in speaking of the action in which his boat was lost, stated that he did not like operating in water as shallow as that off the United States coast. Conversely, one of the surviving petty officers said he preferred shallow water on the theory that it increased the chance of survival in case the submarine was sunk.[25]

During the intervening period between the unsuccessful attacks by the destroyer USS *Broome* and the Coast Guard OS2U Kingfisher patrol aircraft against two enemy submarines, the USCGC *Icarus* sent the *U-352* to the bottom off Cape Lookout, North Carolina. On 9 May, the 165-foot Coast Guard cutter was off the coast of North Carolina, while proceeding alone from New York to Key West, Florida. Throughout the afternoon, she steered a south-southwest course (235°T) at a speed of 14 knots. Although the sky was overcast, visibility was excellent, and only a slight swell disturbed the smooth sea.[26]

In late afternoon, *Icarus* was about 30 miles south of Cape Lookout when her sonar operator obtained a "mushy" contact at 1620, about 1,900 yards (distant) on the port bow. Over the next several minutes, the sonar returns increased in sharpness as the contact drew abaft the beam of the cutter. At 1625, her commanding officer, Lt. Comdr. Maurice David Jester, USCG, was called to the bridge. Four minutes later, there was an explosion about 200 yards on *Icarus*' port quarter.[27]

Photo 8-3

165-foot cutter USCGC *Icarus* (WPC-110) under way, location and date unknown. U.S. Coast Guard photograph

The explosion was the detonation of the warhead of a torpedo which, fired from a bow tube of the *U-352*, had missed its intended target. The German Type VIIC submarine had been commissioned on 18 August 1941, with Kptlt. Hellmut Rathke her commanding officer. On 7 April 1942, she had departed St. Nazaire, France, on her second war patrol under his command. There was no band to "play her away" as she left carrying 14 torpedoes and no mines. Returning from her first patrol (lasting 43 days) on 26 February, her commander and crew had no ships sunk or damaged to their credit.[28]

The April voyage to American waters had taken about three weeks. The submarine cruised at slow speed on the surface, presumably to conserve fuel; and the men were allowed to sunbath on deck, three or four at a time, for short periods. It's believed that *U-352* arrived in American waters about 2 May, a week before her destruction. Misfortune plagued her. She sank nothing and, when on the surface, had to crash-dive several times to elude patrol planes.[29]

When the torpedo exploded off the port quarter of the *Icarus* on 9 May, General Quarters was immediately sounded and Lt. Commander Jester relieved the deck, meaning he took over the duties of officer of the deck (OOD). This action eliminated time delays associated with his providing guidance to the OOD on specifics about maneuvering the cutter in combat, and the OOD relaying these orders to the helmsman and lee helmsman for rudder and engine changes.[30]

Jester had enlisted in the Coast Guard in 1917 as a surfman; one of only 48 such individuals in the Sea Service that year qualified to operate boats in heavy surf. During the next twenty years he served on five cutters, advancing to Chief Boatswain in 1935. In December 1941, at age 52, he received a commission as a lieutenant and a month later was given command of *Icarus*.[31]

Photo 8-4

Lt. Comdr. Maurice David Jester, USCG.
U.S. Coast Guard photograph

The *Icarus* was immediately turned toward the spot where the torpedo had exploded. Jester took this action because propeller noises could be heard in that direction. Arriving at the eastern edge of the swirl created by the blast, the cutter dropped a diamond pattern of five depth charges at 1631. She then reversed course and, at 1645, dropped three addition charges in a V-pattern. As large air bubbles rose to the surface, a single charge was then dropped. *Icarus* once again turned, and returned to the torpedo blast spot, to launch a final depth charge (ten in total).[32]

One minute later, the U-boat, down by the stern, surfaced at a 45-degree angle. *Icarus* immediately opened fire with the machine guns that could be brought to bear, as she maneuvered to bring her 3-inch gun on target. As the cutter closed the submarine, the original range of 1,000 yards decreased rapidly. The first round from the 3-inch gun was short, but skimmed off the water and holed the conning tower. The second round was over (long). After that the gun crew got the range, and made six hits on the submarine.[33]

Throughout the gunfire, the crew of *U-352* were streaming out of the conning tower in clock-like precision, abandoning in order of seniority. At 1714, as the submarine sank, carrying thirteen men with her to the bottom, the cutter ceased firing.[34]

Jester, concerned about the problems that thirty-three enemy combatants (the Germans in the water) might pose aboard his small vessel, sent a series of messages to higher command, inquiring about whether he should recover the Germans. Finally, he received guidance from the commandant, Sixth Naval District, "PICK UP SURVIVORS, BRING THEM TO CHARLESTON."[35]

Photo 8-5

Survivors of *U-352* disembark from USCGC *Icarus* at Charleston, South Carolina, on 10 May 1942, with Marine Corps guards with fixed bayonets providing security. National Archives photograph 80-G-41302

U-352 was the first submarine sunk in American waters in WWII from which survivors were taken. Obtaining information from her crew proved particularly difficult for interrogators. Because of unavoidable circumstances, formal interrogation of her officers and men did not occur until three months after the sinking. Meanwhile, the prisoners, not separated by rank, were subjected to almost constant coaching by Kptlt. Hellmut Rathke. Even while in the water awaiting rescue, Rathke had shouted to his crew warnings about divulging information.[36]

A brief preliminary interrogation was made shortly after the men were landed at Charleston. Thereafter they were taken to a place of temporary internment, where Rathke, a stern disciplinarian, kept a strict surveillance and control over his men. During local, and subsequent interrogation in the United States, the full account of *U-352*'s activities remained concealed behind the crew's reticence. However, the following information, and that previously presented pertaining to her transit from Germany, could be pieced together from statements made by individual prisoners.[37]

The crew complement of *U-352* was 3 officers, 1 midshipman, 18 petty officers, and 24 men, bringing the total complement to 46. The executive officer, engineer officer, and 11 of the crew perished in the sinking; another man, who had lost his leg, died later, aboard the *Icarus*.[38]

Following the submarine's arrival in American waters, it appears she made a few unsuccessful attacks. Several men admitted that ships were sighted, and a coxswain said that a total of seven or eight torpedoes were fired on different occasions, but that the captain never claimed to have sunk anything. This coxswain let it out that they made several attacks one day, one of them on what he presumed to be a refrigerator ship. The next attack made, on the *Icarus*, would be her last.[39]

Additional information about the loss of *U-352* was gleaned by interrogators during the questioning of her crewmembers:

> One prisoner stated that U-*352* had been in the area of her final battle for about 4 days.
>
> When *U-352* sighted *Icarus* she was dead ahead. "Action stations" was sounded. Rathke manoeuvered into position at periscope depth and fired one bow torpedo, believed to have been electric. There is reason to believe that Rathke mistook Icarus for a larger craft. The U-boat crew heard an explosion. Some, at least, thought momentarily that they had scored a hit. If Rathke thought so he could not have been long deceived. In reality, the torpedo broached, sank and exploded, churning mud to the surface.
>
> Rathke believed he was operating in water 95 feet deep. (Actually, it was nearer 120 feet). Apparently hoping to avoid *Icarus'* anti-submarine devices, he took his boat to the approximate position of the torpedo explosion and there grounded her. Ironically, this was precisely the spot *Icarus* chose for her first depth charge attack.
>
> Prisoners stated that they heard a hail of depth charges, some of them extremely close. The first explosions destroyed the periscope and killed an officer in the conning tower. Gauges and glasses were smashed in the control room. The deck was littered with broken gear. Lockers burst open. Crockery and other loose objects were flung about the boat. The crew was shaken up. All lights except the emergency system failed. There is evidence that the electric motors

> failed - perhaps the greatest injury the boat suffered. There apparently was no water or chlorine gas in the boat.[40]

Rathke seems to have concluded that the submarine was damaged beyond hope of saving. He ordered his crew to put on lungs and lifejackets, blew the ballast tanks, and gave the command to abandon ship. Scuttling charges were likely set and detonated. Several prisoners stated that they heard two muffled explosions while swimming in the water. The U-boat's gunner disclosed that they intended to man the 20mm antiaircraft gun on surfacing, but were dissuaded by fire from the *Icarus*. When asked why he did not use his deck gun, Rathke said that the angle of the boat was too great, and that the *Icarus* was firing at his men.[41]

One subject that crewmembers were not reticent about was liberty ashore. German sailors (like those of other navies) generally avoided cafes and restaurants frequented by officers in order to avoid, among other things, the necessity of saluting. Following are some favorite haunts and gathering places of these men.

City	Bars, Cafés, and Restaurants
Lorient, France	The Sechs Titten (presumed to be a bar named Les Trois Soeurs)
St. Nazaire, France	Astoria bar
Gotenhafen, Poland	A dive named Libelle; also, the Berliner Cafe
La Baule, France	Die Giftbude (The Poison Shop), Maritza bar; prisoners complained that champagne cost 6 marks there
Brest, France	Cecilia bar
Kiel, Germany	Metropol, Monopol, Sans Souci, and Bellevue Cafe Delfe, frequented by midshipmen Sans Souci, forbidden to midshipmen Boccacio, where an orchestra named Weiland played Stadt Cafe
Flensburg, Germany	Cafe Haserl, Cafe Meyer, Deutscher Bahnhof Hotel, Haus Deutscher Arbeit, and a cafe near the Marineschule where a singer named Lauria Brandes performed
Stralsund, Germany	Trocadero, and Rathskeller[42]

AWARD OF THE NAVY CROSS

Lt. Comdr. Maurice Jester was awarded the Navy Cross for the destruction of *U-352*; the first Coast Guardsman to earn this award in World War II, and the first to receive it for combat action in direct confrontation with enemy forces. His medal citation reads:

> The President of the United States takes pleasure in presenting the Navy Cross to Maurice D. Jester, Lieutenant Commander, U.S.

> Coast Guard, for extraordinary heroism and distinguished service in the line of his profession as Commanding Officer of the U.S.S. *ICARUS* (WPC-110) during a successful action on 9 May 1942, with an enemy German submarine. The conduct of Lieutenant Commander Jester throughout this action reflects great credit upon himself, and was in keeping with the highest traditions of the United States Naval Service.[43]

Coast Guard Commander Maurice David Jester retired from the sea service in 1944, and returned home to Chincoteague, a town on the island of the same name, in Virginia's Eastern Shore region. He passed away on 31 August 1957, at age 68, after a long illness.[44]

UNITED STATES AND ROYAL NAVY SHIPS SUNK

As previously mentioned, among the vessels sunk by U-boats in May were the patrol yacht USS *Cythera* (1 May) and trawler HMT *Bedfordshire* (12 May). Amidst these losses the trawler HMT *Senateur Duhamel* was struck on 6 May by the auxiliary USS *Semmes* (AG-24), in an accident at sea, and also sunk. Descriptions of these tragedies follow.

LOSS OF PATROL YACHT *CYTHERA*

Photo 8-6

Patrol yacht USS *Cythera* (PY-26) in port, 2 March 1942.
Naval History and Heritage Command photograph #NH 83392

At month's commencement, the patrol yacht *Cythera* (PY-26) left Norfolk, Virginia, on 1 May, en route to Pearl Harbor via the Panama Canal, but was never seen or heard from again. After she failed to arrive at Christobal on 8 May as expected, commander, Offshore Patrol Atlantic of the Panama Sea Frontier received orders to search for the yacht. The resulting hunt for the thirty-five-year-old vessel in the waters of the Panama and Eastern Sea Frontiers produced negative results, as succinctly noted in a 30 May Eastern Sea Frontier patrol log entry:

> Nothing has been heard from *Cythera* (PY-26) which departed Hampton Roads 1 May to arrive Canal Zone May 8. Ship considered lost.[45]

Following an unsuccessful search, a lack of communications with the *Cythera*, and her failure to appear in the Canal Zone, the Navy was forced to announce formally that the ship was lost "due to suspected enemy action." On 2 June notices were sent to family members advising them that their husbands/sons had been placed in a "missing status." It was policy to hold missing personnel in this status for one year before declaring them dead.[46]

However, although the Navy assumed that all seventy-one officers and men aboard the yacht had perished at sea, this presumption was not true for two of her crewmembers. A few weeks after the notices were sent, an article appeared in the German newspaper *Deutsche Zeitung* in Den Niederland, announcing that two American sailors "Charles and James" had been brought back from Atlantic coastal waters.[47]

The *Cythera* was a product of Ramage & Ferguson, a shipbuilding yard in Leith, Scotland. Built as the *Agawa* for William L. Harkness, an oil baron with investments in Standard Oil, newspaper articles about her launching on 20 September 1906 described the yacht's cabins as elegant and her hull lines as graceful.[48]

The Navy bought the yacht from the Harkness family in 1942, three weeks after the attack on Pearl Harbor. Following her delivery, she once again underwent refitting for naval service (she had served in WWI), receiving three 3-inch/50 gun mounts and two stern depth charge racks. The *Cythera* was placed in commission on 3 March 1942, under the command of fifty-six-year-old Lt. Comdr. Thomas W. Rudderow.[49]

After commissioning as an ensign in the Naval Militia of Pennsylvania on 14 July 1916, Rudderow had served during World War I aboard the transport USS *De Kalb* (ID# 3010), and destroyers USS *Allen* (DD-66) and USS *McCall* (DD-28) of the Destroyer Forces based at Queenstown, Ireland. Discharged from active duty on 25 June 1919, he remained in the Naval Reserve until he was transferred to the Honorary Retired List on 1 September 1939. When recalled to active duty on 3 January 1942, he was serving as the superintendent and commanding officer of the Pennsylvania Nautical School ship *Seneca*.[50]

Filling out the wardroom of the *Cythera* were four reserve officers: Lt. Casper L. Zacharias, and Ensigns Robert Earl Brister, William Logan Bunker Jr., and Stratton Christensen.[51]

After departing Norfolk, bound for Pearl Harbor and duty with the Pacific Fleet, the *Cythera* had been at sea for less than twenty-four hours when she was torpedoed by the *U-402.* She quickly sank in the cold North Atlantic. The submarine, commanded by Baron Siegfried von Forstner, had been cruising on the surface some 115 miles off Cape Fear, North Carolina, when around midnight, on 1 May, the bridge lookout spotted the small warship zigzagging on a southerly course.[52]

The submarine submerged and launched a torpedo attack. Two torpedoes struck the *Cythera,* splitting her in half. As she sank, depth charges on her stern exploded, resulting in additional crew casualties. The *U-402* surfaced and plucked the only survivors, Seaman 2nd Class James Monroe Brown and Pharmacist's Mate 1st Class Charles Harold Carter, from the sea. The U-boat's search light, turned on to inspect debris floating in the large oil slick from the ship, had found Brown and Carter covered in oil and clinging to a small raft. Taken aboard as prisoners, they requested to be returned to the water, to which Von Forstner replied: "No, boys, the war's over for you."[53]

During the return voyage to France, the two Americans were treated well, given cigarettes and allowed to go topside for fresh air every day. In the almost three-week trip to the submarine base at St. Nazaire, the U-boat crew and prisoners formed a bond, and the Americans invited the Germans to visit them in the United States after the war.[54]

On reaching port, the prisoners were transported to *Marlag und Milag Nord,* a POW camp for Navy and Merchant Marine personnel located near Westertimke, Germany. Brown was sent to a POW camp in Upper Silesia, Poland, until finally liberated in April 1945 by units of Patton's Third Army. He was later returned to America, along with Carter, who was released in May.[55]

LOSS OF A/S TRAWLER HMT *BEDFORDSHIRE*

Chapter 1 is devoted to the loss on 12 May of the British anti-submarine vessel in combat with the German submarine *U-558.*

LOSS OF A/S TRAWLER HMT *SENATEUR DUHAMEL*

> *Rammed* Senateur Duhamel *on patrol five miles of Lookout Bight buoy No. 2. Our bow torn away back to anchor windlass. Will attempt backing into Bight when all hands from* Senateur Duhamel *accounted for.*
>
> —Message from the auxiliary (ex-destroyer) USS *Semmes* (AG-24), reporting that she had been involved in a collision, in early morning darkness on 6 May 1942, with the British trawler HMT *Senateur Duhamel* (FY327).[56]

On 5 May, the British trawlers HMT *Norwich City*, HMT *Senateur Duhamel*, and HMT *Bedfordshire* were operating in Sector 2 of Fifth Naval District waters. *Norwich City* and *Senateur Duhamel* were assigned convoy duty, escorting vessels south from Norfolk, and *Bedfordshire* to rescue duties.[57]

USS *Semmes* (AG-24) was patrolling a sector off Lookout Bight, North Carolina, guarding anchored merchantmen against the possibility of U-boat attack. The auxiliary was in a darkened condition. In early morning darkness on 6 May, *Semmes* rammed HMT *Senateur Duhamel* at 0344, striking her amidships, forward of the wheelhouse, and damaging her own bow considerably. The crew of the *Senateur Duhamel* was picked up by *Semmes*' boats, and transferred to the destroyer USS *Roper*, patrolling an adjacent sector.[58]

Photo 8-7

Auxiliary USS *Semmes* (AG-24) off the Charleston Navy Yard, 12 April 1945.

The *Semmes* was an old, former *Clemson*-class destroyer (DD-189), first commissioned on 21 February 1920. She had been reclassified an auxiliary (AG-24) on 1 July 1935. As a unit of Experimental Division 1 and, with assigned submarines, she had been testing and evaluating underwater sound equipment into the 1940s before being assigned new duties. Following the entry of the United States into World War II, *Semmes* had been tasked with escort missions, training services for the Key West Sound School, and anti-submarine patrol work in addition to her evaluation duties.[59]

The *Duhamel* sank about 0500, all hands having been rescued. At 0623, *Semmes* began steaming slowly toward Lookout Bight and, at 0658, anchored there. Two and a half hours later, the yard net tender USS *Sandalwood* (YN-27) came alongside and aided in clearing the wreckage from her bow. Early that afternoon, assisted by the tugs *T. E. Moran* and *W. E. Card*, *Semmes* got under way for the Morehead City Terminal Pier, and further emergency repairs to her hull.[60]

COASTAL CONVOY SYSTEM ENACTED

In the middle of May, the coastal convoy system long envisioned by commander, Eastern Sea Frontier was finally placed in operation. Much work still would be required to fit three separate convoy components comprising the whole system, and extending from Key West to Halifax into one, continuous long chain. At either extremity of the chain of protection, adequate cooperation with separate and independent entities was necessary. The southern terminal was the responsibility of commander, Gulf Sea Frontier, while the northern waters were controlled by the British.[61]

In support of the coastal convoy system, it was necessary to develop facilities for the anchorage, inspection, and assembly of ships at many ports along the coast. Most importantly, schedules had to be devised which would permit the limited escort forces available to operate in the most effective fashion. Some of these required actions were completed, others would be forthcoming.[62]

9

U-boats Mine American Waters

The most important convoy system is that protecting our merchant shipping from Canada to England. All the little coastal convoys from Aruba to Trinidad to Key West, from Key West to Hampton Roads or from Hampton Roads to New York exist principally as feeders for the main artery running from Canada to the United Kingdom.

These smaller convoy systems must be laced together in such fashion that they will provide constant protection for shipping; schedules must be so devised as to ensure that vessels move rapidly and steadily along their course.

—Commander, Eastern Sea Frontier War Diary, June 1942.

By this point in the book, nearly halfway through the text, many readers, particularly those with seafarer backgrounds, will appreciate the great burden shouldered by Eastern Sea Frontier naval forces in the first half of 1942, when U-boat attacks in the Frontier were at their highest levels. As expressed by Admiral Andrews in the quoted material, all of the sacrifices borne by his forces were for one purpose only, to shepherd small coastal ship convoys necessary to form larger ones, transporting desperately needed cargos of food, fuel, armaments, and other materiel across the Atlantic to the United Kingdom.

Combatant Ships in Service in the Eastern Sea Frontier
(150 total ships and craft as of 29 June 1942)

Vessel Type	#	Vessel Type	#
Destroyers	10	Coast Guard cutters, 75-83 feet	57
Patrol gunboats (PG)	7	Patrol craft (PC), 173-foot	7
HMT trawlers	16	Yard Minesweepers (YMS)	14
HMS whalers	2		
Sub-chaser (SC), 110-foot (new)	1	Patrol yachts (PY)	2
Sub-chasers (SC), misc. (old)	7	Coastal patrol yachts (PYc)	3
Coast Guard cutters, 165-foot	10	Rescue tugs (ATR)	7
Coast Guard cutters, 125-foot	3	Minelayers (CM)[1]	4

Because large numbers of Atlantic Fleet ships were needed for the transatlantic convoys; to form hunter-killer groups searching for enemy submarines in the vast Atlantic; and to fight at sea and support ground troops in other theaters, Andrews always lacked adequate forces. Moreover, while he gradually was able to obtain additional ships and craft, his area of responsibility kept expanding as shown on the map.

Map 9-1

Progression of Eastern Sea Frontier Boundaries: Area defined nearest the coastline was established in December 1940; an extension southward of this area occurred on 28 February 1942, as shown by fainter S-SW line; and finally, the whole area expanded seaward on 12 June 1942, as defined by the largest perimeter boundary
Commander Eastern Sea Frontier War Diary, June 1942.

In June 1942, U-boats attacked ships in the Eastern Sea Frontier with mines in addition to their torpedoes and guns. German submarine-laid minefields, which accounted for four vessels sunk, were found mid-month at both Cape Henlopen, where the southern boundary of the

Delaware Bay meets the Atlantic; and down the coast at Cape Henry, situated in the northeast corner of Virginia Beach.[2]

LOSS OF TRAWLER HMT *KINGSTON CEYLONITE*

> *The court is of the opinion that H.M.S.* KINGSTON CEYLONITE *was standing on a course which the commanding officer of the ship was fully justified in believing to be safe. In view of the fact that H.M.S.* KINGSTON CEYLONITE *was escorting a slow-moving tow, and the commanding officer's lack of information of the presence of enemy mines, the shorter course appeared to be more reasonable than a course into the channel at Point X-ray Mike where waters were deeper and submarines would have had greater opportunity to drive home an attack.*
>
> *Furthermore, the court is of the opinion that no offense has been committed, nor can serious blame be laid against any of the personnel of the H.M.S.* KINGSTON CEYLONITE *and that the loss of H.M.S.* KINGSTON CEYLONITE *was an unavoidable casualty of war.*

—Findings from "Inquiry into Sinking of HMS *Kingston Ceylonite*."[3]

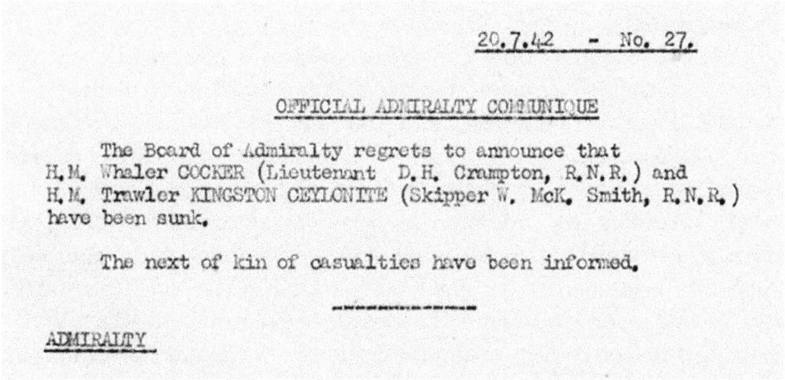

20.7.42 - No. 27.

OFFICIAL ADMIRALTY COMMUNIQUE

The Board of Admiralty regrets to announce that H.M. Whaler COCKER (Lieutenant D.H. Crampton, R.N.R.) and H.M. Trawler KINGSTON CEYLONITE (Skipper W. McK. Smith, R.N.R.) have been sunk.

The next of kin of casualties have been informed.

ADMIRALTY

Early on 15 June, the commodore of Convoy KN 109 (proceeding from Key West, bound for New York) reported that his protected ships would reach the Chesapeake Bay about 1700. At 1650, twelve ships and their six escort vessels arrived off Cape Henry. The below listed ships sailed from Key West on 11 June. USS *Saturn* was the former German freighter *Arauca*, which had put into Port Everglades, Florida, on 19 December 1939, to avoid capture or destruction by the British light cruiser HMS *Orion*, and had remained interned there. Acquired by the

Navy on 20 April 1942, she had been renamed *Saturn* and designated a cargo ship. *Saturn* had sailed from Mobile, Alabama, on 5 June for Boston, with stops planned at Atlantic Coast ports en route.[4]

Convoy KN 109 (Departed Key West, Florida, 11 June 1942)

Convoy Ships	**Convoy Ships**
Cargo ship USS *Saturn* (AK-49)	SS *Robert C. Tuttle*
SS *Delphinola*	SS *Sir James Clark Ross*
SS *Empire Emerald*	SS *Waimarama*
SS *Empire Sapphire*	**Escort Vessels**
SS *Esso Augusta*	Destroyer USS *Decatur* (DD-341)
SS *Hello*	Destroyer USS *Bainbridge* (DD-246)
SS *Ocean Volunteer*	Patrol gunboat USS *Impulse* (PG-68)
SS *Pan Marine*	Coast Guard cutter *Calypso* (WPC-104)
SS *Salomis*	Coast Guard cutter *Dione* (WPC-107)
	British trawler HMS *Lady Elsa* (FY124)[5]

As the commodore, embarked aboard the *Empire Sapphire*, brought his convoy in toward the channel, six miles off Virginia Beach, a summer crowd of bathers, brightly colored in their bathing suits against the shoreline, had gathered to watch the impressive parade of big ships. Fifteen hundred yards on the beam of *Empire Sapphire*, was a red whistle buoy, marked with the white characters 2CB. In times of peace, this buoy, dancing in the shallow water, marked the entrance to Chesapeake Bay.[6]

With the country now at war, it stood in a new position at the southern corner of a swept channel that ran from the sea through a friendly, defensive minefield, into the sheltered waters surrounding Hampton Roads. (A "swept channel" is a navigational channel cleared by minesweepers of any mines present, and maintained safe of any enemy reseeding of ordnance by periodic sweeping of it.) The northern extremity of this channel, which was designated Point XM, lay at the position of a former Chesapeake Light vessel. (Stationary light vessels along the Atlantic Seaboard, being at risk of attack by U-boats, had been removed from their traditional locations.) From there, the channel ran southwest to Buoy 2CB, where it turned sharply into the bay at a 90-degree angle.[7]

At 1655, the commodore awaited a pilot from a nearby pilot vessel to take him through the channel from the whistle buoy, the designated entry point for northbound vessels. He found himself in a comprising situation, without a pilot and without information about when one might be expected. Should he proceed or wait for them? Ahead of him was the dangerous area of an American minefield, while behind him were the members of the convoy strung out in a formation that was very vulnerable to submarine attack. At 1658, he slowed to five knots, and headed toward the pilot vessel that lay stationary in the water. Following astern of the *Empire Sapphire*, the convoy proceeded in the direction of Cape Henry.[8]

At 1702, the quiet of the summer evening was shattered by a loud explosion, and soon the tanker *Robert C. Tuttle*, the fifth ship, started to list to starboard, then fell out of the column. It was a mine blast on her starboard side, about 100 feet aft of the stem, that swung her to port, and stopped her engines, and caused her forward compartments to flood rapidly. As the tanker began to sink slowly, bow first, her crew took to lifeboats. At 1714, she slipped beneath the surface of the bay.[9]

Following the initial confusion caused by the sinking of the *Tuttle*, and subsequent milling about by other ships, the commodore was able to close up the formation and proceed as rapidly as possible to the pilot vessel. Finally, about 1725, *Empire Sapphire* picked up a pilot. Then sequentially, all but one of the other members of the convoy picked up their's and followed the flagship into Hampton Roads. The exception was the tanker *Esso Augusta*, carrying the vice commodore. After the explosion occurred close aboard the *Tuttle*, *Esso Augusta* veered out of the column to starboard, and hoisted signals for the rest of the convoy to zigzag, as she did so. (This action implied belief that the explosion resulted from a submarine attack.)[10]

Esso Augusta increased speed to full, ordered General Quarters set, and for a half-hour maneuvered in the vicinity of Buoy 2CB trying to find a place where she could enter the bay, without passing through the defensive minefield. At 1733, *Esso Augusta* was one-half mile south of the red whistle buoy, when there was an explosion off her port quarter. The resultant damage, although great, was not enough to sink her. HMT *Lady Elsa*, attached to the escort group, made three attempts to tow the 11,237-ton injured ship into port. After the line parted for the third time, shore assistance was requested, and responding tugs sent out towed her to Norfolk, Virginia. She arrived there the next day.[11]

Meanwhile, the escort group, plus several small craft and airplanes, began to search the area for possible submarines.[12]

At 1818, the destroyer USS *Bainbridge* dropped eight depth charges, with considerable repercussion to herself, after gaining a sonar contact 600 yards distant. It was believed that one of these charges set off a mine. Because of damage suffered, *Bainbridge* was ordered to proceed to Navy Yard Norfolk for inspection and repair.[13]

At 1930, HMT *Kingston Ceylonite* blew up; she was the fourth ship that day to fall victim to what would prove to be German submarine-laid mines. Not part of the convoy, she had been en route to Cape

Henry, escorting the freighter SS *Delisle* under tow by the salvage ship USS *Warbler* (ARS-11). Blimp *K-5*, nearby, saw a dark high explosion amidships on the trawler, and dropped a life raft to her. At 2030, Coast Guard lifeboats landed fourteen injured survivors from the trawler at Little Creek, Virginia.[14]

Sadly, twenty members of *Kingston Ceylonite*'s crew of 35 officers and men, including her commanding officer, were killed on 15 June 1942 by the mine blast.

Crew of HMT *Kingston Ceylonite*

	Officers	
William McKenzie Smith	Skipper, Lt., RNR	KIA
Thomas Orford Fletcher Leiper	Skipper, RNR	KIA
Richard Read	Skipper, RNR	
	Ratings	
Leonard Adams	Stoker	
Charles B. Bateson	2nd Hand, RNPS	
Alan L. Bennett	Ordinary Seaman	
Wallace Butt	Ordinary Seaman	
Robert Craig	Ordinary Signalman, RN	KIA
Herbert Deayton	Ordinary Signalman	
John Ernest Farrall	Seaman, RNPS	KIA
Cyril Gibbs	Stoker, RNPS	KIA
Charles Richard Jack Grimmer	Leading Seaman, RNPS	KIA
Albert Hitcham	Stoker, RNPS	KIA
Charles Herbert Edward Hitching	Seaman, RNPS	KIA
David John	2nd Engineer, RNPS	
Joseph R. Kay	Leading Cook	
James Lamplough	Seaman, RNPS	KIA
Norman MacKinnon	Leading Seaman, RNPS	KIA
Kendall Joseph Henry May	Seaman, RNPS	KIA
Frederick Munden	Ordinary Seaman, RNPS	KIA
Percy R. Nunn	Ordinary Seaman	
Albert Edward Palmer	Ordinary Seaman, RNPS	KIA
John H. Payne	Ordinary Telegraphist	
William Pegg	Seaman, RNPS	KIA
Christie Potter	3rd Engineer, RNPS	
Thomas T. Price	Stoker	
Alfred W. Rogers	Stoker	
Samuel A. Shields	Seaman, RNPS	
Joseph Davidson Stubbs	Ordinary Seaman, RNPS	KIA
Harold George Turner	Seaman, RNPS	KIA
Arthur Welby	Ordinary Seaman, RN	KIA
Adam Albert Wharton	Seaman, RNPS	KIA
Charles Edward Williams	Seaman, RNPS	KIA
Jacob Wilson	Chief Engineer, RNPS	
Albert William Wray	Leading Seaman, RNPS	KIA[15]

SOURCE OF THE MINES

On 20 May, *U-701* had sailed from Lorient, France, to carry out a special mission in American waters. A member of 3rd Flotilla, the Type VIIC submarine had been under the command of Kptlt. Horst Degen since her commissioning on 16 July 1941.[16]

Carried in her five torpedo tubes were fifteen magnetic-ground mines, three per tube, the diameter of each roughly that of a torpedo. She was one of three submarines, the others being *U-87* (Kptlt. Joachim Berger) and *U-373* (Kptlt. Paul-Karl Loeser) that were sent to mine Chesapeake Bay, Delaware Bay, and New York Harbor during the new moon period in the middle of June.[17]

On 11 June, *U-87* (a VIIB submarine of 6th Flotilla) laid her ten mines off Boston instead of New York, which remained undiscovered until after a postwar inspection of German naval records. That same day, *U-373*—a 3rd Flotilla VIIC boat like *U-701*—deposited her fifteen mines off Delaware Bay. On 24 June, the 400-ton tug *John R. Williams* detonated one of the mines laid by *U-373* and sank.[18]

INFORMATION GLEANED FROM *U-701* SURVIVORS

After laying her fifteen mines in Chesapeake Bay on 13 June, and later sinking the Yard Patrol Craft *YP-389* on 19 June (discussed in the next section), *U-701* was attacked on 7 July 1942 by a U. S. Army A29 Hudson bomber, and sank about 30 miles off Cape Hatteras.[19]

Photo 9-1

Survivors of *U-701* rescued by a U.S. Coast Guard seaplane, after the submarine was sunk off Cape Hatteras, North Carolina, on 7 July 1942. Naval History and Heritage Command photograph #NH 96587

An interrogation of the seven survivors, which included Kptlt. Horst Degen and the quartermaster (navigator), was begun within three hours after they had been picked up from the sea. The survivors had among them two escape lungs, and one rubber life jacket. Covered with oil, and badly burned by the sun, they had been in the water approximately forty-nine hours when rescued by a Coast Guard plane.[20]

The survivors, with one exception, were fairly security-minded, and as the men recovered, their defenses against interrogation stiffened. Degen had probably admonished his crew not to divulge matters of military importance, but a number of factors—his own garrulousness, his independent interpretation of security, the swiftness of the sinking, and the prompt preliminary interrogation—in the end, contributed to weakening of the resistance of the survivors to questioning.[21]

None of the survivors would admit to having mines aboard, or of laying them at the entrance of the Chesapeake Bay (the doorstep of the Norfolk naval base and of the Newport News port) to close off the shipping lanes at the mouth of the bay. Degen expressed his view that shallow waters presented opportunities for U-boats to lay mines in the paths of convoys and at harbor entrances. He admitted the possibility of U-boats carrying mines, but said such matters are held secret.[22]

Some innocuous information gleaned from survivors related to the submarine, and her last war patrol follows:

- *U-701*'s crew comprised 4 officers, a midshipman, and 38 men
- *U-701* was attached to the Third Flotilla based at La Pallice
- In port the crew was divided into three watches; one watch stayed aboard while the other two had liberty
- Prisoners insisted she carried no mines
- *U-701* left in the company of another U-boat (likely *U-373*)
- *U-701* followed the Great Circle course in crossing to North America; it being the shortest route, and thus the best for fuel economy
- The crossing to the American coast required 22 days. The slow time was due to a number of factors: keeping the engines at slow speed to conserve fuel, heavy weather, and brief pursuits of two east-bound steamers[23]

Information about *U-701* laying mines later came to light from Horst Degen's memoirs and other sources of information; details are as follows: The submarine arrived off Virginia's shores during the day of 11 June. A review of charts by Degen and his officers, revealed there was only one way into Chesapeake Bay, between Cape Henry and Cape

Charles. Because of a bank coming down from Cape Charles, incoming ships had to round the shallows at the southern tip and enter the bay in a single file between Cape Henry and the bank on a northern course.[24]

Degen decided this was the best point to lay the mines, and to do so at night while moving swiftly on the surface. Such an operation was simple. The outer torpedo doors were opened, and mines were released at set time intervals as the submarine moved, providing an equal distance between them. The "ship killers" would then lay inactive for 60 hours before an internal chronometer armed them. This was to ensure that the laying vessel was well clear of the area, and would not be "hoist with their own petard" before the mines became active. Once active, ships passing over or near a magnetic bottom mine would detonate it. No direct contact was required. A sensor in the mine, upon detecting a disturbance to the Earth's magnetic field caused by a passing ship constructed of ferrous metal, or fitted with sufficient machinery or equipment fabricated of metal, would cause it to explode.[25]

At nightfall on 12 June, *U-701* crept in toward the Virginia Beach shoreline. Degen later recalled:

> On port we could see the dark shadows of dunes, lights here and there and as our course brought us by closer to the very beach below Cape Henry it was a breathtaking adventure to see even cars and persons and lighted houses.[26]

To the amazement of the crew, it appeared that their intended area was clearly illuminated and undefended. Degen was able to proceed shoreward aided by lighthouses, which were lit. After entering the mouth of the Chesapeake Bay and reaching Thimble Shoals, minelaying was delayed by the appearance of a patrol vessel running without lights. The submarine and patrol vessel approached each other at right angles, then their courses diverged with the latter continuing on its course toward Cape Charles. Once the patrol vessel had exited the scene, preparations for minelaying continued. As *U-701* advanced, the Cape Henry lighthouse was passed slowly on her port side. When she reached a predetermined bearing, correlated with the starting drop point, Degen gave the order to commence minelaying.[27]

Zig-zagging back and forth, the sub began expelling a mine each 60 seconds into the dark water of the bay. When about half of the ordnance had been laid, the previously mentioned patrol vessel approached on a reverse track to the one it had just taken across the bay entrance. Shutting down the diesel engines to eliminate their "blub, blub, blub" sound but remaining on the surface, *U-701* lay quietly until the "doorkeeper of the Chesapeake" had reached the other side of her assigned route well clear of the sub.[28]

The mining operation resumed, with the submarine operating on battery power, instead of running on its diesels, guaranteeing silence as she finished her secretive mission. The job was completed by 0200 on 13 June. Accordingly, the mines armed themselves at approximately 1400 on 15 June 1942. They had only been active for a little more than three hours when they drew first blood, the mine strike on the tanker *Robert C. Tuttle*.[29]

LOSS OF YARD PATROL CRAFT USS *YP-389*

> *The* YP-389 *reveals the difficulties involved in converting small vessels for war purposes.... She assumed this duty only because no ships adequate to the task were available in the Frontier.*
>
> —Vice Adm. Adolphus Andrews, commander, Eastern Sea Frontier War Diary, June 1942.

Photo 9-2

Fishing schooner *Cohasset*, before her conversion to coastal minesweeper *AMc-202* and later to patrol vessel *YP-389*. National Archives photograph BS-32348

Increased Eastern Sea Frontier requirements—including convoy escort duty, and patrol of defensive minefields (intended to protect anchorages where merchant ships assembled to form convoys) to ensure that friendly vessels did not unknowingly stray into them—were placing an unremitting and increasing strain upon the assets available. Accordingly, YPs assigned to District Inshore Patrols began to be used as escort vessels and in other roles where larger, more heavily-armed ships were not available.[30]

An example was the *YP-389* (assigned to the Montauk Section of the Inshore Patrol, Third Naval District) built as the fishing trawler *Cohasset* for R. O'Brien and Co. of 34 Boston Fish Pier. The Navy had acquired and equipped her and her two 110-foot sister ships, *Salem* and *Lynn*, for use as coastal minesweepers (AMc) before refitting them as patrol vessels, a duty for which they were not particularly well-suited. They were not true sub-chasers by any means, as such vessels had good speed and range, were fitted with sonar to find submarines, and had sufficient armament to dispatch them.[31]

YP-389's top speed was perhaps 10 knots on a good day with a following sea. She had no sound gear and her armament was unimpressive, a single bow-mounted 3-inch deck gun, two .30-caliber machine guns, and four depth charges on racks with two spares. The vessel also had no fresh water tank as her designers had believed she would only remain at sea long enough to bring in a full catch. Thus, crew quarters had no showers, and lacked proper ventilation. The trawler, however, was representative of the types of small vessels that were being pressed into service to meet the emergency conditions that existed on the coast.[32]

Following receipt of orders for new duty in North Carolina, *YP-389* together with her sister *YP-388* proceeded to Section Base, Tompkinsville, New York, where the commanding officer of the *389*, Lt. Roderick Johnstone Philips, presented a list of repairs and alterations his ship required before transit south. The 43-year-old Philips was a naval reserve officer called to active duty the previous January. The *388* and *389* were being sent to the Fifth Naval District, which included the waters of the north coastal region of North Carolina along with those of Maryland and Virginia. The Sullivan Dry Dock and Repair Co. of Brooklyn installed a fresh water tank in the *YP-389*, scraped her bottom, and fitted baffles to prevent light from escaping from the engine room and galley hatches at night. At completion, she stood out of port, bound for Norfolk, as an escort for an "eight and one-half knot" convoy.[33]

On arrival, the YP laid over at Naval Operating Base, Norfolk, for six days, during which Philips tried to get some work done on his engines and obtain information regarding the ship's operating schedule, both to no avail. At the end of this layover, he was ordered to proceed to Section Base, Morehead City, North Carolina, and to report to the senior officer at the Coast Guard station at Ocracoke Island. While at the Section Base, Philips was able to get his engines overhauled.[34]

Soon after, *YP-389* put to sea on her first patrol. On 9 June, she and *YP-388* escorted the American cargo ship SS *West Lashaway* south to waters off Cape Lookout Lighthouse. Philips used this under way period to test fire his 3-inch gun, and found that something was wrong with the firing mechanism. On returning to base for provisioning, a chief gunner's mate inspected the gun and found that the firing spring was broken. This information was passed to "operations" at Morehead City, which agreed to obtain the replacement part. However, necessity soon trumped discretion. Provisions were put aboard the ship and with her only credible weapon inoperative, the *YP-389* was ordered back out on patrol.[35]

Philips' orders were for his ship to operate in the vicinity of Hatteras in order to warn friendly shipping away from a defensive minefield laid to protect the area around Diamond Shoals and Cape Hatteras from submarines. During the time he had been in port, this field had already claimed the SS *F. W. Abrams.* Through a combination of unfortunate circumstances, including a lack of proper navigational information and bad weather in which her master lost sight of the cutter providing escort services, the American tanker strayed into the minefield and was sunk.[36]

Sent to prevent any reoccurrence of such a tragedy, *YP-389* took up her Hatteras patrol on 14 June. In late evening on the 18th, she was five miles west of Diamond Shoals, steering a northeasterly course at six knots on a warm, quiet night, beneath a dark and nearly moonless sky. Mindful of the need to be particularly vigilant near the field—into which he dare not stray, but also could not operate very far from—Philips had posted lookouts on the bridge wings, as well as the flying bridge and on the stern. The ship reached the end of her run around midnight, turned, and began the return leg on a southwesterly course.[37]

In the early morning hours, Philips had the deck (he was the officer of the deck on the bridge) when a cry from the starboard bridgewing caused him to look in that direction. Stunned to see a U-boat appear out of the gloom to shoreward, he ordered battle stations set. As the executive and engineering officers, Ensigns Ray P. Baker Jr. and Robert M. McKellar, raced topside, having been awakened at 0245 by the alarm, the submarine took the ship under fire with its 20mm anti-aircraft gun fitted on the after part of the conning tower, followed by heavier rounds from the 88mm deck gun. The submarine was the *U-701*.[38]

Kptlt. Horst Degen had reported "execution of fouling" to the German Submarine Command on 12 June, signifying that he had laid the mines off the entrance to Chesapeake Bay. With this task completed, he was free to begin hunting shipping in his assigned operational area, which ranged from fifteen miles south of Cape Lookout, north to the Chesapeake Light. (Degen's war diary was later lost when the *U-701* was sunk. References to the following entries are from a U-boat Command Headquarters reconstruction based on information he provided to Admiral Doenitz.)[39]

Degen found that merchant vessels transiting the Cape Hatteras area were moving only during the late afternoon and early evening (when escorts could visually detect periscopes breaking the surface and attack) and that the shipping off Cape Lookout was particularly well protected. On 16 June, he noted:

> Cape Hatteras: traffic only between 1700 and 1900 hours. Cape Lookout: Heavy air, stationary sea patrols, good bombs.[40]

A diary entry for 17 June recorded that *U-701* had been depth-charged that day ("3 destroyers on N-course in formation and a buoy layer. 1 searching destroyer dropping isolated depth charges at position"), which resulted in damage to some gauges and the submarine's main periscope.[41]

Degen received a congratulatory message from Doenitz the next day, informing him that one ship had already been damaged by the minefield he had laid off Virginia. In a 20 June report, Degen summarized conditions encountered over the previous two days, including a chance meeting with, and the ensuing destruction of *YP-389*:

> Situation at Cape Hatteras: Traffic in batches, no longer by day, [shipping] recently [began to] set off far from land, [and] rounds Diamond Shoal 10nm [nautical miles] distant. Sighted 18 June 2 tankers, 1 freighter in line ahead [of] formation without escort, N-course, far out of effective range. Was surprised by [a] guard vessel in the haze. Destroyed in 1-½ hour artillery combat.[42]

Having surfaced off Hatteras and sighted what Degen later indicated he thought was the same vessel that had previously dropped depth charges near *U-701*, he took it under fire. *YP-389* replied with machine gun fire. Over the next hour and a half, the German submarine expended a combination of semi-armor piercing, high explosive, and incendiary rounds, apparently because her gun crew seized every available shell in the ready-use magazine. There were twenty-eight rounds in the magazine, which enabled the gun crew to start firing immediately after surfacing without having to wait for shells to be brought up from the main magazine inside the pressure hull.[43]

As off-watch sailors aboard the YP boiled out of crew's quarters on deck, an 88mm round killed the first to emerge and injured three others, forcing the remaining men to take shelter behind trawling winches. Philips notified the Coast Guard station at Ocracoke that he was under enemy attack and also warned Fifth Naval District ships and aircraft. The Coast Guard replied that help was on the way. With the 3-inch gun unserviceable, Fireman 2nd Class Vincent W. Crabb and 1st Class Robert Wilson returned fire with .30-caliber machine gun mounts in exposed positions on the signal bridge and the boat deck.[44]

Philips had initially turned seaward in order to minimize his ship's cross section by presenting only her stern to the enemy's guns. However, aware that he could neither outgun nor outrun the submarine (which could make nearly 18 knots on the surface), he ordered a westerly course toward the shore, from which he thought help would be coming. The U-boat twice approached the YP sufficiently close for Philips to order Fireman 3rd Class Wilson B. Cole to drop depth charges, but they apparently had no effect. For a time, it appeared that the ex-trawler might escape into shallow water nearer shore, where the larger submarine dared not follow lest it run aground.[45]

The enemy was finding it difficult to score hits on the *YP-389* due to her low profile. However, the longer the one-sided battle lasted, the more likely it was that even in the gloom, the gunners would find the range. Moreover, the YP was no longer returning fire. Philips had ordered his machine gunners to cease fire because small caliber projectiles were not effective against the U-boat and muzzle flashes were pinpointing their location for the Germans.[46]

Another 88mm round hit, activating the engine room fire extinguishing system, flooding the space with CO_2, and forcing the watch team to evacuate to above deck. Thereafter, *U-701* closed to within two hundred yards of the besieged vessel and began to fire pointblank into her starboard side. An incendiary round struck the bridge, setting the chartroom on fire, and a short time later the YP's stern was also in flames.[47]

No further efforts by the officers and men could save the vessel, and the commanding officer thus gave the order to abandon ship. The survivors slipped over the side with only their lifejackets. The life rafts had been shot away and the lifeboats could not be lowered safely due to persistent enemy fire. Philips stayed at the helm until the last crewman was safely away. With the throttles full ahead, he then abandoned as the *U-701* continued its dogged pursuit of the YP in the distance, continuing to shell it until the ship sank at 0414, five to eight miles northeast of Buoy No. 4.[48]

After entering the water, Philips gathered his men around him and helped keep their spirits up until they were rescued by the cutters *CG-462* and *CG-481* at 0800. All but six of the eighteen survivors were injured, some seriously so. They, as well as the body of a crewmember later found washed up on the beach, were taken to Morehead City, from which four grievously hurt men were transferred to Norfolk Naval Hospital. The remaining five missing sailors had been seen killed, or were assumed dead, with likely some of them interred in the hulk of the sunken *YP-389*. A crew list and status of each officer and man aboard the vessel that day is provided in the table.[49]

Crew of USS *YP-389* (19 June 1942)

Officers		
Roderick J. Philips	Lieutenant, USN Officer in Charge	
Ray Palmer Baker Jr.	Ensign, USN Executive Officer	seriously injured
Robert Morrison McKellar	Ensign, USNR Engineering Officer	injured
Deck Force		
Gilbert Leslie MacPherson	Signalman Second Class, USN	
Cornelius Francis MacLean	Seaman First Class, USNR	missing
D. L. Anotil	Seaman Second Class, USN	
Magnus Hia	Seaman First Class, USNR	missing
Anthony Tony Battisti	Seaman Second Class, USNR	
George Behrman	Seaman Second Class, USNR	
Charley Francis Hensley	Seaman Second Class, USNR	missing
Nelson Holt	Seaman Second Class, USNR	injured
Robert J. Long	Seaman Second Class, USN	seriously injured
Robert Lyman Murch	Seaman Second Class, USN	seriously injured
William Walter Nazarsky	Seaman Second Class, USNR	injured
Leroy Albert White	Seaman Second Class, USN	
Engine Room Personnel		
George Tunmer	Machinist's Mate First Class, USNR	injured
Calvin Paul Harris	Motor Machinist's Mate First class, USNR	injured
Robert Wilson	Fireman First Class, USN	seriously injured
Vincent Weathers Crabb	Fireman Second Class, USNR	missing
Eugene Carroll Bonsall	Fireman Third Class, USNR	injured
Wilson Burnett Cole	Fireman Third Class, USNR	missing
John Collins Doucette	Fireman Third Class, USN	killed in action
William John Sesselman	Fireman Third Class, USNR	injured
Other		
W. A. Smith	Ship's Cook Third Class, USN	injured[50]

Crewmember Seaman Second Class J. A. Milot was not aboard on the day of the attack, having shifted to *YP-388* on 12 June 1942.[51]

THE END OF *U-701*

Photo 9-3

A U.S. Army Air Force Lockheed A-29 Hudson in flight, circa 1941.
National Museum of the U.S. Air Force photograph 051122-F-1234P-014

After sending *YP-389* to the bottom, an action more challenging and time consuming than he had envisioned, Degen turned to his principal weapons. Between 26 and 28 June 1942, he torpedoed the Norwegian motor merchant *Tamesis*, and the UK motor tanker *British Freedom*—damaging both but not sinking either—and then sank the American steam tanker *William Rockefeller*. A week later, his luck ran out. On 7 July, a USAAF A29 Hudson out of Cherry Point, North Carolina, caught the submarine surfaced taking in fresh air off Cape Hatteras, and sank her with three 325-lb depth charges.[52]

Two days later, a Coast Guard seaplane recovered seven survivors, including Degen, 110 miles offshore in rafts. The men were first taken to Fort Hunt (an interrogation center for German prisoners at Sheridan Point on the Potomac River in Virginia) and then interned in various POW camps until the end of the war. During interviews, surviving crewmen indicated that they considered the destruction of the little ship (*YP-389*) a wasteful and untidy piece of work, and Degen gave the impression that he was ashamed of it.[53]

LOSS OF MERCHANT AND NAVAL VESSELS

None of the ship losses in June along the Eastern Seaboard occurred off Florida's east coast. Kapitänleutnant Horst Degen was responsible for nine of the ships sunk or damaged identified in the comprehensive table below, following the summary of the victims of *U-701*'s mines, torpedoes, or guns on her last war patrol.

Victims of *U-701* in June 1942

Date	Ship	Mine	Torpedo	Gunfire
15 Jun 42	HMT *Kingston Ceylonite*	sunk		
15 Jun 42	USS *Bainbridge*	damaged		
15 Jun 42	*Esso Augusta*	damaged		
15 Jun 42	*Robert C. Tuttle*	sunk		
17 Jun 42	*Santore*	sunk		
19 Jun 42	USS *YP-389*			sunk
26 Jun 42	*Tamesis*		damaged	
27 Jun 42	*British Freedom*		damaged	
28 Jun 42	*William Rockefeller*		sunk	

Ships Sunk or Damaged off the Eastern Seaboard in June 1942 (Canadian and U.S. East Coast)

Date	Ship/Sub	Registry	Type	Tons	Location
1 Jun 42 unescorted	*West Notus* *U-404*	American	steam merchant	5,492	34°10'N, 68°20'W
1 Jun 42 unescorted	*Westmoreland* *U-566*	British	steam merchant	8,967	35°55'N, 63°35'W
2 Jun 42 unescorted	*Mattawin* *U-553*	British	motor merchant	6,919	40°14'N, 66°01'W
2 Jun 42 unescorted	*Berganger* *U-578*	Norwegian	motor merchant	6,826	39°25'N, 69°50'W
3 Jun 42 unescorted	*Anna* *U-404*	Swedish	steam merchant	1,345	34°10'N, 68°22'W
3 Jun 42 unescorted	*Aeolus* *U-432*	American	fishing vessel	41	43°07'N, 66°51'W
3 Jun 42 unescorted	*Ben and Josephine* *U-432*	American	fishing vessel	102	43°07'N, 66°51'W
7 Jun 42 escorted	USS *Gannet* (AVP-8) *U-653*	American	seaplane tender	840	35°50'N, 65°38'W
8 Jun 42 unescorted	*Pleasantville* *U-135*	Norwegian	motor merchant	4,549	34°12'N, 68°00'W
9 Jun 42 BX-23A	*Kronprinsen* (D) *U-432*	Norwegian	motor merchant	7,073	42°53'N, 67°11'W
9 Jun 42 BX-23A	*Malayan Prince* (D) *U-432*	British	motor merchant	8,593	42°53'N, 67°11'W
15 Jun 42 KN-109	*Esso Augusta* (D) *U-701*	American	motor tanker	11,237	36°52'N, 75°51'W
15 Jun 42 escorted	HMT *Kingston* *Ceylonite* *U-701*	British	A/S trawler	448	36°52'N, 75°51'W
15 Jun 42 escorted	*Robert C. Tuttle* *U-701*	American	steam tanker	11,615	36°52'N, 75°51'W
15 Jun 42 escorted	USS *Bainbridge* (D) *U-701*	American	destroyer	1,190	36°52'N, 75°51'W

16 Jun 42 XB-25	*Cherokee* *U-87*	American	passenger ship	5,896	42°25'N, 69°10'W
16 Jun 42 XB-25	*Port Nicholson* *U-87*	British	steam merchant	8,402	42°11'N, 69°25'W
17 Jun 42 KS-511	*Santore* *U-701*	American	steam merchant	7,117	36°52'N, 75°51'W
19 Jun 42	USS *YP-389* *U-701*	American	patrol vessel	170	34°50'N, 75°20'W
22 Jun 42 unescorted	*Rio Tercero* *U-202*	Argentinian	steam merchant	4,864	39°15'N, 72°32'W
24 Jun 42 unescorted	*Ljubica Matkovic* *U-404*	Yugoslavian	steam merchant	3,289	34°30'N, 75°40'W
25 Jun 42 escorted	*Manuela* *U-404*	American	steam merchant	4,772	34°30'N, 75°40'W
25 Jun 42 escorted	*Nordal* *U-404*	Panamanian	steam merchant	3,845	34°30'N, 75°40'W
26 Jun 42 unescorted	*Tamesis* (D) *U-701*	Norwegian	motor merchant	7,256	34°59'N, 75°41'W
27 Jun 42 unescorted	*Moldanger* *U-404*	Norwegian	motor merchant	6,827	38°03'N, 70°52'W
27 Jun 42 KS-514	*British Freedom* (D) *U-701*	British	motor tanker	6,985	34°45'N, 75°22'W
28 Jun 42 escorted	*William Rockefeller* *U-701*	American	steam tanker	14,054	35°07'N, 75°07'W
29 Jun 42 unescorted	*Everalda* *U-158*	Latvian	steam merchant	3,950	31°00'N, 70°45'W[54]

During June 1942, there were more enemy submarines within the limits of the Eastern Sea Frontier than in any previous month. This increase, however, was deceptive, because it did not reflect the number actually engaged in active operations within Frontier waters. The Germans were increasing their underwater forces along the America coast, but most of their attacking strength was concentrated in the Gulf of Mexico and the Caribbean. Transiting submarines from Europe on their way to the West Indies, passing through the Eastern Seaboard on their journey accounted for the increased numbers.[55]

As shown in the preceding table, with few exceptions, U-boat commanders were extremely reluctant to attack convoys, preferring to concentrate their efforts against slower ships sailing independently. This perhaps is a good reflection on the increased effectiveness of the defending forces.[56]

10

Four U-boats Sunk off Eastern Seaboard in July 1942

During July enemy submarine density in the Eastern Sea Frontier and adjacent waters to 60° W. longitude reached a new high. At the same time, losses of shipping were lower than at any time since the enemy submarine campaign began. This is a clear demonstration of the effectiveness of convoying. Toward the end of the month a decrease in enemy submarines entering the above area was noted.

—Commander, Eastern Sea Frontier War Diary, July 1942.

In July 1942, the efficiency of the Eastern Sea Frontier coastal convoy system when implemented by forces in sufficient strength is clearly demonstrated by the relatively few ship losses, as shown in the following table. Of the incidents of ships being sunk, damaged (D), or declared a total loss (T) as a result of U-boat attack, most occurred in Canadian waters. At that time, there being few unescorted vessels, submarine commanders wanting ship kills were forced to contemplate attacking convoyed ships. Also included in the date column is status regarding whether a particular ship was escorted, escorted as part of a convoy (identified by an alpha-numeric designation), or unescorted.

Ship Losses off the Eastern Seaboard in July 1942

American Waters

Date	Ship/Sub	Registry	Type	Tons	Location
1 Jul 42 escorted	*Warrior* *U-126*	American	passenger ship	7,551	35°10'N, 70°53'W
3 Jul 42 BX-27	*Alexander Macomb U-215*	American	Liberty Ship	7,191	41°48'N, 66°35'W
15 Jul 42 KS-520	*Bluefields* *U-576*	Nicaraguan	motor merchant	2,063	34°46'N, 75°22'W
15 Jul 42 KS-520	*Chilore* (D) *U-576*	American	steam merchant	8,310	34°47'N, 75°22'W
15 Jul 42 KS-520	*J. A. Mowinckel* (D) *U-576*	Panamanian	motor tanker	11,147	33°44'N, 75°19'W

Canadian Waters

6 Jul 42 QS-15	*Anastassios Pateras U-132*	Greek	steam merchant	3,382	49°30'N, 66°30'W
6 Jul 42 QS-15	*Dinaric U-132*	British	steam merchant	2,555	49°30'N, 66°30'W
6 Jul 42 QS-15	*Hainaut U-132*	Belgian	steam merchant	4,312	49°30'N, 66°30'W
20 Jul 42 QS-19	*Frederika Lensen* (T) *U-132*	British	steam merchant	4,367	49°22'N, 65°12'W
25 Jul 42 unescorted	*Lucille U-89*	Canadian	fishing vessel	54	42°02'N, 65°38'W
28 Jul 42 unescorted	*Ebb U-754*	American	fishing vessel	260	43°18'N, 63°50'W
30 Jul 42 ON-113	*Pioneer U-132*	British	motor merchant	6,734	43°30'N, 60°35'W[1]

Greatly contributing to the increased protection given to merchant vessels, in addition to convoying them, was the growing air strength in the Frontier, which reduced the sphere of effective action by enemy submarines. These measures were desperately needed given the many U-boats known to be operating in Frontier waters—July was the most active month to date for interactions of surface and air forces with submarines. As noted by Vice Admiral Andrews:

> There were more sightings (62), more sound contacts (23), and more actual attacks (41) by all forces of the air and surface than ever before.[2]

However, robust and stealthy U-boats, whose activities were then being contested by greater numbers of Allied forces bent on searching for and attacking them, remained hard to kill. Only four of the attacks in July by Eastern Sea Frontier forces resulted in the actual destruction of a submarine. The minelayer *U-215* fell victim to depth charges from HMT *Le Tigre*. Details about this action begin on the following page. A successful attack by an Army bomber against the *U-701* was described in the preceding chapter. Destruction of a third submarine, *U-576*, came at the hands of two Kingfisher aircraft attacks and gunfire from the American motor ship *Unicoi*. A fourth submarine, *U-754*, was depth charged and sunk south of Nova Scotia by a Canadian Hudson aircraft.

U-boats Sunk off the Eastern Seaboard in July 1942

Date	U-boat	Location	Disposition
3 Jul 42	*U-215*	41°48'N, 66°38'W east of Boston	Sunk by HMT *Le Tigre* with depth charges; 48 dead (all hands lost)
7 Jul 42	*U-701*	34°50'N, 74°55'W off Cape Hatteras	Sunk by depth charges from a U.S. Army A-29 Hudson aircraft; 39 dead and 7 survivors
15 Jul 42	*U-576*	34°51'N, 75°22'W off Cape Hatteras	Sunk by depth charges from two USN Kingfisher aircraft and gunfire from the American motor ship MS *Unicoi*; 45 dead (all hands lost)
31 Jul 42	*U-754*	43°02'N, 64°52'W South of Nova Scotia	Sunk by depth charges of a Canadian Hudson aircraft (113 Sqn RCAF/625); 43 dead (all hands lost)[3]

DESTRUCTION OF *U-215*

> *It is significant that the attacking planes were able to locate submarines lying on the surface and to deliver in a very short space of time well developed and extensive attacks. Surface vessels have rarely found the U-boat on the surface and by their nature have been prevented from delivering concentrated attacks within a short space of time. They must, ordinarily, wait until the submarine comes to them while they are escorting a convoy, and then they must develop a complicated attack against an unseen enemy.*
>
> —Commander, Eastern Sea Frontier War Diary, July 1942.

On the morning of 3 July 1942, the American Liberty ship SS *Alexander Macomb* was proceeding from Boston to Halifax as part of Convoy BX 27. On her maiden voyage, during the previous night, heavy fog and fear of collision had resulted in her falling astern of the convoy. Her master, Carl Monsen Froisland, while maintaining an intermittent zigzag course, as a defense against a possible U-boat attack, was attempting to catch the convoy in the daylight. It comprised thirty-two merchant ships that had departed either from Buzzards Bay, the Cape Cod Canal, or Boston on 2 July. (The Cape Cod Canal in Massachusetts connects Buzzards Bay to the southwest, with Cape Cod Bay to the northeast, at a point south-southeast of Boston.)[4]

Alexander Macomb had just reached the rear of the convoy with about seven ships and an escort vessel in sight, when at 0630, a torpedo from *U-215* struck her between No. 4 and 5 Holds, causing her cargo of explosives to ignite and burst into flames. Most of the eight officers,

33 crewmen and 25 Navy Armed Guards (the ship was armed with one 4-inch, one 3-inch, four 20mm and two .30-caliber guns) abandoned ship in three lifeboats and one raft but, unfortunately because the ship was still making way, one boat capsized. Other crew members leapt overboard into the Atlantic, and swam to and hung onto pieces of wreckage.[5]

Photo 10-1

Anti-submarine trawler HMT *Le Tigre* (FY243) location and date unknown. Source: http://www.harwichanddovercourt.co.uk/warships/trawlers/

The ship was about 175 miles east of Cape Cod, Massachusetts, when attacked. The trawler HMT *Le Tigre*, a unit of the escort group, immediately made a radar sweep, and gained contact on two objects, reported bearing 000 degrees relative—dead ahead of her. At 0655, a firm Asdic (sonar) contact was made on what was believed to be a submarine. *Le Tigre* maneuvered for attack. When the submerged, unseen contact was 300 yards away, it suddenly turned toward its attacker, and approached at high speed. As it passed down the starboard side of *Le Tigre*, the trawler fired a full pattern of depth charges at the appropriate moment. She then turned and came in again on the contact, delivering a second attack from her starboard depth-charge thrower.[6]

Asdic information indicated that the submarine, after these two attacks, remained stationary. The whole incident took place close to the survivors of the sunken Liberty ship, who were bobbing around in the water, in lifeboats or on the raft. When they were picked up by ships in the escort group, the survivors indicated they considered that the submarine had been destroyed. This belief was not concurred with by commander, Eastern Sea Frontier, as indicated in a war diary entry for July 1942:

> Some of them said definitely that they had seen the boat come to the surface for a few seconds after the second attack before she rolled over and disappeared. Official analysis failed to bear out this estimate of the men on the scene. It was ultimately decided that the submarine had probably been damaged.[7]

Photo 10-2

Painting by Richard DeRosset of HMT *Le Tigre* carrying out a depth charge attack, and sinking the German submarine *U-215* east of Cape Cod, Massachusetts.

HMT *Le Tigre* rescued 23 crew members and eight Armed Guards and brought them to Woods Hole, Massachusetts, on 4 July. The corvette HMCS *Regina* (T/Lt. Roy Stanley Kelley, RCNR) picked up 14 crew members and 11 Armed Guards and landed them at Halifax. Sadly, six Armed Guards and four crew members perished in the attack.[8]

BELATED AWARD FOR VALOUR

HMT *Le Tigre*'s commanding officer was Temporary Lt. Colin Arthur Hoodless, RNR. In May 1946 (following British Admiralty post-war examination of German records related to U-boat losses), he was awarded a Distinguished Service Cross. As will be explained, this was in relation to the destruction of *U-215*.

Numb. 37564 2285

THIRD SUPPLEMENT

TO

The London Gazette

Of FRIDAY, the 10th of MAY, 1946

Published by Authority

Registered as a newspaper

TUESDAY, 14 MAY, 1946

For outstanding services while in command of H.M. Ships engaged in anti-submarine operations during the war in Europe:

The Distinguished Service Cross.

Temporary Lieutenant-Commander Colin Arthur HOODLESS, R.N.R.

U-215 FOUND AND MISSION DISCOVERED

Long after the war, any remaining doubt about *Le Tigre*'s success in destroying *U-215* was removed. In July 2004, the wreckage of the *U-215* was found. The submarine, missing from the time of her first patrol, was located by a team of divers and marine archeologists at a depth of 270 feet about 130 miles SSW of Shelburne, Nova Scotia.[9]

The identification of the submarine as *U-215* revealed that she was a unique under-sea vessel, one of only six built, specially designed to lay mines. In the summer of 1942, she was on a secret mission to sow mines in Boston harbor. Mike Fletcher, project leader and chief diver for Eco-Nova Productions, the Halifax-based TV production company involved with the find, conveyed that she was found in a difficult area with strong tides, and described visiting the wreckage:

> I've never had a more challenging dive.... The vessel has five distinctive tubes that rise up out of the deck.... In fact, you can look inside and see the live mines still there.[10]

TYPE VIID MINELAYING U-BOATS

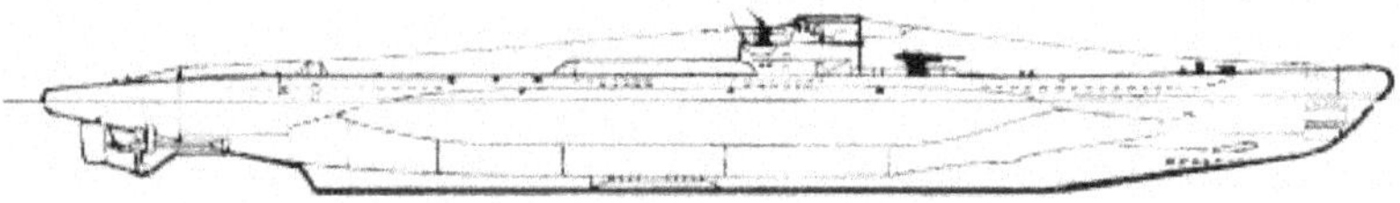

The six German type VIID submarines, of which *U-215* was one, were a version of the VIIC lengthened by 32 feet, 10 inches to accommodate their minelayer function. Using the layout of the VIIC, a new section was inserted aft of the control room. Five vertical mine launchers, each holding three SMA mines were housed in this new section. Remaining space in the section was used to accommodate additional bunks and two refrigerators. The saddle tanks were also lengthened, allowing additional diesel fuel storage capacity.[11]

The VIID submarine had been designed to lay SMA type mines in British coastal waters. This type of mine had to be deployed vertically, and differed from other TMA and TMB mines which were torpedo launched. Introduced in 1942, the SMA was a moored, influence mine, fabricated with an aluminum alloy shell to reduce sonar detection. It could be moored in either 219 fathoms (1,314 feet) or 328 fathoms (1,968 feet) deep and had a 772-lb explosive charge.[12]

Photo 10-3

Beached German SMA moored influence mine with, to its left, a diagram of a deployed SMA mine from the Admiralty's Technical Staff Monographs 1939-1945, German Minelaying, dated 1949.

The Type VIID submarine was unique in its expanded ability. Because the mine launchers were housed in a new section, the existing structure of the boat remained unchanged with the torpedo and armament functions of the boat fully operable. This enabled the VIID to serve in a dual role, as minelayer or attack boat. However, due to their increased size and weight, maneuverability, speed, and diving time were diminished. Of these type submarines—*U-213*, *U-214*, *U-215*, *U-216*, *U-217*, and *U-218*—only *U-218* managed to survive the war; all of the other five were sunk, with the loss of their entire crews.[13]

LE TIGRE'S OFFICERS

Temporary Lt. Colin Arthur Hoodless, RNR, was in command of the 188-foot, 516-ton trawler HMT *Le Tigre* from 6 November 1940 to 7 July 1943, when he assumed command of the Flower-class corvette HMS *Jasmine* (K23) which he captained until 10 November 1944. *Jasmine* was larger at 205 feet and 925 tons, and more heavily armed—boasting one 4-inch gun, one 2-pounder AA gun, and four .303-caliber machine guns, as well as depth charges.[14]

Two other officers who served aboard *Le Tigre* during Hoodless' tenure in command are listed below. Lt. Geoffrey Frank Bedford, RANVR, was seconded (on temporary loan) from the Royal Australian Navy. He would later command HMT *Northern Duke* from 12 August to October 1943.[15]

Date Reported	Officer
27 January 1941	Temp. Lt. Peter Arnold Tunbridge, RNVR
17 February 1941	Lt. Geoffrey Frank Bedford, RANVR

11

Vice Adm. Adolphus Andrews, USN

Photo 11-1

Then Rear Adm. Adolphus Andrews, confers with Capt. Hans Nielson, master of the Norwegian freighter MS *Reinhol*, circa 1942.
Naval History and Heritage Command photograph #NH 96399

In July 1942, Vice Admiral Andrews was finally "on top" of U-boats in the Eastern Sea Frontier, after months of exacerbating work, prying loose additional forces from Navy leadership, and implementing practices needed for the safeguarding and escorting of merchant vessels. As such, this is a good time in the book to leave his Frontier, although there is some reference to it and him in the following chapter.

The next chapter takes readers aboard Royal Canadian Navy corvettes under Andrews' command, plying between New York and Guantanamo Bay, escorting convoys. The remainder of the book follows the "King's Ships" to South African waters, to join their South African Navy counterparts in combating enemy submarines and shepherding merchantmen in that area. This requirement was spurred by U-boat emphasis moving sequentially from North America's Eastern Seaboard, south-southwest into the Gulf of Mexico and Caribbean, then southeast across the narrows of the Atlantic to African waters.

Before proceeding to those waters, a little more about Vice Adm. Adolphus Andrews, who commanded the Eastern Sea Frontier until his relief by Vice Adm. Herbert Fairfax Leary on 1 November 1943 is in order. Leary remained in this capacity until 2 September 1945. (A listing of the commanders of subordinate Naval Districts may be found in Appendix D. Separately, Appendix E. provides a list of Sea Frontier commanders during the war, including the only two, Andrews and Leary, of the Eastern Sea Frontier.)

Adolphus Andrews was born in Galveston, Texas, 7 October 1879. He graduated from the Naval Academy on 7 June 1901, and served (the two years at sea then required by law before commissioning) in the battleship USS *Maine* operating with the Atlantic Fleet, and was commissioned Ensign on 7 June 1903.[1]

Over the next thirty-five years, Andrews progressed rapidly upward through a succession of ever more prestigious and important duties, including:

- Duty aboard USS *Dolphin*, the yacht assigned for the use of the Secretary of the Navy, and additional duty as aide at the White House
- Commanding officer of the gunboat USS *Villalobos*
- Executive officer of the presidential yacht USS *Mayflower*
- Aide to the superintendent of the U.S. Naval Academy
- Gunnery officer of the battleship USS *Michigan*, then battleship USS *Utah*
- Navigator of the battleship USS *Oklahoma*
- Executive officer of the battleship USS *Mississippi*
- Naval aide to Prince Axel of Denmark
- Commanding officer of the battleship USS *Massachusetts*
- Commanding officer of the repair ship USS *Prometheus*
- Assistant chief of staff to the commander in chief, Atlantic Fleet

- Commanding officer of the presidential yacht *Mayflower* and naval aide to the president
- Commanding officer of the Submarine Base at New London, Connecticut
- Commanding officer of the battleship USS *Texas*
- Chief of staff of the Naval War College[2]

After the above service, Andrews served as commander, Scouting Force, with the accompanying rank of vice admiral, from 13 July 1938 until 1 February 1941, when he reverted to the rank of rear admiral. The United States Fleet had previously been organized into Battle Force, Scouting Force, Submarine Force, and Base Force components; with the Asiatic Fleet remaining independent. On 1 February 1941, the United States Fleet organization was abolished, and replaced by the U.S. Atlantic Fleet and the U.S. Pacific Fleet, while the Asiatic Fleet organization remained independent as before.[3]

On 10 March 1941 he reported for duty for a new dual assignment as commandant of the Third Naval District, New York, New York, and commander of the North Atlantic Naval Coastal Frontier. The latter command became the Eastern Sea Frontier. At the completion of his tour of duty for the Frontier, Vice Admiral Adolphus Andrews was awarded the Distinguished Service Medal. The associated citation reads:

> For exceptionally meritorious and distinguished service to the Government of the United States in a position of great responsibility as Commander Eastern Sea Frontier. During a period of intense enemy submarine activities, Vice Admiral Andrews displayed the highest qualities of leadership, judgment, and planning, and initiated and put into effect the anti-submarine organization of this Sea Frontier which proved to be highly effective in driving German submarines from our coastal waters and which became the model for the anti-submarine organization of other sea frontiers.

Andrews transferred to the Retired List of the Navy on 11 November 1943, in the rank of vice admiral. He died at the age of 68, on 19 June 1948, at the Naval Hospital, Houston, Texas.[4]

FRONTIER NAVAL SURFACE FORCES, JULY 1942

Vice Admiral Andrews' most important legacy, in the face of superior enemy forces assaulting shipping off America's East Coast, was finally muzzling and extracting costs to the German submarines. This was accomplished on a shoestring budget," while utilizing Ad hoc forces he assembled, trained, and led. One need only compare his force to those assigned forward combat commanders in Europe and the Pacific to gain admiration for Andrews' performance.

On 27 July 1942, one hundred fifty-six ships were assigned to the Eastern Sea Frontier. Of this total, the status of sixty (38 percent) was "overhaul," which meant they were in port for regular maintenance, or were undergoing actual overhaul (extended repair period). Allocation of the ships to the various Eastern Sea Frontier subordinate commands is shown in the table, from the one farthest north on America's East Coast to that farthest south within the Frontier. The locations of the headquarters of the Naval Districts are also identified.[5]

A quick review of the force levels (types and quantities of ships) of each Naval District, Naval Operating Base Newport, Rhode Island, or Norfolk, Virginia to Key West Florida convoy escort duty, reveals where Eastern Sea Frontier forces were most required. For each command, the employment of ships, and area of operations are also identified. The long titles of the ship types listed are provided following the table.

Surface Vessels, Eastern Sea Frontier (27 July 1942)

First Naval District (HQ: Boston, Massachusetts)
(7 of 19 ships in overhaul on this date)

No.	Type	Employment	Area
1	CGC 125'	Escort & Patrol	Massachusetts Bay Area
3	CGC 75'	Escort & Patrol	Massachusetts Bay Area
2	Trawlers		Massachusetts Bay Area
1	SC 93'	Escort & Patrol	Massachusetts Bay Area
1	PYc	Escort & Patrol	Massachusetts Bay Area
3	YMS	Sweep	Massachusetts Bay Area
2	IX	Escort & Patrol	Massachusetts Bay Area
5	YP	Escort & Patrol	Buzzard Bay Area
1	AMb		Buzzard Bay Area

Naval Operating Base Newport, Rhode Island
(0 of 3 ships in overhaul)

1	CGC 125'	Escort & Patrol	Vineyard Sound – Block Island Area
1	PYc	Escort & Patrol	Vineyard Sound – Block Island Area
1	SC 110'	Escort & Patrol	Vineyard Sound – Block Island Area

Third Naval District (HQ: New York, New York)
(8 of 29 ships in overhaul)

6	Trawlers	Escort & Patrol	New York – Cape May Area
3	SC 110'	Escort & Patrol	One: New York – Cape May Area One: New York Area One: New London Area
1	PY	Sound School	New London Area
6	CGC 75'	Escort & Patrol	Five: New York – Long Island Area One: New London Area
2	CGC 80'	Escort & Patrol	New York – Cape May
5	CGC 83'	Escort & Patrol	New York – Cape May
1	PGCG	Escort & Patrol	New York – Cape May
1	YP	Escort & Patrol	New York – Cape May
4	YMS	Escort, Patrol & Sweep	New York – Cape May

Fourth Naval District (HQ: Philadelphia, Pennsylvania)
(7 of 13 ships in overhaul)

4	CGC 75'	Patrol	Atlantic City Area
1	CGC 79'	Escort & Patrol	Cape May Area
4	CGC 83'	Escort & Patrol	New York – Cape May
2	PYc	Escort & Patrol	Cape May – North & South
2	YP	Escort & Patrol	Cape May – North & South

Fifth Naval District (HQ: Naval Operating Base, Norfolk, Virginia)
(23 of 53 ships in overhaul)

4	PC 173'	Escort & Patrol	Cape Henry – North & South
6	Trawlers	Escort & Patrol	Chesapeake to Cape Lookout
2	SC 110'	Escort & Patrol	Cape Henry Area
1	CGC 125'	Escort & Patrol	Cape Henry – North & South
1	CGC 165'	Escort & Patrol	Cape Henry – North & South
6	CGC 75'	Escort & Patrol	Little Creek – Morehead City
3	CGC 80'	Escort & Patrol	Little Creek – Morehead City
22	CGC 83'	Escort & Patrol	Little Creek – Morehead City
3	YP	Escort & Patrol	Little Creek – Morehead City
5	YMS	Patrol - Sweep	Cape Henry Area

Sixth Naval District (HQ: Charleston, South Carolina)
(1 of 7 ships in overhaul)

3	Trawlers	Escort & Patrol	Charleston – Cape Lookout
2	CGC 75'	Escort & Patrol	Charleston – Savannah
1	CGC 165'	Escort & Patrol	Charleston – Cape Lookout
1	PY	Escort & Patrol	Charleston – Jacksonville

Convoy Escort – Norfolk, Virginia, to Key West, Florida (14 of 32 ships in overhaul)

No.	Type	No.	Type
10	Destroyers	7	PG
	USS *Broome* (DD-210)	8	CGC 165'
	USS *Bainbridge* (DD-246)	7	PC 177'
	USS *Decatur* (DD-341)		
	USS *Dickerson* (DD-157)		
	USS *Du Pont* (DD-152)		
	USS *MacLeish* (DD-220)		
	USS *McCormick* (DD-223)		
	USS *Overton* (DD-239)		
	USS *Roper* (DD-147)		
	USS *Simpson* (DD-221)[6]		

AMb: Base minesweeper
CGC: Coast Guard cutter
IX: Miscellaneous unclassified
PC: Patrol craft
PG: Patrol gunboat
PGCG: Coast Guard patrol gunboat
PY: Patrol yacht
PYc: Coastal patrol yacht
SC: Sub-chaser
YMS: Yard minesweeper
YP: Yard patrol craft

12

Royal Canadian Navy "Ready Aye Ready"

The wholesome sea is at her gates, her gates both east and west.

—Words inscribed above the four doors to the entrance of Canada's Parliament Building in Ottawa.

Photo 12-1

Corvette HMCS *Oakville* (K178) on passage from Saint John, New Brunswick, to Halifax, Nova Scotia, as an escort to Convoy FH-70 on 7 August 1943.
National Defence - Canadian Navy Heritage website, Image Number CN-6040

During World War II, the Royal Canadian Navy shouldered a large portion of critical Allied convoy escort work. Canadian destroyers and corvettes were most famous for escorting trans-Atlantic convoys, whose member ships were marshalled in Bedford Basin (a large enclosed bay forming the northwestern end of Halifax Harbour) before departure. They also formed a major part of the mid-ocean force that took convoys between Newfoundland and British waters, braving German submarine 'wolfpack' offensives. Halifax-based warships shepherded HX Convoys (New York to UK) during their first leg between New York and Newfoundland, and brought westbound convoys from Newfoundland to New York. These tasks were in addition to supporting a comprehensive network of coastal convoys between Canadian and northern United States ports.[1]

Additional tasking for a period of time, beginning on 27 August 1942, involved the six RCN corvettes identified in the table, working directly under the orders of Vice Admiral Andrews, commander, Eastern Sea Frontier. The specific duty of these ships was to escort NG Convoys from New York to Guantanamo.[2]

Corvette	Commanding Officer	WWII Battle Honours
HMCS *Fredericton* (K245)	T/A/Lt. Comdr. John H. S. MacDonald, RCNR	Atlantic 1942-45
HMCS *Halifax* (K237)	T/A/Lt. Comdr. Charles Copelin, RCNR	Atlantic 1942-45
HMCS *Oakville* (K178)	T/A/Lt. Comdr. Clarence A. King, DSC RCNR	Atlantic 1942-45
HMCS *Snowberry* (K166)	T/A/Lt. Comdr. Philip John Bowin Watts, RCNVR	Atlantic 1941-44 Biscay 1943 Gulf of St. Lawrence 1944 English Channel 1945
HMCS *Sudbury* (K162)	T/Lt. Alexander McAllister McLarnon, RCNR	Atlantic 1941-1944
HMCS *The Pas* (K168)	T/A/Lt. Comdr. Ernest George Old, RCNR[3]	Atlantic 1942-44

Sudbury, a favorite vessel on Canada's West Coast was later converted to long distance tug that performed several famous long distant tows after the war.[4]

Tasking of the RCN corvettes (along with some RN ones, supplemented by the destroyers HMS *Churchill*, HMS *Havelock*, and HMS *Warwick*) occurred because the British trawlers did not have "the legs" (fuel endurance) for extended convoys, such as those between New York and Guantanamo. The trawlers continued to be employed by Naval Districts for local escort work and patrol until autumn 1942. By then, rapidly developing plans for an Allied invasion of North Africa required an increase of escort and patrol vessels along the western coast of Africa—and by the middle of October, all the British trawlers had been detached from the Eastern Sea Frontier.[5]

SHIFT IN U-BOAT EMPHASIS TO OTHER FRONTIERS

Although this arrangement of escorts was adequate in the Eastern Sea Frontier, one important reason for our perfect no-sinking score from July 1942 through January 1943 was the land-based aircraft patrols. In the North Atlantic and in any areas where aircraft could not operate successfully, enemy submarines concentrated their attacks with such success that shipping losses continued alarmingly.

—Commander, Eastern Sea Frontier War Diary, January 1943.

There was always close correlation between sinkings and the number of U-boats operating, no matter how great the protection. But anti-submarine measures were a major influence on the number operating, because as soon as they became effective in a given area, Admiral Doenitz pulled his boats out.

—Samuel Eliot Morison in *The Battle of the Atlantic 1939-1943.*[6]

Map 12-1

Western Atlantic Defense Areas as of 1 August 1942
https://www.ibiblio.org/hyperwar/AAF/I/maps/AAF-I-26.jpg

As noted by Vice Admiral Andrews in January 1943 war diary entries, the Eastern Sea Frontier benefited in the latter half of 1942 from increased escort of convoys by ships and availability and operations of patrol aircraft. It also benefited from a change in geographic focus of U-boat operations. Early in that year, enemy submarines in the Western Atlantic had concentrated their operations in the nearly wide-open and heavily traveled Eastern Sea Frontier. With the commencement of convoy operations on 14 May, and other defense measures greatly increased, Doenitz shifted attention to the largely unprotected Gulf, Caribbean, and Panama Sea Frontiers.[7]

As shown in the table, Andrews' Frontier suffered the loss of only three ships, "sunk in convoy" (SIC), between mid-May and year's end.[8]

East Coast Convoys, 14 May – 31 December 1942

Designation/Period	Convoys	Ships	Escorts	SIC	S	D
KS 500/533 14 May-28 Aug 42	34	719	219	3	0	1
KN (old) 100/136 15 May-8 Sep 42	37	773	216	0	0	0
NK 500/515 28 Aug-31 Dec 42	16	318	81	0	0	0
KN (new) 200/214 8 Sep-30 Dec 42	15	368	80	0	0	0
NG 300/331, Spec. 1 27 Aug-29 Dec 42	33	722	160	0	0	0
GN Spec. 1/29 1 Sep-26 Dec 42	30	733	149	0	0	0
Total Eastern Sea Frontier	165	3,633	905	3	0	1

Legend: Average Ships per Convoy/Escorts per Convoy Figures
KS: Norfolk to Key West (SPC: 21/EPC: 6.4)
KN: (Old) Key West to New York or Key West to Norfolk (SPC: 21/EPC: 5.8)
KN: (New) Key West to New York or Key West to Norfolk (SPC: 20/EPC: 5.1)
NK: New York to Key West (SPC: 25/EPC: 5.3)
NG: New York to Guantanamo (SPC: 22/EPC: 4.8)
GN: Guantanamo to New York (SPC: 24/EPC: 5.0)
SIC: Sunk in convoy S: Sunk as a straggler D: Damaged

CONVOY TAW-15 (TRINIDAD-ARUBA-KEY WEST)

Since no Allied ships were lost on the NG (New York to Guantanamo) convoys in which the Canadian corvettes participated under Eastern Sea Frontier command, no discussion of those operations follow. Instead, the next few pages will introduce readers to three of the six corvettes, which were part of the escort force of a Trinidad-Aruba-Key West convoy immediately prior to their assignment to Andrews' command.

In particular, the mettle of HMCS *Oakville* and her intrepid commanding officer, Lt. Comdr. Clarence A. King, DSC RCNR, is highlighted.

Map 12-2

Caribbean Basin

In July, August, and September 1942, submarines sank 75 ships in the Caribbean Sea Command area, the majority of them under escort in those waters. The two most dangerous spots were along the eastern approaches to Trinidad, and the Windward Passage between Cuba and Haiti. While east- and southbound tankers were being attacked around Trinidad, those bound to and from New York from Trinidad, Venezuela, and Aruba were struck by U-boats between Haiti and Cuba. In August 1942, the approaches to the Windward Passage were as dangerous for shipping as any part of the Atlantic.[9]

Four RCN corvettes and two British destroyers under Canadian control were in the Caribbean, ordered there by Admiral Percy Nelles, to escort Canadian oil tankers through U-boat infested waters. Lacking pipelines to its western resources, despite its vast and expansive territory, Canada's war effort relied on crude oil deliveries from Colombia, Venezuela, and Texas. Its increased wartime production caused an associated increased demand for oil at a time when merchant shipping losses to U-boats was increasing. Oil shipments from South America to refineries in Montreal and Halifax were necessary to help quench Eastern Canada's thirst for petroleum. Despite authorities having imposed fuel rationing, naval fuel stocks had decreased to 45,000 tons, a mere 15-day supply.[10]

Shortly before noon on 23 August 1942, twelve merchant ships sortied from Trinidad, formed a convoy with escort vessels, and proceeded on base course 304° true. The convoy escort under Comdr. John Franklin Walsh, USN, captain of the destroyer USS *Lea* (DD-118), consisted of she and the submarine chasers USS *PC-559*, *SC-499*, *SC-506*, and *SC-522*.[11]

Photo 12-2

President Franklin D. Roosevelt, fishing off Aves Island, Port of Spain, Trinidad, 12 December 1936, while relaxing at the conclusion of his "Good Neighbor" cruise to South America.
Naval History and Heritage Command photograph #NH 68192

Two days later, at 1503 on 25 August, two ships left the convoy for the Aruba- Curaçao area, and nineteen fast tankers joined with escorts HNMS *Jan van Brakel* (M80)—a Dutch minelayer—and the Canadian corvettes HMCS *Halifax*, *Snowberry*, and *Oakville*.[12]

Consolidated Convoy TAW-15, en route from Trinidad to Key West, then comprised twenty-nine ships in six columns. The escorts were stationed in reference to the body of the convoy as follows:

- *Jan van Brakel* ahead
- *Halifax* on starboard bow
- *SC-506* starboard beam
- *PC-559* starboard quarter
- *Lea* rear and quarters[13]
- *SC-522* astern
- *Oakville* port quarter
- *SC-499* port beam
- *Snowberry* port bow

Lea, the escort commander, was patrolling the outer screen, across the entire rear and quarters, distance 6,000 to 9,000 yards.[14]

Following rendezvous of the two groups of ships, TAW-15 altered course north in preparation to pass between Jamaica and Haiti, before turning northeast for transit of the Windward Passage separating Cuba and Haiti. Unbeknownst to the convoy, *U-94*, a Type VIIC U-boat on her 10th wartime patrol, was in the area searching for Allied shipping. Fortunately, U.S. Navy PBY Catalina patrol bomber flights from the airfield at Guantanamo Bay had been increased in advance of the vulnerable tankers' arrival.[15]

Photo 12-3

The Windward Passage was no stranger to naval battles. Painting by Warren of the privateer American schooner *Joseph and Mary* captured on 24 November 1812 by a boarding party in boats dispatched from the British 32-gun frigate HMS *Narcissus*. Naval History and Heritage Command photograph #USN 902778

PBY CATALINA AND HMCS *OAKVILLE* SINK *U-94*

An account of the destruction of *U-94* by PBY Catalina-dropped depth charges, and corvette depth charges, ramming, and gunfire follows. Because 1 officer, 1 senior midshipman, 9 petty officers, and 15 enlisted men survived of the submarine's crew complement of 45, many details about her operations were gleaned during interrogations that followed the action.[16]

SUBMARINE'S ATLANTIC CROSSING

The *U-94* left St. Nazaire under the command of Oblt. Otto Ites on 2 August, bound for the Caribbean. She was attached to the 7th Flotilla, and carried its insignia the Snorting Bull on its sail. The crew was not surprised to learn that they were headed to the Caribbean in their "500-tonner". One sailor recalled that they had been promised this trip to southern waters inasmuch as previously they had operated only in the cold waters of the North Atlantic.[17]

During the ocean crossing, crewmen were allowed to sunbath topside, and no contacts were sighted until reaching Caribbean waters. *U-94* made landfall in the Windward Passage, probably about 20 August, and finally after intercepting a convoy they prepared to attack. Ites suspected the approach of a convoy on 27 August, when still undetected himself, he sighted flying boats (PBYs) which he presumed to be serving as convoy scouts. He spent a good part of that day avoiding these planes. The 20mm anti-aircraft gun fitted in U-boats was a formidable weapon, particularly with red tracer chemicals in every cartridge, but its use, except as required for self-defense, would have disclosed the submarine's presence prematurely.[18]

U-94 PLANNED ATTACK ON CONVOY THWARTED

Photo 12-4

Catalina PBY-5A patrol plane in flight, with wheels down, 28 June 1942.
National Archives photograph #80-G-16013

Later that night, after contacting Convoy TAW-15 east of Jamaica, Ites maneuvered *U-94* into position within the convoy screen to fire a torpedo at one of the escort vessels, when one of his lookouts sighted a plane. There was a full moon, with the wind and sea from the east. The submarine immediately began a crash dive, but PBY Catalina (*92-P-5*)—piloted by Lt. Gordon R. Fiss, USN, from Patrol Bombing Squadron VP-92—had spotted it. He made an attack run and straddled the conning tower with his bombs, then dropped a flare. The explosive force of the four 650lb depth charges was not enough to sink the submarine, but damaged its diving planes.[19]

HMCS *Oakville* had seen the airplane flashing "S's" by signal lamp as well as the flare, and proceeded at full speed toward the flare. Arriving at that spot, she dropped five depth charges set at 100 feet, and shortly afterwards, obtained an Asdic (sonar) contact. Aboard the destroyer *Lea*, the explosions of depth charges had been heard at 2300, followed by the sighting of an aircraft flare on the port quarter of the convoy, then another barrage of depth charges (*Oakville*'s).[20]

U-94, her hydroplanes blown away by depth charges and unable to dive, was forced to surface. A lookout aboard the corvette sighted her bow, corresponding with the Asdic (sonar) bearing, about 100 yards distant, and slowly opening (drawing away). HMCS *Oakville* altered course to ram, but the submarine passed under her bow, then bumped against her port side when the corvette turned hard to port. *Oakville* opened with 4-inch and machine gun fire and altered course in another attempt to ram. Her gunners scored a hit on the conning tower and carried away the sub's deck gun. *U-94* then increased speed in an apparent avoiding action. *Oakville* then rammed her starboard side and, determined to finish off the enemy, opened the range, turned, increased speed and rammed the submarine a second time—this time squarely abaft her conning tower.[21]

Oakville reported to *Lea* via voice communications that she had rammed a submarine twice, and was now firing at it. Asked if she needed help, *Oakville* replied that none was required. *Lea* then headed for the port quarter of the convoy to take *Oakville*'s screening station.[22]

Earlier, forced to surface, and unable to either fight or escape, Ites had directed vents opened to scuttle the submarine, then gave the order to abandon, "Alle Mann aus dem Boot." Ites, on deck, was shot in the right leg by machine-gun fire which *Oakville* was employing to prevent the Germans from manning their still in place deck gun. The crew, when able, began leaving the U-boat through the conning tower.[23]

Lieutenant Commander King laid *Oakville* alongside the submarine in a moderately heavy swell, and a boarding party comprising a sub-lieutenant and a petty officer leapt aboard. Two Germans, one the engineer officer Muller, appeared in the conning tower hatch. When they ignored the boarding officer's order to stop, he shot one of them. The second lunged toward the petty officer and also was shot.[24]

The boarding officer allowed the remaining Germans in the submarine to come up on deck and placed them under guard of the petty officer aft. He then descended the conning tower, found all of the lights out below, and the lower deck flooded to about four feet from the overhead part of the hull. The submarine then lurched and appeared to be settling by the stern. The boarding officer, unable to find any of the U-boat's confidential papers, quickly collected four pairs of binoculars and emerged from the conning tower. He ordered the large numbers of survivors on deck overboard. When they were about fifty feet clear, *U-94* sank, her bow first rising high into the air, before she slipped stern first beneath the surface. Sometime during all this, *Oakville* retrieved her boarding party and five survivors.[25]

The destroyer USS *Lea* arrived on the scene shortly before the submarine sank. *Oakville* had requested *Lea* to close her as the corvette was taking water badly. As the destroyer approached, the submarine was visible off her port beam with conning tower and forward deck awash. In the water, many people were swimming near the sinking sub. One of *Lea*'s boats was lowered, and sent to the submarine to pick up survivors and possible recovered information. When the boat arrived, only the conning tower was visible, and it soon disappeared.[26]

At 0040 aboard *Lea*, while awaiting return of her boat, a burst of flame illuminated the sky in the direction in which the convoy had disappeared, followed by many flares and rockets. The boat, which had picked up 21 survivors, was immediately recalled and hoisted. Lieutenant Commander King after investigating the extent of damage to *Oakville*, signaled that although one boiler was flooded, and the hull forward leaking, he could proceed cautiously to Guantanamo Bay at very slow speed. *Lea* then departed at full speed to rejoin the convoy.[27]

Upon rejoining, *SC-522* reported that the Dutch motor tanker *Rotterdam* and the British steam tanker *San Fabian*—the second and third ships in the second column from the left—had been sunk. The American steam tanker *Esso Aruba*, which was leading the third column, had been hit, but was able to continue with the convoy.[28]

During *Oakville*'s action with *U-94*, the *U-511* (Kptlt. Friedrich Steinhoff)—a type IXC submarine—fired a spread of four torpedoes at the convoy, then about 120 miles south-southeast of Guantanamo. She then escaped undected.[29]

Convoy TAW-15 arrived in Key West without further incident.

ADDITIONAL INFORMATION GLEANED

Photo 12-5

Ships at anchor at Guantanamo Bay, Cuba, year unknown.
Naval History and Heritage Command photograph #NH 109396

The twenty-one *U-94* survivors picked up by *Lea*, and the remaining five aboard HMCS *Oakville*, were delivered to the naval base at Guantanamo Bay. Two of the Germans had been slightly burned when chemicals from their bullet-punctured escape lungs had come into contact with seawater.[30]

During interrogation, Oberfähnrich zur See (Senior Midshipman) Rolf-Kurt Gebeschus disclosed that a U-boat at sea was always under radio control of headquarters. He said if *U-94* suddenly became silent for some reason, the B.d.U. (Admiral Doenitz, commander of the submarines would send out a series of messages—"U-Ites Lage angeben" (give position), "U-Ites Wettersignale" (give weather signal) in an effort to determine what had happened to the boat. Thus, Gebeschus believed that within three or four days the loss of their U-boat would become known in Germany. No announcement would be made to the crew's families, however, for at least three months.[31]

Gebeschus also confirmed statements by other officer prisoners-of-war that operations in American waters were becoming more and more difficult, remarking that "Commanders are now hard put to sink 50,000 tons in the Gulf of Mexico" (as compared with the high tonnage which U-boats were sinking in American waters early in 1942). He insisted that U-boat commanders were able to gauge accurately the tonnage of their victims. Night silhouette disclosed their distinguishing features which could be recognized readily from a U-boat on the surface a few hundred yards distant. Further, U-boats carried as references, Groener's list of merchant ships as well as Weyer's naval registry.[32]

Ites stated, when asked why he hadn't ordered the use of explosives, that setting off scuttling charges in a U-boat was a dangerous operation which almost invariably resulted in loss of life. He agreed with members of his crew that had they set off charges in *U-94*, it would have required two men to do it, would have taken them at least one minute, and they undoubtedly would have been killed or drowned.[33]

An enlisted prisoner, with a flair for phrase-making, said, in describing tactics of night attacks: "Destroyers are our great enemy—night our great weapon."[34]

CATALINA PILOT AWARDED DFC FOR HEROISM

United States Distinguished Flying Cross

Established 2 July 1926

Presented by Military Departments
For heroism or extraordinary achievement while participating in an aerial flight

Lieutenant Gordon R. Fiss, USN, the pilot of the PBY-5A Catalina was awarded the Distinguished Flying Cross; the associated citation follows:

> The President of the United States of America takes pleasure in presenting the Distinguished Flying Cross to Lieutenant Gordon R. Fiss, United States Navy, for heroism and extraordinary achievement while participating in aerial flight during World War II. Although he had just returned from a long and arduous patrol flight, Lieutenant Fiss volunteered to take his Catalina Patrol Bomber out again to provide protection for a convoy moving out the same night. As the convoy moved slowly along, Lieutenant Fiss spotted a submarine on the surface, coming up astern of the group of ships. He immediately put his plane into a dive and dropped down upon the U-boat. The submarine attempted to crash dive, but so swift was Lieutenant Fiss' attack that only her bow was awash as he released his depth charges. The charges severely damaged the U-boat, making it impossible for her to submerge, and she was destroyed shortly thereafter by gunfire from surface vessels accompanying the convoy.

CLARENCE A. KING DECORATED IN TWO WARS

 **DSO**	Distinguished Service Order Established by: Queen Victoria, 6 September 1886 For meritorious or distinguished service by officers during war	Distinguished Service Cross Established by: King Edward VII, 28 June 1901 For meritorious or distinguished service before the enemy 'by men of His Majesty's Fleet'	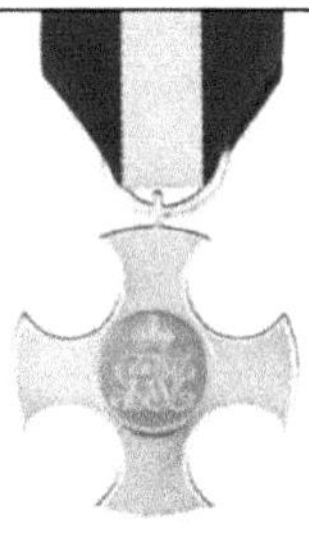 **DSC**
 **LOM**	United States Legion of Merit Established by President Franklin D. Roosevelt, 20 July 1942 For exceptionally meritorious conduct in the performance of outstanding services and achievements	To be mentioned in despatches describes a member of the armed forces whose name appears in an official report in which their gallant or meritorious action in the face of the enemy is described.	 **War Medal**

Clarence Aubrey King, RCNR, one of Canada's finest naval officers, retired with the rank of Captain. From the time he was 13 years old, in 1899, until the end of World War II, King spent most of his life at sea. He, 53 years old when World War II broke out, was decorated in both the First and Second World Wars for destroying German U-boats. His very distinguished record of naval service is worthy of recognition.

Born at Islington on the outskirts of London in 1886, King attended the Conway Merchant Marine School and went to sea at age thirteen. By twenty-five he had earned his foreign-going steamship Master's certification.[35]

In 1913, King married Olive Hill, who had emigrated to Canada in April 1912, and settled on a fruit farm at Kamloops, British Columbia. After the First World War broke out, he relocated his wife and daughters to Winnipeg to be with her brother, and returned to England and joined the Royal Naval Volunteer Reserve as a sub-lieutenant.[36]

In January 1917, King was assigned to a motor launch carrying out submarine patrols in the English Channel, before being transferred to the Special Service steel barquentine *Merops*. This sailing vessel, fitted with hidden armament, was designed to attract attack by U-boats believing her harmless; she then engaged them with gunfire. Built in 1892 as the Danish-flagged *Maracaibo*, she was taken into Q-ship service on 2 February 1917 operating under the names *Bellmore*, *Ilma*, *Maracaibo*, *Merope/Merops*, *Q28*, *Steady* and *Toofa*, until returned to mercantile service on 11 February 1919 and renamed *Bellmore*.[37]

Outwardly, "Q-ships" might be scruffy colliers, tramp steamers, fishing smacks, or luggers. However, they carried concealed 12-pounder and Maxim guns and twice the crew that a similar commercial vessel would need. The decoy ships endeavored to lure submarines to surface, approach to within close range, and use their guns—thereby saving one of the precious few torpedoes they carried. Once the sub's conning tower and deck presented a sure enough target, concealment of weapons was abandoned as the mystery ship opened fire.

Following her selection for decoy work, *Merops* was fitted out in the Firth of Forth with a couple of 12-pounders and a 4-inch gun. At the end of May 1917, she was in an engagement with a submarine, in which both she and the U-boat were considerably damaged. When not trying to attract enemy attention, *Merops* and similar vessels were employed in a dual-role as freighters. In late September 1917, after being repaired, *Merops* was at Runcorn (a port in Cheshire, England) discharging cargo preparatory to loading coal for delivery to Cherbourg.[38]

Serving in 'Q' ships as navigator, first lieutenant and captain successively, King was credited with one kill and two probable submarine sinkings, and was awarded his first Distinguished Service Cross (DSC).[39]

In 1919, King returned home to a farm south of Winnipeg where two sons were born. Nine years later, he moved to a fruit farm near Oliver, British Columbia, and in 1935 moved into a home on Lake Ossoyos, located about two miles from the fruit farm.[40]

In April 1939, King offered his services to the Admiralty, and was ordered to Panama where he joined the staff of the British Consul as shipping adviser. In 1941, he was appointed commander of the anti-submarine base in Bermuda. In 1942, he transferred to the Royal Canadian Naval Reserve and commanded for a short period the corvette HMCS *Saskatoon* (5-14 February) and minesweeper HMCS *Nipigon* (15 February to 11 May). Soon after he assumed command of the corvette HMCS *Oakville* (12 May 1942 to 21 April 1943). For the destruction of *U-94*, King was awarded a Distinguished Service Order and the U.S. Legion of Merit (the first American decoration to be awarded to a Canadian in World War II).[41]

COMMAND OF HMCS *SWANSEA*

Several months later, King was appointed to command HMCS *Swansea* (K328), a River-class frigate, commissioning her on the West Coast and then sailing her to Halifax in October 1943 to begin her war service. He served as her commanding officer from 4 October 1943 to 4 November 1944.[42]

During this period, King was twice Mentioned in Despatches. The first, announced in the *London Gazette* of 15 August 1944, was "For good service in action with enemy destroyers."[43]

His second Mention in Despatches (*London Gazette* of 15 August 1944) was "For good service in the destruction of an enemy submarine on 10 March 1944. For leadership, skill and determination in H.M. Ships *Affleck*, *Brecon* and *Forester*, and H.M. Canadian Ships *St. Laurent*, *Swansea* and *Owen Sound* in operations against U-boats." Depth charges from the British destroyer HMS *Forester*, the Canadian destroyer HMCS *St. Laurent*, the Canadian corvette HMCS *Owen Sound*, and the Canadian frigate HMCS *Swansea* had sunk *U-845* on 10 March 1944 in the North Atlantic southwest of Ireland.[44]

Commander Clarence Aubrey King was awarded a Bar to his Distinguished Service Cross (DSC*) per the *London Gazette* of 24 October 1944, "For good service in the destruction of an enemy submarine." On 14 April 1944, HMCS *Swansea* and the sloop HMS *Pelican* sank *U-448* with depth charges in the North Atlantic northeast of the Azores. Four and one-half months later, HMCS *Swansea* and the frigate HMCS *St. John* sank *U-247* off Cornwall, in the English Channel near Lands End.[45]

FINAL ASSIGNMENTS AND PROMOTION

King continued to escort convoys, and eventually finished the war as senior officer of C-5 Escort Group. From 9 June to 22 October 1945, he commanded the frigate HMCS *Runnymede* (K678).[46]

Clarence Aubrey King was promoted to Captain on 1 January 1946, while serving as Staff Officer (Operations) to the Commanding Officer Pacific Coast at Esquimalt. He was demobilized at the end of July 1946 and returned to his home in the Okanagan Valley where he died in February 1964. His wife Olive died in Penticton, a city also located in the Okanagan Valley of British Columbia, in 1983.[47]

13

U-boats arrive in South African Waters

By the latter half of 1942, the effectiveness of German submarines against shipping in the North Atlantic had decreased considerably owing to improved and expanded Allied anti-submarine warfare efforts. As a result, Admiral Doenitz decided that an operation off the coast of Southern Africa would prove viable, and cause a diversionary effect whereby the Allies would be forced to split their defensive forces between protecting the North Atlantic, the American Eastern Seaboard and the vital sea route around Africa.[1]

The Allied response to the extensive U-boat threat had improved considerably by the latter half of 1942, through:

- increasing skill of convoy and escort commanders
- greater numbers of escorts
- ready availability of shipboard Asdic (sonar) equipment
- great improvement of anti-submarine weapons
- Diminished "air-gap" in the North Atlantic (area beyond the range of land-based aircraft)[2]

Additionally, Allied ability to read German naval ciphers, provided information about where to search for enemy submarines with land-based aircraft and dedicated anti-submarine (ASW) hunter-killer groups. This ability came about after the Royal Navy captured *U-110* on 9 May 1941 in the North Atlantic east of Cape Farewell, Greenland, after being badly damaged by depth charges from the British destroyers HMS *Bulldog* and *Broadway* and the corvette HMS *Aubretia.* The German crew abandoned their damaged submarine, and a boarding party from *Bulldog* went aboard her and was able to recover a working Enigma machine, its cipher keys, and codebooks, which allowed codebreakers to read German signal traffic. Although taken under tow by the British, *U-110* flooded and sank the following day, about 100 miles from Iceland, preserving the secret of her capture.[3]

The ASW groups were formed around small escort carriers with several destroyers, frigates, destroyer escorts, or corvettes acting as screens and performing underwater searches. Freed from protecting merchant ship convoys, these groups were able to move independently, and hunt for submarines rather than just react to attacks. Once prey was found, they had the time necessary to fully prosecute contacts.

TARGETS ABOUND IN SOUTH AFRICAN WATERS

Map 13-1

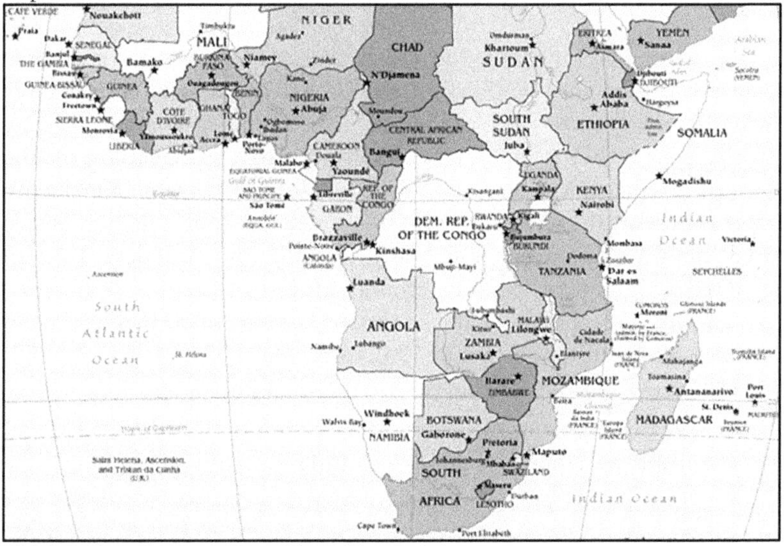

Middle and southern portion of the African continent

Doenitz well appreciated the fact that the Freetown-Cape Town convoy route and beyond, up the east coast of South Africa, was an excellent target for a concentrated U-boat offensive. The port of Freetown, in Sierra Leone on Africa's west coast (upper left of map), served as an assembly point for all merchant shipping going to and coming from Europe, the Middle East and the Far East. This route passed along the strategic maritime nodal point of the Cape of Good Hope (about 31 miles south of Cape Town, South Africa). At Freetown, when escort availability permitted use of convoys, slower merchantmen were formed into them for their onward transit north, while faster ships and other less fortunate vessels not able to join convoys sailed independently.[4]

Shipping using the Cape route around the southern tip of Africa had to stop over at one of the key South African ports of Saldanha Bay, Cape Town, East London, Port Elizabeth or Durban for refueling and replenishing. But, because of the limited number of escorts available, only large troop transports and other important ships could be escorted. All other shipping rounding the Cape was independently routed.[5]

Photo 13-1

Wartime Cape Town with the converted troopship *Nieuw Amsterdam* alongside the Duncan Dock.
SA Naval Museum

OPERATION EISBAR

Operation EISBAR (Polar Bear) was the first German submarine offensive in South African waters. It began in October 1942 and was intended to strike a devastating blow to shipping off the African coast—which it did. At that time, Allied usage of most of its escort ships (not engaged in North Atlantic convoys) to protect North African and Mediterranean waters in support of the campaign in North Africa, enticed Admiral Doenitz to strike the 'soft underbelly' of South Africa.[6]

Between 7 October and 14 December, fifty-one ships were attacked (48 sunk, two damaged, and one that was afloat but a total loss). As shown in the table, all of these victims were unescorted when attacked, including SS *Aegeus* and SS *Scottish Chief*, the only ships which had earlier been in convoy. (Appendix F provides a complete list of ships sunk in African waters during war.)

Aegeus had been a part of Convoy TRIN-16 (convoys from Trinidad to dispersal in southeast). She was lost after being detached, while proceeding independently to her destination. *Scottish Chief* was similarly dispersed from Convoy PA-8 (Bandar Abbas to Aden), and proceeding to her destination when torpedoed and sunk.[7]

51 Ships Sunk or Damaged in South African Waters (7 October – 14 December 1942)

Date	Ship/Sub	Registry	Type	Tons	Location
7 Oct 42 unescorted	*Boringia* *U-159*	British	motor merchant	5,821	35°09'S, 16°32'E
7 Oct 42 unescorted	*Chickasaw City* *U-172*	American	steam merchant	6,196	34°15'S, 17°11'E
7 Oct 42 unescorted	*Firethorn* *U-172*	Panamanian	motor merchant	4,700	34°13'S, 17°21'E
8 Oct 42 unescorted	*Clan Mactavish* *U-159*	British	steam merchant	7,631	34°53'S, 16°45'E
8 Oct 42 unescorted	*City of Athens* *U-179*	British	steam merchant	6,558	33°40'S, 17°03'E
8 Oct 42 unescorted	*Koumoundouros* *U-68*	Greek	steam merchant	3,598	34°10'S, 17°07'E
8 Oct 42 unescorted	*Gaasterkerk* *U-68*	Dutch	steam merchant	8,679	34°20'S, 18°10'E
8 Oct 42 unescorted	*Swiftsure* *U-68*	American	steam tanker	8,207	34°40'S, 18°25'E
8 Oct 42 unescorted	*Sarthe* *U-68*	British	steam merchant	5,271	34°50'S, 18°40'E
8 Oct 42 unescorted	*Pantelis* *U-172*	Greek	steam merchant	3,845	34°20'S, 17°50'E
9 Oct 42 unescorted	*Coloradan* *U-159*	American	steam merchant	6,557	35° 47'S, 14° 34'E
9 Oct 42 unescorted	*Examelia* *U-68*	American	steam merchant	4,981	34°52'S, 18°30'E
9 Oct 42 unescorted	*Belgian Fighter* *U-68*	Belgian	steam merchant	5,403	35°00'S, 18°30'E
10 Oct 42 unescorted	*Orcades* *U-172*	British	troop transport	23,456	35°51'S, 14°40'E
13 Oct 42 unescorted	*Empire Nomad* *U-159*	British	steam merchant	7,167	37°50'S, 18°16'E
17 Oct 42 unescorted	*Empire Chaucer* *U-504*	British	steam merchant	5,970	38°12'S, 20°04'E
23 Oct 42 unescorted	*City of Johannesburg* *U-504*	British	steam merchant	5,669	33°20'S, 29°30'E
26 Oct 42 unescorted	*Anne Hutchinson* *U-504* (T)	American	Liberty ship	7,176	33°10'S, 28°30'E
29 Oct 42 unescorted	*Ross* *U-159*	British	motor merchant	4,978	38°51'S, 21°40'E
29 Oct 42 unescorted	*Laplace* *U-159*	British	steam merchant	7,327	40°35'S, 21°35'E
31 Oct 42 unescorted	*Empire Guidon* *U-504*	British	steam merchant	7,041	30°48'S, 34°11'E
31 Oct 42 unescorted	*Reynolds* *U-504*	British	steam merchant	5,113	30°02'S, 35°02'E

1 Nov 42 unescorted	*Mendoza* *U-178*	British	troop transport	8,233	29°20'S, 32°13'E
2 Nov 42 Convoy TRIN-16	*Aegeus* *U-177*	Greek	steam merchant	4,538	32°30'S, 16°00'E
3 Nov 42 unescorted	*Porto Alegre* *U-504*	Brazilian	steam merchant	5,187	35°27'S, 28°02'E
3 Nov 42 unescorted	*East Indian* *U-181*	American	motor merchant	8,159	37°23'S, 13°34'E
4 Nov 42 unescorted	*Hai Hing* *U-178*	Norwegian	steam merchant	2,561	25°55'S, 33°10'E
4 Nov 42 unescorted	*Trekieve* *U-178*	British	steam merchant	5,244	25°46'S, 33°48'E
7 Nov 42 unescorted	*La Salle* *U-159*	American	steam merchant	5,462	40°00'S, 21°30'E
8 Nov 42 unescorted	*Plaudit* *U-181*	Panamanian	steam merchant	5,060	36°00'S, 26°32'E
9 Nov 42 unescorted	*Cerion* (D) *U-177*	British	motor tanker	2,588	35°58'S, 26°37'E
10 Nov 42 unescorted	*K.G. Meldahl* *U-181*	Norwegian	steam merchant	3,799	34°59'S, 29°45'E
13 Nov 42 unescorted	*Excello* *U-181*	American	steam merchant	4,969	32°23'S, 30°07'E
13 Nov 42 unescorted	*Louise Moller* *U-178*	British	steam merchant	3,764	30°50'S, 35°54'E
15 Nov 42 unescorted	*Adviser* (D) *U-178*	British	steam merchant	6,348	32°03'S, 33°52'E
19 Nov 42 unescorted	*Gunda* *U-181*	Norwegian	steam merchant	2,241	25°48'S, 33°15'E
19 Nov 42 Convoy PA-8	*Scottish Chief* *U-177*	British	steam tanker	7,006	30°39'S, 34°41'E
20 Nov 42 unescorted	*Pierce Butler* *U-177*	American	Liberty ship	7,191	29°40'S, 36°35'E
20 Nov 42 unescorted	*Corinthiakos* *U-181*	Greek	steam merchant	3,562	25°42'S, 33°27'E
22 Nov 42 unescorted	*Alcoa Pathfinder* *U-181*	American	steam merchant	6,797	26°45'S, 33°10'E
24 Nov 42 unescorted	*Mount Helmos* *U-181*	Greek	steam merchant	6,481	26°38'S, 34°59'E
24 Nov 42 unescorted	*Dorington Court* *U-181*	British	steam merchant	5,281	27°00'S, 34°45'E
27 Nov 42 unescorted	*Jeremiah Wadsworth* *U-178*	American	Liberty ship	7,176	39°25'S, 22°23'E
28 Nov 42 unescorted	*Evanthia* *U-181*	Greek	steam merchant	3,551	25°13'S, 34°00'E
28 Nov 42 unescorted	*Nova Scotia* *U-177*	British	troop transport	6,796	28°30'S, 33°00'E

30 Nov 42 unescorted	*Llandaff Castle* *U-177*	British	troop transport	10,799	27°20'S, 33°40'E
30 Nov 42 unescorted	*Cleanthis* *U-181*	Greek	steam merchant	4,153	24°29'S, 35°44'E
2 Dec 42 unescorted	*Amarylis* *U-181*	Panamanian	steam merchant	4,328	28°14'S, 33°24'E
7 Dec 42 unescorted	*Saronikos* *U-177*	Greek	steam merchant	3,548	24°46'S, 35°30'E
12 Dec 42 unescorted	*Empire Gull* *U-177*	British	steam merchant	6,408	26°15'S, 34°40'E
14 Dec 42 unescorted	*Sawahloento* *U-177*	Dutch	steam merchant	3,085	31°02'S, 34°00'E[8]

D: Damaged T: Total loss (uneconomical to repair/return to service)

Doenitz, appreciative of the logistical challenges associated with operations in the central and southern Atlantic, had initiated the use of U-tankers (Milch Cows). In receipt of this support at several rendezvous points with supply ships or U-tankers established across the Atlantic, the U-boats could remain at sea for twice the time they could before it was established.[9]

Photo 13-2

At sea transfer in the South Atlantic.
SA Naval Museum

By August 1942, Doenitz had a large number of IXC long-range 1,200-ton U-boats at his disposal. These U-boats, supported by the Milch Cows, enabled deployment of German submarine forces to areas previously devoid of any sustained U-boat operations. Spearheading the commencement of Operation EISBAR, four 1,200 tonners—*U-68*, *U-*

172, *U-504*, *U-156*—left Lorient on 19 and 20 August. Their supporting Milch Cow *U-459* had departed St. Nazaire a day earlier. The attack submarines had to journey approximately 6,000 miles before reaching the waters off Cape Town. During this transit, *U-156* was damaged by a USAAF bomber and was recalled (an account of that action follows this section). She was replaced with *U-159*, which had separately left Lorient on 24 August.[10]

The following table identifies the parent flotillas of the submarines, the commanders of the submarines, and provides a summary of the number of ships sunk by each during this patrol in African waters.[11]

2nd Flotilla
2. Unterseebootsflottille
Lorient, France

U-68 (IXC)
U-156 (IXC)
U-504 (IXC)

10th Flotilla
10. Unterseebootsflottille
Lorient, France

U-159 (IXC)
U-172 (IXC)
U-459 (XIV)

Date Left	U-boat/ Type	Commander	Ships Hit
18 Aug 42	*U-459*/XIV Milch Cow	KrvKpt. Georg von Wilamowitz-Möllendorf	0 S
19 Aug 42	*U-172*/IXC	Kptlt. Carl Emmermann	4 S
19 Aug 42	*U-504*/IXC	KrvKpt. Hans-Georg Friedrich Poske	5 S, 1 T
20 Aug 42	*U-68*/IXC	KrvKpt. Karl-Friedrich Merten	6 S
20 Aug 42	*U-156*/IXC	KrvKpt. Werner Hartenstein	0 S
24 Aug 42	*U-159*/IXC	Kptlt. Helmut Friedrich Witte	7 S
		Total	22 S, 1 T

S: Sunk T: Total loss owing to extensive damage suffered

SINKING OF *LACONIA* WITH GREAT LOSS OF LIFE

In the lead-up to the first U-boat offensive in South African waters, *U-156*, while on passage, torpedoed and sank the unescorted 19,695-ton British troop transport *Laconia*, about 360 miles northeast of Ascension Island on the night of 12 September. This small, isolated scrap of British territory (situated in the middle of the Atlantic almost halfway between the continents of South America and Africa) hosted an important naval and air station. From it, Allied aircraft and ships could carry out anti-submarine operations against enemy forces.[12]

Photo 13-3

The British troop transport *Laconia*.
SA Naval Museum

Photo 13-4

Survivors from the *Laconia* on the casing of *U-156*.
SA Naval Museum

Operating partly under the dictates of the old prize rules, the U-boat captain, Korvettenkapitän Werner Hartenstein, immediately began picking up survivors, took lifeboats in tow and notified the BdU (Doenitz) about her rescue operation. He also broadcast the submarine's position on open radio channels in English to all ships nearby requesting assistance with the rescue effort and promising not to attack. On 15 September, *U-506*, *U-507*, and the Italian submarine *Cappellini* also arrived and participated in the rescue. The following day, *U-156*, which was prominently displaying a Red Cross banner, was controversially attacked by an American B-24 Liberator bomber operating from Ascension.[13]

The attack killed dozens of *Laconia*'s survivors who were crammed below decks and on the U-boats foredeck, forcing *U-156* to cast them into the sea, set the lifeboats adrift and crash dive to avoid being destroyed. *U-156* was severely damaged, Doenitz was forced to recall her, and the incident had far-reaching consequences. In response to the incident, he issued an order prohibiting U-boat crews from attempting rescues or providing humanitarian support to survivors, as had previously been the practice. Survivors were to be left in the sea. The era of unrestricted German submarine warfare had arrived.[14]

Map 13-2

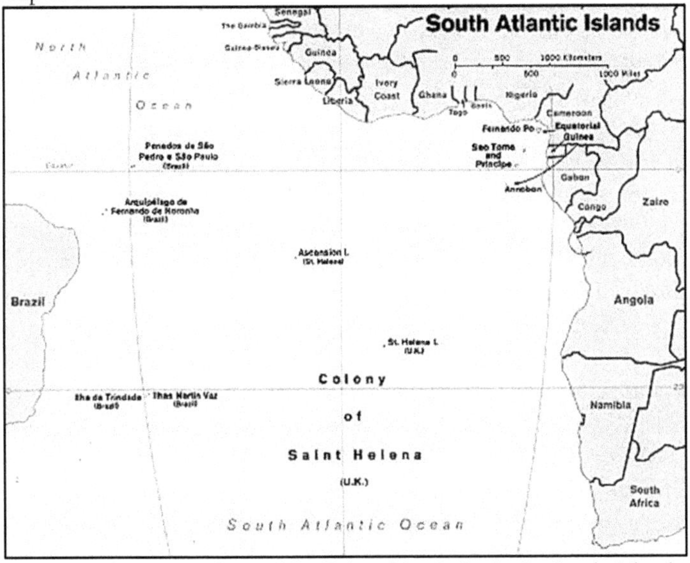

UK possessions Ascension and St. Helena islands, lay in the South Atlantic "narrows," between the coastlines of Brazil and West Africa
www.lib.utexas.edu/maps/islands_oceans_poles/southatlanticislands.jpg

Between 17 and 20 September, 1,083 survivors (among them 415 Italian prisoners of war) were picked up from lifeboats or directly from the U-boats by the Vichy French warships *Gloire*, *Dumont d'Urville* and *Annamite*, and were taken to Dakar in French West Africa (today Senagal). *Gloire* brought her 668 Allied survivors to Casablanca on 26 September. They consisted of one officer and 178 ratings of the Royal

Navy, 17 officers and 87 ratings from the British Army, nine officers and 70 ratings from the Royal Air Force, and eight officers and 178 men from the Merchant Navy. Among the survivors were also one officer and 69 ratings from the Free Polish Army, and 50 women and children.[15]

Sadly, the master of the *Laconia*, 97 crew members, 133 passengers, 33 Polish guards and 1,394 prisoners perished.[16]

ARRIVAL IN SOUTH AFRICAN WATERS

U-159 was available to replace *U-156*, because she was in the equatorial area making her way to an operational area off the mouth of the Congo River on a separate operation. Between 22 and 24 September, the Operation EISBAR boats rendezvoused with *U-459* to the south of St. Helena (see preceding map) where they were replenished. The new fuel and logistic supplies they received enabled them to continue their patrols for a further thirty days. The remainder of the journey south was without incident, and the Eisbar boats arrived off Cape Town during the first week of October 1942.[17]

On the night of 6 October, *U-172* successfully crept into the Table Bay roadstead off Cape Town harbour to reconnoiter for targets, but found it empty of Allied merchant shipping. This was not of concern as shipping offshore was plentiful, and South African defences deficient, as the following two summaries of merchant vessels sunk by *U-68*, *U-159*, and *U-172*, and *U-504* amply demonstrates. (These ships are subsets of the 51 total ships sunk or damaged, identified in the previous table.)

While *U-68*, *U-159*, and *U-172* concentrated their efforts in the Cape Town area (waters off Cape Town, the Cape of Good Hope, Cape Point, and Cape Agulhas), *U-504* hunted mostly off the Eastern Cape ports of Port Elizabeth, East London, and Durban.

The first sinking of the offensive occurred at 0500 on 7 October. The American freighter *Chickasaw City* was torpedoed and sunk 60 miles west-by-south from Cape Town by *U-172*, followed at 0900 by the Panamanian ship *Firethorn* 8 miles farther west. Late that night the British ship *Boringia* and the Greek *Koumoundouros* were lost, and, during the 8th and 9th, nine more ships were added to the list. On the 10th, the Orient lines *Orcades* of 23,456 tons, carrying about 1,000 passengers and crew and independently routed for Britain, went down in a position 220 miles WSW from Cape Town after being torpedoed by *U-172*. About 40 lives were lost, the survivors being picked up by the Polish ship *Narwik*—a gallant effort on her part as the U-boat, which did not attack her, was surfaced a few miles away.[18]

As soon as it was established that the sinkings had been caused by submarines, diversion signals were made and some sailings were deferred, but not all. At least one ship, the British *Sarthe*, torpedoed on the evening of the 8th by *U-68*, had failed to take in the diversion signal. Very few of the ships attacked managed to get off an SOS distress message, as in nearly all cases the first torpedo, usually closely followed by a second, was the first danger in an area which had been considered a particularly safe one. The attacks which followed certainly indicated a very wide dispersion of the U-boats.[19]

Vessels sunk in the Cape Town, South Africa Area by *U-68*, *U-159*, *U-172*, and *U-504* (7 October to 7 November 1942)

Date	Ship	U-boat	Torpedoed/Sunk
7 Oct 42	*Boringia*	*U-159*	~120 miles WSW of Cape Town
7 Oct 42	*Chickasaw City*	*U-172*	~85 miles SSW of Cape Town
7 Oct 42	*Firethorn*	*U-172*	~60 miles NW of Cape Town
8 Oct 42	*Clan Mactavish*	*U-159*	~100 miles WSW of Cape Town
8 Oct 42	*Koumoundouros*	*U-68*	~20 miles SW of Cape Point
8 Oct 42	*Gaasterkerk*	*U-68*	~15 miles W of the Cape of Good Hope
8 Oct 42	*Swiftsure*	*U-68*	~25 miles SE of the Cape of Good Hope
8 Oct 42	*Sarthe*	*U-68*	~35 miles SSW of the Cape of Good Hope
8 Oct 42	*Pantelis*	*U-172*	~40 miles SW of Cape Town
9 Oct 42	*Coloradan*	*U-159*	~200 miles SW of Cape Town
9 Oct 42	*Examelia*	*U-68*	~20 miles S of the Cape of Good Hope
9 Oct 42	*Belgian Fighter*	*U-68*	~80 miles SSE of Cape Town
10 Oct 42	*Orcades*	*U-172*	~220 miles SW of Cape Town
13 Oct 42	*Empire Nomad*	*U-159*	~230 miles S of Cape Point
17 Oct 42	*Empire Chaucer*	*U-504*	~450 miles S of Cape Town
29 Oct 42	*Ross*	*U-159*	~370 miles SSE of Cape Agulhas
29 Oct 42	*Laplace*	*U-159*	~350 miles SSE of Cape Agulhas
7 Nov 42	*La Salle*	*U-159*	~350 miles SE of the Cape of Good Hope

South Africa's Eastern Cape Area
Vessels sunk by *U-504* (23 October-3 November 1942)

Date	Ship	U-boat	Torpedoed/Sunk
23 Oct 42	*City of Johannesburg*	*U-504*	~80 miles ESE of East London
26 Oct 42	*Anne Hutchinson* (T)	*U-504*	~60 miles E of East London
31 Oct 42	*Empire Guidon*	*U-504*	~180 miles ESE of Durban
31 Oct 42	*Reynolds*	*U-504*	~210 miles E of Durban
3 Nov 42	*Porto Alegre*	*U-504*	~150 miles SE of Port Elizabeth

T: Total loss (uneconomical to repair/return to service as a result of damage suffered)
~: About

Map 13-3

The Cape of Good Hope is a rocky headland on the Cape Peninsula south of Cape Town; Cape Point lies at the tip of this peninsula; Cape Agulhas, marking the southern tip of Africa, is to the southeast of Cape Town

SIGNIFICANTLY TOO FEW PATROL VESSELS

The situation facing British and South African naval forces in South African waters upon the onslaught of U-boat attacks in October 1942 while similar to that experienced earlier in the U.S. Eastern Sea Frontier, was even more acute. One Flower-class corvette, which was three to four knots faster than the A/S trawlers and whalers, was the only A/S vessel belonging to the South Atlantic Station operationally available when the offensive began. She was, however, soon joined by two more RN Flower-class corvettes which were normally involved in the escort of troopships and other important convoys rounding the Cape. While, by good fortune, two destroyers had just arrived from the Eastern Fleet to refit, but had not yet been taken in hand, two more destroyers had also put into Simon's Town on passage to Freetown. The South African Naval Forces (SANF), which had responsibility for local A/S patrols in the vicinity of South Africa's principal ports, was also able to initially provide the converted A/S whaler HMSAS *Vereeniging*, while increased air patrols were provided by South African Air Force (SAAF) Ventura and Anson coastal patrol aircraft.[20]

Photo 13-5

A South African Airforce Avro Anson conducting a coastal patrol.
SAAF Museum

Following the outbreak of war in 1939, the development of anti-submarine protection measures in South African waters had proved to be agonizingly slow, mainly because of an initial shortage of Asdic sets to equip the fifteen requisitioned SANF trawlers and whalers identified for conversion to A/S vessels to guard anchorages. As a result, anti-submarine measures were initially limited to local patrols off Cape Town and Durban—the principal areas through which a majority of merchant shipping passed—until more Asdic-equipped A/S ships became available.[21]

Moreover, after four South African Southern-class A/S whalers which had been intended for local service were sent instead to the Mediterranean in December 1940, only eleven converted whalers and trawlers were available to serve as anti-submarine vessels in the Cape Town and Durban areas. This necessitated limiting the scope of activities and patrol areas that could be covered until replacements could be commissioned. This number was further reduced by one, in April 1942, when HMSAS *Sydostlandet* (unit of the Durban A/S Flotilla) ran aground near the Umgeni River mouth during rough weather.[22]

During the first half of 1942, the almost unchecked successes of Japan on land and at sea had appeared to present the more serious threat, including attacks by carrier-borne aircraft and attacks by midget submarines like those used in the attacks on Pearl Harbor and Sydney. As a result, anti-submarine indicator loops were laid across the entrance channel to Durban harbour and an anti-torpedo boom was installed across the entrance to the dry-dock to protect the caisson against torpedo bombers. Arrangements were also made for the laying of A/S loops which would enclose the anchorages at Cape Town and Durban. But these were extensive installations and took many months to complete.[23]

At Durban, the anti-submarine (A/S) patrol line was approximately six miles from the shore and nearly six miles in length. His Majesty's South African Ships *Blaauwberg*, *Cedarberg*, *Odberg*, *Rondevlei*, *Smalvlei*, and *Tordonn* comprised the Durban A/S Flotilla from May 1942 onward (*Tordonn* having replaced *Sydostlandet*). This allowed for three vessels to conduct patrols at any one time, while the other three refueled, reprovisioned, completed needed maintenance and repairs, and allowed for some crew rest.[24]

Durban Anti-Submarine Flotilla

Ship	Type	Displ.	Fuel	In Service
HMSAS *Rondevlei*	whaler	247 tons	oil	8 Jun 40
HMSAS *Smalvlei*	whaler	233 tons	oil	8 Jun 40
HMSAS *Blaauwberg*	whaler	307 tons	oil	27 Dec 40
HMSAS *Sydostlandet* (lost)	whaler	258 tons	oil	4 Jan 41
HMSAS *Cedarberg*	whaler	307 tons	oil	14 Mar 41
HMSAS *Odberg*	whaler	351 tons	oil	1 May 41
HMSAS *Tordonn*[25]	whaler	314 tons	oil	25 Nov 41

While six A/S vessels were similarly needed at Cape Town, only four vessels were available to patrol the northern approaches to Table Bay between Robben Island and Bloubergstrand, as well as the main approaches between Robben Island and Green Point after HMSAS *Tordonn* was sent to Durban to replace HMSAS *Sydostlandet* in April 1942. A sixth vessel, the converted A/S whaler HMSAS *Protea*, which had been intended to serve at Cape Town, had instead been sent to the Mediterranean the previous year as a replacement for HMSAS *Southern Floe* which had been lost off Tobruk.

Photo 13-6

The converted SANF A/S Trawler HMSAS *Mooivlei*.
Du Toit Collection

The situation at Cape Town had only improved when a further four vessels—HMSA Ships *Pretoria*, *Vereeniging*, *Turffontein*, and *Standerton*—were commissioned between May and October 1942. This brought the total number of SANF A/S vessels in South African waters to fourteen for the remainder of the war. Their addition, just before the U-boats arrived, had also allowed for the provision of anti-submarine protection at Saldanha Bay, located 70 miles north of Cape Town, without reducing the Cape Town patrols.[26]

Fortunately, the use of Saldanha Bay, South Africa's only natural protected anchorage, as an overflow anchorage since June 1942, had reduced the average number of ships at anchor in Table Bay. And when the U-boat offensive began, ten extra berths were formed inside the harbour at Cape Town by double-banking ships. But, while Saldanha Bay served as a defended lay-by anchorage, its limited supply of water and harbour facilities prevented it from handling many ships at any one time.[27]

From 1942, the South African authorities attempted to correct these shortfalls by a variety of measures. Fresh water was conveyed by sea from Cape Town by a water-tanker on a temporary basis, until lighters and temporary bunker facilities could be utilized on a more permanent basis. Subsequently, a pipeline was built from the Berg River to supply 1 million gallons of water per day, and existing meagre port facilities improved via the construction of a reinforced concrete jetty, a ship-repair depot and oil storage tanks. Ironically, most of these improvements reached completion after the port's greatest need had passed.[28]

Cape Town Anti-Submarine Flotilla

Ship	Type	Displacement	Fuel	In Service
HMSAS *Blomvlei*	trawler	252 tons	coal	11 Oct 39
HMSAS *Mooivlei*	trawler	252 tons	coal	13 Nov 39
HMSAS *Sonneblom*	whaler	335 tons	oil	14 Aug 41
HMSAS *Immortelle*	whaler	335 tons	oil	5 Nov 41
HMSAS *Pretoria*	whaler	374 tons	oil	8 May 42
HMSAS *Vereeniging*	whaler	355 tons	oil	27 Jun 42
HMSAS *Turffontein*	whaler	355 tons	oil	17 Aug 42
HMSAS *Standerton*[29]	whaler	357 tons	oil	26 Oct 42

As well as the A/S vessels, it was usually possible at both Cape Town and Durban to provide one ship of the local minesweeping flotilla to carry out a surface patrol in the anchorage. This ship usually patrolled well inside the patrol perimeter, ready to back up an anti-submarine attack with her two depth charges or, at night, to assist in engaging small enemy surface craft or submarines coming in on the surface. Although their threat to the U-boats was small, they no doubt helped to restrict their activities. And they frequently helped pick up survivors from the nearer sinkings during the U-boat offensive, saving other shipping from taking the additional risk of stopping to do so.[30]

ADDITIONAL U-BOATS ARRIVE

On the enemy side, a batch of newly constructed IXD2 U-boats was commissioned between August and September 1942, enabling Doenitz to extend submarine operations to cover African ports in the Indian Ocean. With these additional long-range submarines available, he dispatched four boats—*U-177*, *U-178*, *U-179*, *U-181*—to relieve the Eisbar group so as to maintain constant pressure on the shipping off South Africa. The first, *U-179*, sailed from the German naval base at Kiel on 15 August, and caught up to the Eisbar boats in the waters off Cape Town in early October.[31]

On 8 October, *U-179* sank the unescorted British steam merchant *City of Athens* about 60 miles west-northwest of Cape Town, but this would be her only victory in a very short life. She was sunk with the loss of all hands later that day by depth charges from the British destroyer HMS *Active* (H14).[32]

Photo 13-7

British destroyer HMS *Active* under way.
SA Naval Museum

The destroyer had sighted the survivors of the merchantman in five rafts towed by a motor boat at dusk. Their recovery, along with a cat retrieved by survivors from the wreckage, took until 2200. Shortly afterwards, *Active* picked up a radar contact, and after illuminating it with star shells and a searchlight, opened fire on it. The contact proved to be the surfaced *U-179*. As the shells rained down, the submarine crash dove, but failed to escape an ensuing depth-charge attack by the destroyer. It was sunk, as evidenced by as a large amount of oil that came to the surface soon afterwards.[33]

The three remaining IXD2 boats—*U-177*, *U-178*, and *U-181*—left Kiel between 8 and 17 September bound for the waters off Cape Town and then into the Indian Ocean. During a six-week period off the east coast of South Africa, they travelled as far north as the Portuguese port of Lourenço Marques in the Mozambique Channel. Between 1 November and 14 December, as shown in the table below, they collectively sank 26 merchant vessels and damaged two additional ships.[34]

10th Flotilla
10. Unterseebootsflottille
Lorient, France

U-177 (IXD2)
U-178 (IXD2)
U-179 (IXD2)
U-181 (IXD2)

Date Left	U-boat	Commander	Ships Hit
15 Aug 42	*U-179*	FrgKpt. Ernst Sobe	1 S
8 Sep 42	*U-178*	Kpt. Hans Ibbeken	5 S, 1 D
12 Sep 42	*U-181*	KrvKpt. Wolfgang Luth	12 S
17 Sep 42	*U-177*	KrvKpt. Robert Gysae[35]	8 S, 1 D
		Total	26 S, 2 D

S: Sunk D: Damaged

Between 7 October and 14 December 1942, the two groups of four U-boats each, previously identified, together with a German-allied Italian submarine, the *Ammiraglio Cagni*, sank 50 vessels in African waters and damaged another three—one of which was a total loss. The *Ammiraglio Cagni*'s contribution to this horrific loss of shipping, and associated deaths of merchant mariners of various nations, as well as gun crews and/or passengers aboard some ships, was two vessels sunk, is described in the next section.

ITALIAN SUBMARINE *AMMIRAGLIO CAGNI*

The *Ammiraglio Cagni*, more commonly referred to as *Cagni*, was one of the four submarines of the Ammiragli-class ("Admirals"); identified by the surnames of famous admirals of the Italian Navy: Saint Bon, Millo, Caracciolo, and Cagni. Of the four, only the *Cagni* survived the war. The Ammiragli boats were designed for the guerre de course ("war of the chase") on distant oceans and met very high operational requirements. They could range from their home base for up to six continuous months, or about 20,000 miles. Because of their endurance, armament, and reliability, the Ammiragli were, overall, the best Italian submarines produced up to that period.[36]

The *Cagni* was under the command of Lieutenant Commander Carlo Liannazza and, because of her large carrying capacity, had mostly been employed previously for transport missions to North Africa, where fuel and ammunitions were desperately needed. Following a decision to take advantage of her exceptional range, she underwent a long period of repairs in Taranto to prepare for war in the Atlantic. On 6 October, the ocean boat departed La Maddalena, Sardinia, Italy, en route to the South African coast and possibly the Indian Ocean.[37]

Photo 13-8

The Italian submarine *Ammiraglio Cagni* (Lt. Comdr. Joseph Roselli Lorenzini) going alongside in Durban harbour flying a black flag of surrender following the Italian Armistice on 8 September 1943. She was passing near Durban and learning of the Italian armistice she entered Durban harbour under the escort of the corvette HMS *Jasmine* (K23). She had been at sea for 84 days.
SA Naval Museum

On 3 November, she sank the British motor vessel *Dagoma* off Freetown, Sierra Leone, followed, three-and-one-half weeks later, by the Greek sloop *Argo* off the Cape of Good Hope. Later during this voyage, the submarine was re-provisioned by *U-459*, after which she operated off the St. Peter and St. Paul Archipelago in the central equatorial Atlantic, before returning to BETASOM (Bordeaux Sommergibile or Sommergibili), the Italian submarine base in Bordeaux, France.[38]

REPRESENTATIVE U-BOAT ATTACK / SINKING

At 2202 hours on 8 Oct 1942, the unescorted British steam merchant *Sarthe* (Master Charles Ernest Mason) which, as previously mentioned, had failed to take in the diversion signal from Cape Town, was hit on the port side amidships underneath the bridge by one torpedo from *U-68* while proceeding at 7.5 knots 35 miles south-southwest of the Cape of Good Hope. The ship had witnessed the sinking of the American tanker SS *Swiftsure* about 8 miles ahead. She had tried to flee by altering her course towards the coast at full speed, but was too slow to escape and unable to evade the torpedo track spotted by a lookout. The explosion stopped the vessel, destroyed the port side of the bridge and the port forward lifeboat, wrecked the accommodation in that area, damaged the davits of the starboard forward lifeboat, and opened a great split on the foredeck. As the *Sarthe* settled quickly by the bow with a slight list to port, her crew of 49 and eight gunners (she was armed with one 4-inch, one 40mm and five machine guns) quickly abandoned ship in the two after lifeboats.[39]

Photo 13-9

The Clyde-built British merchant ship *Sarthe*, torpedoed and sunk by *U-68*, 35 miles south-southwest of the Cape of Good Hope.
www.photoship.co.uk

At 2239, a second torpedo struck the settling ship starboard side, just forward of the bridge, broke her in two and blasted debris and wreckage into the air that fell into the water around the lifeboats. The bow sank at once, followed a few minutes later by the after part of the ship. The survivors observed the surfaced U-boat twice during the night and saw it leaving at high speed afterwards. The submarine had been on the surface, reloading two torpedoes from the upper deck containers, when she spotted her next victim, the American steam merchant *Examelia*. At a little after dawn, 0700 on 9 October, the South African A/S whaler HMSAS *Vereeniging* (T62) picked up the survivors. She landed them at Simon's Town later that day.[40]

Photo 13-10

South African A/S whaler HMSAS *Vereeniging*.
Du Toit Collection

HMSAS *VEREENIGING*

HMSAS *Vereeniging*, formerly the *Vikingen VII*, was built in 1936 by Smith's Dock Company at Middlesborough, England, for the Vestford Whaling Company of Panama. Shortly before the war, her name had been changed to *Vestfold IX*. Requisitioned from the South Georgia Whaling Station in December 1941 by the Admiralty, she was commissioned on 27 June 1942 as HMSAS *Vereeniging* after her transfer to South Africa. The big whale catcher, and her sister ship HMSAS *Turffontein* were fine-looking craft, offering comforts far superior to that of smaller vessels of the SANF.[41]

These included forecastle messes in which a man of normal height could stand erect without banging his head on the deckhead beams.

The officers' accommodation was also better; cabins had running water, albeit only cold water, and showers with hot and cold water were provided which, unfortunately ran only very hot or very cold, rarely at a bearable temperature either way.[42]

Powerful and sleek in appearance, the whalers were sea-kindly vessels (easy on their crew and gear) except in the roughest weather. Until the procurement of frigates, they were the South African Naval Forces 'big ships.'[43]

ESCORT VESSELS DESPERATELY NEEDED

As previously noted, of the 51 ships sunk or damaged by German U-boats and the two by the Italian submarine *Cagni* in South African waters, all were sailing independently when attacked. Here for the most part, the undersea boats had the luxury of picking off easy prey, unescorted and, in some cases unarmed, ships, which included Greek merchantmen. Escorted coastal convoys were desperately needed to shepherd vessels between South African ports. To form them, additional escort vessels were required. Patrol duties off Cape Town, nearby Saldanha Bay, and Durban occupying much of the efforts of the fourteen SANF anti-submarine whalers and trawlers prevented them from being dedicated for this purpose, so other vessels would be required.

Help began to appear in December 1942, as the first of the surviving eighteen Royal Navy A/S trawlers and whalers previously employed in American waters began to arrive in South Africa.

ROLE OF WHALERS AND TRAWLERS EXPANDED

The arrival of the first four British A/S trawlers from American waters at the Cape on 24 December, was the vanguard of a group of eighteen, covered in the following chapters. These, in addition to the fourteen SANF A/S vessels, and the limited number of RN escorts available in South African waters, made it possible to introduce Group Sailings for the slower merchant ship traffic traveling between South African ports and along its coastline. These convoys were officially termed 'Group Sailings' to distinguish them from the more important 'through convoys' which were already being escorted by destroyers and larger warships.[44]

Ships bound for the east, including the Middle East, India and Australia routes, were assembled at Walvis Bay, where they were placed in two classes. The first was comprised of ships with cargo for South African ports, together with those of low speed and endurance. These went in coastal convoy—Group Sailings—to Cape Town and then along the South African coast, touching at Port Elizabeth, East London and Durban. From there, they were escorted to a deep-sea dispersal point. The second class consisted of ships which had no cargo for South African ports and were of high speed and endurance. These travelled with the others as far as Cape Town where they were formed into a separate convoy and sailed directly to a deep-sea dispersal point.[45]

West-bound ships were put into convoy at either Lourenço Marques or at Durban where ships for West Africa and South African ports, together with those of low speed and endurance were put into coastal convoy which touched at the intervening South African ports before finally proceeding to the dispersal point west of Walvis Bay. All other ships sailed direct from Durban to a dispersal point from which they took the Southern Route—a wide detour to the south of the Cape to evade the waiting U-boats. The special ships, troopers (troop ships) and all those whose speed was too much for the ordinary convoy were brought into Cape Town, whichever way they were bound, from where they sailed independently with air, and perhaps surface, escort to the dispersal point.[46]

The number of escort vessels was, however, still inadequate, and some of the newly arrived trawlers began to break down rather badly, while others were so slow that convoy speeds had to be reduced to enable them to keep station. Although the original policy at the outbreak of hostilities in 1939 made the A/S protection of South African anchorages a primary SANF commitment, it was now agreed that there was no logical reason why an exchange of RN ships equally suitable for this task, should not take place. As a result, whenever the larger and more suitable oil-burning South African A/S whalers involved in anchorage patrols were released to reinforce the newly formed RN escort groups, their place on local patrols was taken over by some of the recently arrived coal-burning RN A/S vessels which were placed under South African operational control.[47]

When the Group Sailing scheme commenced on 20 January 1943, one of the five escort groups was comprised entirely of SANF vessels. Functioning under RN operational control, these escort groups were mainly employed sheparding merchantmen between Cape Town and Durban. On 23 January, *Standerton*, *Vereeniging*, and *Turffontein* sailed with the first of these convoys to leave Cape Town for Durban and *Immortelle*, *Sonneblom* and *Pretoria* began escorting soon afterwards. Although the system of keeping the SANF ships together was not adhered to for long, partly because it was preferable to have one corvette in each group, one or two SANF ships sailed between Cape Town and Durban every week—sometimes together, sometimes with different convoys until the end of the submarine offensive in September, when Group Sailings ceased for the time being.[48]

The arrangement for SANF/RN ship exchanges was not, however, strictly carried out. Owing to rather frequent mechanical breakdowns among the recently arrived RN trawlers and with the number of escorts for most convoys soon being increased to four or more, there were frequent occasions when the Cape Town A/S patrol system was reduced by one ship.[49]

Photo 13-11

When the Group Sailing scheme commenced in January 1943, one of the five escort groups was comprised entirely of SANF vessels. Seen here is HMSAS *Pretoria*. Du Toit Collection

Photo 13-12

The Flower-class corvette HMS *Honesty* (K285) departing Port Elizabeth, South Africa. The Flower-class, together with SANF and RN anti-submarine whalers and trawlers, formed the backbone of the coastal convoy system.
FW Neaveto

14

RN Trawlers Dispatched to South African Waters

Map 14-1

Northern half of South America; Recife, capital of Pernambuco state in northeastern Brazil, is an Atlantic seaport

In autumn 1942, the bulk of the eighteen surviving British trawlers loaned to the U.S. Navy were withdrawn to West African waters, to combat growing U□boat activity there. (In early 1943, the remaining ones were also withdrawn and followed the others.) From the U.S. East Coast the trawlers traversed the Caribbean Sea to Trinidad, then on to the Brazilian port of Pernambuco (today Recife). There, they coaled ship (loaded coal required for fuel) for passage to West Africa. En route to Pernambuco, some trawlers engaged in a fruitless reconnaissance off the French penal settlement of Devil's Island (penal colony of Cayenne in the Salvation Islands of French Guiana), where the presence of U□boats had been suspected. From Pernambuco, they set out across the "narrows of the Atlantic" to Freetown, Sierra Leone, from where they proceeded down the African west coast.[1]

Map 14-2

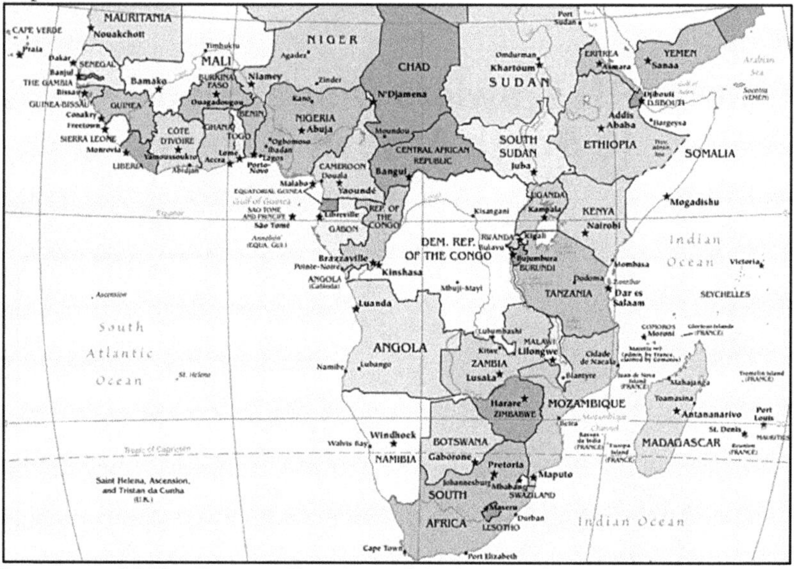

Lower part of Africa; Freeport, Sierra Leone is in the upper left portion of the map

Eighteen Royal Naval Patrol Service Trawlers and Whalers

A/S Trawlers	**A/S Trawlers**	**A/S Trawlers**
HMT *Arctic Explorer*	HMT *Le Tigre*	HMT *St. Loman*
HMT *Cape Warwick*	HMT *Northern Chief*	HMT *St. Zeno*
HMT *Coventry City*	HMT *Northern Dawn*	HMT *Stella Polaris*
HMT *Hertfordshire*	HMT *Northern Duke*	HMT *Wellard*
HMT *Lady Elsa*	HMT *Northern Isles*	**A/S Whalers**
HMT *Lady Rosemary*	HMT *Norwich City*	HMS *Buttermere*
		HMS *Wastwater*

ARRIVAL AT TAKORADI HARBOUR, GOLD COAST

It's not clear when the RN trawlers first arrived in African waters. One of the groups—HMTs *Hertfordshire*, *Cape Warwick*, *St. Loman*, *Northern Isles*, and *Le Tigre*—had departed Cape Henry, Virginia bound for Trinidad, on 26 October 1942, upon their transfer from the U.S. Fifth Naval District, headquartered in Norfolk, Virginia.[2]

Northern Isles arrived at Pointe Noire (a port on the Atlantic, 95 miles north of the mouth of the Congo River) on 27 November. Pointe Noire, then the capital of French Equatorial Africa, is today in the Republic of Congo. A West Africa Command, Freetown War Diary entry which noted that *Northern Isles* arrived "from Takoradi escorting," did not identify her escorted vessel(s), nor the date on which she had stood out of Takoradi well up the west coast of Africa.[3]

Map 14-3

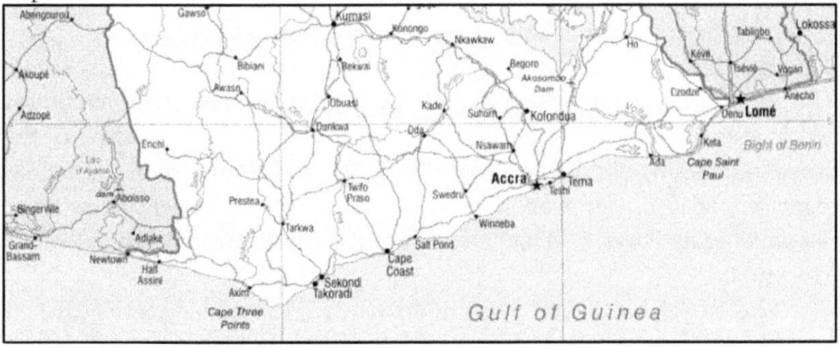

Coastline of Ghana (formerly British Colony of the Gold Coast), Takoradi is located on the map directly above the word "British" in the preceding line

Map 14-4

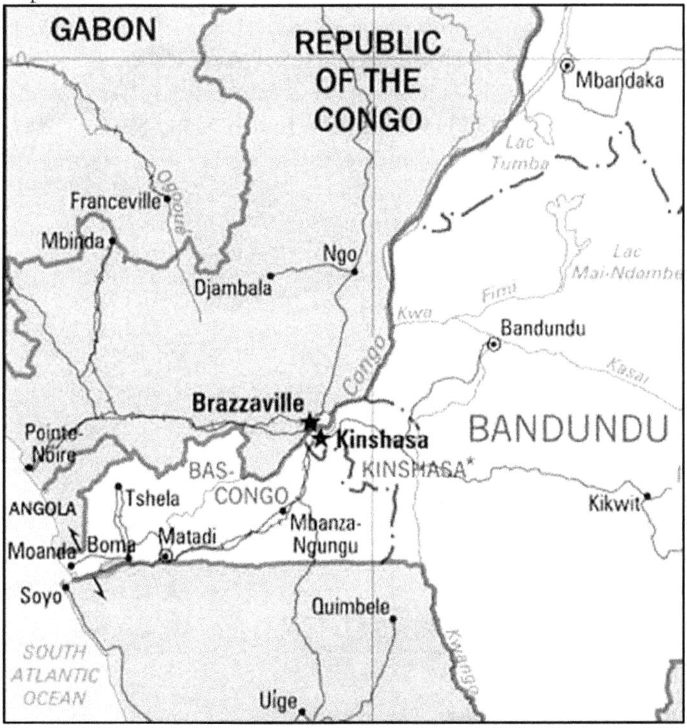

Pointe Noire is situated 95 miles northward of the mouth of the Congo River;
the important river port of Matadi lies up the Congo River near the border with Angola

The port city of Takoradi was the site of a Royal Navy base created during the war as part of its South Atlantic Station. Under the command of Naval Officer-in-Charge, Takoradi, the base existed from 1943 to 1945, during which its harbour served as an important staging point for British Atlantic convoys and protection patrols.[4]

The trawlers *Northern Dawn* and *Coventry City* arrived at Takoradi Harbour on 22 November 1942. Soon after, they began coastal convoy work, escorting with *St. Zeno*, a convoy to Pointe Noire consisting of the Royal Navy M/S trawler *Magnolia* (T31) and boom defense vessel *Barbrake* (Z173), as well as the Turkish ferry vessel *Tuzia* with accompanying tugs. This small group arrived safely there on 7 December.[5]

The Royal Navy had just employed *St. Zeno* to help safeguard its naval vessels and mobile port equipment. She had arrived at Takoradi on 24 November with His Majesty's A/S trawler *Spaniard* (FY144), A/S whaler *Southern Gem* (K247), M/S trawlers *Magnolia* (T31) and *Canna* (T161), M/S tugs *Empire Pat* and *Empire Sam*, and a floating crane.[6]

On the same day that *Northern Dawn*, *Coventry City*, and *St. Zeno* made Pointe Noire, 7 December 1942, the trawlers *St. Loman*, *Stella Polaris*, and *Northern Chief*, arrived at Takoradi with HM A/S trawler *Sphene* (FY249) and the minesweeper HMIS (His Majesty's Indian Ship) *Khyber* (J190). The group had journeyed there from Freetown, Sierra Leone, farther up the coast.[7]

Map 14-5

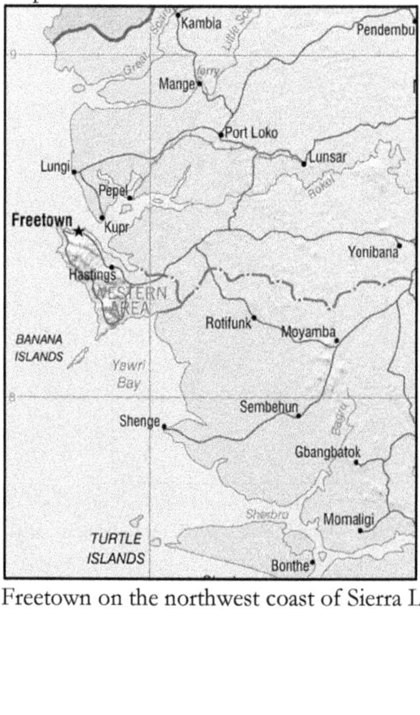

Freetown on the northwest coast of Sierra Leone

By this time, a majority of the eighteen Royal Navy A/S vessels that were being withdrawn from American waters had arrived in African waters. Before progressing further in describing their patrol and escort activities, a review of Royal Navy nomenclature, and an explanation of the Royal Navy/South African military command structure then in effect in Africa is in order.

RN SOUTH ATLANTIC STATION, 1939-1958

The Royal Navy's South Atlantic Station (also known as South Atlantic Command) was a major naval command area created in 1939 from the then existing Africa Station, as one of the geographical divisions into which the RN divided its worldwide responsibilities.[8]

Shortly before war broke out in 1939, the Commander-in-Chief, South Atlantic Station, Vice Adm. Sir. George Lyon, RN, was ordered by the Admiralty to move his headquarters from Simon's Town, South Africa, to Freetown in Sierra Leone. Located midway between Britain and the South African Cape, Freetown was favorably situated for protecting shipping in the South Atlantic during the early stages of the war. Lyon left Captain (later Commodore) Charles Gage Stuart, RN, as the senior officer at Simon's Town.[9]

The South Atlantic Station's area of responsibility covered the Atlantic Ocean south of a line drawn between the northern French West African (now Mauritanian) border and French Guiana and the Southern Ocean and Indian Ocean east of a line drawn south from the western entrance to the Magellan Strait and west of a line drawn south from the South African/Mozambican border. The South Atlantic Station had bases at Freetown, Sierra Leone (HMS Eland); Simon's Town, South Africa (HMS Afrikander); and Port Stanley, Falklands (HMS Pursuivant).[10]

Local Area Command	Active
Bathurst (today, Banjul, Gambia, West Africa)	1942-1944
Durban, South Africa	1942-1948
Falkland Islands	1939-1946
Freetown	1939-1944, 1945-1946
Lagos, Nigeria	1941-1944, 1945-1946
Simon's Town/Cape Town, South Africa	1939-1967*
Takoradi, Gold Coast (today Ghana)[11]	1944-1946

* South Atlantic and South America Station from 1960-1967

Map 14-6

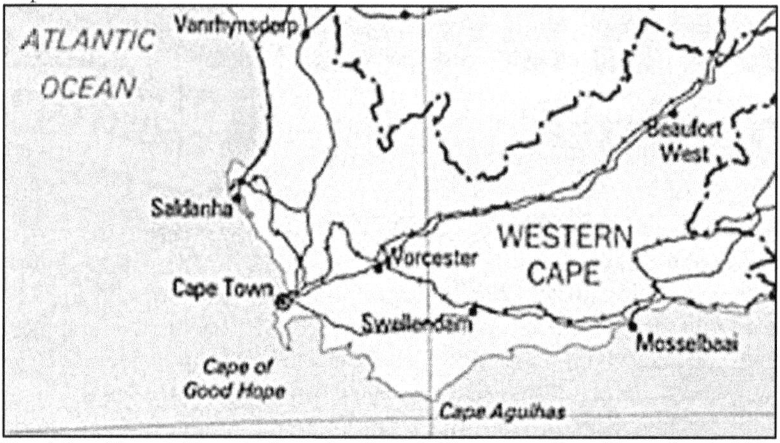

Naval Base Simon's Town is situated at Simon's Town, near Cape Town, South Africa

Photo 14-1

HM Naval Base and Dockyard, Simon's Town.
Du Toit Collection

ROYAL NAVY WEST AFRICAN COMMAND, 1942-1945

In March 1942, the Royal Navy established a West African Command at Freetown, headed by a vice admiral with the title of Flag Officer, West Africa. This new command was created—as part of a larger Admiralty re-organisation of commands worldwide—as a result of the growing importance of Freetown as a major base for convoy escorts.[12]

ROYAL NAVY SOUTH ATLANTIC STATION (SOUTH ATLANTIC COMMAND) HEADQUARTERS MOVED TO CAPE TOWN

Photo 14-2

Shipping off Cape Town, South Africa, circa 1939-1945.
Australian War Memorial photograph 302824

The headquarters of the West African Command, previously mentioned, was firmly established on 26 March 1942 at Freetown, after the Commander-in-Chief, South Atlantic (South Atlantic Station), Vice Adm. William Eric Campbell Tait, RN, had relocated himself and his staff, back to Simon's Town as ordered, in February 1942. In April he began to make arrangements to transfer his operational headquarters to Cape Town to be in closer touch with the South African Prime Minister General Smuts and military authorities, although he continued to fly his flag at Simon's Town where his administrative headquarters remained for the rest of the war. In Cape Town, Tait headed a Combined Headquarters (at the end of Orange Street) where the South African General Officer Commanding Coastal Area, Maj. Gen. Isaac Pierre de Villiers, and his staff were co-located. Within the headquarters' integrated Combined Operations Room, and War Room, the Royal Navy, and South African land, air and naval forces shared all relevant information regarding shipping movements, intelligence and reconnaissance. This on-site interaction between members of the Royal Navy and South African military services, facilitated Tait and de Villiers to cooperate closely and take swift, collective actions when necessary.[13]

Photo 14-3

Maj. Gen. Isaac Pierre de Villiers, General Officer Commanding 2nd South African Infantry Division, discussing plans with some of his officers, Brigadier F. W. Cooper, Colonel H. B. Klopper and Lieutenant T. W. Charles, at Sidi Omar, Libya, 1941. Australian War Memorial photograph 022152

RELATED COASTAL AREA COMMAND

Soon after movement of the headquarters of the South Atlantic Station to Cape Town, Prime Minister Jan Smuts decided to establish a Coastal Area Command to centralise control over South Africa's coastal defences. The Coastal Area Command under Maj. Gen. de Villiers was responsible for the defence of an area roughly 100 miles wide along the entire South African coast. The coastline was divided into several smaller sectors, each with its own commander. These commands, commonly referred to as 'Fortresses,' corresponded with the principal South African ports:

- Cape Town
- Walvis Bay
- Outeniqua
- Port Elizabeth
- East London
- Durban[14]

Each Fortress had a Combined Operations Room, which gathered local information on the movement of shipping, reports from coastal air patrols, radar plots, troop locations, and the positions of patrol vessels. Anti-submarine measures and fixed defences were also linked to various area Ops Rooms, including the combined one in Cape Town. The analysis and display of this information allowed for accurate military decision making, resulting in minimum delays when dealing with emergencies or false alarms. As a rule, the various Operations Rooms passed all their information to the Coastal Area Command, which could then allocate military forces to the Fortresses when necessary.[15]

The formation of the Coastal Area Command coincided with the formal establishment on 1 July 1942, of the South Atlantic Station Headquarters Combined Operations Room in Cape Town.[16]

RAF HELPS FILL PATROL AIRCRAFT SHORTFALL

While the South African Coastal Area Command, in conjunction with the Royal Navy South Atlantic Command at Cape Town, expended efforts to combat the German U-boats, they were not entirely adequate and considerable assistance was still required. RN trawlers arriving from American waters in late 1942 and taking up both coastal convoy escort duties and local A/S patrol duties, relieved some of the strain on the South African whalers and trawlers that were previously limited to A/S patrol duties. There remained still too few escort and patrol vessels, but the greatest need, after the arrival of the additional ships, was for anti-submarine patrol aircraft to conduct exhaustive searches of ocean waters, and to find and attack U-boats before they could target shipping.

Photo 14-4

A Consolidated PBY Catalina aircraft of No. 240 Squadron RAF moored on Loch Ryan, Scotland, circa March 1941.
Australian War Memorial photograph 009102

The South African Air Force (SAAF), which was limited to coastal patrol missions, had no long-range maritime patrol or associated anti-submarine capability at that stage, and was unable to carry out a defence of the Cape Sea route on its own. This untenable situation was similar to that which commander, Eastern Sea Frontier faced during the early months of the U-boat onslaught on the U.S. Eastern Seaboard—he had too few patrol and escort vessels, and fewer still, patrol aircraft to even slow the enemy's efforts.[17]

This situation improved markedly in early 1943, when the Royal Air Force began operating long-range PBY Catalinas from a new flying boat base at Congellas in Durban Harbour. After Cape Town, Durban was the most important South African port. Its facilities were considerably expanded as the war progressed. Durban guarded the eastern end of the long coastline that stretched between it and Cape Town; it was the first port of call for ships from Australia and India; and was well placed for the protection of ships transiting the Mozambique Channel while plying the Middle East Route towards/from the Suez Canal.[18]

Forward RAF PBY operating bases were also established at Lake St. Lucia, and later Lake Umsingazi at Richards Bay on the northeast coast of Natal, South Africa, for long-range Indian Ocean operations. Plane detachments were sent to Langebaan on the western Cape coast for operations to the south. The sturdy long endurance twin-engined Catalinas flying from these locations would be available to patrol the Cape sea route, escort convoys, and counter the submarine threat to shipping with other RAF squadrons and detachments based in Kenya and Tanganyika in East Africa, and the Indian Ocean islands of Madagascar and Mauritius.[19]

Photo 14-5

The seaplane base at Congella in Durban at the end of World War II, with Sunderland maritime patrol aircraft staged at the facility.
Du Toit Collection

TWO A/S TRAWLERS WHICH ARRIVED BEFORE THE SUBMARINE LULL

Two trawlers, HMT *Norwich City* and HMT *Arctic Explorer*, whose arrival dates are unknown, were plying African coastal waters before the Dutch merchant vessel SS *Sawahloento* became the last victim of an Operation EISBAR boat (*U-177*) on 14 December 1942.

On 8 December, the Free French corvette *Commandant d'Estienne d'Orves* (K93), HMT *Norwich City*, HMT *Stella Polaris*, and motor launches ML *302* and *209* sailed from Takoradi. Two days later, *Norwich City* and *Stella Polaris* arrived at Lagos, Nigeria, from Takoradi escorting four ships, then sailed for Walvis Bay escorting the Norwegian motor ship *Hai Lee*. Their destination was Matadi, 93 miles up the Congo River from the port of Banana at its mouth. On 14 December, returning down river, the trawlers arrived with *Hai Lee* at Banana. The Banana Peninsula, a sandy piece of land jutting into the mouth of the river at the southern tip of the Belgian Congo's (today, Democratic Republic of Congo) tiny sliver of coastline was the site of a naval base.[20]

On 9 December, the six vessels of Convoy ST 46—*Belgian Fisherman*, *Biafra*, *Camerata*, *Hudson*, *James Turner*, and *Lorca*—sailed from Freetown, escorted by HM trawlers *Arctic Explorer*, *Cape Warwick*, *Le Tigre*, and *Indian Star* (FY208). All of the escorted ships were British, except for the *Belgian Fisherman*, and American *James Turner*. All arrived safely at Takoradi on 14 December 1942.[21]

DUNEDIN STAR GROUNDING

HMT *Northern Duke*, (T/Lt. George William Osborne Howe, RNR), which had departed Charleston, South Carolina, for Freetown on 19 October 1942 in company with HM trawlers *Stella Polaris* and *Northern Dawn*, while on passage to Simon's Town was tasked with assisting in the salvage of the Blue Star liner *Dunedin Star* cargo. Rather than being torpedoed, *Dunedin Star* had struck a poorly charted reef just south of the boundary between Portuguese Angola and South West Africa on the evening of 29 November 1942.[22]

Northern Duke arrived on the scene on 20 December after the rescue of survivors had been completed and was tasked, together with the SANF minesweeping trawlers HMSAS *Crassula* and *Nerine*, with the salvage and transportation of the *Dunedin Star*'s vital war cargo. The *Dunedin Star*, which had been on passage from Britain to Cape Town and the Middle East, had been independently routed close to the coast as an anti-submarine measure. She had remained afloat, but as she was in danger of sinking, her master had beached her a few hours later at a point 350 miles north of Walvis Bay.[23]

Map 14-7

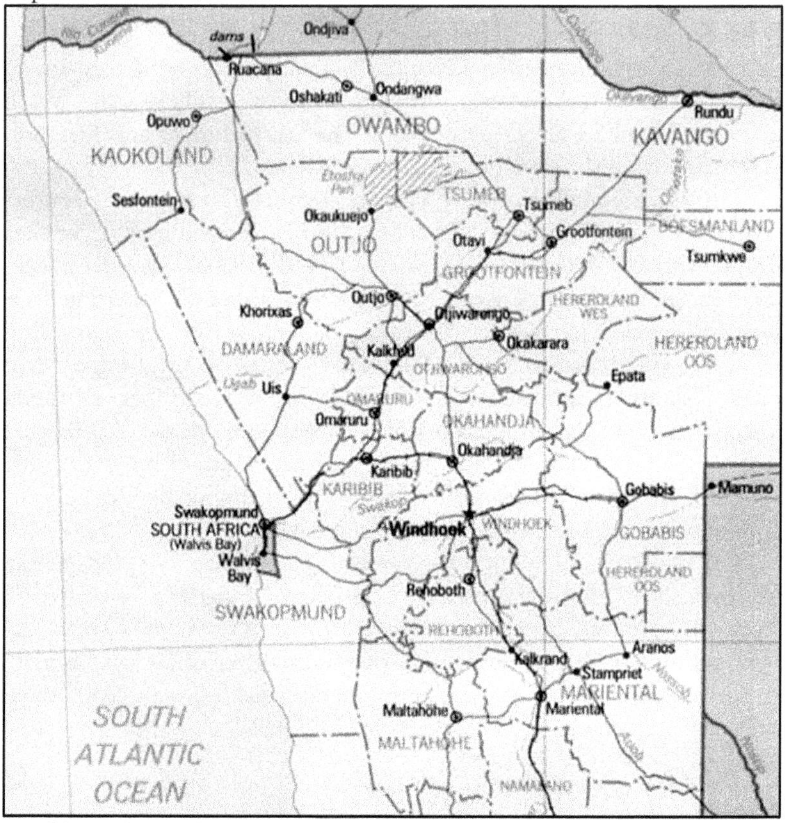

Namibia northern and central coastline

Walvis Bay was a port town on the west coast of South West Africa (today Namibia). Britain had occupied Walvis Bay in 1838 to keep the deep-water harbour out of the Kaiser's hands in the early colonisation days. The territory was formally annexed by Britain in 1884 as part of the Cape Colony and became part of the newly formed Union of South Africa in 1910. After being briefly taken by the Germans in 1915, South African forces recaptured Walvis Bay during the early part of World War I. This occurred during the South West Africa campaign, involving the conquest and occupation of German South West Africa by forces from the Union of South Africa acting on behalf of the British imperial government. South Africa was later awarded a mandate by the League of Nations to administer the territory. Even after Namibia gained its independence in 1990, Walvis Bay remained South African sovereign territory until ceded to Namibia as an act of African solidarity after Nelson Mandela was elected president of South Africa in 1994.[24]

Unnecessarily, as it turned out, 63 persons, of which 21 were fare paying passengers, including eight women and three young children, were landed on the open beach. They were then stranded with little food and water, without shelter and far from help after the ship's only motorboat was driven ashore and put out of action by the heavy surf, a permanent feature of that coastline. The remaining 43 of the crew, including the master, were later rescued by two passing merchant ships.[25]

Water and provisions had been floated ashore on rafts by *Nerine* in early December. She returned with a surf-boat on the 9th, and 26 of those ashore were subsequently brought off through the heavy surf with much difficulty before the surf-boat capsized and was damaged beyond repair. The remainder of survivors were rescued with considerable difficulty by a land rescue expedition the following week. The SAAF after unsuccessfully attempting to drop water containers had dropped dry provisions but one of the Ventura bombers, which had decided to land near the survivors to provide water, got bogged down in the sand and the crew joined the survivors. Although it eventually was able to take off, it crashed on its way back to Walvis Bay and became a total loss. Another loss was the government tug *Sir Charles Elliot*, which hugged the coast too closely and ran ashore on her return voyage to Walvis Bay with the loss of two lives.[26]

Dunedin Star remained largely intact long enough for a sizeable amount of her valuable war cargo to be salvaged by *Crassula, Nerine* and *Northern Duke. Northern Duke* was at first employed on patrolling to seaward of the wreck. Later she embarked some of the liner's deck cargo and sailed on the 27th. In all, the three ships salvaged about 300 tons of cargo which included 139 packages of confidential documents, 3,795 bags of navy, army and civilian mail and a vast assortment of equipment which ranged in size from Oerlikon guns and aircraft tyres (tires) to charts and wireless valves.[27]

Photo 14-6

British cargo liner *Dunedin Star* hard aground on the Skeleton Coast.
SA Naval Museum

15

Operation SEEHUND U-boats sent to South African Waters

Photo 15-1

Gross Admiral Karl Doenitz, German Navy.
National Archives photograph #208-PU-52P-1

In December 1942, Admiral Doenitz dispatched a third group of U-boats to the South African coast to attack shipping along the extended Allied supply routes. The type IXC U-boats that constituted those of the second Eisbar group, had proved ill-suited for operations in the distant waters. Their limited fuel capacity was insufficient even when refueled along the way by Milch Cows, and this restraint significantly reduced their time in South African waters.[1]

Despite their limitations, Doenitz was again forced to deploy four more type IXC U-boats for operations off Cape Town, as there was only one of the more desirable type IXD2 available, for the five boat deployment. These submarines, identified below, along with their commanders and numbers of ships hit, launched Operation SEEHUND, a new German submarine offensive in South African waters. They were supported by the Milch Cow *U-459*.[2]

12th Flotilla
12 Unterseebootsflottille
Bordeaux (France)

U-459 **(XIV)**
U-182 **(IXD2)**

10th Flotilla
10 Unterseebootsflottille
Lorient, France

U-160 (IXC)
U-506 **(IXC)**
U-509 **(IXC)**
U-516 **(IXC)**

Date Left	U-boat/ Type	Commander	Ships Hit
20 Dec 42	*U-459*/XIV Milch Cow	KrvKpt. Georg von Wilamowitz-Möllendorf	
14 Dec 42	*U-506*/IXC	Kptlt. Erich Würdemann	2 S
23 Dec 42	*U-516*/IXC	KrvKpt. Gerhard Wiebe	4 S
23 Dec 42	*U-509*/IXC	KrvKpt. Werner Witte	1 S, 1 T
6 Jan 43	*U-160*/IXC	Kptlt. Georg Lassen	6 S, 2 D
9 Dec 42	*U-182*/IXD2	Kptlt. Asmus Nicolai Clausen	3 S
		Total	16 S, 2 D, 1 T

S: Sunk D: Damaged T: Total loss owing to extensive damage suffered

The four type IXC boats from the 10th Flotilla—*U-506*, *U-516*, *U-509*, and *U-160*—left Lorient, France, between 14 December 1942 and 6 January 1943 for South African waters. They were joined by *U-182*, the long-range submarine which had departed Horten, in the Oslo Fjord in German-occupied Norway, on 9 December. Norway was invaded by German forces in April 1940 and, even before she fell to Germany in the spring, U-boats had begun to operate from her many favorable and poorly defended ports.[3]

Photo 15-2

German light cruiser *Emden* in Oslo Fiord, Norway, in the late summer of 1941, with a camouflage scheme of black and white stripes breaking up her grey paint. Naval History and Heritage Command photograph #NH 80887

CONDITIONS CHANGING IN AFRICAN WATERS

The Seehund boats arrived off Cape Town during February 1943 to find that operational conditions in the South Atlantic, and more notably off the coast of South Africa, had changed drastically since October 1942. The lull of nearly two months after the sinking of *Sawahloento* on 14 December 1942 had given South Atlantic Command an opportunity to overhaul the anti-submarine defences. The Royal Navy and South African Union Defence Force (UDF), and the Allies in general, had now adopted a number of defensive anti-submarine measures, aimed at curtailing the losses of merchant ships around the South African coast. One important measure, as previously mentioned, involved the implementation of a coastal convoy escort system.[4]

ADDITIONAL ROYAL NAVY A/S TRAWLERS ARRIVE

During the lull in the U-boat merchant vessel sinkings—between 14 December 1942, when the last victim fell prey to an Eisbar boat, and 10 February 1943, when the first was sunk by a Seehund boat—a few additional Royal Navy trawlers arrived from American waters. The thirteen vessels in the table below were already on hand, engaged in escort and local patrol duties.

Royal Navy A/S Trawlers

HMT *Arctic Explorer*	HMT *Northern Chief*	HMT *Norwich City*
HMT *Cape Warwick*	HMT *Northern Dawn*	HMT *St. Loman*
HMT *Coventry City*	HMT *Northern Duke*	HMT *St. Zeno*
HMT *Hertfordshire*	HMT *Northern Isles*	HMT *Stella Polaris*
HMT *Le Tigre*		

The three additional A/S trawlers and two A/S whalers that arrived later were as follows:

RN A/S Trawlers	RN A/S Trawlers	RN A/S Whalers
HMT *Lady Elsa*	HMT *Wellard*	HMS *Buttermere*
HMT *Lady Rosemary*		HMS *Wastwater*

The new arrivals travelled in pairs. For example, on 17 December 1942, HM trawlers *Lady Elsa* and *Wellard* sailed southward from Freetown on passage down the West African coast to Simon's Town with stops along the way. They arrived at the RN base at Takoradi on the 22nd, and stood out again on Christmas Eve, bound for Pointe Noire, which lay a little to the north of the Congo River mouth. The trawlers then proceeded up the Congo to the river port of Bomba, arriving there on 4 January. After several replenishment days, they sailed south from Bomba for Walvis Bay. War diary entries do not reveal when *Lady Elsa* and *Wellard* left Walvis Bay and arrived at Simon's Town.[5]

Continuing the theme of RN trawlers operating in pairs, HMT *Lady Rosemary* (a new arrival) sailed from Freetown on 27 December 1942. It's likely that she stood out with *Hertfordshire* (an earlier arrival in African waters) because on 4 January, they reached Takoradi together. The two departed there on the 6th with the Royal Navy motor launches *ML 263*, and *ML 1078*. It's not clear where they were bound. The next two pieces of information about the vessels based on pertinent war diary entries are a little muddled, but document the trawlers were working their way down the West African coast, carrying out Royal Navy tasking while en route. Thereafter, their duties appeared to mostly involve escorting other RN vessels between coastal bases:

- Tuesday, 12 January 1943: H.M. Ships *Hertfordshire* and *Lady Rosemary* arrived and sailed for Pointe Noire
- Wednesday, 13 January 1943: H.M. Ships *Hertfordshire* and *Lady Rosemary* arrived Banana from Pointe Noire and sailed again for Walvis Bay having disembarked balance of the crew of the barquentine HMS *Mercator* (which functioned as a rest home for submariners)[6]

LAST TWO ROYAL NAVY A/S VESSELS ARRIVE

The whalers HMS *Buttermere* and HMS *Wastwater* were the final Royal Navy A/S vessels to be recalled from American waters. (Because these two "King's Ships" were whalers and not trawlers, HMS is used in lieu of the conventional HMT for trawlers.) They arrived at Freetown in early April 1943. As they were nearing the end of their Atlantic crossing, *Wastwater* was tasked with rescuing survivors of the SS *Celtic Star*, sunk southwest of Freetown on the afternoon of 29 March 1943 by the Italian submarine *R.Smg. Giuseppe Finzi*. Before describing this rescue action, some background information is in order.

Several weeks earlier, HMS *Buttermere* had departed U.S. Naval Operating Base, Trinidad, on 4 February, escorting the British motor minesweepers *M/S 102*, *103*, *105*, *106*, and *107* to Pernambuco, Brazil. As noted by an Admiralty War Diary entry, *Wastwater* was prevented from departing with this group as planned, owing to an engineering casualty:

> 4 February 1943: Sailed *Buttermere* escorting HM M/S *107*, *102*, *103*, *105*, *106*... *Wastwater* prevented sailing by boiler defect delay four days and will be sailed independently when ready by similar route to overtake group at Pernambuco.[7]

Repaired more quickly than expected, *Wastwater* was able to depart on the morning of 7 February, to join HM motor minesweepers and *Buttermere*.[8]

Photo 15-3

One of two A/S whalers deployed to Cape waters, HMS *Wastwater*.
SA Naval Museum

It's not clear when *Wastwater* and *Buttermere* left Pernambuco, but it seems they sailed independently of each other across the Atlantic, each escorting a group of minesweepers. On 30 March, as noted previously, *Wastwater*, escorting the BYMS (British Yard Minesweepers) *J805*, *J806*, *J807*, and *J808*, was ordered to search for survivors from the British refrigerated cargo liner SS *Celtic Star*. The old vessel, completed in 1918, was outbound from Freetown, on passage to Montevideo and Buenos Aires, when torpedoed near the track of *Wastwater* and the minesweepers.[9]

Searching in conjunction with the Royal Air Force, *Wastwater* found and rescued 60 survivors from the *Celtic Star*, and also picked up 3 aircrew from a plane that crashed after sighting the *Celtic Star* survivors. All personnel recovered by *Wastwater* were landed at Freetown on 2 April. Two *Celtic Star* crewmembers died in the attack by the Italian submarine *Finzi* (Mario Rossetto), a Canadian was captured, but all the remaining survivors, left in boats or in the sea, were rescued. (Presumably, the Canadian was the master, as the captains of sunken vessels were routinely taken prisoner in an effort to try to gain information about Allied shipping). *Wastwater*'s escorted minesweepers, continuing on their own, had arrived earlier at Freetown on 31 March.[10]

Photo 15-4

HMS *J808* (later reclassified *BYMS-2008*) at Whitestone, New York, 18 October 1942.
Mystic Seaport, Rosenfeld Collection

On 8 April, HMS *Buttermere* with HM MMS (Motor Minesweepers) *102*, *103*, *105*, *106*, and *107* arrived at Freetown from Recife, capital of Pernambuco on the northeast coast of Brazil. All these motor minesweepers, except for *107*, which was slated for the Persian Gulf, were on passage to the Levant in the Mediterranean.[11]

OPERATION SEEHUND COMMENCES

During operations in South African waters between 10 February and 5 April 1943, the Seehund Group sank only 16 vessels, and damaged three others. One of the damaged ships later became a total loss, broken by wave action after being abandoned and drifting ashore. As shown in the table, while operating off the South African coast in February (between Cape Town and Port Elizabeth), sinking results were exceptionally poor. Over a period of eighteen days, only five ships—MS *Queen Anne*, SS *Helmspey*, SS *Deer Lodge*, SS *Llanashe*, and the Dutch submarine tender HNMS *Colombia*—were sent to the bottom.[12]

All the victims were unescorted, with the exception of the British *Queen Anne* (Master Charles Hicking Radford), which was part of Convoy CA-11. On the morning of 9 February, *U-509* (KrvKpt.

Werner Witte) had sighted a convoy of six ships steering west from the Agulhas Bank, and a single ship next day, but he could not get into a firing position against either of these targets. That evening he identified three ships steering southeast, and later two more moving in the opposite direction. He surfaced and closed, and at 0219 hit the *Queen Anne*, 4,937 tons, with a single torpedo at 400 metres, some eight miles south-southwest of Cape Agulhas.[13]

Photo 15-5

The *Queen Anne*, sunk by *U-509* on 10 February 1943. 17 survivors were picked up by HMT *St. Zeno* and landed at Cape Town.
Old Ship Photo Galleries

Photo 15-6

HMT *St. Zeno* about to be slipped at Port Elizabeth, South Africa, circa 1943.
Frank W. Neave

The RN escort trawler HMT *St. Zeno* (T/Lt. John Kirke Craig, RNVR) fired a star-shell and, on sighting the U-boat, followed with two rounds of gunfire and then seven depth charges after she dived. Undamaged, *U-509* surfaced a little over an hour later. Witte was questioning survivors from the *Queen Anne*, when his radar detector picked up radar waves and he quickly submerged. The master and four crewmembers were lost; but the remaining 30 crewmembers and nine gunners survived. Seventeen of the survivors were picked up by *St. Zeno* and landed at Cape Town. The remaining 22 survivors in a lifeboat made landfall at Bredasdorp near Cape Agulhas.[14]

By the beginning of March, the Seehund boats had moved northeastward toward the waters off Durban and Lourenço Marques, Mozambique, where they anticipated more shipping. However, during the whole of March, only ten merchantmen were sunk, and two damaged. Five of the vessels sunk were unescorted. Of the remaining seven: *U-160* sank four ships of Convoy DN-21 and damaged two others, while *U-516* sank one member of Convoy CN-13. Descriptions of these actions follow the table.[15]

Vessels sunk in the South Africa Waters by *U-160*, *U-182*, *U-506*, *U-509*, and *U-516* (10 February-5 April 1943)

Date	Ship	U-boat	Torpedoed/Sunk
10 Feb 43 Convoy CA-11	*Queen Anne*	*U-509*	torpedoed and sunk eight miles SSE of Cape Agulhas
11 Feb 43 unescorted	*Helmspey*	*U-516*	torpedoed and sunk 11 miles south of Cape St. Francis, Cape Colony
17 Feb 43 unescorted	*Deer Lodge*	*U-516*	torpedoed and sunk about 60 miles east of Port Elizabeth
17 Feb 43 unescorted	*Llanashe*	*U-182*	torpedoed and sunk south of Cape St. Francis, Cape Colony
27 Feb 43 escorted	*Colombia*	*U-516*	torpedoed and sunk near Simon's Town
3 Mar 43 Convoy DN-21	*Harvey W. Scott*	*U-160*	torpedoed and sunk 40 miles south of Port St. Johns, South Africa
3 Mar 43 DN-21	*Nirpura*	*U-160*	torpedoed and sunk 40 miles south of Port St. Johns, South Africa
3 Mar 43 DN-21	*Tibia* (D)	*U-160*	torpedoed and damaged 40 miles south of Port St. Johns, South Africa
4 Mar 43 DN-21	*Empire Mahseer*	*U-160*	torpedoed and sunk ENE of East London
4 Mar 43 DN-21	*Marietta E.*	*U-160*	torpedoed and sunk ENE of East London
4 Mar 43 DN-21	*Sheaf Crown* (D)	*U-160*	torpedoed and damaged ENE of East London

7 Mar 43 unescorted	*Sabor*	*U-506*	torpedoed and sunk SE of Mossel Bay
8 March unescorted	*James B. Stephens*	*U-160*	torpedoed and sunk about 150 miles NE of Durban
9 Mar 43 unescorted	*Tabor*	*U-506*	torpedoed and sunk SE of Cape Agulhas
10 Mar 43 unescorted	*Richard D. Spaight*	*U-182*	torpedoed and sunk about 270 miles NNE of Durban
11 Mar 43 unescorted	*Aelybryn*	*U-160*	torpedoed and sunk ENE of Durban
20 Mar 43 Convoy CN-13	*Nortun*	*U-516*	torpedoed and sunk about 70 miles southwest of Luderitz Bay, South West Africa (today Namibia) after dispersal from Convoy CN-13
2 Apr 43 Convoy NC-9	*City of Baroda* (T)	*U-509*	torpedoed 90 miles south of Luderitz Bay; abandoned and drifted ashore, a total loss after waves broke up the wreck
5 Apr 43 unescorted	*Aloe*	*U-182*	torpedoed and sunk 420 miles SE of Durban[16]

A CONVOY IN TROUBLE

On 3 March, Convoy DN-21—consisting of eleven merchantmen—departed Durban. The 21st such convoy sailing from Durban to the deep-sea dispersal point, it was escorted by the corvette HMS *Nigella* (K19), HM trawlers *Norwich City* and *Viviana* (FY23), and HM A/S whaler *Sondra* (FY355). The convoy was supposed to disperse on 4 March, with its member merchant vessels then proceeding on their own to various ports with cargos of essential war materiel.[17]

Convoy DN-21 Merchantmen

Baron Maclay	*Harvey W. Scott* (S)	*San Francisco*
Benvannoch	*Marietta E.* (S)	*Sheaf Crown* (D)
Carolinian	*Nirpura* (S)	*Tibia* (D)
Charles F. Meyer	*Ocean Vespers*	
Empire Mahseer (S)	*Sabor*[18]	

S: Sunk D: Damaged

At 1400 on 3 March, *U-160*, under the command of Kptlt. Georg Lassen, met the convoy while patrolling off Port Shepstone south of Durban, and turned and ran along a parallel course. Lassen lost contact with the convoy at dusk but pursued on the surface, and easily overtook the 8-knot convoy which was pinpointed by escorting aircraft showing their navigation lights.[19]

The night was dark and cloudy, with a slight swell running, and Lassen was able to come in on the surface, escaping the Asdic search of the escorts and penetrating between two lines of ships. Shortly before midnight, about 40 miles south of Port St. Johns, he fired three tubes in succession, sinking the American SS *Harvey W. Scott* and the British SS *Nirpura*, and damaging the Dutch motor tanker *Tibia.*[20]

The lack of convoy discipline was immediately apparent. *Viviana* switched on her searchlight and began picking up survivors, leaving the convoy open on her side; *Nigella* sent up star-shells; and the American freighter *Carolinian* fired indiscriminate tracer, to the discomfort of everyone except *U-160* which quietly retired into the background. The Convoy Commodore made light signals ordering two successive 45 degree turns to port, but not all ships saw or understood them, and the escort trawler *Norwich City* (Lt. Leslie Hugh Stammers, RNVR) lost contact with the convoy altogether.[21]

Less than two hours later, after some calm had been restored within the convoy, Lassen went in again and made a second attack at 0110 on 4 March, east-northeast of East London. This time, he sank the British SS *Empire Mahseer* and SS *Marietta E.*, and damaged the British SS *Sheaf Crown.* At dawn, having achieved the enemy's greatest success of the offensive, Lassen abandoned the pursuit and moved northward to Cape St. Lucia.[22]

Survivors of the four freighters sunk were picked up by shipping in the area, the SAAF crash launch *R-8*, convoy escorts, or made landfall in lifeboats. HMT *Norwich City* picked up *Empire Mahseer*'s master, 29 crew members and six gunners, and landed them at Durban.[23]

The *Sheaf Crown* which caught fire after being torpedoed, was quickly abandoned by her crew, as they feared the flames might reach her cargo of explosives. One crewmember and two gunners were lost as a result of the attack. The survivors were picked up by the whaler HMS *Sondra* (T/Lt. W. P. Hart, RNR) and taken to Durban. After three days adrift, *Sheaf Crown* was taken in tow to East London and eventually returned to service after being repaired.[24]

The misadventures which befell DN-21 caught the attention of Mr. Churchill, who addressed a formal reminder to the Admiralty that "We simply cannot afford losses of this kind on this route."[25]

FINAL SHIP SINKINGS BY SEEHUND SUBS / *U-182* SUNK BY DESTROYER

After the successful attack on Convoy DN-21, six more ships were sunk by the Seehund Group—two off Cape St. Lucia also by U-160, one 350 miles northeast of Durban, one 25 miles south of Knysna, and another 240 miles southwest of Port Elizabeth. The final victim in South African waters was the unescorted British steam merchant *Aloe*, which was torpedoed by *U-182*, 420 miles southeast of Durban on 5 April 1943. The ship's master, Captain Angus Maclennan, was taken prisoner but lost on 16 May when the submarine was sunk with no survivors, northwest of the Madeira Islands by depth charges from the destroyer USS *MacKenzie* (DD-614). After departing South African waters to return to their base at Lorient, *U-516* and *U-509* sank the SS *Nortun* (Convoy CN-13) and damaged the SS *City of Baroda* (Convoy NC-9), respectively, off Luderitz Bay, South West Africa.[26]

HMT *CAPE WARWICK* RESCUES SURVIVORS

The RN trawlers were to remain in South Africa until the war's end, with their crews being relieved after a long spell of duty. They were joined by a handful of other trawlers to make up for their previous losses suffered in American waters, and were employed on anti-submarine patrols and as escorts for convoys from Walvis Bay rounding the Cape of Good Hope and up to Durban and Mombasa. It was generally wearisome work, though occasionally eventful. One example was when HMT *Cape Warwick* rescued survivors of the SS *City of Baroda*.[27]

Photo 15-7

HMT *Cape Warwick* at Port Elizabeth, South Africa.
IWM photograph HU 110616

Cape Warwick's captain was Lt. William Edward 'Paddy' Goggin, an Irishman of great renown among RN trawler commanders, with his ship and jaunty and strong-hearted crew. It was aboard her that an officer was about to tuck into his lunch when the steward shot into the wardroom and suggested that he skip the soup, as they had just got to the bottom of the pot and found a black sock resting among the remains.[28]

In late afternoon on 2 April 1943, HM trawlers *Cape Warwick* and *Northern Dawn* set out from Walvis Bay, then a known hot-bed of German spies, as escorts to a small convoy of three ships bound for Cape Town. Two of these were cargo vessels, one, the French *Ville d'Amiens.* The third was the 7,000-ton passenger ship *City of Baroda*, with more than 338 passengers and crew aboard. Comprising this total were: the master and 130 crewmembers, four gunners, and 203 passengers. Among the passengers were ninety Europeans and a hundred lascars. (Lascars were sailors from the Indian Subcontinent, Southeast Asia, the Arab world, British Somaliland, or other lands east of the Cape of Good Hope, who were employed on European ships from the 16th century until the middle of the 20th century.) At nightfall, a thick fog descended, and the speed of the convoy was reduced. Jack Clegg, formerly a coder aboard *Cape Warwick*, later described the ensuing events:

> About 9 p.m. a dull thud was heard from what appeared to be a considerable distance. The ships in convoy were not visible owing to the fog. Shortly afterwards a mysterious SOS was received from a ship whose identify was unknown, and whose position given was on dry land! At the first, light of dawn, when it was discovered that *City of Baroda* was not in line with the convoy, *Cape Warwick* was ordered to make a search.[29]

Photo 15-8

The 7,000-ton passenger ship *City of Baroda.*
SA Naval Museum

Until she found a lifeboat with survivors, it was unbeknownst to *Cape Warwick*, that without warning, a torpedo from *U-509* had struck

City of Baroda starboard side, exploding and destroying one of her lifeboats. Almost immediately, she was hit by a second torpedo, again on her starboard side. The captain gave the order to abandon ship and six lifeboats were quickly filled and lowered; a seventh boat upended, throwing the occupants into the sea, and five people were drowned.[30]

The attacking submarine was never seen. Five hours after beginning her search, *Cape Warwick* came upon the first lifeboat, and within a few hectic hours she found other boats and picked up a total of 260 people. Among them were scores of lascars, as well as European crew and passengers, among them three children and a dozen women, including some Quaker nurses on their way to Burma. Gallantly, Paddy Goggin turned his cabin over to the ladies.[31]

Paddy and his officers, with salvage in mind, wanted to take the stricken *City of Baroda* in tow as she appeared to be floating fairly well, but orders came for him to abandon the hulk and proceed to Cape Town with the survivors. After four days of hardship during the journey, there was great celebration following the trawler's arrival at Cape Town, as recounted by Clegg:

> Conditions on board with 300 souls were terrible, and everything that could possibly be jettisoned went over the side. Every inch of deck space, chartroom, wireless cabin, officers' quarters, was occupied during waking and sleeping hours. The crew gave up their bunks to survivors and slept on deck, but even here people had to sleep sitting up because there was insufficient room to lie down. The lascars were accommodated in an unused fish hold and the for'ard messdeck, and the scenes here were unbelievable.
>
> The trawler men distributed all the clothing they could "rake up" among the survivors, but food was a different problem. It was perilously short and the only way they could give everyone a meagre two meals a day was by using up all the concentrated rations kept in the lifeboats for emergency use. For some of *City of Baroda*'s crew who had been torpedoed before — one man had been sunk nine times since war began — every discomfort was small. Even so, there was hearty relief when the grossly over laden *Cape Warwick* reached Cape Town and a pleasant surprise.
>
> While there were supposed to be security restrictions in force, every ship in the harbour sounded their welcoming hooters as we sailed alongside. Even more remarkable was the sight of trestle tables laid out on the quayside laden with food, and more than 300 chairs. The food had been provided by the WVS [Women's Voluntary Service] of South Africa. All 260 survivors, together with our forty

> crewmembers sat down unshaven, unwashed, and in many cases only partly clothed, to enjoy their first real meal for four days. Before leaving, all the survivors expressed their thanks to us by singing *Auld Lang Syne.*[32]

Captain "Paddy" Goggin subsequently received a letter of gratitude from the High Commissioner's office in Cape Town. It thanked him for the manner of the survivors' rescue and the 'overwhelming kindness and hospitality displayed by his officers and crew.'[33]

LASSEN RECOGNIZED UPON RETURN TO BASE

Georg Lassen's *U-160*, having not departed Lorient until 6 January 1943, had the necessary supplies and fuel to remain on patrol longer than the other boats. After sinking two additional ships, the unescorted SS *James B. Stephens* on 8 March, and SS *Aelybryn* on 11 March, he arrived at Bordeaux, France, on 10 May. In recognition of his great success in South African waters, Lassen was awarded Oak Leaves to his Knight's Cross.[34]

Photo 15-9

Georg Lassen.
Willi Schumacher Collection

16

U-boats Depart, Other Submarines take their Place

U-boat successes were at their peak. The number of the U-boats was continually increasing, losses were slight; and the reinforcement by boats from home, considerable. The radius of action of all the boats was considerably extended by the use of supply U-boats, from each of which, about 10 U-boats could each draw 40 tons of oil and additional provisions .... The U-boats also fueled by surface tankers when such were available. These could also supply torpedoes. Operations in the South American area, in the area around Cape Town, and in the Indian Ocean were thus made possible.

—Admiral Karl Doenitz describing in *The Conduct of the War at Sea*, reasons for greater U-boat successes in late-1942/early-1943.[1]

By April 1943, of the five attack boats of the Seehund Group, only *U-182* remained off the South African coast. She was the only Type IXD2 of the five boats, with a range of nearly double that of the Type IXCs, the other four (*U-160*, *U-506*, *U-509*, *U-516*) being Type IXCs.

German Long Range Attack U-boats

Characteristics	**Type IXC**	**Type IXD1**	**Type IXD2**
Length	252 feet	287.4 feet	287.4 feet
Displacement (submerged)	1,257 tons	1,799 tons	1,804 tons
Top speed (surf /submerged)	18.3/7.3 kts	20.8/6.9 kts	19.2/6.9 kts
Max range (surfaced at 12 kts)	11,400 nm	9,900 nm	23,700 nm
(submerged at 4 kts)	63 nm	57 nm	57 nm
Torpedo tubes (bow/stern)	4/2 (21-inch)	4/2 (21-inch)	4/2 (21-inch)
Deck gun	One 105mm	One 105mm	One 105mm
Anti-aircraft guns	One 37mm One 20mm	One 37mm One 20mm	One 37mm One 20mm
Crew size	48 O & E	55 O & E	57 O & E

Surf: surfaced O: Officers E: Enlisted[2]

The other boats were en route back to their bases and arrived at Bordeaux (*U-160*) or Lorient (*U-506*, *509*, *516*) between 4 and 11 May.

Photo 16-1

Port of Bordeaux, France. Stipple engraving, by Wells after Owen.
Published in the *Naval Chronicle*, vol. 7, 1802, by Bunney and Gold, London.
Naval History and Heritage Command photograph #NH 65997

Photo 16-2

U-428 being welcomed home at her base at Lorient,
France, following a cruise off the U.S. Coast, date unknown.
Naval History and Heritage Command photograph #NH 111251

REPLACEMENTS HAVE GREATER CAPABILITIES; TWO U-BOATS CARRY OUT "SPECIAL MISSIONS"

Replacement U-boats in addition to the remaining *U-182* were already in the "hunting grounds" off South Africa, as their predecessors voyaged home. When a number of the long-range type IXD U-boats from the 12th Flotilla became available in February and March, Doenitz dispatched them to relieve the Seehund Group. The extended fuel capacity of these U-boats allowed for greater operational freedom in distant waters—more time on station to search for and attack shipping. Two additional IXD boats to those sent in February and March were deployed to African waters in April; as well as in May, a single IXC from the 10th Flotilla bound for Kure, Japan, operated briefly there.[3]

As summarized below, these submarines collectively achieved much success, sinking 35 Allied ships and damaging another.

12th Flotilla
12 Unterseebootsflottille
Bordeaux, France

U-177 **(IXD2)**
U-178 **(IXD2)**
U-180 **(IXD1)**
U-181 **(IXD2)**
U-182 **(IXD2)**
U-195 **(IXD1)**
U-196 **(IXD2)**
U-197 **(IXD2)**
U-198 **(IXD2)**

10th Flotilla
10 Unterseebootsflottille
Lorient, France

U-511 **(IXC)**
Handed over to Japan on 16 September 1943 at Kure, and became the Japanese submarine ***RO-500***

Date Left	U-boat/ Type	Commander	Ships Hit
9 Dec 42	*U-182*/IXD2	Kptlt. Asmus Nicolai Clausen	0 S
9 Feb 43	*U-180*/IXD1	FrgKpt. Werner Musenberg	1 S
9 Mar 43	*U-198*/IXD2	Kpt. Werner Hartmann	7 S
13 Mar 43	*U-196*/IXD2	KrvKpt. Eitel-Friedrich Kentrat	2 S
20 Mar 43	*U-195*/IXD1	KrvKpt. Heinz Buchholz	0 S
23 Mar 43	*U-181*/IXD2	KrvKpt. Wolfgang Luth	10 S
28 Mar 43	*U-178*/IXD2	KrvKpt. Wilhelm Dommes	6 S
1 Apr 43	*U-177*/IXD2	KrvKpt. Robert Gysae	6 S
3 Apr 43	*U-197*/IXD2	KrvKpt. Robert Bartels	2 S, 1 D
10 May 43	*U-511*/IXC	Kptlt. Fritz Schneewind	1 S
S: Sunk	D: Damaged	Total	35 S, 1 D

U-180 TASKED WITH SPECIAL MISSION

The first replacement submarine to sail had orders to carry out a special mission relating to technology transfer and payment between Germany and its Axis partner Japan. On 9 February, *U-180* (a type IXD1 cargo-configured combat submarine) under the command of FrgKpt. Werner Musenberg, left Kiel, a port city on Germany's Baltic Sea coast. Aboard her was Netaji Subhas Chandra Bose, the leader of the anti-British Indian National Army, and his aide. Chandra Bose had become disillusioned that Nazi Germany would be of much assistance in helping India to rid itself of British rule. Hoping to gain better support from Imperial Japan, he had procured transport aboard to meet Japanese officials as part of the mission.[4]

On 18 April, while en route to Madagascar to rendezvous with the Japanese submarine *I-29*, *U-180* sank the unescorted British motor tanker *Corbis* about 500 miles east-southeast of Port Elizabeth, South Africa. Eight days later, on 26 April, the German and Japanese submarines met up in the Mozambique Channel for an at-sea transfer of their respective cargos to one another. Over a difficult two days, while employing rubber boats and open torpedo tubes, *I-29* transferred 11 tons of cargo to *U-180*, which included:

- two tons of gold as payment for previous transfer of German technology
- four torpedoes
- blueprints for the carrier *Akagi* (to assist the Germans with the *Graf Zeppelin*, their carrier under construction)
- plans for the Type A midget submarine (used at Pearl Harbor)[5]

In return, *U-180* transferred blueprints for the type IXC/40 submarine, quinine samples (to assist the Japanese with anti-malaria drugs), various other weapon and radar technology, as well as Bose and his aide. After the successful transfer, the German submarine remained operational off the South African coast until 26 May without achieving any further vessel sinkings.[6]

The *I-29* delivered the two Indians to Sabang, Sumatra. They were then flown to Tokyo and met with Japanese Prime Minster Hideki Tojo and Emperor Hirohito. Bose later led the Indian National Army (composed mostly of Indian troops of the British Indian Army who had been captured by the Japanese, then sided with their captors) in an action against British forces in India in 1944, but was decisively defeated. He subsequently died as a result of burns suffered in a plane crash on 18 August 1945, in Japanese Taihoku (present day Taiwan).[7]

The special mission of the German *U-511*, involving her transfer to the Imperial Japanese Navy, is taken up at the end of the chapter.

ITALIAN SUBMARINE *LEONARDO DA VINCI*

As additional German U-boats were being deployed to South African waters in February and March 1943, so too were the Italian submarines *Leonardo da Vinci* and *R.Smg. Giuseppe Finz* (previously discussed), which increased the enemy threats to Allied shipping.

After leaving Bordeaux on 20 February, the *Leonardo da Vinci* arrived off West Africa in late March. (Her patrol was conducted in collaboration with *R.Smg. Giuseppe Finz*.) *Da Vinci* was the most successful non-German Axis submarine in World War II. She was commanded by Italy's most effective submarine ace, Lt. Gianfranco Gazzana-Priaroggia. During her 11 war patrols, she sank seventeen ships.[8]

Photo 16-3

The Italian submarine *Leonardo da Vinci* was the most successful non-German Axis submarine in World War II.
SA Naval Museum

Launched on 16 September 1939, she was one of six Marconi-class submarines. This type of boat was fairly large (251 feet long with 1,510 tons submerged-displacement) requiring a crew of 57 men. Their armament consisted of four bow and four stern 21-inch torpedo tubes, one 3.9-inch deck gun and four 13.2mm anti-aircraft machine guns. With these weapons, a top surface speed of just over 17 knots (8.2 submerged), and a range of nearly 3,000 miles, they were formidable weapons capable of operating far from home.[9]

Despite these attributes, *Da Vinci* and other Italian submarines had significant weaknesses. The Regia Marina's (Italian Navy's) ocean-going submarines were, for the most part, more massive than their German counterparts, making them easier to detect and more likely to come under attack by Allied forces. Their large size resulted from Italian submarine warfare doctrine which called for their subs to operate beneath the surface while engaging a vessel. Initial torpedo attacks were made while submerged, after which the sub could rise to the surface to finish off the target if applicable. However, this type of submerged warfare required longer periscopes, necessitating Italian submarines to have larger conning towers in comparison to the German U-boats.[10]

Because German submarines mostly engaged their targets on the surface and with their smaller conning towers, their silhouette was minimized. An added advantage of their more svelte profiles was that they could crash dive more quickly than Italian submarines—a critical feature in avoiding attack by Allied aircraft or surface ships. Regia Marina submarines were not optimally designed to make a quick escape.[11]

During this, her 11th and last deployment, *Leonardo da Vinci* sent six merchantmen (identified in the table) to the bottom in West and South African waters. On her return voyage, the Italian submarine was sunk on 23 May 1943, northeast of the Azores, through the efforts of the British destroyer HMS *Active* (H14) and frigate HMS *Ness* (K219).[12]

Ships Sunk by the Italian submarine *Leonardo da Vinci* in African Waters, 16 March – 25 April 1943

Date	Ship	Registry	Type	Tons	Location
14 Mar 43 unescorted	RMS *Empress of Canada*		troop ship	21,500	01°13'S 09°57'W
18 Mar 43 unescorted	SS *Lulworth Hill*		freighter	7,628	10°10'S 01°00'E
17 Apr 43	SS *Sembilan*		freighter	6,566	31°30'S 33°30'E
18 Apr 43	SS *Manar*		freighter	8,007	31°30'S 33°30'E
21 Apr 43	SS *John Drayton*		Liberty ship	7,177	32°10'S 34°50'E
25 Apr 43	MS *Doryessa*		motor tanker	8,078	32°03'S, 34°04'E[13]

Leonardo da Vinci's first victim in African waters was the 21,500-ton RMS *Empress of Canada*, an ocean liner of the Canadian Pacific Steam Ship Company, which had been converted to a troop transport. The massive ship was sunk off Freetown, while en route from Durban to the

United Kingdom via Takoradi on the Gold Coast. Aboard her were 1,346 persons including Greek and Polish refugees, as well as 499 Italian prisoners of war (unbeknownst to Gazzana-Priaroggia).[14]

Just after midnight, a torpedo impacted the *Empress of Canada* and exploded. Gazzana-Priaroggia gave her master, Captain George Goold, half an hour to abandon ship. After this period expired, she sank about 20 minutes after a second torpedo struck her. A total of 392 people were lost because of exposure, drowning and sharks, including 90 women and 44 crew. The survivors were picked up by the destroyer HMS *Boreas* (H77), corvettes HMS *Petunia* (K79) and HMS *Crocus* (K49), and the Ellerman Line cargo ship SS *Corinthian*.[15]

The Italian submarine's next victim was the SS *Lulworth Hill* off the northwest coast of South West Africa (now Namibia). On 18 March, *Da Vinci* torpedoed and sank the British freighter, which was on passage from Cape Town to Freetown, bound for the UK.[16]

By mid-April 1943, the Italian submarine had rounded the Cape and was in the Indian Ocean, just off Durban, South Africa. In quick succession, she sank another two freighters—the Dutch SS *Sembilan* (east of Durban) and British SS *Manar* (east of Port Elizabeth) and the American Liberty ship SS *John Drayton* (east of Durban). The *Drayton* had previously survived after being torpedoed twice and shelled while sailing alone from Bahrain to Cape Town.[17]

On 21 April 1943, when the *John Drayton* was 300 miles east of Durban, the lookout posted on the bow yelled the warning, "Torpedo coming! The captain on the bridge ordered hard right rudder, and the torpedo sliced through the water past the Liberty ship. But, a second one followed. Decades later, Herman "Hank" Rosen, a 23-year-old cadet midshipman at the time of attack, described how the ship trembled and died in rough seas, on a dark, cloudy night:

> The torpedo hit, and simultaneously a huge ball of flames came out of the smokestack. Everybody in the engine room must have been fried.
>
> The ship shook, like that (he said, clenching two fists.) And then there was dead silence. It was eerie, because before we could hear the engines.[18]

The torpedo blast destroyed one of the *Drayton*'s four lifeboats; another capsized when being launched, drowning everyone aboard; a third lifeboat was launched with just 11 men. The final boat was packed with 23 men when Rosen stepped on board. Thirty days later, when a ship finally arrived to rescue them, only Rosen and four others in the boat were still alive.[19]

Leonardo da Vinci's final victim was the MS *Doryessa*, a British oil tanker, which she sank in a position very close to that of the *John Drayton*.[20]

On 6 May, Tenente di Vascello (Vessel Lieutenant) Gazzana-Priaroggia received word that he was promoted "for service in war" to the rank of Capitano di Corvetta (Corvette Captain). Several days later, on 22 May, he sent the last radio message that would be received from *Da Vinci*; informing her base that she would begin "hidden" navigation the following day.[21]

The U-boat was expected to make Bordeaux within a week, but she never arrived. In 1945, the British Admiralty confirmed that at 1135 on 23 May 1943, the destroyer HMS *Active* and frigate HMS *Ness* had conducted an attack on the submarine off Cape Finestrelle. Gazzana-Priaroggia's decision to radio home his intentions proved fatal. The submarine's position was fixed by Allied direction-finding equipment, the warships subjected it to an intense depth charge attack and sank it; there were no survivors.[22]

MOST U-BOATS HUNT FURTHER OUT TO SEA AND CONTINUE TO ATTACK, ALMOST EXCLUSIVELY, UNESCORTED MERCHANT VESSELS

While the German submarines operating in African waters in spring and early-summer of 1943, collectively achieved much success, they had to venture farther afield in order to escape Allied patrol aircraft and surface ship attacks. With South African waters patrolled by South African and Royal Air Force planes, and coastal convoys under escort by RN and SANF trawlers and whalers, the U-boats focused most of their efforts on the Mozambique and Madagascar Island areas.

A review of the table on the following page reveals that a majority of attacks against shipping occurred well to the east or northeast of the South African coastline and adjacent waters. The following summary, and associated map, identifies the number of attacks in different areas; many took place long distances out to sea:

- 1 off Tanganyika (present-day Tanzania)
- 10 off Mozambique, or in the Mozambique Channel
- 11 off Madagascar Island
- 2 off Mauritius Island, to the east of Madagascar
- 7 off Durban
- 1 off Port St. Johns
- 1 off Port Elizabeth
- 2 off Cape Town

Attacks off the South African coastline; most occurred at great distances out to sea

- 1 southwest of Freetown, Sierra Leone (not shown on map)

Map 16-1

Southern part of the African Continent

Ships sunk in Africa Waters by *U-177*, *U-178*, *U-180*, *U-181*, *U-196*, *U-197*, *U-198*, and *U-511* (11 April-17 August 1943)

Date	Ship	U-boat	Torpedoed/Sunk
11 Apr 43 unescorted	SS *Empire Whimbrel*	*U-181*	about 420 miles SW of Freetown, Sierra Leone
18 Apr 43 unescorted	MS *Corbis*	*U-180*	about 500 miles ESE of Port Elizabeth, South Africa
11 May 43 unescorted	SS *Tinhow*	*U-181*	in the Mozambique Channel
11 May 43 unescorted	SS *Nailsea Meadow*	*U-196*	40 miles south of Port St. Johns, Cape Colony
17 May 43 Convoy LMD-17	SS *Northmoor*	*U-198*	north of Durban
27 May 43 unescorted	MS *Sicilia*	*U-181*	off Mozambique, after departing Lourenço Marques

28 May 43 Convoy CD-20	SS *Agwimonte*	*U-177*	off Cape Town
28 May 43 Convoy CD-20	MS *Storaas*	*U-177*	off Cape Town
29 May 43 unescorted	MS *Hopetarn*	*U-198*	about 450 miles east of Durban
1 Jun 43 Convoy CD-20	SS *Salabangka*	*U-178*	off the coast, south of Durban
5 Jun 43 unescorted	MS *Dumra*	*U-198*	northeast of Durban
6 Jun 43 unescorted	SS *William King*	*U-198*	about 200 miles east of Durban
7 Jun 43 unescorted	SS *Harrier*	*U-181*	about 200 miles east of Durban
27 Jun 43 unescorted	SS *Sebastian Cermeno*	*U-511*	about 290 miles southeast of Madagascar
2 Jul 43 unescorted	SS *Hoihow*	*U-181*	105 miles WNW of Mauritius
4 Jul 43 Convoy DN-50	SS *Breiviken*	*U-178*	off Mozambique, dispersed from Convoy DN-50
4 Jul 43 unescorted	SS *Michael Livanos*	*U-178*	in the Mozambique Channel
6 Jul 43 unescorted	SS *Jasper Park*	*U-177*	SSW of Cap Sainte Marie, Madagascar
6 Jul 43 unescorted	SS *Hydraios*	*U-198*	13 miles south of Ponta Zavora Lighthouse, Mozambique
7 Jul 43 unescorted	SS *Leana*	*U-198*	about 40 miles SE of Zavora Point, Mozambique
10 Jul 43 unescorted	SS *Alice F. Palmer*	*U-177*	south of Madagascar
11 Jul 43 unescorted	SS *Mary Livanos*	*U-178*	in the Mozambique Channel
14 Jul 42 unescorted	SS *Robert Bacon*	*U-178*	about 35 miles off the Mozambique Light
15 Jul 43 unescorted	SS *Empire Lake*	*U-181*	about 240 miles east of Madagascar
16 Jul 43 unescorted	SS *Fort Franklin*	*U-181*	southwest of the island of Reunion, east of Madagascar
17 Jul 43 unescorted	SS *City of Canton*	*U-178*	northeast of Beira, Mozambique
19 July 43 Convoy DN-53	MS *Cornish City*	*U-177*	southeast of Madagascar, dispersed from Convoy DN-53
24 Jul 43 unescorted	MS *Pegasus*	*U-197*	southwest of Madagascar

30 Jul 43 unescorted	SS *William Ellery* (D)	*U-197*	300 miles ESE of Durban
1 Aug 43 Convoy BC-2	SS *Mangkalihat*	*U-198*	torpedoed off Mozambique, foundered three days later while under tow
3 Aug 43 Convoy CB-1	SS *City of Oran* (scuttled)	*U-196*	about 100 miles northeast of Memba Bay, Tanganyika (present-day Tanzania)
4 Aug 43 unescorted	SS *Dalfram*	*U-181*	east of Madagascar
5 Aug 43 unescorted	SS *Efthalia Mari*	*U-177*	east of Madagascar
7 Aug 43 Convoy DN-54	SS *Umvuma*	*U-181*	southwest of Port Louis, Mauritius, after dispersed from Convoy DN-54
12 Aug 43 Convoy DN-55	SS *Clan Macarthur*	*U-181*	east of Farafangan, Madagascar, after dispersed from Convoy DN-55
17 Aug 43 unescorted	MS *Empire Stanley*	*U-197*	SSE of Cap Sainte Marie, Madagascar

SOUTH AFRICAN / ROYAL NAVY ANTI-SUBMARINE MEASURES WORKING

It had now been proved unmistakably by years of war experience that the directing of the U-boats from another boat away at sea or in the neighborhood of the convoy was impossible. The whole direction had to be conducted by a U-boat commander ashore and often a thousand miles away.... The battle at the convoy position itself was waged by the U-boats in tactical cooperation and with a high standard of individual performance in attack.

—Admiral Karl Doenitz describing in *The Conduct of the War at Sea*, the importance of centralized control of U-boats on patrol.[23]

As indicated in the above quoted material, while Admiral Doenitz exercised centralized control over U-boats on combat patrols, he assigned boats to areas or against targets he believed to be most conducive of success. Given this, it is reasonable to believe that, when given the opportunity, he would assign his most experienced and aggressive submarine commanders to the most dangerous prey.

With anti-submarine measures inducing most U-boat commanders to attack unescorted shipping, his commanders with the most hits on shipping between 11 April-17 August, were directed to attack convoys as well. In the following table the third column records the total hits on shipping, while the fourth, escorted ships sunk by these commanders:

U-boat	Commander	Ships hit	Convoys/ # Ships Sunk
U-181	KrvKpt. Wolfgang Luth	10 S	DN-54 (D): 1 S DN-55 (D): 1 S
U-198	Kpt. Werner Hartmann	7 S	LMD-17: 1 S BC-2: 1 S (F)
U-177	KrvKpt. Robert Gysae	6 S	CD-20: 2 S DN-53 (D): 1 S
U-178	KrvKpt. Wilhelm Dommes	6 S	CD-20: 1 S DN-50(D): 1 S
U-196	KrvKpt. Eitel-Friedrich Kentrat	2 S	CB-1: 1 S (S)

S: Sunk (D): Convoy dispersed (F): Foundered (S): Scuttled by RN warship

In total, 10 of the 36 ships sunk were, or had been in convoy. However, this number is misleading because 4 of the 10 ships were unescorted at the time of attack, their convoys (DN-50, DN-53, DN-54, and DN-55) having dispersed. (Dispersed means that the ships had been released to proceed to their respective destination ports and were no longer under escort.) Moreover, 1 ship each in Convoys BC-2 and CB-1, counted as being sunk by enemy actions were only damaged. One later foundered (sank) while under tow, and the other was scuttled (purposely sunk, owing to damage suffered) by Allied forces. So, only four ships of the thirty-six sunk were actually under escort at the time of their loss, and sunk solely as a result of the attacking U-boat.

RN AND SANF A/S TRAWLERS AND WHALERS

Photo 16-4

British anti-submarine trawler HMT *Wellard* departing Port Elizabeth.
FW Neave

As German U-boats and Italian submarines searched for prey, Royal Navy and South African Naval Forces A/S trawlers and whalers continued to ply dangerous waters, shepherding their charges. The following accounts pay tribute to the efforts of their sailors aboard these small, converted vessels, in rescuing survivors of sunken ships from inhospitable waters and delivering them to safe havens.

In mid-afternoon on 17 May 1943, *U-198* after firing two spreads of two torpedoes at convoy LMD-17 (Lourenço Marques to Durban) north of Durban, and hearing four detonations and sinking noises, reported one ship sunk and another probably sunk. However, only the British merchant vessel SS *Northmoor* (Master Arthur Peters) was hit and sunk. HMT *St. Loman* (Lt. Richard Colin Warwick, RNR) picked up the master, 20 crewmembers, four gunners and two passengers and landed them at Durban. Sadly, the remaining eleven members of the crew and one gunner were lost.[24]

In another afternoon attack, at 1318 on 6 June, against an unescorted ship, the American Liberty ship SS *William King* (Master Owen Harvey Reed) was hit on the port side in No. 3 hold by a torpedo fired by *U-198*. The ship had been steaming on a zigzag course at 10 knots about 200 miles east of Durban. After the first hit, a second torpedo was seen by her crew to pass astern of her. The explosion opened a large hole in the ship's hull, killing all three engineers on watch, destroying the port boiler, and setting fire to the engine room, the hold and the midships house. Two lifeboats were also destroyed. Most of the eight officers, 34 crewmen and 23 armed guards quickly abandoned ship in two lifeboats and two rafts.[25]

At 1346, the submarine fired a torpedo that missed, followed by another at 1404, which struck on the ship's starboard side, sending flames high into the air and causing her to sink by the stern about 10 minutes later. *U-198* surfaced shortly after the sinking and fired two short bursts from a machine gun to induce the lifeboats to come alongside, questioned the survivors, and took the master as prisoner on board before leaving. All others in the lifeboat and rafts, save two who died from explosion injuries, were picked up by British naval craft after trying for several days to find land. Three crew members had been killed when the torpedo exploded in the engine room of the Liberty Ship, while another was blown from the bridge and never seen again.[26]

Survivors on two rafts were picked up a day and a half later by HMT *Northern Chief*, which also picked up the survivors in one of the lifeboats and landed them at Durban on 10 June. The survivors in the other boat were found after six days by the destroyer HMS *Relentless* (H85), and landed in Durban the same day.[27]

CONVOY CD-20 (CAPE TOWN TO DURBAN)

African Star	*Duke of Athens*	*Roger Griswold*
Agwimonte	*Empire Silver*	*Salabangka*
Banffshire	*Glenstrae*	*Storaas*
British Vigour	*Griqua*	*Turkistan*
Cape Romano	*Hoegh Scout*	*Wilful*[28]
Castalia	*Hoogkerk*	
City of Canton	*Kota Gede*	

In darkness, at a little before midnight on 28 May 1943, *U-177* attacked Convoy CD-20, escorted by six RN and SANF ships, firing a spread of two bow torpedoes at the freighter SS *Agwimonte* and two minutes later, a spread of two stern torpedoes at the tanker MS *Storaas*. The submarine had earlier missed the same freighter with four torpedoes. This time, one hit each was observed on *Agwimonte* and *Storaas*. Shortly after midnight, *U-177* fired a torpedo at 0046, on 29 May, which hit and sank the abandoned *Agwimonte*. It took two additional torpedoes—one at 0110 and another at 0153—to put the *Storaas* down.[29]

The South African whaler HMSAS *Vereeniging* (T72), which on the night was zigzagging astern of the convoy, carried out a brief A/S search before picking up 61 survivors of the *Agwimonte* from a lifeboat and two rafts, and the survivors of the *Storaas*. Despite three A/S searches, at no time did *Vereeniging* obtain a contact or sight a submarine, but the survivors in the boats did, and reported that the U-boat was proceeding at high speed on the surface. The survivors were landed at Port Elizabeth on 30 May. Two other boats from *Agwimonte* were sighted by a SAAF aircraft in the afternoon of 29 May. An Air Force crash boat rescued their occupants 18 hours after the attack.[30]

As it was approaching Durban, Convoy CD-20 was attacked again when, at 1000 on 1 June, *U-178* fired a spread of two torpedoes at the Dutch merchant vessel SS *Salabangka* (Master H. A. Broere). One of the torpedoes struck her starboard side in the engine room, killing ten men and destroying the starboard lifeboats. The ship lost all electrical power and stopped "dead in the water." She then developed a heavy list to port from sea water rushing in through the breech in her hull, and surviving crewmembers abandoned ship.[31]

At 1030, the British rescue tug HMS *Masterful* (W20), which accompanied the convoy, began picking up the survivors from two boats and a raft, seven of them injured. The crew of the tug, the master and some men from *Salabangka* managed to secure a towing line to the badly damaged ship after several attempts failed. At 1330, the tug began to proceed with her "waterlogged tow" at 1.5 knots. Early that evening, after there was a heavy explosion aboard *Salabangka*; she sank by the bow, south-southwest of Durban. Fortunately, the towing line parted, and the tug with survivors safely reached Durban that night.[32]

Photo 16-5

Dutch merchant vessel *Salabangka*.
SA Naval Museum

To collect and make full use of all information in the form of 'lessons learnt,' an A/S Committee (with sub-committees at each of the South African ports) had been formed in February and held extensive inquiries into the three convoy attacks that had occurred since Group Sailings were introduced. The inquiry into the June attack found that *Vereeniging* should have continued her A/S search and not stopped to pick up survivors, especially in view of the rescue tug being close at hand.[33]

WEATHER MOST FOUL

During the winter months of 1943 the convoys had their full share of foul weather. In August, HMSAS *Turffontein*, while escorting a convoy from Cape Town to Durban, encountered a particularly heavy gale, which is recorded in the following abbreviated extract from her captain's report of proceedings:

> Until early on the night of the 23rd the voyage to Durban was without incident though after passing East London the weather deteriorated with reduced visibility. As the night drew on the wind increased until, by 2300, the coxswain (after a life at sea) remarked that he had seldom, if ever, seen it blow harder. The sea was ugly and confused, and the ship began to labour heavily. Shortly before

midnight the wind was blowing between 75 and 100 miles an hour and an impenetrable wall of howling darkness surrounded the blacked-out ship. The convoy vanished. Green seas broke over the ship despite the fact that she was running almost before the gale; the seamen's messdeck and wardroom were flooded. The rolls became alarming and one in particular, about midnight, caused those on the messdecks to grab their lifejackets and prepare to scramble up the ladder to the hatch.[34]

Photo 16-6

Anti-submarine whaler HMSAS *Turfontein.*
Du Toit Collection

U-177 SUNK BY AIRCRAFT IN FEBRUARY 1944

The service to the German Navy of *U-177* ended abruptly on 6 February 1944, when she was sunk in the South Atlantic west of Ascension Island, by depth charges from a U.S. Liberator PB4Y aircraft. All but fourteen members of her crew were killed, including her commanding officer, KrvKpt. Heinz Buchholz. Considerable information was obtained from her survivors, including some associated with her preceding patrol in which she attacked Convoy CD-20.[35]

Ten months earlier, on 1 April 1943, *U-177* had put to sea from Bordeaux on her second patrol, escorted, by two coastal patrol vessels and several planes to where she could dive to safer deeper waters. Passage of the Bay of Biscay was made submerged, except for essential surfacing, on course 240° true. She proceeded to the South Atlantic without incident, even enjoying a traditional ceremony for the Equator crossing.[36]

U-177 arrived in the shipping lanes off the Cape of Good Hope, during the last week of May 1943. Her commander, KrvKpt. Robert Gysae, gained visual contact with Convoy CD-20 shortly after it left Cape Town the morning of the attack, and followed it throughout the day. He attacked about midnight, sinking the freighter *Agwimonte* and tanker *Storaas*, as previously described.[37]

Toward the end of July, *U-177* was ordered to meet the blockade runner *Charlotte Schliemann* at a point southeast of Madagascar to take on fuel and provisions together with other U-boats. The *Schliemann* was functioning as a refueling and supply ship for 1,200-ton U-boats operating in the Indian Ocean. The rendezvous with the combined oiler/supply ship involved six 1,200 tonners (*U-177*, *U-178*, *U-181*, *U-196*, *U-197*, and *U-198*), and lasted about two and one-half days. As each U-boat refueled on the surface, the others circled the area as lookouts for enemy surface ships or aircraft.[38]

Map 16-2

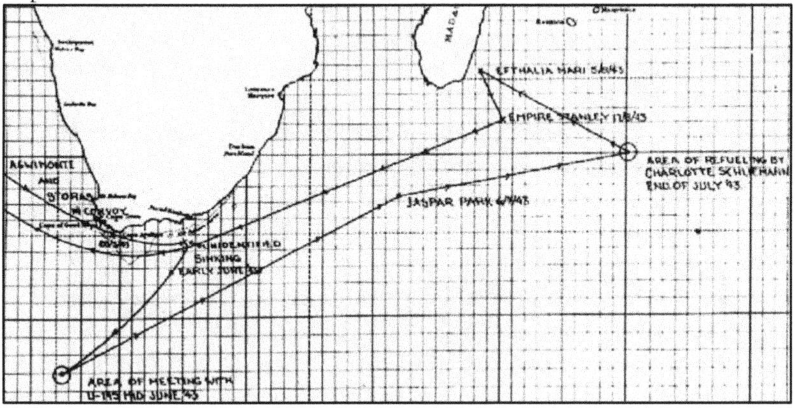

U-177's area of operations on her second patrol

U-177 under Gysae sank six ships in African waters. When only one torpedo remained aboard the submarine, he proceeded homeward. The northward passage through the Atlantic was without incident except that, when at the approximate latitude of Walvis Bay, South Africa, a freighter was sighted steering a northwest course toward St. Helena. Gysae fired his final torpedo, but because it had a damaged tail piece (which could not be repaired on board), it ran wide of the mark.

Passage of the Bay of Biscay was without incident and *U-177* reached Bordeaux on 1 October 1943.[39]

Two weeks later, KrvKpt. Robert Gysae (Knights Cross), was relieved by KrvKpt. Heinz Buchholz in command of *U-177*. She was lost, as previously noted, in the South Atlantic on 6 February 1944, to an Allied aircraft depth charge attack.[40]

U-511'S MISSION

On 10 May 1943, the *U-511* (Kptlt. Fritz Schneewind) departed Lorient with a cargo that included the German ambassador to the Japanese puppet-government in China, the Japanese representative to the Tripartite Commission (Vice Adm. Naokuni Nomura), and German scientists and engineers bound for Japan. While en route, *U-511* sank two unescorted U.S. Liberty ships in the Indian Ocean, the SS *Sebastion Cermeno* on 27 June (290 miles southeast of Madagascar), and SS *Samuel Heintzelman* (much farther out in the Indian Ocean) on 9 July.[41]

On 16 July, *U-511* reached Penang, Malaysia, the first German submarine to arrive at the base. Penang subsequently becomes home for the "Monsun Gruppe," a submarine group that would operate very far from Germany, and its occupied countries, in the Indian Ocean. These U-boats operated from Japanese-provided bases in Indonesia—Penang, Jakarta and Sabang in 1943-1945—and had some success against Allied shipping.[42]

U-511 reached Kure, Japan, on 7 August 1943. On 16 September 1943, she was handed over to the Japanese Navy as a "Present of the Fuehrer," and re-commissioned as *RO-500*. A second type IXC German submarine, *U-1224*, was re-commissioned into the Japanese Navy as *RO-501* by a Japanese crew on 15 February 1944 at Kiel.[43]

The voyages of U-boats between Europe, Southeast Asia and Japan—including the operations of German U-boats from Japanese bases in Japanese occupied South East Asia—were based on German-Italian-Japanese tripartite agreements. Separately from the Italian involvement, it had been agreed to donate to Japan, two German U-boats for study and test purposes.[44]

EAST AFRICAN CONVOYS

Although the general situation had allowed for the resumption of independent sailings between South African ports in September 1943, group sailings continued north of Durban. This was partly because less intelligence was available on the approach of U-boats from the East than from the West but chiefly because, while strong air cover and A/S protection could be provided at short notice in South African waters, most of the 1,600-mile passage between Durban and Kilindini (Mombassa), which skirted neutral territory and lacked air cover, was vulnerable to enemy submarine attack.[45]

Until November 1943, the small convoy escorts on this route consisted of the coal-burning RN trawlers but owing to a shortage of coal at Kilindini the Commander-in-Chief, South Atlantic approached the South African Defence authorities with the request that an exchange of ships, on the same lines as previously operated in South African waters, might be made. This was readily agreed to and the eight best SANF A/S whalers (all oil-burners) were formed into two groups and placed under RN operational control, their places in the local patrol systems being taken by the coal-burning RN trawlers which were placed under SANF operational control. This secondment of SANF A/S vessels to the Royal Navy lasted until the defeat of Germany.[46]

Photo 16-7

The locally built SANF Harbour Defence Motor Launches, which were equipped with Asdic and depth charges, supplemented A/S trawlers and whalers for local A/S patrols in the approaches to South African ports.
Du Toit Collection

At the beginning of 1944, however, the Commander-in-Chief, South Atlantic stated that the number of A/S trawlers which he had provided for local patrol duties in exchange for the SANF whalers forming the 3rd and 4th Escort Groups would have to be reduced from eight to six. He suggested that this could best be effected by replacing two of them in Cape Town with two of the new locally-built Harbour Defence Motor Launches (HDML), equipped with a light form of Asdic and depth charges, which were being introduced into SANF service. This was agreed to, and HDMLs *1197* and *1200*, which had recently been built in Durban, arrived in Cape Town at the end of January 1944. By June 1944, eleven HDMLs were in service with the SANF. Two were stationed at East London, and three at each of the other three larger ports of Cape Town, Durban, and Port Elizabeth. One of the Cape Town HDMLs, was usually stationed at Saldanha Bay.[47]

INTERCEPTION OPERATIONS

From September 1943 onward, Admiral Doenitz had ceased to regard the waters off the South African coast as a viable targeted operational area, although any U-boats earmarked for offensive operations in the Far East which would inevitably pass through South African waters before reaching their bases at Penang and Surabaya could use the opportunity to attack shipping enroute.

Between the end of October 1943 and March 1944 there were no sinkings of merchant ships in South African waters. By this time, anti-submarine measures in the Southern Oceans (Atlantic and Indian) had improved so markedly that U-boats found it increasingly difficult to operate successfully against merchant shipping even while transiting.[48]

With indications that enemy submarines were passing south of the Cape on passage to and from the Far East, the Commander-in-Chief, South Atlantic proceeded to employ some of his A/S forces to intercept them. Operation BARRAGE was organized for the interception of a Japanese submarine expected to pass well to the south of Agulhas, eastward bound in mid-November. The force consisted of an RN frigate and corvette, about ten Catalina and Ventura aircraft, and the SANF A/S vessels *Turffontein* and *Pretoria* and minesweepers *Southern Barrier* and *Brakpan*. Although the mission failed, the frigate did get a weak HF/DF bearing of the submarine, but the resulting search was unsuccessful.[49]

The second operation, to intercept an east-bound German submarine, was cancelled in the light of updated intelligence before ships were sailed, while the third operation, also to intercept an eastbound U-boat, failed to make any contact with the enemy. The surface forces employed for this operation included one destroyer, four RN A/S trawlers and two South African minesweeping whalers, the best ships that the SANF could provide after the departure of all the larger A/S vessels for east coast convoy work.[50]

Early in March 1944 it became apparent, from information based on DF bearings, that one or possibly two submarines were approaching the Cape from the east and one from the west. Later information caused the Commander-in-Chief to concentrate his forces on the former, of which a fairly accurate position was obtained on 6 March, resulting in Operation WICKETKEEPER. The SANF provided the minesweeping whalers *Southern Barrier* and *Roodepoort*, while the RN contributed one destroyer and two A/S trawlers. The establishment of strong air patrols was soon rewarded when a SAAF Ventura sighted a U-boat on the surface steering west, 300 miles southeast of Port Elizabeth. Although five depth-charges were released 20 seconds after the submarine dived, nothing further was seen before the Ventura had to return to base.[51]

While inconclusive, this attack gave great encouragement to all forces involved in the interception, and three days later a Catalina sighted the U-boat on the surface 410 miles southwest of Cape Agulhas. When still four miles away the enemy opened fire and slightly damaged the aircraft which nevertheless pressed home the attack and dropped its first pattern of depth-charges. The U-boat, which had not dived, temporarily disappeared amongst the explosions, and was observed to have a decided list as the Catalina ran in for her second attack. The last charge exploded close to the submarine's starboard bow and an air-bubble appeared as she dived. By this time, two more Catalinas had arrived, which allowed the damaged aircraft, whose captain was anxious to return to base, to depart. The two recently arrived aircraft circled the area until the U-boat was again sighted with only her conning tower showing. The U-boat was effectively straddled by one of the Catalinas and, by the time the depth-charge explosions subsided, she had disappeared. Soon afterwards wreckage, together with a steadily increasing oil patch was observed by both Catalinas.[52]

Although nothing could be found by the RN destroyer and A/S trawlers which arrived and carried out a lengthy search that evening, the destruction of one enemy submarine was assessed at the time as highly probable. The sinking of the ex-Italian blockade-runner *UIT-22* was subsequently confirmed from German records post-war.[53]

GROUP SAILING REINTRODUCED

On 1 April 1944, the British ship *Dahomian* was sunk 10 miles WSW of Cape Point by *U-852*. The sinking was observed by the SANF minesweepers HMSAS *Natalia* and *Soetvlei* which were sweeping the Cape Town to Simon's Town channel and the minesweeper HMSAS *Krugersdorp* on passage from Simon's Town arrived shortly afterwards. The frigate HMS *Test*, which was near enough to sight *Dahomian* sinking, closed the position and commenced an A/S search. She was joined later by an RN destroyer and two A/S trawlers from Simon's Town, and aircraft were soon on the scene. The sea-air search continued until the evening of the 3rd and was recommenced on a smaller scale on the 4th because of a DF fix 150 miles ESE of Agulhas, but no sighting or A/S contact took place in either position. *U-852* did not remain in South African waters and after heading east, was subsequently sunk 32 days later by British aircraft, 400 miles ESE of Socotra, in the northwest Indian Ocean near the Gulf of Aden.[54]

As a result of the sinking, the Cape Town to Durban convoy system was immediately reintroduced. And, during the latter part of April, DF and other intelligence placed four U-boats in the South Atlantic, the most southerly of them being about 700 miles due west of the Cape. Further reports indicated that the others were moving south and that some had arrived in the same area.[55]

On 26 May the SANF minesweeping trawler HMSAS *Arum* was sweeping the Walvis Bay searched channel in flat calm conditions with high visibility. At 1355, when 20 miles WSW from Pelican Point, her captain sighted a periscope moving at the same speed as the ship and on a parallel course. *Arum* immediately slipped her sweep and steered for the submarine, which turned away at once, increasing speed considerably. The minesweeper opened fire with her six-pounder and fired ten rounds before the periscope disappeared. At the same time, what appeared to be rails and stanchions were seen awash near the periscope until the submarine submerged. *Arum* then dropped a depth-charge ahead of where the U-boat had dived and circled the position. She was later joined by the minesweeping trawler HMSAS *Bluff* and both ships, which were not fitted with Asdic, conducted a surface search of the area until after dark but without result.[56]

FURTHER INTERCEPTION OPERATIONS

As a direct result of *Arum*'s sighting, plans were prepared to intercept the submarine on the assumption that she was about to attack coastal shipping north of Cape Town and would therefore pass close to Cape Columbine. This operation, named THROTTLE, lasted from 31 May until 2 June. Ships taking part included seven RN A/S vessels, the SANF Mine Clearance Flotilla and aircraft. Nothing was sighted and no A/S contact was made, but a loop-crossing occurred at Saldanha Bay on the night of 1 June and two of the controlled mine-loops were fired.[57]

Meanwhile, intelligence had been received that another German submarine, believed to be one of the 1,200-ton class, was heading south. As a result, Operation STEADFAST was planned and implemented to intercept her if she passed close to the Cape. Despite a coordinated RN and SANF surface search in the area between Cape Columbine and

Table Bay between 13-17 June, supported by air patrols, no contact was made with the enemy. However, on 19 June, four survivors from the SS *Columbine* came ashore in a lifeboat near the cape of the same name and gave the first news of the sinking of their ship. *Columbine* had been hit by two torpedoes fired by *U-198* at 2000 on the 16th in a position 20 miles northwest of Saldanha Bay and only 20 miles north of the northern end of the line on which the three RN A/S trawlers were patrolling during the last night of the operation. It was unfortunate that no distress message had been received, which would have allowed immediate countermeasures to have been taken and more lives saved, with 23 persons perishing out of a total of fifty-two.[58]

The sinking of the *Columbine*, together with other intelligence received at about the same time, including reports on two Japanese submarines returning from Europe, suggested that the enemy might soon be expected off the east coast of South Africa. As a result, Operation TRICOLOUR was initiated after a DF report placed a German submarine about 270 miles ESE of Durban on 4 July. And the next day, a Catalina attacked a surfaced U-boat in this area. Five depth charges were dropped and there was an exchange of machine-gun fire in which the aircraft was hit but was able to return to base. The submarine did not dive until 15 minutes after the depth-charge attacks but did not appear to have suffered significant damage at the time, although an oil patch was later sighted in the position.[59]

A second attack, 120 miles north of the first, was made at 0901 the following day, this time by two SAAF Venturas. The first of these, which sighted the U-boat on the surface, was hit twice and driven off by heavy anti-aircraft fire before releasing her depth charges. The second Ventura, homed to the position by the first, arrived in time to depth charge the submarine 10 seconds after she crash-dived. Seven minutes later several life-saving dinghies came to the surface together with a considerable quantity of oil. Further searches on 7 and 8 July revealed nothing further, nor does the official list of U-boat losses show a "kill" in this area.[60]

Photo 16-8

SAAF Lockheed PV-1 Ventura from 25 Squadron conducting a coastal patrol. Ventura's were also used to provide aerial cover for coastal convoys. SAAF Museum

MORE SINKINGS

At 0057 on 15 July, the British ship *Director* was sunk near the coast 186 miles ENE of Lourenço Marques by *U-198*. This was followed in August by the losses of five more ships – all British. Four of these were sunk by *U-862* in the Mozambique area and the last, which was also the nearest to South Africa, took place on the night of the 20th when a slow east-bound convoy was attacked by *U-861* 420 miles ESE of Durban. SS *Berwickshire* was sunk by three torpedoes but the tanker *Daronia*, though hit twice, reached Durban under her own steam escorted during the last two days by the A/S whaler HMSAS *Immortelle* of the 3rd Escort Group.[61]

Meanwhile, on the 19th, the sloop HMS *Banff*, one of a group of four RN vessels, obtained a submarine contact 35 miles east of Cape St. Lucia. Not long afterwards, one of her consorts sighted two torpedo tracks and counter-attacked without result. It appeared probable that this was the same submarine that had sunk the *Director* four days earlier and that she had now moved south to attack shipping near the focal point off Durban. At dawn on 20 July, the 3rd Escort Group sailed from Durban to commence a search for the submarine. This continued all next day, in company with two RN A/S trawlers which had meanwhile arrived, but no contact was made, and they set course for Durban later that night.[62]

In addition to these losses, two other British ships were sunk by *U-198* outside South African waters, between Mozambique and Zanzibar, also in August, before she in turn was sunk by British surface vessels 170 miles northwest of the Seychelles.[63]

With the threat from enemy submarines continuing until the end of the war, the six remaining RN A/S trawlers, which had replaced SANF A/S whalers for patrol work at Cape Town and Durban, remained under SANF operational control. However, at 1000 on 19 January 1945, one of these trawlers, HMT *Northern Isles*, in fine clear weather, ran on the rocks right under the Durban Bluff, 100 feet from shore. She was then some 1.25 miles from her patrol line and there was no operational or mechanical reason for her leaving it. A tug arrived within half-an-hour, but her engine room was flooded, and the ship became a total loss. The Board of Inquiry decided that the grounding was "quite inexcusable" and the Commanding Officer and Officer of the Watch were both sentenced to loss of seniority and dismissed from their ship.[64]

THE FINAL SINKING

The brief "blitz" in August was almost the last appearance of enemy submarines near the coasts of South Africa but, because of submarines occasionally being reported in the South Atlantic and far out in the Indian Ocean, escort work involving both SANF and RN A/S trawlers and whalers continued for several months. As it turns out, the U-boats had yet to strike their final blow.[65]

This was the sinking of the Canadian steamship *Point Pleasant Park* on the afternoon of 23 February 1945, 510 miles NW of Cape Town. Hit by one torpedo, which killed nine men, and then shelled by the submarine, she went down two hours later. Although the submarine was seen on the surface by the survivors, there is no record of her number.[66]

So ended the enemy submarine offensive, or series of offensives, in waters within 1,000 miles of South Africa which had claimed one allied warship and 132 merchant ships with a gross tonnage of 743,544 tons, while six ships were severely damaged but safely reached port. Against these losses of merchant ships, despite extensive anti-submarine measures, only two operational submarines—*U-179* and *U-197*—as well as the ex-Italian blockade-runner *UIT-22* were sunk within 1,000 miles of the South African coast, although the mortality rate was high among the remaining 24 U-boats known to have entered the area. Of these, two more were sunk soon afterwards farther up the east coast of Africa; two more were destroyed in the Atlantic on their way home; and twelve others were subsequently lost before the end of the war.[67]

Postscript

The U-boat losses, which previously had been 13 percent of all the boats at sea, rose rapidly to 30 to 50 percent. In 1943 alone, 43 U-boats were lost. These losses were suffered not only in convoy attacks, but everywhere at sea. There was no part of the Atlantic where the boats were safe from being located day and night by aircraft....

Under these circumstances, the previous surface war on convoys could not be continued because, in the meantime, the favorable conditions in the American sphere of activity had also changed and U-boat successes had diminished considerably in that theater. The enemy air force with its modern methods of searching had produced this change in U-boat warfare.

—Admiral Karl Doenitz describing in *The Conduct of the War at Sea*, that although in March 1943, the major attacks on convoys could still be carried out, by May it was evident that Allied air strength in the Atlantic had increased enormously. Moreover, U-boats could be located at a great distance by Allied radar, without previous warning on the submarines' own receivers.[1]

Of the twenty-four King's Ships that sailed from Britain in February 1942, to serve under U.S. Navy command on America's East Coast, seventeen of these "minor war vessels" found their way back home to England after the war. Six trawlers were lost in American waters in 1942. A seventh one, HMT *Northern Isles*, grounded off Durban, South Africa, on 19 January 1945, and was a total loss. The other trawlers and whalers returned to Britain from South Africa in 1945.

HMT (Trawler)	HMT (Trawler)	HMT (Trawler)	HMS (Whaler)
Arctic Explorer	*Lady Rosemary*	*Norwich City*	*Buttermere*
Cape Warwick	*Le Tigre*	*St. Loman*	*Wastwater*
Coventry City	*Northern Chief*	*St. Zeno*	
Hertfordshire	*Northern Dawn*	*Stella Polaris*	
Lady Elsa	*Northern Duke*	*Wellard*	

All seventeen vessels were paid off by the Royal Navy in 1945, and disposed of. They were either returned to their original owners—if requisitioned (taken) by the Admiralty for naval service—or placed on the Disposal List for sale to mercantile (commercial interests)—if they had, instead, been purchased for naval service.

As shown in the tables at the end of this postscript, the six oldest surviving "King's Ships" had been launched at their builders' yards in 1936. (The oldest of the original twenty-four vessels, HMT *Senateur Duhamel* launched 1927, was among the seven trawlers lost.) Many, perhaps all, of the surviving ships (records are sketchy for some) served as fishing vessels post-World War II into the early 1960s. Operating from the fishing ports of Hull or Grimsby, they had easy access to the North Sea fishing grounds. Hull (or Kingston upon Hull) is a port city in East Yorkshire, England, situated where the River Hull meets the Humber Estuary. The port town of Grimsby, in Northeast Lincolnshire, is on the South Bank of the Humber Estuary.

At the end of these vessels' useful lives, they were broken up (scrapped); some in Belgium, either at Ghent or Antwerp. *Buttermere* was sold in May 1946 and her fate thereafter is unknown. *Wastwater* was sold in 1946 and possibly converted into a salvage tug. She was listed as *Tiern* in Lloyd's Register 1957-58 and sold in April 1958 to Nor-West Whaling Co Ltd, Freemantle, Western Australia. She was renamed *Robert Moore* in 1959 and still listed in Lloyds Register 1969-70. She was reported scuttled on 10 July 1968 off Rottnest Island, Western Australia. Prior to scuttling, the vessel was listed as a Steam Lighter. Of the trawlers, *St. Loman* may have had the most combined years of naval and fishing service. Launched in 1936, she remained a hardworking fishing vessel until her tragic end in 1964. On 8 December, she suffered a boiler explosion ninety miles off the Scottish coast, which killed three engine-room men. Towed back to Hull, the cost and benefits of the necessary work and expense to repair her was considered uneconomical, and so she was broken up at Ghent, Belgium, the following year.

TRAWLERS AT HULL, ENGLAND

Le Tigre, of "U-boat killer in American waters" fame, was a special ship even from the beginning. Upon the completion of her construction by Cochrane Shipbuilders at Selby, England, in 1937, her proud owners, Earl SF Co. of Grimsby, had commemorated the building of what they considered to be an exceptional vessel, by presenting each man at the builder's yard with a shilling. After returning to the UK after war's end, being paid off and placed on the Disposal List, *Le Tigre* was acquired in October 1945 by The Hull Ice Company. In July 1947, she was renamed *Regal*, and then a few months later, *Othello* in September. Following 36 years of naval and commercial service, she was broken up in 1963, this time with no ceremony and exchange of coins.

In a mercantile sale in January 1946, *Lady Elsa* was acquired by her previous owners, Jutland Amalgamated Trawlers of Hull, from which the Royal Navy had purchased her in August 1939. In 1950, she was acquired by Associated FTC of Hull and renamed *Lord Tay.* Three years later, Lord Line of Hull purchased her and converted her to use fuel oil. In September 1964, she was damaged by an engine room fire in port at Hull. Shortly afterward, in November, she was broken up by Thomas Ward at Grays in Essex, England.

Lady Rosemary was returned to Kingston STC of Hull in May 1946, and renamed *Kingston Ruby.* She was scrapped at Ghent in 1963.

St. Loman was returned to her owner, T. Hamling of Hull in July 1946. In 1951, she was acquired by Boyd Line of Hull and renamed *Arctic Adventurer.* As previously mentioned, a boiler explosion in 1964 prematurely ended her service; she also was broken up at Ghent.

St. Zero, also originally owned by T. Hamling of Hull, had been purchased into the Royal Navy, and not requisitioned as had *St. Loman.* As such, she was sold to mercantile in May 1946 being acquired by Firth ST Co. of Hull. In 1952, she was renamed *Banyers.* Fourteen years later, she was broken up in Belgium, at Antwerp, in 1966.

After returning to the UK and being paid off, *Stella Polaris* was returned to Charleson & Smith Trs. of Hull in October 1945.

TRAWLERS AT GRIMSBY, ENGLAND

Cape Warwick was sold to mercantile on 26 January 1946. Purchased by Consolidated Fisheries of Grimsby and renamed *Lincoln City*, she plied fishing waters until broken up in 1963. Consolidated Fisheries of Grimsby, also gained back *Coventry City*, which returned to the UK in 1945. The following year, she was returned to her original owner from whom she had been requisitioned by the Admiralty for naval service.

Hertfordshire was returned to The Rutlandshire SF Co. Ltd. of Grimsby in 1945. Six years later, she was acquired in 1951 by Northern Trawlers of Hull, and renamed *Northern Gift.*

The five "Northern ships" that had sailed for American in 1942 were constructed at Bremerhaven, as part of the German World War I Reparation Programme. As one of the terms of the Treaty of Versailles at the conclusion of World War I, the Central Powers were compelled to give war reparations to the Allied Powers. Each of the defeated powers were required to make payments in either cash or kind; the latter included these vessels.

The three survivors of these reparation ships had all been requisitioned from Mac Line of London, and were returned to same. *Northern Chief* was returned to Mac Line of London in July 1945, then acquired by Northern Trawlers Ltd. of London and based at Grimsby. In 1947, she was sold to Icelandic owners. Sister ship *Northern Dawn* was likewise returned to her owners in February 1946, acquired by Northern Trawlers and based at Grimsby. She was broken up in 1964. The same story applied with *Northern Duke*; she was returned to her owners a month earlier in January 1946, acquired by Northern Trawlers and based at Grimsby.

Norwich was returned to Consolidated Fisheries of Grimsby in 1946 and, at the end of her service, broken up in 1964.

Wellard returned to the UK in 1945, and was sold to mercantile the following year. She was reacquired by the Crampins Steam Fishing Company of Grimsby, which had originally sold her to the Royal Navy. Of the eleven ships of Crampins originally taken up for naval service, only five returned from the war. *Wellard* retaining her original name, took up her intended vocation of trawling, and was eventually broken up in September 1961.[2]

BUILDERS OF 24 KING'S SHIPS SENT TO AMERICA, INCLUDING THE 17 SURVIVORS AND 7 LOST

Cochrane Shipbuilders, Shelby, England

Trawler	Launched	Disposition
HMT *Arctic Explorer*	1937	Sold to mercantile in 1945
HMT *Cape Warwick*	May 1937	Sold to mercantile on 26 January 1946
HMT *Le Tigre*	Apr 1937	Returned to UK 1945, sold to mercantile
HMT *Stella Polaris*	1936	Returned to UK and to owners, in 1945

Smith's Dock Company, South Bank on the River Tees, England

Trawler / Whaler	Launched	Disposition
HMT *Bedfordshire*	1937	Sunk by *U-558* on 11 May 1942
HMT *Coventry City*	1937	Returned to UK in 1945; to owners 1946
HMT *Hertfordshire*	Sep 1936	Returned to UK and to owners, in 1945
HMT *Norwich City*	1937	Returned to UK in 1945; to owners 1946
HMS *Buttermere*	Jun 1939	Sold in May 1946
HMS *Wastwater*	Aug 1939	Sold in May 1946

CWG (Cook, Welton & Gemmell), Beverley, England

Trawler	Launched	Disposition
HMT *Kingston Ceylonite*	1935	Sunk on 15 June 1942, in a minefield laid off Virginia Beach by *U-701*
HMT *Lady Elsa*	1937	Returned to UK in 1945; sold to mercantile in January 1946
HMT *Lady Rosemary*	1937	Returned to UK in 1945; to owners 1946
HMT *Pentland Firth*	1934	sunk in collision on 19 September 1942
HMT *St. Cathan*	1936	sunk in collision on 11 April 1942
HMT *St. Loman*	1936	Returned to UK in 1945; to owners 1946
HMT *St. Zero*	1940	Returned to UK in 1945; to owners 1946
HMT *Wellard*	1937	Returned to UK in 1945; to owners 1946

Bremerhaven, Germany

Trawler	Launched	Disposition
HMT *Northern Chief*	1936	Returned to UK and owners in 1945
HMT *Northern Dawn*	1936	Returned to UK in 1945; to owners 1946
HMT *Northern Duke*	1936	Returned to UK in 1945; to owners 1946
HMT *Northern Isles*	1936	Stranded near Durban on 19 January 1945, and was lost; no casualties
HMT *Northern Princess*	1936	Sunk off Newfoundland on 8 March 1942 by *U-587*

Hall, Russell and Company, Aberdeen, Scotland

Trawler	Launched	Disposition
HMT *Senateur Duhamel*	1927	sunk in collision on 6 May 1942

Appendix A: Ship Characteristics of RNPS Vessels sent to American Waters

Royal Naval Patrol Service Anti-Submarine Vessels

Ship Name **Ship Type** **Commanding Officer**	**Launch** **Comm**	**Length / Speed** **Displacement /** **Weapons**	**Remarks**
Arctic Explorer (FY162) A/S trawler – no class	1937 Nov 39	167 feet 501 tons 4-inch gun, depth charges	Battle Honour ATLANTIC 42
Bedfordshire (FY141) A/S trawler – no class	1935 Oct 39	162.3 feet 443 tons 4-inch gun, .303 Lewis machine gun, twin .50-cal. machine guns, Holman Projector AA weapon, depth charges	Sunk on 12 May 1942 by *U-558* off Cape Lookout, North Carolina; no survivors
Buttermere (FY205) A/S whaler – Lake class	18 Oct 39	148 feet 568 tons 12pdr AA gun, 20 mm AA gun, twin .5" AA gun (1x2) depth charges	
Cape Warwick (FY167) A/S trawler – no class	1937 Oct 39	173 feet 516 tons 4-inch gun, depth charges	Battle Honour ATLANTIC 41-42
Coventry City (FY267) A/S trawler – no class	1937 Jan 1940	546 tons 12 knots 4-inch gun, depth charges	Battle Honour ATLANTIC 41
Hertfordshire (FY176) A/S trawler – no class	1936 Nov 39	458 tons 4-inch gun, depth charges	Battle Honour ATLANTIC 43

Kingston Ceylonite (FY214) A/S trawler – no class	1935 Nov 39	448 tons 12.3 knots 4-inch gun, depth charges	Sunk on 15 June 1942 in a minefield laid off Virginia Beach on 11 June by *U-701*; 18 of the 32-man crew went down with the ship
Lady Elsa (FY124) A/S trawler – no class	1937 Oct 39	518 tons 4-inch gun, depth charges	Battle Honour ATLANTIC 40-42
Lady Rosemary (FY253) A/S trawler – no class	1937 Jun 40	472 tons 4-inch gun, depth charges	
Le Tigre (FY243) A/S trawler – no class	1937 Dec 39	173 feet 516 tons 12 knots 4-inch gun, depth charges	On 3 July 1942, *Le Tigre* depth-charged and sank *U-215* east of Cape Cod
Northern Chief (4.34) A/S trawler – no class	1936 Sep 39	655 tons 4-inch gun, depth charges	
Northern Dawn (FY146) A/S trawler – no class	1936 Sep 39	655 tons 4-inch gun, depth charges	Battle Honour ATLANTIC 40-42
Northern Duke (4.11) A/S trawler – no class	1936 Sep 39	655 tons 4-inch gun, depth charges	
Northern Isles (4.25) A/S trawler – no class	1936 5 Sep 39	655 tons 4-inch gun, depth charges	Beached and lost off Durban, South Africa on 19 January 1945
Northern Princess (4.06) A/S trawler – no class	1936 Sep 39	655 tons 4-inch gun, depth charges	Sunk on 8 March 1942 by *U-587* off the Grand Banks
Norwich City (FY229) A/S trawler – no class	1937 Nov 39	541 tons 4-inch gun, depth charges	Battle Honour ATLANTIC 40-42

Pentland Firth (FY108) A/S trawler – no class	1934 Oct 39	485 tons 4-inch gun, depth charges	Battle Honour ATLANTIC 40 Sunk on 19 September 1942 in a collision with the minesweeper USS *Chaffinch* (AM-81), between Ambrose Lightship and Sandy Hook, New Jersey
Senateur Duhamel (FY327) A/S trawler – no class	1927 Jan 41	192.3 feet 913 tons 4-inch gun, depth charges	On 6 May 1942, accidentally rammed and sunk by the auxiliary USS *Semmes* (AG-24) off Cape Lookout, North Carolina
St. Cathan (FY234) A/S trawler – no class	1936 Nov 39	565 tons 4-inch gun, depth charges	Battle Honour ATLANTIC 41 On 11 April 1942, sunk in a collision with the Dutch merchant *Hebe* south-southeast of Little River, South Carolina
St. Loman (FY276) A/S trawler – no class	1936 Oct 39	565 tons 4-inch gun, depth charges	Battle Honour ATLANTIC 40
St. Zeno (FY280) A/S trawler – no class	1940 18 Jul 40	155 feet 608 tons 4-inch gun, depth charges	Battle Honour ATLANTIC 40-41
Stella Polaris (4.258) A/S trawler – no class	1936 Sep 40	498 tons 4-inch gun, depth charges	
Wastwater (FY239) A/S whaler – Lake class	7 Nov 39	148 feet 568 tons 12pdr AA gun, 20 mm AA gun, twin .5" AA gun (1x2), depth charges	

Wellard (FY137)	1937	514 tons
A/S trawler – no class	Sep 39	4-inch gun, depth charges[1]

Appendix B: Officers Serving in RNPS Anti-submarine Vessels, post-March 1942

HMT *Arctic Explorer*

Officer	Seniority	Aboard
T/Sub Lt. Robert Murray Jackson, RNVR	18 Sep 41	29 Nov 41-1 Oct 43
T/Lt. Frederick Victor Storey, RNVR	28 Oct 41	12 Feb 42-Apr 43
T/Lt. Christopher Pawley, RNVR (In Command) Gazetted for the award of the DSC on 14 August 1945 while serving in HMS *La Malouine for distinguished service, efficiency and zeal in the clearance of the Aegean and the relief of Greece during the period 1944-1945.*	9 Dec 39	Mar 42-Feb 44
T/Sub Lt. Kenneth William Esswood, RNVR	5 Jun 41	Apr 43-16 Nov 44
T/Lt. Gordon Chapman Edwards, RNVR	17 Jan 42	Jul 43-4 Aug 44
T/Lt. Denis Hugh Crampton, RNR (In Command)	21 Apr 41	Feb 44-4 Aug 44
T/Sub Lt. William Hawthorne Tennant Llewellyn, RNVR/SANF(V)	18 Dec 43	From 29 Feb 44
T/Sub Lt. David Baxter, RNVR/SANF(V)	18 Aug 44	From 17 Mar 44
T/Lt. Rupert Edward Ellis-Brown, RNVR/SANF(V)	20 Mar 44	From 10 Dec 44
T/Lt. Arthur Robert James Tilston, DSC SANF(V) (In Command) Gazetted for the award of the DSC on 6 January 1942 *for courage and skill in action against the Enemy in the Mediterranean.* This was probably for his performance while commanding the whaler *Kos XXI.*	10 Jan 41	4 Aug 44-Jun 45

HMT *Bedfordshire* (sunk 12 May 1942)

Lt. Russell Bransley Davis, RNR (In Command)	27 May 40	26 Feb 41-11 May 42 †
T/Sub Lt. Bruce Hall, RNVR	28 Jun 40	4 Jul 41-11 May 42 †
T/Sub Lt. Henry Clutterbuck, RNVR	28 Aug 41	12 Feb 42-11 May 42 †
T/Sub Lt. Thomas Cunningham, RNVR	17 Jul 41	13 Feb 42-11 May 42 †

HMS *Buttermere*

Officer	Seniority	Aboard
Lt. George William Farrow, RNR (In Command) Gazetted for the award of a Mention in Despatches on 2 July 1946 *for distinguished services during the war in the Far East* while serving at HMIS *Feroze*.	15 Aug 40	30 May 40-Dec 42
T/Sub Lt. William John Connacher Cleland, RNVR	20 Mar 41	17 Apr 41-30 Aug 43
T/A/Sub Lt. William Lawrence Wright, RNVR	9 May 41	22 Aug 41-30 Aug 43
T/Sub Lt. Forrest Smyth Scott, RNVR	11 Sep 42	Oct 42-5 Apr 43
Lt John Dudley Edward Lewis, RNR (In Command)	9 Sep 40	Dec 42-early 44
T/Sub Lt. Geoffrey Brian Rogers, RNVR	23 Oct 41	From Apr 43
T/A/Sub Lt. John Arthur Pemberton Morris, RNVR	21 Nov 43	18 Jun 43-7 Jul 43
T/Sub Lt. John Barnard Butchers, RNZNVR (In Command)	5 Mar 43	Early 44-20 Dec 44
T/A/Sub Lt. Ralph Seymour Dickins, RNVR	22 Aug 44	From Sep 44
T/Sub Lt. Josias Toulmin Esterhuizen, SANF(V) (In Command)	9 Oct 43	20 Dec 44-7 Mar 45
T/Lt. Colin Gordon McKenzie, SANF(V) (In Command)	6 Aug 43	7 Mar 45-late 1945
T/Lt. (Sp. Br.) John Geoffrey Hall, SANF(V)	1 Jan 45	From 12 Mar 45
T/A/Sub Lt. Roy Arthur Dunkley, RNVR	18 Feb 44	From 1 May 45

HMT *Cape Warwick*

Sub Lt. John Patrick Geaney, RANVR	14 Mar 40	18 Oct 40-25 Apr 43
Sub Lt. Arthur Lloyd Hargreaves, RANVR	15 Aug 40	From 5 Aug 41
T/Lt. William Edward Goggin, RNR (In Command)	28 Feb 40	10 Sep 41-Aug 43
T/Lt. George Arthur Hartnell, RNR	23 Sep 40	From 17 Feb 42
T/Sub Lt. John Alexander Smith, SANF(V)	13 Mar 41	From 2 Jul 43
T/Lt Kenneth Joseph Stern, RNVR (In Command) Gazetted for the award of a Mention in Despatches on 29 Jul 1941 *for good services in rescue work* while in Command of HMT *St Zeno*.	1 Mar 42	Aug 43-29 Dec 44
T/Sub Lt. Colin Gordon McKenzie, SANF(V)	6 Nov 42	From 1 Oct 43
T/A/Sub Lt. Robert Angus Munro Wilson, RNVR	18 Aug 44	From Mar 44
T/Sub Lt. Eric Hargreaves, RNVR	18 Aug 44	From 15 Aug 44
T/Lt Charles William Leslie Moser, RNVR (In Command)	15 Nov 40	From 29 Dec 44

HMT *Coventry City*

Officer	Seniority	Aboard
T/Lt. John Coade Grose, RNR (In Command)	1 Feb 40	24 Nov 41-Aug 43
T/Sub Lt. Albert Brady, RNVR	2 Dec 41	From 21 May 41
T/Lt. Norman Kingsley Baynes, RNVR	1 Feb 41	3 Jul 41-Jul 43
T/Lt. James Norman Balliol Laine, RNVR	3 Oct 40	From 13 Dec 41
T/Sub Lt. Thomas Alexander Gale, RNVR	26 Jun 41	From Apr 43
T/A/Sub Lt. Anthony Michael Craven Whitaker, SANF(V)	9 Jul 43	From 12 Aug 43
T/Lt. Robert Murray Jackson, RNVR	5 Jul 43	1 Oct 43-30 Jul 44
T/Lt. John Wells, RNVR (In Command)	7 Dec 42	Aug 43-Jun 44
T/Lt. Willie Morris, RNVR (In Command)	5 Jun 41	Jun 44-Apr 45
T/Lt. David Hamilton Graham, RNZNVR	31 Dec 43	From 2 Aug 44
T/Sub Lt. Joseph Lingard Bregami/Bregazzi, RNVR	18 Feb 44	From 15 Aug 44
T/Lt. Alec Charles Stevenson, RNVR	9 Apr 44	From Oct 44
T/Lt. Kenneth Stephen Hook, RNVR (In Command)	2 Jan 43	From Apr 1945
T/Sub Lt. Peter Louw, SANF(V)	1 Jul 43	From Apr 45
T/Sub Lt. Paul Delville Mallett, SANF(V)	30 Oct 43	From Jun 45

HMT *Hertfordshire*

T/Lt. Colin Sawyer Pirie, RNVR (In Command as A/Lt. Cdr.)	6 Oct 39	From 14 Nov 41
T/Lt. Raymond Shrimpton, RNVR	31 May 40	From 14 Nov 41
T/Sub Lt. Thomas Alexander Gale, RNVR	26 Jun 41	14 Nov 41-Apr 43
T/Sub Lt. Thomas Thornton Hodgson, RNVR	13 Nov 41	From 13 Feb 42
T/Lt. Frederick Lorraine Mackenzie, RNVR	17 May 41	From Apr 43
T/Lt. Norman Kingsley Baynes, RNVR	1 Feb 41	From Jul 43
T/Sub Lt. George William Henderson Gordon, SANF(V)	26 Feb 43	From Jul 43
T/A/Sub Lt. Henry Thomas Dockrall, SANF(V)	25 Apr 44	From 3 Oct 43
T/Lt. Elkan Maurice Green, SANF(V) (In Command) Gazetted for the award of the BEM on 11 December 1945 *for Distinguished Service during the war in Europe* while in command of HMT *Hertfordshire*.	13 Jun 41	From 17 Mar 44
T/Sub Lt. Warwick Landon Fletcher, SANF(V)	21 Jun 43	From 27 Jul 44

HMT *Kingston Ceylonite* (sunk 15 June 1942)

Officer	Seniority	Aboard
Skr. Richard Read, RNR	29 Mar 40	From 3 Aug 40
Skr. Stanley Charles Larner, RNR Gazetted for the award of the BEM on 11 September 1945 *for bravery and devotion to duty in firefighting and rescue work after an explosion in a Merchant Vessel in the Port of Bari on the 9th April, 1945* while serving in HMT *Bream.*	5 Jan 39	11 Jan 42-12 Feb 42
Skr. William McKenzie Smith, RNR (In Command)	28 Dec 37	13 Feb 42-15 Jun 42 †
T/Skr. Thomas Orford Fletcher Leiper, RNR	1 Dec 41	13 Feb 42-15 Jun 42 †

HMT *Lady Elsa*

T/Lt. Sidney George Phillips, RNVR (In Command) Gazetted for the award of the DSC in New Year Honours 1 January 1942 *for outstanding zeal, patience and cheerfulness, and for setting an example of wholehearted devotion to duty, without which the high traditions of the Royal Navy could not have been upheld while in Command of HMT Lady Elsa.*	9 Dec 39	Jun 40-Aug 43
T/Lt Geoffrey John Younghusband Thorpe, RNVR (In Command) Gazetted for the award of a Mention in Despatches 11 September 1945 *for skill and enterprise in command of H.M.S. Northern Spray, which salvaged a tanker off Iceland on 4th-5th May, 1945.*	1 Apr 42	11 Feb 41-Aug 43
T/Sub Lt. Reginald George Pritchard, RNVR	27 Feb 41	3 Apr 41-Jul 43
T/Lt. Alexander Weston, RNVR	31 Jul 42	From Nov 42
T/Sub Lt. John Cameron Louis Davidson, RNVR	18 Dec 43	From 12 Aug 43
T/Lt. Arthur Marchant Brown (In Command)	19 Oct 40	Aug 43-24 Jun 44
T/Lt. David LeFleming Dobson, RNVR	21 Jul 42	1 Oct 43-1 Aug 44
T/Lt. Charles Alfred Power, SANF(V) (In Command)	6 Aug 43	24 Jun 44-10 May 45
T/Sub Lt. Peter Gordon Buckley, SANF(V)	15 Oct 43	From Sep 44
T/Lt Alfred Kenneth Scholes, RNVR (In Command)	14 Aug 43	10 May 45-13 Aug 45
T/Sub Lt. Ernest Locksley Cross, RNVR (In Command)	25 Jun 43	13 Aug 45-late 45

HMT *Lady Rosemary*

Officer	Seniority	Aboard
T/Lt. Brian Thomas Borthwick, RNVR	28 Jun 40	From 9 Jan 41
T/Lt. Henry Brown, RNR (In Command)	3 Oct 40	4 Feb 41-Aug 43
T/Sub Lt. James Leonard Warwick, RNVR	2 Feb 42	From 14 Feb 42
T/Lt Gilbert Neville Jones, RNVR	2 Jun 42	From 3 Jul 43
T/Sub Lt. James Arthur Farber, SANF(V)	17 Jul 41	From 15 Nov 43
T/Lt Geoffrey John Younghusband Thorpe, RNVR (In Command) Gazetted for the award of a Mention in Despatches 11 September 1945 *for skill and enterprise in command of H.M.S. Northern Spray, which salvaged a tanker off Iceland on 4th-5th May, 1945.*	1 Apr 42	Aug 43-5 Jun 44
T/A/Sub Lt. John Arnold Farr, RNVR	18 Aug 44	From Mar 44
T/Lt. Denis Louis Simpson, RNVR	1 Mar 45	From 10 May 44
T/Lt. Thomas Toft, SANF(V) (In Command)	5 Sep 39	5 Jun 44-30 Sep 44
T/Sub Lt. William Graham Holder, RNZNVR	25 Dec 42	From Jun 44
T/Lt. James Leonard Warwick, RNVR (Back again but in Command this time)	25 Mar 44	From 30 Sep 44

HMT *Le Tiger/Tigre*

T/Lt. Colin Arthur Hoodless, RNR (In Command) Gazetted for the award of a DSC on 14 May 1946 *for outstanding services while in command of H.M. Ships engaged in anti-submarine operations during the war in Europe.*	23 Oct 40	6 Nov 40-7 Jul 43
T/Lt. Peter Arnold Tunbridge, RNVR	17 Jun 42	From 27 Jan 41
Lt. Geoffrey Frank Bedford, RANVR	22 May 41	From 17 Feb 41
T/Lt. George Murray Oliver, RCNVR	17 Jun 41	From Apr 43
T/Lt. Robert Fulton Walker, RNVR (In Command)	24 Nov 40	7 Jul 43-21 Mar 44
T/Sub Lt. Thomas John Vincent, RNVR	9 Jan 44	From 12 Aug 43
T/Lt. Albert Brady, RNVR (In Command)	17 Jul 43	From 21 Mar 44
T/Sub Lt. Royden Alfred Main, SANF(V)	20 Feb 44	From 1 Aug 44

HMT *Northern Chief*

Officer	**Seniority**	**Aboard**
T/Sub Lt. John Rutherford Hutchinson Fletcher, RNVR	16 Jan 40	From 16 Jan 40
T/Sub Lt. William Millward Russell, RNVR Gazetted for the award of a DSC on 3 Apr 45 as an A/Lt. Cdr while Senior Officer 15th ML Flotilla and in Command of the motor launch HM *ML 454 for great gallantry and endurance in clearing the estuary of the Scheldt of mines during, the period of October to November 1944.*	2 Mar 40	From 2 Mar 40
T/Sub Lt. Robert John St. Aubyn Latham, RNVR	21 Oct 39	From 17 Apr 40
Sub Lt. Donald Stewart Watson, RNR	24 Aug 41	From 26 Sep 41
T/Lt. George William Osborne Howe, RNR (In Command)	27 May 41	14 Feb 42-Oct 42
T/Sub Lt. John Frederick Forester Gardner, RNVR	1 May 41	From 14 Feb 42
Lt. John Dudley Edward Lewis, RNR (In Command)	9 Sep 40	Oct 42-Dec 42
T/Lt. George Arthur Hartnell, RNR (In Command)	23 Sep 40	Dec 42-mid 43
T/A/Sub Lt. Douglas Morier Porter, RNVR	19 Mar 43	Apr 43-Oct 44
T/Lt. Leonard Griffin Gillham, SANF(V) (In Command)	1 Apr 41	Dec 43-25Aug 44
T/Lt. Gerald Arthur Nel, SANF(V)	2 Jul 43	From Feb 44
T/Sub Lt. John Reginald Crowden, RNVR	7 Jul 44	From 15 Apr 44
T/Lt. Alfred Kenneth Scholes, RNVR (In Command)	14 Aug 43	25 Aug 44-9 May 45
T/Lt. Charles Alfred Power, SANF(V) (In Command)	6 Aug 43	From 10 May 45
T/Sub Lt. Oliver Ashe Francis, RNR	1 Jul 43	From 11 May 45

HMT *Northern Dawn*

Officer	Seniority	Aboard
T/Lt. Gordon Chapman Edwards, RNVR	17 Jan 42	8 Feb 41-Jul 43
T/Lt. Arthur Marchant Brown, RNVR	19 Oct 40	19 Feb 41-Aug 43
T/Lt. Reginald Beaumont Belas, RNVR	18 Jan 41	From Apr 41
Lt. Joseph Oswald Williams, RNR (In Command)	20 Jun 40	May 41-Aug 43
T/Sub Lt. Donald Hugh Fisher, RNVR Gazetted for the award of a Mention in Despatches in New Year Honours on 1 January 1944 *for gallantry or outstanding service in the face of the Enemy, or for zeal, patience and cheerfulness in dangerous waters and for setting an example of wholehearted devotion to duty, upholding the high traditions of the Royal Navy* while serving in HMT *Northern Chief*.	21 Aug 41	From 30 Oct 41
T/Lt John Patrick Geaney, RANVR	25 Apr 43	25 Apr 43-31 Jul 44
T/Lt. Frederick Victor Storey, RNVR	28 Oct 41	From Apr 43
T/Lt. Denis Louis Simpson, RNVR	1 Mar 45	May 43-10 May 44
T/Lt. Reginald George Pritchard, RNVR	27 Aug 43	From Jul 43
Lt. Stuart Faithful Fell, RANVR (In Command)	2 May 41	12 Aug 43-Sep 44
T/Lt. Robert Murray Jackson, RNVR (In Command)	5 Jul 43	From Sep 44
T/Sub Lt. (Sp. Br.) Sidney Phillip Alban Newhouse, SANF(V)	18 Aug 44	From 30 Sep 44
T/Sub Lt. Douglas Morier Porter, RNVR	19 Sep 43	From Oct 44

HMT *Northern Duke*

Officer	Seniority	Aboard
Lt. Norman Peter McLeod, RD RNR	12 Jan 35	Mar 40-31 Jan 41
T/Sub Lt. James Farquharson MacLaren Anderson, RNR	4 Dec 39	4 Apr 40-27 Jul 40
Sub Lt. George Lachlan Fraser, RNR	11 Jan 40	27 May 40-13 Apr 41
T/Sub Lt. Thomas Jobling, RNVR	21 Oct 39	24 Jan 41-6 Mar 41
Sub Lt. Alan Percival Bunce, RNVR	20 Jun 38	29 Jan 41-6 Feb 43
T/Lt. William Carl McDonnell, RNVR	21 Feb 41	20 Mar 41-Aug 43
T/Lt. Harold Gott, RNVR	1 Jun 43	1 Jan 42-Nov 43
T/Lt. James Alfred Wright, RNR (In Command) Gazetted for the award of a Mention in Despatches on 10 July 1945 *for outstanding courage, skill and endurance whilst serving in HMS Honeysuckle, in escorting convoys, frequently in severe weather, to North Russia.*	30 Dec 40	Feb 42-12 Aug 43
T/Sub Lt. Charles Alfred Power, RNVR Later transferred to SANF(V)	6 Nov 42	21 Jan 43-24 Jun 44
T/Lt. Geoffrey Frank Bedford, RANVR (In Command)	22 May 41	12 Aug 43-29 Oct 43
T/Lt. Richard Dirk van der Byl, SANF(V) (In Command)	13 Jun 41	29 Oct 43-31 Jul 44
T/Lt William Barrowcliffe Atkin, SANF(V)	7 Feb 42	From 29 Oct 43
T/A/Sub Lt. Tom Spencer, RNR	1 Sep 43	Nov 43-15 Jun 44
T/Lt. John Patrick Geaney, RANVR (In Command)	25 Apr 43	From 31 Jul 44

HMT *Northern Isles* (grounded and lost 19 January 1945)

Sub Lt. Ernest John Adams, RANVR	28 Oct 40	From 8 Jul 41
T/Lt. John Maurice Baldry, RNVR (In Command)	5 Jan 41	Feb 42-Jan 44
T/Lt. Cyril Garrett Layland, RNVR	23 Jan 42	From 5 Feb 42
Lt. Robert Arthur Groom, RNVR	1 Apr 42	14 Feb 42-Aug 43
T/Lt. Peter Eric Studd, RNVR	5 Jun 42	From Oct 42
T/Lt. Arthur Robert James Tilston, DSC SANF(V) (In Command) Gazetted for the award of a DSC on 6 January 1942 *for courage and skill in action against the Enemy in the Mediterranean.* This was probably for his performance while commanding the whaler *Kos XXI.*	10 Jan 41	Jan 44-1 Aug 44
T/Sub Lt. Arthur Cole Fairbrother, RNVR	4 Aug 44	From 1 Jul 44
T/Lt. David LeFleming Dobson, RNVR (In Command)	21 Jul 42	From 1 Aug 44

HMT *Northern Princess* (sunk 8 March 1942)

Officer	Seniority	Aboard
T/Sub Lt. Herbert Edward James, RNR	4 Dec 39	From 22 Apr 40
Lt. Dryden Byrne Phillipson, RNR (In Command)	16 May 40	Mar 41-7 Mar 42 †
T/Sub Lt. Edward Shepherd, RNVR	6 Mar 41	From 3 Mar 41 †
T/Sub Lt. Jack MacDonnell, RNVR	21 Feb 41	From 20 Mar 41 †
T/Lt. Leslie William Kevis, RNR	29 Jan 41	From 14 Feb 42 †

HMT *Norwich City*

T/Lt. Leslie Hugh Stammers, RNVR (In Command)	21 Sep 40	12 Apr 41-Aug 43
T/Sub Lt. John Alexander Smith, SANF(V)	13 Mar 41	14 Apr 41-2 Jul 43
A/Sub Lt. Eric Allan Hamilton, RNR	15 Aug 40	1 Jul 41-6 Feb 43
T/Sub Lt. James Farmer, RCNVR Gazetted for the award of a Mention in Despatches on 4 July 1944 *for courage, resolution and skill in H.M.C.S. Waskesiu in successful operations against U-boats in the Atlantic.*	30 Dec 40	Feb 42-13 Sep 43
T/Lt. Richard Dirk van der Byl, SANF(V)	13 Jun 41	8 Jun 42-29 Oct 43
T/Sub Lt. James Leonard Warwick, RNVR	2 Feb 42	From 2 Jul 43
T/A/Sub Lt. John Arthur Pemberton Morris, RNVR	21 Nov 43	From 7 Jul 43
Lt. Robert Arthur Groom, RNVR (In Command)	1 Apr 42	Aug 43-Oct 44
T/Lt. Leslie Gordon Wright, DSC RNVR Gazetted for the award of a DSC on 30 November 1943 *for great courage and vigour in action with enemy submarines in HMS Test in the escort of a convoy.*	3 Jul 43	From 31 Aug 44
T/Lt. Leonard Griffin Gilham, SANF(V) (In Command)	unknown	From Oct 44
T/Sub Lt. Harry Dennis Jennett, RNVR	1 Mar 44	From 19 Mar 45

HMT *Pentland Firth* (sunk 19 September 1942)

Skr. Edward John Lockwood Davies, RNR (In Command)	1 May 40	Aug 41-19 Sep 42

HMT/FFS *Senateur Duhamel* (sunk 6 May 1942)

Officer	Seniority	Aboard
Lt. Innes Athole Thorpe, MBE RNVR Gazetted for appointment as an MBE on 19 May 1942 *for bravery in the salvage of a tanker* [*Lucellum* on 19 December 1941] *and in saving many men from her* while serving in HMT/FFS *Senateur Duhamel.*	3 May 41	Aug 41-Feb 42
Sub Lt. Peter Eric Studd, RNVR	5 Jun 41	Aug 41-May 42
Lt. Richard Wallace Hart, RCNVR Gazetted for award of Mention in Despatches in King's Birthday Honours 8 June 1944 while serving in HMCS *Canada.*	4 Sep 40	Apr-May 42
Lt Alexander Michael Sullivan, RNVR	18 Apr 40	Apr-May 42

HMT *St. Cathan* (sunk 11 April 1942)

T/Lt. Frederick Twomey, RNR (In Command)	13 Mar 40	27 Mar 40-11 Jun 41
T/Lt. Alexander Michael Sullivan, RNVR	18 Apr 40	From 4 Feb 41
Lt. John Mackay, RNR (In Command)	11 Jan 40	12 Jun 41-11 Apr 42
T/Sub Lt. Henry Bleby Hodgeshon, RNVR	26 Nov 40	From 10 Jan 42
T/Sub Lt. Alexander Weston, RNVR	31 Jul 41	From 16 Jan 42

HMT *St. Loman*

T/Lt. Oswald Thomas Dodwell, RNR	22 Nov 40	From 27 Jan 41
T/Lt. Gilbert Neville Jones, RNVR	2 Jun 42	From 28 Mar 41
T/Lt. Thomas Alfred Willis, RCNVR	21 Dec 39	From 30 Jun 41
T/Lt. Richard Colin Warwick, DSC RNR (In Command) Gazetted for the award of a DSC on 19 August 1940 for service in the 15th Anti-Submarine Striking Force off the Norwegian Coast. Gazetted for a bar to his DSC in the 1941 New Year Honours *for outstanding zeal, patience and cheerfulness, and for never failing to set an example of wholehearted devotion to duty, without which the high tradition of the Royal Navy could not have been upheld* while *in command of HMT St Loman.*	31 Jan 40	17 Apr 40-Aug 43
T/A/Sub Lt. Roy Moores, RNVR	18 Jun 43	From 12 Aug 43
T/Lt. William Carl McDonnell, RNVR (In Command)	21 Feb 41	Aug 43-16 Jan 45
T/Lt. Richard Henry Maynard, SANF(V) (In Command)	2 Oct 43	From 16 Jan 45
T/Sub Lt. Edward Dunn Thorburn, SANF(V)	24 Sep 43	From 4 May 45

HMT *St. Zeno*

Officer	Seniority	Aboard
T/Lt. John Kirke Craig, RNVR (In Command) Gazetted for the award of a Mention in Despatches on 11 June 1942 *for outstanding zeal, patience and cheerfulness, and for never failing to set an example of wholehearted devotion to duty, without which the high tradition of the Royal Navy could not have been upheld* while serving in HMT *St Zeno.* Gazetted for the award of a Mention in Despatches on 14 June 1945 *for gallantry or outstanding service in the face of the enemy, or for zeal, patience and cheerfulness in dangerous waters, and for setting an example of wholehearted devotion to duty, upholding the high tradition of the Royal Navy* while serving in HMS *Oxlip.*	22 Nov 39	25 Sep 40-Jul 43
T/Sub Lt. Walter Herbert Robertson, RNVR	17 Jan 41	21 May 41-Jan 43
T/Sub Lt. Alec Alfred Trotter, RNVR	14 Aug 41	8 Nov 41-Feb 43
T/Lt. Raymond Shrimpton, RNVR (In Command)	31 May 40	Jul 43-30 Mar 44
T/Lt. Colin Gordon McKenzie, SANF(V) (In Command)	6 Aug 43	31 Mar 44-7 Mar 45
Sub Lt. Gordon MacAllister Douglas, SANF(V)	18 Aug 44	From 6 Mar 45

HMT *Stella Polaris*

Skr. Thomas Normandale, RNR (In Command)	1 Jun 40	11 Jul 41-31 Mar 44
Skipper Ernest Thomas Sanders, RNR	17 May 39	From Sep 41
Skipper William Jesse Jones, RNR	1 Dec 40	From Dec 43
T/Sub Lt. Barry Mervyn Stacey, SANF(V) (In Command)	1 Mar 44	31 Mar 44-14 Mar 45
T/Lt. David Hamilton Graham, RNZNVR (In Command) Gazetted for the award of a Mention in Despatches on 1 August 1943 for action against a Japanese submarine at Guadalcanal on 29 January 1943 while serving in HMNZS *Kiwi.*	31 Dec 43	14 Mar 45-Jul 45
T/Lt. Alec Charles Stevenson, RNVR	9 Apr 44	From 16 Mar 45
T/Sub Lt. Joseph Mervyn Kendal, SANF(V)	5 May 44	From 4 May 45

HMS *Wastwater*

Officer	Seniority	Aboard
T/Sub Lt. Geoffrey Holder Jones, RNVR	20 Mar 41	From 4 Apr 41
T/Lt. John Henry Louis May, OBE RNVR (In Command) Gazetted for appointment as OBE on 11 July 1940 *in recognition of distinguished services during the War* while serving in HMT *Northern Sun.*	11 Oct 39	Aug 41-Apr 43
T/Lt. Michael Rayner Thwaites, RNVR	15 Dec 40	From Aug 41
T/Sub Lt. John Rattenbury, RNVR	6 Mar 41	Aug 42-Aug 43
Y/Sub Lt. Richard Christopher Wright, RNVR	11 Sep 42	From Oct 42
T/Lt. William John Lewis Storey, RNVR (In Command)	7 Sep 40	Apr 43-13 Jul 45
T/Lt. Alan John Nicol, RANVR	13 Jan 42	From Apr 43
T/Sub Lt. John Damien Stott, RNVR	29 Jan 43	From Apr 43
T/Lt. Andrew Miller Anderson, RNVR (In Command)	17 Oct 42	13 Jul 45-late 45

HMT *Wellard*

Lt. Robert Fletcher Turnbull, RNVR (In Command)	Retired	May 41-Oct 42
Lt. Stuart Faithful Fell, RANVR	2 May 41	14 Feb 41-13 Jul 43
T/Lt. Graham Hellyer, RNVR (In Command)	20 Oct 40	14 Jul 43-Nov 43
T/Lt. Harold Gott, RNVR	1 Jun 43	Nov 43-24 Oct 44
T/A/Lt. Cdr. Harold Moxley Pinnell, RNVR (In Command)	7 May 41	25 Oct 44-11 May 45
T/Lt. William Carl McDonnell, RNVR (In Command)	21 Feb 41	From 11 May 45

† Killed in Action

Appendix C: Officers Serving in SANF Anti-submarine Vessels

RNVR (SAD): RNVR (South African Division) formed in 1922
SANF (V): South African Naval Forces (Voluntary) created in 1942 with the amalgamation of South Africa's SDF (Seaward Defence Force, ex-South African Naval Service) and the RNVR (SAD)

HMSAS *Blaauwberg*

Officer	Seniority	Aboard
Lt Oswald Richard Dudley Stephen, SDF	22 Jul 40	Jun 41-Apr 42
Sub Lt Robert Thomas Park, SDF	1 Jul 40	Jun 41-Apr 42
Sub Lt Kenneth William Dartnell Shuttleworth	8 Dec 40	Dec 41-Apr 42
Lt Allan Thomas Gazetted for the award of the DSC on 9 September 1941 *for courage, resolution and devotion to duty in the face of Enemy air attacks* while in command of HMSAS *Southern Sea* with the Mediterranean 22nd Anti-Submarine Group.	25 Nov 40	Jun-Dec 42
Sub Lt John Douglas Stephens	1 Jul 40	Jun-Dec 42
Sub Lt Kenneth William Dartnell Shuttleworth	8 Dec 40	Jun-Dec 42
Eng Sub Lt George Henry Nash	22 Nov 41	Jun-Dec 42
Sub Lt Peter Hartog	18 Jun 41	Apr-Aug 43
Lt Harry Jeffrey	1 Oct 42	Apr 43-Apr 44
Sub Lt Jan Andre Beyers	16 Jan 41	Oct 43-Apr 44
Sub Lt John Duncan	1 Apr 43	Oct 43-Apr 44
Midshipman John Alexander Clark	1 Dec 42	Oct 43-Apr 44
Lt Casper Becker Dreyer	1 Apr 43	Oct 44
Sub Lt John Griffiths Robertson	2 Jan 42	Oct 44
Sub Lt A J Picton	unknown	Oct 44
Lt Richard Carrington Cousens	1 Oct 42	Jan-Jul 45
Lt Thomas Fletcher Shenfield	1 Oct 44	Jan-Jul 45
Sub Lt Robert Frank Monson	4 Dec 42	Jan-Jul 45
Sub Lt John Whewell Dickinson	20 Apr 44	Jan-Jul 45
Eng Sub Lt Philip Charles Preston-Whyte	30 Aug 44	Jan-Jul 45

HMSAS *Blomvlei*

Officer	Seniority	Aboard
Skipper Stephen Benjamin Petzer, RNVR (SAD)	28 Mar 37	From 10 Oct 39
Lt Henry Edelbert Fougstedt, RNVR(SA)	15 Jan 40	Jun-Oct 41
Sub Lt Edward John Raymond Walker, SDF Gazetted for the award of the DSC on 17 November 1942 *for skill and resource in action against enemy Submarines while serving in HMSAS Southern Maid.*	26 Jun 40	Jun-Oct 41
Sub Lt Harold Ray Tyler, SDF	19 Jun 40	Jun-Oct 41
Lt William Lynedoch Graham, SDF (CO)	15 Jan 40	Dec 41-Apr 42
Sub Lt J Alexander, SDF	unknown	Dec 41-Apr 42
Sub Lt Robert Ivan Easton, SDF	17 Mar 41	Dec 41-Apr 42
Lt Cdr Duncan Livingstone MacKinnon	1 Jan 42	Jun-Dec 42
Lt William Lynedoch Graham	7 Aug 40	Jun-Dec 42
Sub Lt Robert Ivan Easton	17 Mar 41	Jun-Dec 42
Sub Lt Peter Douglas Kockott	21 Jan 42	Jun-Dec 42
Lt Douglas Hocking Clarkson	22 Apr 42	Apr-Aug 43
Sub Lt Neil Frederick Carlisle	20 Sep 40	Apr-Aug 43
Sub Lt Robert Freeland Barrie	21 Jan 42	Apr-Aug 43
Sub Lt Percival Durie James	8 May 41	Oct 43-Apr 44
Sub Lt Clifford Andrew Perkins	19 Mar 43	Oct 43-Apr 44
Sub Lt George Arthur Heard	9 Nov 42	Oct 43-Apr 44
Lt Alec Woodford Solomon Gazetted for the award of the DSC on 17 November 1942 *for skill and resource in action against enemy Submarines while serving in HMSAS Protea.*	1 Jul 44	Oct 44-Jul 45
Sub Lt Ernest Brian Carter	27 Jan 41	Oct 44
Sub Lt John Ray Whiting	17 Jul 44	Oct 44
Sub Lt Douglas Windsor Pett	20 Apr 44	Jan-Jul 45
Sub Lt John Smalberger Murray	5 Aug 44	Jan-Jul 45

HMSAS *Cedarberg*

Officer	Seniority	Aboard
Eng Sub Lt Harold Ronaasen, SDF	11 Jul 40	Jun-Oct 41
Lt Eric Victor Brown (CO)	1 Jan 41	Dec 41-Apr 42
Sub Lt Leonard John Bangley, SDF Gazetted for the award of the DSC on 17 November 1942 *for skill and resource in action against enemy Submarines while serving in HMSAS Southern Maid.*	11 Jan 42	Dec 41-Apr 42
Sub Lt Edward John Raymond Walker, SDF Gazetted for the award of the DSC on 17 November 1942 *for skill and resource in action against enemy Submarines while serving in HMSAS Southern Maid.*	26 Jun 40	Dec 41-Apr 42
Sub Lt James Bevan McLoughlin, SDF	4 Oct 40	Dec 41-Apr 42
Lt Eric Victor Brown	1 Jan 41	Jun-Dec 42
Sub Lt James Bevan McLoughlin	4 Oct 40	Jun-Dec 42
Sub Lt Peter Hartog	18 Jun 41	Jun-Dec 42
Eng Sub Lt Arthur Orazio Mario Antonio Bonfa	6 Oct 41	Jun-Dec 42
Sub Lt Harold Orffer	21 Jan 42	Apr-Aug 43
Sub Lt William John Hume	4 Aug 41	Apr-Aug 43
Sub Lt Spencer Joseph Newton Richards	3 Feb 41	Apr-Aug 43
Lt Louis Botha Ribbink Gazetted for the award of the DSC on 9 September 1941 *for courage, resolution and devotion to duty in the face of Enemy air attacks* while serving in HMSAS *Southern Isles.*	16 Jan 40	Oct 43-Apr 44
Sub Lt Kenneth Noel Woolley	15 Sep 41	Oct 43-Apr 44
Lt John Cunningham Govan	23 Apr 42	Oct 44
Sub Lt Johannes Jacobus Floris Carstens	1 Jul 42	Oct 43-Oct 44
Sub Lt George Clifford Smart	8 May 42	Oct 44
Sub Lt (E) Arthur Orazio Mario Antonio Bonfa	6 Oct 41	Oct 43-Oct 44
Midshipman Henry John van der Heever	1 Apr 43	Oct 44
Lt Ernst Ronald Eriksen	1 Jul 44	Jan-Jul 45
Sub Lt Leon Gluckman	1 Jul 43	Jan-Jul 45
Sub Lt George Clifford Smart	8 May 42	Jan-Jul 45
Sub Lt (E) Allan Maurice Drinkwater	2 Sep 44	Jan-Jul 45
Midshipman Terence Creagh Stevens	24 Aug 43	Jan-Jul 45

HMSAS *Immortelle*

Officer	Seniority	Aboard
Lt David Alfred Hall, SANF(V) Gazetted for the award of the DSC on 9 September 1941 *for courage, resolution and devotion to duty in the face of Enemy air attacks* while serving in HMSAS *Southern Maid.* Gazetted for the award of a bar to his DSC on 24 July 1945 *for courage, skill and devotion to duty whilst serving in HMSAS Natal in the destruction of enemy submarines and midget submarines.*	28 Nov 40	Jun-Dec 42
Sub Lt Kenneth Devenish Parsons	10 Oct 40	Jun-Dec 42
Sub Lt Robert Freeland Barrie	21 Jan 42	Jun-Dec 42
Eng Sub Lt Robert Dunsire Bruce	12 Jan 42	Jun-Dec 42
Lt Robert Thomas Park	1 Oct 42	Apr-Aug 43
Sub Lt Geoffrey Comer Bluett	5 Jan 42	Apr-Aug 43
Sub Lt William Ebstol Bellad-Ellis	4 Aug 42	Apr-Aug 43
Lt Thomas Endersby	24 Apr 42	Oct 43-Apr 44
Sub Lt James Preston	22 Apr 42	Oct 43-Apr 44
Sub Lt Cecil Alfred Hughes	5 Oct 42	Oct 43-Apr 44
Sub Lt Andrew Bryson	4 Dec 42	Oct 43-Apr 44
Sub Lt (E) James Harting Shepherd	3 Oct 42	Oct 43-Apr 44
Lt Andrew MacBride Martin	1 Oct 42	Oct 44-Jul 45
Sub Lt George Arthur Heard	9 Nov 42	Oct 44
Sub Lt Andrew Bryson	4 Dec 42	Apr-Oct 44
Midshipman Ray Alexander Lock	1 Apr 43	Oct 44
Sub Lt Albert James Picton	8 Nov 43	Jan-Jul 45
Sub Lt Gordon Duncan Ellis-Brown	20 Apr 44	Jan-Jul 45
Sub Lt Andrew Bryson	4 Dec 42	Jan-Jul 45
Sub Lt (E) Owen Charles Scrutton	20 Nov 42	Jan-Jul 45

HMSAS *Mooivlei*

Officer	Seniority	Aboard
Skipper Hendrik Albertus Crous, RNVR (SAD)	12 Aug 39	From 9 Oct 39
Sub Lt W S Thompson, SDF	unknown	Jun-Oct 41
Lt Merddyn Ray Terry-Lloyd, RNVR (SA)	29 Jul 38	Jun 41-Apr 42
Sub Lt Kenneth Devenish Parsons	10 Oct 40	Dec 41-Apr 42
Sub Lt Thomas Patrick Simpson, SANF(V)	1 Feb 41	Dec 41-Apr 42
Lt Christopher Bertram Bidwell Watson Gazetted for the award of the DSC on 9 September 1941 *for courage, resolution and devotion to duty in the face of Enemy air attacks* while serving in HMSAS *Southern Maid.*	16 Sep 41	Jun-Dec 42
Sub Lt Thomas Patrick Simpson	1 Feb 41	Jun-Dec 42
Sub Lt Robert Nuttall	21 Jan 42	Jun-Dec 42
Sub Lt Percival Durie James	8 May 41	Jun-Dec 42
Sub Lt B Gardner	unknown	Apr-Aug 43
Sub Lt Patrick Hamilton	19 Nov 40	Apr 43-Apr 44
Sub Lt Ernst Ronald Erikson	21 Jan 42	Apr 43-Apr 44
Sub Lt Robert Frank Monson	4 Dec 42	Oct 43-Apr 44
Sub Lt Edward John Raymond Walker, SDF Gazetted for the award of the DSC on 17 November 1942 *for skill and resource in action against enemy Submarines while serving in HMSAS Southern Maid.*	26 Jun 40	Oct 44
Sub Lt Ernest Murton Taylor	27 Jul 42	Oct 44
Midshipman Andrew Cecil McMurray	24 Aug 43	Oct 44
Sub Lt Robert Freeland Barrie	21 Jan 42	Jan-Jul 45
Sub Lt George Arthur Young	8 Nov 43	Jan-Jul 45

HMSAS *Odberg*

Officer	Seniority	Aboard
Eng Sub Lt Alexander Murray Wishart, SDF	10 Jul 41	Jun 41
Lt Duncan Livingstone MacKinnon, SDF	1 Feb 40	Jun 41-Apr 42
Sub Lt Lewis Lester Adams, SDF	15 Sep 41	Aug 41-Apr 42
Lt Cdr Aubrey Charles Matson	16 Sep 41	Jun-Dec 42
Sub Lt Alec Woodford Solomon Gazetted for the award of the DSC on 17 November 1942 *for skill and resource in action against enemy Submarines while serving in HMSAS Protea.*	1 Jul 44	Jun-Dec 42
Sub Lt Harry Dalgarno Milne	4 Aug 41	Jun-Dec 42
Eng Sub Lt Rene Bennett Randall	14 Jan 42	Jun-Dec 42
Lt Eric Victor Brown	1 Jan 41	Apr 43-Apr 44
Sub Lt David Adrian Ferris Smuts	1 Feb 41	Apr 43-Apr 44
Sub Lt Jerry Michael Fox Maule	18 Jun 41	Oct 43-Apr 44
Sub Lt (E) Gordon Johnston Dickie	30 Sep 42	Oct 43-Apr 44
Lt Cdr Richard Paul Dryden-Dymond	1 Oct 42	Oct 44
Lt Spencer Joseph Newton Richards	1 Oct 43	Oct 44
Lt Richard Gerald Gardner	1 Apr 44	Oct 44
Lt E J Miller	unknown	Oct 44
Lt Cdr William Edward Rojohn Scott	1 Oct 42	Jan-Jul 45
Lt Peter Neville Ryder Crowder	17 Dec 43	Jan-Jul 45
Lt Peter Gundry Morris May	8 Nov 43	Jan-Jul 45
Lt Peter Douglas Kockott	1 Jan 45	Oct 44-Jul 45
Midshipman Adrian Ernest Forsyth-Thompson	24 Aug 43	Oct 44-Jul 45
Eng Lt George Henry Nash	1 Jul 42	Jan-Jul 45

HMSAS *Pretoria*

Officer	Seniority	Aboard
Lt Christopher Bertram Bidwell Watson Gazetted for the award of the DSC on 9 September 1941 *for courage, resolution and devotion to duty in the face of Enemy air attacks* while serving in HMSAS *Southern Maid.*	16 Sep 41	Apr-Aug 43
Sub Lt William Ernest Sutton Mansfield	19 Nov 40	Apr-Aug 43
Sub Lt Ernest Murton Taylor	27 Jul 42	Apr-Aug 43
Sub Lt (E) John George Lee	27 Aug 41	Apr-Aug 43
A/Sub Lt Dudley Amyas Ramsay Lewis	6 Oct 42	Oct 43-Feb 44
Sub Lt Edward John Raymond Walker, SDF Gazetted for the award of the DSC on 17 November 1942 *for skill and resource in action against enemy Submarines while serving in HMSAS Southern Maid.*	26 Jun 40	Oct 43-Apr 44
Sub Lt Arthur Raymond Coulter	4 Aug 41	Oct 43-Apr 44
Sub Lt (E) Norman Raymond Laidlow Curry	1 Oct 42	Oct 43-Oct 44
Lt Julius Henry Davids	21 Apr 42	Oct 44-Jul 45
Sub Lt Peter Hartog	18 Jun 41	Oct 44
Sub Lt Thomas Fletcher Shenfield	27 Nov 42	Oct 44
Sub Lt Edwin William Uren (Sometimes Wren)	5 Aug 44	Jan-Jul 45
Sub Lt (E) Alexander James McCall	29 Aug 44	Jan-Jul 45
Midshipman Albert Samuel Davis	17 Dec 43	Oct 44-Jul 45

HMSAS *Rondevlei*

Lt Richard Paul Dryden-Dymond, RNVR(SA)	17 Jun 37	Jun-Oct 41
Sub Lt William Edward Gleave, SDF	21 Jun 40	Jun-Oct 41
Lt Ronald McDonald, SDF	1 Sep 41	Dec 41-Apr 42
Sub Lt Stanley V Brooks, SDF	17 Mar 41	Dec 41-Apr 42
Sub Lt Raymond Ryecroft Mitchell, SDF	8 May 41	Dec 41-Apr 42
Lt Ronald McDonald	1 Sep 41	Jun-Dec 42
Sub Lt Stanley V Brooks	17 Mar 41	Jun-Dec 42
Sub Lt Arthur Raymond Coulter	4 Aug 41	Jun-Dec 42
Sub Lt John Griffiths Robertson	2 Jan 42	Apr-Aug 43
Lt John Cunningham Govan	23 Apr 42	Apr 43-Apr 44
Sub Lt Spencer Joseph Newton Richards	3 Feb 41	Oct 43-Apr 44
Sub Lt Thomas Frederick Bywater	9 Nov 42	Oct 43-Apr 44
Lt Frederick Martin Kamke	1 Oct 43	Oct 44-Jan 45
Sub Lt Gordon Melhuish Dixon	17 Dec 43	Oct 44
Sub Lt Dudley Amyas Ramsay Lewis	6 Oct 42	Oct 44
Sub Lt P S Langermann	20 Aug 43	Jan 45
Sub Lt Jack Herbert French	17 Jul 44	Jan 45
Lt Herbert Henry Cook	26 May 41	Jul 45
Sub Lt (E) Francis Cecil Nott	1 Sep 44	Jul 45

HMSAS *Smalvlei*

Officer	Seniority	Aboard
Lt John Leask, SDF	16 Jul 40	Jun-Oct 41
Sub Lt Fred Duncum, SDF	1 Jul 40	Jun-Oct 41
Lt John Kennaway Mallory, SDF	1 Sep 41	Dec 41-Apr 42
Sub Lt Neville William Jones, SDF	15 Jan 41	Dec 41-Apr 42
Sub Lt George Nelson Wooley	15 Sep 41	Jun-Dec 42
Lt Louis Botha Ribbink Gazetted for the award of the DSC on 9 September 1941 *for courage, resolution and devotion to duty in the face of Enemy air attacks* while serving in HMSAS *Southern Isles*	16 Jan 40	Apr-Aug 43
Sub Lt Neville William Jones	15 Jan 41	Apr-Aug 43
Sub Lt Harold Orffer	21 Jan 42	Oct 43-Feb 44
Lt William Ernest Sutton Mansfield	1 Oct 42	Oct 43-Apr 44
Sub Lt Leslie John Downing	17 Mar 41	Oct 43-Apr 44
Sub Lt Roy Edwin Patrick	8 May 41	Apr 44
Lt Patrick Hamilton	1 Oct 42	Oct 44-Jul 45
Sub Lt Charles Francis Brooks	2 Oct 42	Oct 44
Sub Lt Roy Charles Osborne	5 Aug 44	Jan-Jul 45
Sub Lt Eric Stanley Wynne Simpson	17 Jul 44	Jan-Jul 45

HMSAS *Sonneblom*

Lt John Leask, SDF	16 Jul 40	Dec 41-Apr 42
Sub Lt John Cunningham Govan, SDF	22 Jun 40	Dec 41-Apr 42
Sub Lt Dudley Raymond Burton, SDF	8 May 41	Dec 41-Apr 42
Eng Lt Donald Herbert Brooks, SDF	18 Jun 41	Dec 41-Apr 42
Lt Louis Botha Ribbink Gazetted for the award of the DSC on 9 September 1941 *for courage, resolution and devotion to duty in the face of Enemy air attacks* while serving in HMSAS *Southern Isles.*	16 Jan 40	Jun-Dec 42
Sub Lt Thomas Endersby	19 Jun 40	Jun-Dec 42
Sub Lt Douglas Hocking Clarkson	19 Jun 40	Jun-Dec 42
Eng Sub Lt Donald Herbert Brooks	18 Jun 41	Jun-Dec 42
Sub Lt Harold Theodore Bailey	1 May 42	Apr-Aug 43
Lt Thomas Endersby	24 Apr 42	Apr-Aug 43
Sub Lt Dudley Raymond Burton	8 May 41	Apr 43-Apr 44
Lt Nelson Albert Tomalin	1 Jul 42	Oct 43-Apr 44
Sub Lt (E) Kenneth Barton Yuill	15 Feb 43	Oct 43-Apr 44
Midshipman Eric Stanley Wynne Simpson	1 Dec 42	Oct 43-Oct 44
Lt Harry Jeffrey	1 Oct 42	Oct 44-Jul 45
Lt William John Hume	1 Oct 44	Oct 44-Jul 45
Sub Lt John Duncan	1 Apr 43	Oct 44
Sub Lt Geoffrey Kenneth Harris	6 Aug 44	Jan-Jul 45
Sub Lt Marthinus Philipus van Zyl	18 Apr 44	Jan-Jul 45
Lt (E) Robert McDonald Tolmie	1 Apr 44	Jan-Jul 45

HMSAS *Standerton*

Officer	Seniority	Aboard
Lt David Alfred Hall, SANF(V) Gazetted for the award of the DSC on 9 September 1941 *for courage, resolution and devotion to duty in the face of Enemy air attacks* while serving in HMSAS *Southern Maid.* Gazetted for the award of a bar to his DSC on 24 July 1945 *for courage, skill and devotion to duty whilst serving in HMSAS Natal in the destruction of enemy submarines and midget submarines.*	28 Nov 40	Apr-Aug 43
Lt Oswald Richard Dudley Stephen	22 Jul 40	Oct 43-Apr 44
Lt Edward Kent Watkins	1 Oct 42	Oct 43-Apr 44
Sub Lt George Clifford Smart	8 May 42	Oct 43-Apr 44
Sub Lt Bernard Denny Pickles	1 Feb 41	Oct 43-Apr 44
Sub Lt James Gilmour Faulds Watts	6 Nov 42	Oct 43-Apr 44
Lt (E) Fred Hutton	1 Oct 42	Oct 43-Apr 44
Lt Walter John Toddun	28 Jun 40	Oct 44
Sub Lt Alexander Benjamin Corbett	4 Dec 42	Oct 44
Lt (E) George Mulke Oertel	14 Sep 42	Oct 44
Sub Lt Geoffrey Kenneth Harris	6 Aug 44	Oct 44
Lt Gordon Burn-Wood Gazetted for the appointment of Companion of the DSO on 17 November 1942 *for skill and resource in action against enemy Submarines while serving in HMSAS Protea.*	1 Sep 41	Jan-Jul 45
Sub Lt Charles Francis Brooks	2 Oct 42	Jan-Jul 45
Sub Lt Peter John Baxter Williams	20 Aug 43	Oct 44-Jul 45
Lt (E) Charles Stewart Parnell	1 Oct 43	Jan-Jul 45
Midshipman Ronald Frederick Webber	24 Aug 43	Jan-Jul 45

HMSAS *Sydostlandet*

Lt Alex Shelton Bowyer, RNVR(SA)	22 Jul 40	Jun-Oct 41
Sub Lt Gordon Burn-Wood, SDF	1 Jul 40	Jun-Oct 41
Lt Gordon Burn-Wood, SDF (CO) Gazetted for appointment as Companion of the DSO on 17 Nov 1942 *for skill and resource in action against enemy Submarines while serving in HMSAS Protea.*	1 Sep 41	Dec 41-Apr 42
Sub Lt Jan Andre Beyers, SDF	16 Jan 41	Dec 41-Apr 42
Lt Joshua Portal Fielden	16 Sep 41	Jun-Dec 42
Sub Lt Casper Becker Dreyer	1 Apr 43	Jun-Dec 42
Eng Sub Lt Julian Darlington Vowles	12 Dec 41	Jun-Dec 42

HMSAS *Tordonn*

Officer	Seniority	Aboard
Lt Merddyn Ray Terry-Lloyd, RNVR (SA)	29 Jul 38	Jun-Dec 42
Sub Lt John Cunningham Govan	22 Jun 40	Jun-Dec 42
Sub Lt Clifford Jack Bawden	17 Nov 41	Jun-Dec 42
Sub Lt Ernst Ronald Erikson	21 Jan 42	Jun-Dec 42
Lt Nelson Albert Tomalin	1 Jul 42	Apr-Aug 43
Sub Lt (E) Arthur Orazio Mario Antonio Bonfa	6 Oct 41	Apr-Aug 43
Lt Christopher Bertram Bidwell Watson Gazetted for the award of the DSC on 9 September 1941 *for courage, resolution and devotion to duty in the face of Enemy air attacks* while serving in HMSAS *Southern Maid.*	16 Sep 41	Oct 43-Apr 44
Sub Lt William John Hume	4 Aug 41	Oct 43-Apr 44
Lt Percival Durie James	1 Oct 43	Oct 44-Jul 45
Sub Lt Harold Orffer	21 Jan 42	Oct 44-Jul 45
Lt Dennis John Cronin	1 Jan 45	Oct 44-Jul 45

HMSAS *Turffontein*

Lt Cdr Richard Paul Dryden-Dymond	1 Oct 42	Apr-Aug 43
Sub Lt Frederick Martin Kamke	22 Apr 42	Apr-Aug 43
Sub Lt John Hamilton Dyer	27 Jun 42	Apr-Aug 43
Lt Douglas Hocking Clarkson	22 Apr 42	Oct 43-Oct 44
Lt Julius Henry Davids	21 Apr 42	Oct 43-Apr 44
Sub Lt Patrick Roland Montague Furber	24 Dec 42	Oct 43-Apr 44
Sub Lt W E P Stephen	unknown	Oct 43-Apr 44
Sub Lt Ronald Mackie	19 Mar 43	Oct 44
Lt (E) Percy Clifford Paul	1 Apr 43	Jun 43-Oct 44
Midshipman P D Fuller	unknown	Oct 44
Lt Casper Becker Dreyer	1 Apr 43	Jul 45
Lt Aubrey McGregor Matthews	1 Oct 44	Oct 44- Jul 45
Sub Lt Dudley Aymas Ramsay Lewis	11 Dec 43	Jul 45
Midshipman Warren Peter Goodwin	24 Aug 43	Jul 45

HMSAS *Vereeniging*

Officer	Seniority	Aboard
Lt Alex Shelton Bowyer	22 Jul 40	Apr-Aug 43
Lt David Gonyne Roberts	1 Oct 42	Apr-Aug 43
Sub Lt Bernard Denny Pickles	1 Feb 41	Apr-Aug 43
Sub Lt (E) Charles Stewart Parnell	11 Jun 42	Apr-Aug 43
Lt David Gonyne Roberts	1 Oct 42	Oct 43-Apr 44
Sub Lt Peter Francis Blair	23 Jan 42	Oct 43-Apr 44
Sub Lt Ronald Victor Mowlam	8 May 41	Oct 43-Apr 44
Lt David Alfred Hall, SANF(V) Gazetted for the award of the DSC on 9 September 1941 *for courage, resolution and devotion to duty in the face of Enemy air attacks* while serving in HMSAS *Southern Maid.* Gazetted for the award of a bar to his DSC on 24 Jul 1945 *for courage, skill and devotion to duty whilst serving in HMSAS Natal in the destruction of enemy submarines and midget submarines.*	28 Nov 40	Oct 44
Lt (E) Bastraan Pieter de Groot	1 Nov 41	Oct 43-Oct 44
Sub Lt Ronald John Pedley	14 Aug 43	Oct 44
Sub Lt John Duncan Moir	17 Jul 44	Oct 44

Appendix D: USN Commandants, Naval Districts and River Commands

First Naval District

Rear Admiral William T. Tarrant: 7 December 1941--15 July 1942
Vice Admiral Wilson Brown Jr.: 15 July 1942--8 February 1943
Rear Admiral Robert A. Theobald: 9 February 1943--28 October 1944
Rear Admiral Felix X. Gygax: 28 October 1944--2 September 1945

Third Naval District

Rear Admiral Adolphus Andrews: 7 December 1941--16 March 1942
Rear Admiral Edward J. Marquart: 17 March 1942--31 March 1944
Rear Admiral William R. Munroe: 31 March 1944--6 November 1944
Rear Admiral Monroe Kelly: 6 November 1944--2 September 1945

Fourth Naval District

Rear Admiral Adolphus E. Watson: 7 December 1941--30 August 1942
Rear Admiral Milo F. Draemel: 30 August 1942--2 September 1945

Fifth Naval District

Rear Admiral Manley H. Simons: 7 December 1941--31 May 1943
Rear Admiral Herbert Fairfax Leary: 1 June 1943--30 October 1943
Rear Admiral David M. LeBreton: 30 October 1943--20 August 1945
Rear Admiral Walden L. Ainsworth: 20 August 1945--2 September 1945

Sixth Naval District

Rear Admiral William H. Allen: 7 December 1941--2 June 1942
Rear Admiral William A. Glassford: 2 June 1942--14 May 1943
Rear Admiral Jules James: 14 May 1943--2 September 1945

Seventh Naval District

(Combined with Sixth until 1 February 1942)
Captain Russell S. Crenshaw (A): 1 February 1942--3 June 1942
Rear Admiral James L. Kauffman: 3 June 1942--3 February 1943
Captain Howard H.J. Benson (A): 3 February 1943--1 April 1943
Rear Admiral William R. Munroe: 1 April 1943--25 March 1944
Captain Howard H.J. Benson (A): 25 March 1944--17 July 1944
Vice Admiral Walter S. Anderson: 17 July 1944--2 September 1945

Eighth Naval District

Captain Thaddeus A. Thomson (A): 7 December 1941--22 April 1942
Rear Admiral Frank T. Leighton: 22 April 1942--18 March 1943
Captain Eugene T. Oates (A): 18 March 1943--14 June 1943
Rear Admiral Andrew C. Bennett: 14 June 1943--2 September 1945

Ninth Naval District

Rear Admiral John Downes: 7 December 1941--3 January 1944
Vice Admiral Arthur S. Carpender: 3 January 1944--2 September 1945

Tenth Naval District

Vice Admiral John H. Hoover: 7 December 1941--12 August 1943
Vice Admiral Arthur B. Cook: 12 August 1943--14 May 1944
Vice Admiral Robert C. Giffen: 14 May 1944--20 August 1945
Vice Admiral William R. Munroe: 20 August 1945--2 September 1945

Eleventh Naval District

Rear Admiral Charles A. Blakely: 7 December--9 December 1941
Rear Admiral John S. McCain (A): 9 December 1941--22 December 1941
Rear Admiral Ralston S. Holmes: 22 December 1941--31 December 1942
Captain George M. Ravenscroft (A): 31 December 1942--30 March 1943
Rear Admiral David W. Bagley: 30 March 1943--31 January 1944
Rear Admiral Wilhelm L. Friedell: 31 January 1944--2 September 1945

Twelfth Naval District

Vice Admiral John W. Greenslade: 7 December 1941--1 February 1944
Rear Admiral Carlton H. Wright: 1 February 1944--2 September 1945

Thirteenth Naval District

Vice Admiral Charles S. Freeman: 7 December 1941--21 November 1942
Vice Admiral Frank Jack Fletcher: 21 November 1942--12 October 1943
Rear Admiral Sherwoode A. Taffinder: 12 October 1943--15 December 1944
Rear Admiral Robert M. Griffin: 15 December 1944--2 September 1945

Fourteenth Naval District

Rear Admiral Claude C. Bloch: 7 December 1941--4 April 1942
Rear Admiral David W. Bagley: 4 April 1942--17 February 1943
Vice Admiral Robert L. Ghormley: 17 February 1943--25 October 1944
Rear Admiral William R. Furlong (A): 25 October 1944--28 November 1944
Vice Admiral David W. Bagley: 28 November 1944--25 July 1945
Vice Admiral Sherwoode A. Taffinder: 25 July 1945--2 September 1945

Fifteenth Naval District

Rear Admiral Frank H. Sadler: 7 December 1941--15 April 1942
Rear Admiral Clifford E. Van Hook: 15 April 1942--14 October 1943
Rear Admiral Harold C. Train: 14 October 1943--10 June 1944
Captain Ellis S. Stone (A): 10 June 1944--3 November 1944
Rear Admiral Howard F. Kingman: 3 November 1944--9 July 1945
Captain Schuyler Mills (A): 9 July 1945--23 August 1945
Rear Admiral John R. Beardall: 23 August 1945--2 September 1945

Sixteenth Naval District
(Ceased to exist on 6 May 1942)

Rear Admiral Francis W. Rockwell: 7 December 1941--18 March 1942
Captain Kenneth M. Hoeffel: 18 March 1942--6 May 1942

Seventeenth Naval District
(Created on 15 April 1944)

Rear Admiral Francis E.M. Whiting: 15 April 1944--12 August 1944
Rear Admiral Allan E. Smith (T): 12 August 1944--24 August 1944
Rear Admiral Ralph F. Wood: 24 August 1944--2 September 1945

Potomac River Naval Command
(Established 8 December 1941)

Rear Admiral George T. Pettengill (Ret): 8 December 1941--15 September 1942
Rear Admiral Ferdinand L. Reichmuth: 15 September 1942--2 September 1945.

Severn River Naval Command
(Established 8 December 1941)

Rear Admiral Russell Willson: 8 December 1941--30 December 1941
Captain Thomas S. King (A): 30 December 1941--31 January 1942
Rear Admiral John R. Beardall: 31 January 1942--8 August 1945
Vice Admiral Aubrey W. Fitch: 8 August 1945--2 September 1945

Appendix E: USN Sea Frontier Commanders

Alaskan
(Established 15 April 1944)
Vice Admiral Frank Jack Fletcher: 15 April 1944--2 September 1945

Caribbean
(Naval Coastal Frontier until 6 February 1942)
Vice Admiral John H. Hoover 7 December 1941--12 August 1943
Vice Admiral Arthur B. Cook: 12 August 1943--14 May 1944
Vice Admiral Robert C. Giffen: 14 May 1944--20 August 1945
Vice Admiral William R. Munroe: 20 August 1945--2 September 1945

Eastern
(North Atlantic Naval Coastal Frontier until 6 February 1942)
Vice Admiral Adolphus Andrews: 7 December 1941--1 November 1943
Vice Admiral Herbert Fairfax Leary: 1 November 1943--2 September 1945

Gulf
(Southern Naval Coastal Frontier until 6 February 1942)
Rear Admiral William H. Allen: 7 December 1941--3 February 1942
Captain Russell S. Crenshaw (A): 3 February 1942--3 June 1942
Rear Admiral James L. Kauffman: 3 June 1942--3 February 1943
Captain Howard H.J. Benson (A): 3 February 1943--1 April 1943
Rear Admiral William R. Munroe: 1 April 1943--25 March 1944
Captain Howard H.J. Benson (A): 25 March 1944--17 July 1944
Rear Admiral Walter S. Anderson: 17 July 1944--2 September 1945

Hawaiian
(Naval Coastal Frontier until 6 February 1942)
Rear Admiral Claude C. Bloch: 7 December 1941--2 April 1942
Rear Admiral David W. Bagley: 2 April 1942--17 February 1943
Vice Admiral Robert L. Ghormley: 17 February 1943--25 October 1944
Commodore Marion C. Robertson (A): 25 October 1944--28 November 1944
Vice Admiral David W. Bagley: 28 November 1944--25 July 1945
Vice Admiral Sherwoode A. Taffinder: 25 July 1945--2 September 1945

Moroccan
(Established 19 November 1942 as Sea Frontier Forces, Western Task Force.
Name changed 17 February 1943.
Disestablished 1 August 1945)
Rear Admiral John L. Hall: 19 November 1942--9 February 1943
Captain Chester L. Nichols (T): 9 February 1943--19 February 1943
Rear Admiral Frank J. Lowry: 19 February 1943--20 September 1943
Captain Chester L. Nichols (T): 20 September 1943--13 October 1943
Commodore Benjamin V. McCandlish: 13 October 1943--1 August 1945

Northwest

(Pacific-Northern Naval Coastal Frontier until 6 February 1942
Disestablished 15 April 1944)

Vice Admiral Charles S. Freeman: 7 December 1941--21 November 1942
Vice Admiral Frank Jack Fletcher: 21 November 1942--15 April 1944

Panama

(Naval Coastal Frontier until 6 February 1942)

Rear Admiral Frank H. Sadler: 7 December 1941--15 April 1942
Rear Admiral Clifford E. Van Hook: 15 April 1942--14 October 1943
Rear Admiral Harold C. Train: 14 October 1943--10 June 1944
Captain Ellis S. Stone (A): 11 June 1944--3 November 1944
Rear Admiral Howard F. Kingman: 3 November 1944--9 July 1945
Captain Schuyler Mills (A): 9 July 1945--23 August 1945
Rear Admiral John R. Beardall: 23 August 1945--2 September 1945

Philippine

(Naval Coastal Frontier until 6 February 1942)
Inactive from 6 May 1942 to 13 November 1944)

Rear Admiral Francis W. Rockwell: 7 December 1941--18 March 1942
Captain Kenneth M. Hoeffel: 18 March 1942--6 May 1942
Vice Admiral James L. Kauffman: 13 November 1944--2 September 1945

Western

(Pacific-Southern Naval Coastal Frontier until 6 February 1942)

Vice Admiral John W. Greenslade: 7 December 1941--1 February 1944
Vice Admiral David W. Bagley: 1 February 1944--17 November 1944
Admiral Royal E. Ingersoll: 17 November 1944--2 September 1945[1]

Appendix F: Ships Sunk or Damaged in African Waters

Date	Ship/Sub	Registry	Type	Tons	Location
21 Aug 42 unescorted	*City of Wellington* *U-506*	British	steam merchant	5,733	7°29'N, 14°40'W
23 Aug 42 unescorted	*Hamla* *U-506*	British	steam merchant	4,416	5°30'N, 15°0'W
5 Sep 42 escorted	*Myrmidon* *U-506*	British	motor merchant	6,278	0°45'N, 6°27'W
13 Sep 42 unescorted	*Lima* *U-506*	Swedish	motor merchant	3,764	2°35'N, 11°22'W
30 Sep 42 unescorted	*Siam II* *U-506*	British	motor merchant	6,637	3°25'N, 15°46'W
7 Oct 42 unescorted	*Boringia* *U-159*	British	motor merchant	5,821	35°09'S, 16°32'E
7 Oct 42 unescorted	*Chickasaw City* *U-172*	American	steam merchant	6,196	34°15'S, 17°11'E
7 Oct 42 unescorted	*Firethorn* *U-172*	Panamanian	motor merchant	4,700	34°13'S, 17°21'E
8 Oct 42 unescorted	*Clan Mactavish* *U-159*	British	steam merchant	7,631	34°53'S, 16°45'E
8 Oct 42 unescorted	*City of Athens* *U-179*	British	steam merchant	6,558	33°40'S, 17°03'E
8 Oct 42 unescorted	*Koumoundouros* *U-68*	Greek	steam merchant	3,598	34°10'S, 17°07'E
8 Oct 42 unescorted	*Gaasterkerk* *U-68*	Dutch	steam merchant	8,679	34°20'S, 18°10'E
8 Oct 42 unescorted	*Swiftsure* *U-68*	American	steam tanker	8,207	34°40'S, 18°25'E
8 Oct 42 unescorted	*Sarthe* *U-68*	British	steam merchant	5,271	34°50'S, 18°40'E
8 Oct 42 unescorted	*Pantelis* *U-172*	Greek	steam merchant	3,845	34°20'S, 17°50'E
9 Oct 42 unescorted	*Coloradan* *U-159*	American	steam merchant	6,557	35° 47'S, 14° 34'E
9 Oct 42 unescorted	*Examelia* *U-68*	American	steam merchant	4,981	34°52'S, 18°30'E
9 Oct 42 unescorted	*Belgian Fighter* *U-68*	Belgian	steam merchant	5,403	35°00'S, 18°30'E
10 Oct 42 unescorted	*Orcades* *U-172*	British	troop transport	23,456	35°51'S, 14°40'E
13 Oct 42 unescorted	*Empire Nomad* *U-159*	British	steam merchant	7,167	37°50'S, 18°16'E
17 Oct 42 unescorted	*Empire Chaucer* *U-504*	British	steam merchant	5,970	38°12'S, 20°04'E

23 Oct 42 unescorted	*City of Johannesburg* *U-504*	British	steam merchant	5,669	33°20'S, 29°30'E
26 Oct 42 unescorted	*Anne Hutchinson* *U-504*	American	Liberty ship	7,176	33°10'S, 28°30'E
29 Oct 42 unescorted	*Ross* *U-159*	British	motor merchant	4,978	38°51'S, 21°40'E
29 Oct 42 unescorted	*Laplace* *U-159*	British	steam merchant	7,327	40°35'S, 21°35'E
31 Oct 42 unescorted	*Empire Guidon* *U-504*	British	steam merchant	7,041	30°48'S, 34°11'E
31 Oct 42 unescorted	*Reynolds* *U-504*	British	steam merchant	5,113	30°02'S, 35°02'E
1 Nov 42 unescorted	*Mendoza* *U-178*	British	troop transport	8,233	29°20'S, 32°13'E
2 Nov 42 Convoy TRIN-16	*Aegeus* *U-177*	Greek	steam merchant	4,538	32°30'S, 16°00'E
3 Nov 42 unescorted	*Porto Alegre* *U-504*	Brazilian	steam merchant	5,187	35°27'S, 28°02'E
3 Nov 42 unescorted	*East Indian* *U-181*	American	motor merchant	8,159	37°23'S, 13°34'E
4 Nov 42 unescorted	*Hai Hing* *U-178*	Norwegian	steam merchant	2,561	25°55'S, 33°10'E
4 Nov 42 unescorted	*Trekieve* *U-178*	British	steam merchant	5,244	25°46'S, 33°48'E
7 Nov 42 unescorted	*La Salle* *U-159*	American	steam merchant	5,462	40°00'S, 21°30'E
8 Nov 42 unescorted	*Plaudit* *U-181*	Panamanian	steam merchant	5,060	36°00'S, 26°32'E
9 Nov 42 unescorted	*Cerion* (D) *U-177*	British	motor tanker	2,588	35°58'S, 26°37'E
10 Nov 42 unescorted	*K.G. Meldahl* *U-181*	Norwegian	steam merchant	3,799	34°59'S, 29°45'E
13 Nov 42 unescorted	*Excello* *U-181*	American	steam merchant	4,969	32°23'S, 30°07'E
13 Nov 42 unescorted	*Louise Moller* *U-178*	British	steam merchant	3,764	30°50'S, 35°54'E
15 Nov 42 unescorted	*Adviser* (D) *U-178*	British	steam merchant	6,348	32°03'S, 33°52'E
19 Nov 42 unescorted	*Gunda* *U-181*	Norwegian	steam merchant	2,241	25°48'S, 33°15'E
19 Nov 42 Convoy PA-8	*Scottish Chief* *U-177*	British	steam tanker	7,006	30°39'S, 34°41'E
20 Nov 42 unescorted	*Pierce Butler* *U-177*	American	Liberty ship	7,191	29°40'S, 36°35'E
20 Nov 42 unescorted	*Corinthiakos* *U-181*	Greek	steam merchant	3,562	25°42'S, 33°27'E

22 Nov 42 unescorted	*Alcoa Pathfinder* *U-181*	American	steam merchant	6,797	26°45'S, 33°10'E
24 Nov 42 unescorted	*Mount Helmos* *U-181*	Greek	steam merchant	6,481	26°38'S, 34°59'E
24 Nov 42 unescorted	*Dorington Court* *U-181*	British	steam merchant	5,281	27°00'S, 34°45'E
27 Nov 42 unescorted	*Jeremiah Wadsworth* *U-178*	American	Liberty ship	7,176	39°25'S, 22°23'E
28 Nov 42 unescorted	*Evanthia* *U-181*	Greek	steam merchant	3,551	25°13'S, 34°00'E
28 Nov 42 unescorted	*Nova Scotia* *U-177*	British	troop transport	6,796	28°30'S, 33°00'E
30 Nov 42 unescorted	*Llandaff Castle* *U-177*	British	troop transport	10,799	27°20'S, 33°40'E
30 Nov 42 unescorted	*Cleanthis* *U-181*	Greek	steam merchant	4,153	24°29'S, 35°44'E
2 Dec 42 unescorted	*Amarylis* *U-181*	Panamanian	steam merchant	4,328	28°14'S, 33°24'E
7 Dec 42 unescorted	*Saronikos* *U-177*	Greek	steam merchant	3,548	24°46'S, 35°30'E
12 Dec 42 unescorted	*Empire Gull* *U-177*	British	steam merchant	6,408	26°15'S, 34°40'E
14 Dec 42 unescorted	*Sawahloento* *U-177*	Dutch	steam merchant	3,085	31°02'S, 34°00'E
10 Feb 43 Convoy CA-11	*Queen Anne* *U-509*	British	motor merchant	4,937	34°53'S, 19°51'E
11 Feb 43 unescorted	*Helmspey* *U-516*	British	steam merchant	4,764	34°22'S, 24°54'E
17 Feb 43 unescorted	*Deer Lodge* *U-516*	American	steam merchant	6,187	33°46'S, 26°57'E
17 Feb 43 unescorted	*Llanashe* *U-182*	British	steam merchant	4,836	34°00'S, 28°30'E
27 Feb 43 escorted	*Colombia* *U-516*	Dutch	submarine tender	10,782	33°36'S, 27°9'E
3 Mar 43 Convoy DN-21	*Harvey W. Scott* *U-160*	American	Liberty ship	7,176	31°54'S, 30°37'E
3 Mar 43 DN-21	*Nirpura* *U-160*	British	steam merchant	5,961	32°47'S, 30°48'E
3 Mar 43 DN-21	*Tibia* (D) *U-160*	Dutch	motor tanker	10,356	32°00'S, 30°21'E
4 Mar 43 DN-21	*Empire Mahseer* *U-160*	British	steam merchant	5,087	32°01'S, 30°48'E
4 Mar 43 DN-21	*Marietta E.* *U-160*	British	steam merchant	7,628	31°49'S, 31°11'E
4 Mar 43 DN-21	*Sheaf Crown* (D) *U-160*	British	steam merchant	4,868	31°49'S, 31°11'E

7 Mar 43 unescorted	*Sabor* *U-506*	British	steam merchant	5,212	34°30'S, 23°10'E
8 March unescorted	*James B. Stephens* *U-160*	American	Liberty ship	7,176	28°53'S, 33°18'E
9 Mar 43 unescorted	*Tabor* *U-506*	Norwegian	motor merchant	4,768	37°30'S, 23°15'E
10 Mar 43 unescorted	*Richard D. Spaight* *U-182*	American	Liberty ship	7,177	27°39'S, 35°28'E
11 Mar 43 unescorted	*Aelybryn* *U-160*	British	steam merchant	4,986	29°08'S, 34°05'E
20 Mar 43 Convoy CN-13	*Nortun* *U-516*	Panamanian	steam merchant	3,663	27°35'S, 14°22'E
28 Mar 43 Convoy RS-3	*Silverbeech* *U-159*	British	motor merchant	5,319	25°30'N, 15°55'W
29 Mar 43 Convoy RS-3	*Moanda* *U-172*	Belgian	motor merchant	4,621	24°44'N, 16°48'W
2 Apr 43 Convoy NC-9	*City of Baroda* *U-509* (T)	British	steam passenger ship	7,129	27°56'S, 15°21'E
5 Apr 43 unescorted	*Aloe* *U-182*	British	steam merchant	5,047	32°37'S, 37°50'E
11 Apr 43 unescorted	*Empire Whimbrel* *U-181*	British	steam merchant	5,983	2°31'N, 15°55'W
18 Apr 43 unescorted	*Corbis* *U-180*	British	motor tanker	8,132	34°56'S, 34°03'E
11 May 43 unescorted	*Tinhow* *U-181*	British	steam merchant	5,232	25°15'S, 33°30'E
11 May 43 unescorted	*Nailsea Meadow* *U-196*	British	steam merchant	4,962	32°04'S, 29°13'E
17 May 43 Convoy LMD-17	*Northmoor* *U-198*	British	steam merchant	4,392	28°27'S, 32°43'E
27 May 43 unescorted	*Sicilia* *U-181*	Swedish	motor merchant	1,633	24°31'S, 35°17'E
28 May 43 Convoy CD-20	*Agwimonte* *U-177*	American	steam merchant	6,679	34°57'S, 19°33'E
28 May 43 Convoy CD-20	*Storaas* *U-177*	Norwegian	motor tanker	7,886	34°57'S, 19°33'E
29 May 43 unescorted	*Hopetarn* *U-198*	British	motor merchant	5,231	30°50'S, 39°32'E

1 Jun 43 Convoy CD-20	*Salabangka* *U-178*	Dutch	steam merchant	6,586	31°08'S, 30°18'E
5 Jun 43 unescorted	*Dumra* *U-198*	British	motor merchant	2,304	28°15'S, 33°20'E
6 Jun 43 unescorted	*William King* *U-198*	American	Liberty ship	7,176	30°25'S, 34°15'E
7 Jun 43 unescorted	*Harrier* *U-181*	South African	steam merchant	193	25°50'S, 33°20'E
27 Jun 43 unescorted	*Sebastian Cermeno U-511*	American	Liberty ship	7,194	29°00'S, 50°10'E
2 Jul 43 unescorted	*Hoihow* *U-181*	British	passenger ship	2,798	19°30'S, 55°30'E
4 Jul 43 Convoy DN-50	*Breiviken* *U-178*	Norwegian	steam merchant	2,669	21°50'S, 37°50'E
4 Jul 43 unescorted	*Michael Livanos* *U-178*	Greek	steam merchant	4,774	22°52'S, 36°47'E
6 Jul 43 unescorted	*Jasper Park* *U-177*	Canadian	steam merchant	7,129	32°52'S, 42°15'E
6 Jul 43 unescorted	*Hydraios* *U-198*	Greek	steam merchant	4,476	24°44'S, 35°12'E
7 Jul 43 unescorted	*Leana* *U-198*	British	steam merchant	4,742	25°06'S, 35°33'E
10 Jul 43 unescorted	*Alice F. Palmer* *U-177*	American	Liberty ship	7,176	26°30'S, 44°20'E
11 Jul 43 unescorted	*Mary Livanos* *U-178*	Greek	steam merchant	4,771	15°40'S, 40°45'E
14 Jul 42 unescorted	*Robert Bacon* *U-178*	American	Liberty ship	7,197	15°25'S, 41°13'E
15 Jul 43 unescorted	*Empire Lake* *U-181*	British	steam merchant	2,852	21°27'S, 51°47'E
16 Jul 43 unescorted	*Fort Franklin* *U-181*	British	steam merchant	7,135	22°36'S, 51°22'E
17 Jul 43 unescorted	*City of Canton* *U-178*	British	steam merchant	6,692	13°52'S, 41°10'E
19 July 43 Convoy DN-53	*Cornish City* *U-177*	British	motor merchant	4,952	27°20'S, 52°10'E
24 Jul 43 unescorted	*Pegasus* *U-197*	Swedish	motor tanker	9,583	28°05'S, 37°40'E
30 Jul 43 unescorted	*William Ellery* (D) *U-197*	American	Liberty ship	7,181	32°00'S, 36°00'E
1 Aug 43 Convoy BC-2	*Mangkalihat* *U-198*	Dutch	steam merchant	8,457	25°06'S, 34°14'E
3 Aug 43 Convoy CB-1	*City of Oran* (S) *U-196*	British	steam merchant	7,323	13°45'S, 41°16'E

4 Aug 43 unescorted	*Dalfram* *U-181*	British	steam merchant	4,558	20°53'S, 56°43'E
5 Aug 43 unescorted	*Efthalia Mari* *U-177*	Greek	steam merchant	4,195	24°21'S, 48°55'E
7 Aug 43 Convoy DN-54	*Umvuma* *U-181*	British	steam merchant	4,419	20°18'S, 57°14'E
12 Aug 43 Convoy DN-55	*Clan Macarthur* *U-181*	British	steam merchant	10,528	23°00'S, 53°11'E
17 Aug 43 unescorted	*Empire Stanley* *U-197*	British	motor merchant	6,921	27°08'S, 48°15'E
21 Oct 43 escorting	*HMS Orfasy* (T204) *U-68*	British	minesweep trawler	545	5°58'N, 11°30'W
22 Oct 43 unescorted	*Litiopa* *U-68*	Norwegian	steam tanker	5,356	6°18'N, 11°55'W
31 Oct 43 unescorted	*New Columbia* *U-68*	British	steam merchant	6,574	4°25'N, 5°03'E
30 Nov 43 escorted	*Fort de Vaux* *U-68*	French	steam merchant	5,186	6°32'N, 12°20'W
1 Apr 44 unescorted	*Dahomian* *U-852*	British	steam merchant	5,277	34°25'S, 18°19'E
16 Jun 44 unescorted	*Columbine* *U-198*	S. African	steam merchant	3,268	32°44'S, 17°22'E
15 Jul 44 unescorted	*Director* *U-198*	British	steam merchant	5,107	24°30'S, 35°44'E
6 Aug 44 unescorted	*Empire City* *U-198*	British	motor merchant	7,295	11°33'S, 41°25'E
7 Aug 44 unescorted	*Empire Day* *U-198*	British	motor merchant	7,242	7°06'S, 42°00'E
13 Aug 44 unescorted	*Radbury* *U-862*	British	steam merchant	3,614	24°20'S, 41°45'E
16 Aug 44 unescorted	*Empire Lancer* *U-862*	British	steam merchant	7,037	15°00'S, 44°00'E
18 Aug 44 unescorted	*Nairung* *U-862*	British	steam merchant	5,414	15°00'S, 42°00'E
19 Aug 44 unescorted	*Wayfarer* *U-862*	British	steam merchant	5,068	14°30'S, 42°20'E
20 Aug 44 Convoy DN-68	*Berwickshire* *U-861*	British	steam merchant	7,464	30°58'S, 38°50'E -
20 Aug 44 Convoy DN-68	*Daronia* (D) *U-861*	British	motor tanker	8,139 tons	31°10'S, 38°00'E
5 Sep 44 unescorted	*Ioannis Fafalios* *U-861*	Greek	steam merchant	5,670 tons	4°20'S, 43°57'E
23 Feb 45 unescorted	*Point Pleasant Park* *U-510*	Canadian	steam merchant	7,136	29°42'S, 9°58'E

D: Damaged T: Total loss

Bibliography/Chapter Notes

Bruhn, David D. *Battle Stars for the "Cactus Navy": America's Fishing Vessels and Yachts in World War II.* Berwyn Heights, MD: Heritage Books, 2014.

—*Wooden Ships and Iron Men: The U.S. Navy's Coastal and Motor Minesweepers, 1941-1953.* Westminster, MD: Heritage Books, 2009.

Chatterton, Edward Keble. *Q-Ships and Their Story.* London: Sidgwick and Jackson, Ltd, 1922.

Doenitz, Karl. *The Conduct of War at Sea.* Washington, DC: Division of Naval Intelligence, Office of the Chief of Naval Operations, 1946.

Du Toit, Allan. *South Africa's Fighting Ships Past and Present.* Garden City, NY: Ashanti, 1992.

Emery, K. O. *Atlantic Continental Shelf and Slope of The United States Geologic Background.* Washington, DC: Government Printing Office, 1966.

Farb, Nathan. *The Adirondacks.* New York, NY: Rizzoli International, 1985.

Goldman, Kenneth Howard. *American Yachts in Naval Service: A History from the Colonial Era to World War II.* Jefferson, NC: McFarland & Company Inc., 2021.

Hickam Jr., Homer H. *Torpedo Junction: U-boat War Off America's East Coast, 1942.* Annapolis, MD: U.S. Naval Institute, 1989.

Holland, Brett Leo. *The Tidewater confronts the storm: antisubmarine warfare off the capes of Virginia during the first six months of 1942 (Master's Thesis).* Richmond, VA: University of Richmond, 1994.

Kleynhans, Evert. *The Axis and Allied Maritime Operations around Southern Africa, 1939-1945.* Stellenbosch University. Thesis for: PhD in Military Science, December 2018.

Lott, Arnold S. *Most Dangerous Sea.* Annapolis, MD: U.S. Naval Institute, 1959.

Lund, Paul, Harry Ludlam. *Trawlers Go to War.* Los Angeles, CA: New English Library, 1975.

Maton, Michael. *Honour The Navies – Honours & Awards to the British & Dominion Navies During WWII.* Honiton, UK: Token Publishing Ltd, 2007.

Morison, Samuel Eliot. *The Battle of the Atlantic 1939-1943.* Edison, NJ: Castle Books, 2001.

Naisawald, L. VanLoan. *In Some Foreign Field: Four British Graves and*

Submarine Warfare on the North Carolina Outer Banks. Raleigh, NC: University of North Carolina Press, 1997.
Office of the Chief of Naval Operations, *Post Mortems on Enemy Submarines Division of Naval Intelligence, Final Report of Interrogation of Survivors from U-352 Sunk by U.S.C.G. Icarus on May 9, 1942, in Approximate Position Latitude 34.12.05 N., Longitude 76.35 W.* Washington, D.C.: U.S. Government Printing Office. 1942.
Office of the Chief of Naval Operations, *Post Mortems on Enemy Submarines Division of Naval Intelligence, Report of Interrogation of Survivors of U-701 Sunk by U.S. Army Attack Bomber No. 9-29-322, Unit 296 B.S. on July 7, 1942* (Washington, D.C.: U.S. Government Printing Office, 1942).
Parker, Tim. *Signalman Jones: Based on the Recollections of Geoffrey Holder-Jones*. Woodbridge, UK: Seafarer Books, 2010.
Poland, Nicho. *The Torpedomen – HMS Vernon's Story 1872-1986*. Westbourne, UK: Kenneth Mason Publications Ltd, 1993.
Smith, Gordon, Don Kindell, Donald A. Bertke. *World War II Sea War, Vol 9: Wolfpacks Muzzled*. Dayton, OH: Bertke Publications, 2016.
Thwaites, Michael. *Atlantic Odyssey*. Oxford, U.K., 1999.
Toghill, Gerald. *Royal Trawlers: Part Two: Requisitioned Trawlers*. Cornwall, UK: Maritime Books Liskeard, 2004.

PREFACE NOTES:

[1] Samuel Eliot Morison, *The Battle of the Atlantic 1939-1943*, 198.
[2] Ibid, 114.
[3] Morison, *The Battle of the Atlantic 1939-1943*, 125-127; "Reinhard Hardegen" (https://uboat.net/men/hardegen.htm: accessed 5 June 2021).
[4] "Adolphus Andrews" (https://www.history.navy.mil/research/library/research-guides/modern-biographical-files-ndl/modern-bios-a/andrews-adolphus.html: accessed 5 June 2021).
[5] Morison, *The Battle of the Atlantic 1939-1943*, 200-201.
[6] "H-008-5: Admiral Ernest J. King—Chief of Naval Operations, 1942" (https://www.history.navy.mil/content/history/nhhc/about-us/leadership/director/directors-corner/h-grams/h-gram-008/h-008-5.html: accessed 5 June 2021).
[7] Ibid.
[8] Ibid.
[9] Morison, *The Battle of the Atlantic 1939-1943*, 130.
[10] Ibid, 131.

[11] "RNPS Association" (http://rnpsa.co.uk/cms/?History); "Sparrow's Nest, Lowestoft, UK" (https://productforums.google.com/forum/#!msg/gec-history-illustrated-moderated/mtvvUuqzAZs/O0Sjenfm_bEJ: accessed 10 April 2018).
[12] "The Royal Naval Patrol Service at War" (http://www.harry-tates.org.uk/history1.htm: accessed 8 July 2018).
[13] Ibid.
[14] "Invasion of Norway, Battles of Narvik, Blitzkrieg on Western Europe, Dunkirk Evacuation Starts" (http://www.naval-history.net/WW2RN04-194004.htm: accessed 10 April 2018).
[15] "RNPS Association" (http://rnpsa.co.uk/cms/?History: accessed 10 April 2018).
[16] Morison, *The Battle of the Atlantic 1939-1943*, 134.
[17] Ibid, 132.
[18] Ibid.
[19] Ibid, 133.
[20] Ibid.
[21] ComEastSeaFron War Diary, April 1942.
[22] Ibid.
[23] "USS *Roper* (DD-147/APD-20)" (http://www.navsource.org/archives/05/147.htm: accessed 7 June 2021).
[24] "German U-boat Casualties in World War Two" (https://www.history.navy.mil/research/library/online-reading-room/title-list-alphabetically/u/united-states-submarine-losses/german-U-boat-casualties-in-world-war-two.html); "*Unicoi*" (https://www.history.navy.mil/research/histories/ship-histories/danfs/u/unicoi.html): accessed 7 June 2021.
[25] Morison, *The Battle of the Atlantic 1939-1943*, 199.
[26] Ibid, 198.
[27] Morison, *The Battle of the Atlantic 1939-1943*, 136-137; Arnold Lott, *Most Dangerous Sea*, 48-49.
[28] Morison, *The Battle of the Atlantic 1939-1943*, 303.
[29] Ibid, 308-309.
[30] ComEastSeaFron War Diary, January 1943.
[31] Ibid.
[32] Ibid.
[33] Ibid.
[34] Morison, *The Battle of the Atlantic 1939-1943*, 257-258.
[35] Evert Kleynhans, *The Axis and Allied Maritime Operations around Southern Africa, 1939-1945*, Thesis for: PhD in Military Science (Military History), Stellenbosch University, December 2018, 65
[36] Ibid, 168-169.
[37] Ibid.
[38] "Michael Wilfred Tomkinson DSC, RN" (https://uboat.net/allies/commanders/2481.html: accessed 8 June 2021).

[39] "Obituaries"
http://www.trinity.unimelb.edu.au/publications/trinity_today/december2005/TTDec2005_pp_52-53.pdf); "Book Review" by Harold Adams (https://www.tandfonline.com/doi/abs/10.1080/07266472.1999.10878571?journalCode=ramo19: accessed 8 June 2021).
[40] Ut supra.

CHAPTER 1 NOTES:

[1] "Sam Nutt" (https://royalnavalpatrolservicehistory.net/2019/01/15/sam-nutt/: accessed 16 April 2021).
[2] L. VanLoan Naisawald, *In Some Foreign Field: Four British Graves and Submarine Warfare on the North Carolina Outer Banks* (Raleigh, NC: North Carolina Office of Archives & Hi-Story, 1997), 48.
[3] Karl Doenitz, *The Conduct of War at Sea* (Washington, DC: Division of Naval Intelligence, Office of the Chief of Naval Operations, 15 January 1946), 17.
[4] Ibid.
[5] Ibid.
[6] National Register of Historic Places Register Form (https://nmsmonitor.blob.core.windows.net/monitor-prod/media/archive/shipwrecks/bedfordshire_nrn.pdf: accessed 17 April 2021).
[7] Smith's Dock Co., Ltd., 1935.
[8] Ibid.
[9] Ibid.
[10] National Register of Historic Places Register Form; The Daily Mail, 9 August 1939.
[11] Gerald Toghill, *Royal Trawlers: Part Two: Requisitioned Trawlers* (Cornwall, UK: Maritime Books Liskeard, 2004), 39.
[12] Naisawald, *In Some Foreign Field: Four British Graves and Submarine Warfare on the North Carolina Outer Banks*, 20-22.
[13] Ibid.
[14] Toghill, *Royal Trawlers: Part Two: Requisitioned Trawlers*, 14-15.
[15] Ibid, 39.
[16] ComEastSeaFron War Diary, March 1942; Toghill, *Royal Trawlers: Part Two: Requisitioned Trawlers*, 39; Paul Lund and Harry Ludlam, *Trawlers Go to War* (Los Angeles, CA: New English Library, 1975), 155; Naisawald, *In Some Foreign Field: Four British Graves and Submarine Warfare on the North Carolina Outer Banks*, 27-30.
[17] Ut supra.
[18] Ut supra.
[19] Nathan Farb, *The Adirondacks* (New York, NY: Rizzoli International, 1985), 163-164; Homer H. Hickam Jr., *Torpedo Junction: U-boat War Off America's East Coast, 1942* (Annapolis, MD: Naval Institute, 1989), 204.
[20] Farb, *The Adirondacks*, 163-164; Hickam Jr., *Torpedo Junction: U-boat War Off America's East Coast, 1942*, 204.

[21] Hickam Jr., *Torpedo Junction: U-boat War Off America's East Coast, 1942*, 204-205.
[22] Naisawald, *In Some Foreign Field*, 52.
[23] ComEastSeaFron War Diary, May 1942; Naisawald, *In Some Foreign Field*, 52.
[24] Naisawald, *In Some Foreign Field*, 70.
[25] "The sinking of HMS *Bedfordshire*" (http://www.bbc.co.uk/threecounties/content/articles/2005/02/15/hms_bedfordshire_feature.shtml: accessed 16 April 2021).
[26] "HMS *Bedfordshire* (FY 141)" (https://uboat.net/allies/merchants/crews/ship1626.html: accessed 16 April 2021).
[27] National Register of Historic Places Register Form (https://nmsmonitor.blob.core.windows.net/monitor-prod/media/archive/shipwrecks/bedfordshire_nrn.pdf: accessed 17 April 2021).
[28] "Newfoundland Casualties of the Royal Navy WW II" (http://ngb.chebucto.org/NFREG/WWII/ww2-casualties-royal-nav.shtml: accessed 18 April 2021).

CHAPTER 2 NOTES:

[1] Commander, North Atlantic Naval Coastal Frontier War Diary, December 1941.
[2] Ibid.
[3] Ibid.
[4] Ibid.
[5] Ibid.
[6] *Dubuque*, *DANFS*.
[7] *Paducah*, *DANFS*.
[8] "Submarine Chasers" (https://www.history.navy.mil/content/history/museums/nmusn/explore/photography/wwi/wwi-submarine-chasers.html: accessed 21 April 2021).
[9] "Eagle-class Patrol Craft (PE)" (http://www.hazegray.org/danfs/patrol/eagles.htm: accessed 21 April 2021);
[10] Ibid.
[11] Ibid.
[12] Ibid.
[13] "USS *PE-56 (PE-56)*" (https://uboat.net/allies/warships/ship/8481.html: accessed 22 April 2021.
[14] Kenneth Howard Goldman, *American Yachts in Naval Service: A History from the Colonial Era to World War II* (Jefferson, NC: McFarland & Company Inc., 2021), 124; "*Sialia* (American Steam Yacht, 1914). Was USS *Sialia* (SP-543) in 1917-1920" (https://www.ibiblio.org/hyperwar/OnlineLibrary/photos/sh-civil/civsh-s/sialia.htm: accessed 22 April 2021).
[15] Ut supra.

[16] Up supra.
[17] David D. Bruhn, *Battle Stars for the "Cactus Navy": America's Fishing Vessels and Yachts in World War II* (Berwyn Heights, MD: Heritage Books, 2014), 39.
[18] Ibid, 40.
[19] Ibid.
[20] Commander, North Atlantic Naval Coastal Frontier War Diary, December 1941.
[21] Ibid.
[22] Ibid.
[23] Ibid.
[24] Ibid.
[25] Ibid.

CHAPTER 3 NOTES:

[1] Commander, North Atlantic Naval Coastal Frontier War Diary, January 1942.
[2] Ibid.
[3] "Operation Drumbeat" by Guomundur Helgason (https://uboat.net/ops/drumbeat.htm: accessed 22 April 2021).
[4] "Ships hit by U-boats in WWII" (https://uboat.net/allies/merchants/: accessed 23 April 2021).
[5] National Security Agency OP-20-G publication, "Battle of the Atlantic Volume IV Technical Intelligence from Allied Communications Intelligence." (https://www.history.navy.mil/content/history/nhhc/research/library/online-reading-room/title-list-alphabetically/b/battle-of-the-atlantic-volume-3-technical-intelligence-from-allied-communications-intelligence.html); "The Torpedoes" (https://uboat.net/technical/torpedoes.htm): both accessed 29 January 2021.
[6] Ut supra.
[7] "Type IX" (https://uboat.net/types/ix.htm: accessed 23 April 2021).
[8] "Germany Mines" (http://www.navweaps.com/Weapons/WAMGER_Mines.php); "Mines" (http://www.uboataces.com/weapon-mines.shtml): accessed 24 April 2021.
[9] "Deck Guns" (http://www.uboataces.com/weapon-deck-gun.shtml: accessed 23 April 2021).
[10] Ibid.
[11] "The Anti-aircraft guns" (https://uboat.net/technical/flak.htm: accessed 24 April 2021).
[12] "U-boat types" (https://uboat.net/types/: accessed 24 April 2021).
[13] Bruhn, *Battle Stars for the "Cactus Navy": America's Fishing Vessels and Yachts in World War II*, 131-132.
[14] "U-boat types."
[15] K. O. Emery, *Atlantic Continental Shelf and Slope of The United States Geologic Background* (Washington, DC: Government Printing Office, 1966), A4 (https://pubs.usgs.gov/pp/0529a/report.pdf: accessed 25 April 2021).

[16] David D. Bruhn, *Wooden Ships and Iron Men: The U.S. Navy's Coastal and Motor Minesweepers, 1941-1953* (Westminster, MD: Heritage Books, 2009), 30-31; Morison, *The Battle of the Atlantic 1939-1943*, 129.
[17] Bruhn, *Wooden Ships and Iron Men: The U.S. Navy's Coastal and Motor Minesweepers, 1941-1953*, 30-31.
[18] Commander, North Atlantic Naval Coastal Frontier War Diary, January 1942.
[19] Ibid.
[20] Ibid.
[21] Commander, North Atlantic Naval Coastal Frontier War Diary, January 1942; Morrison, *The Battle of the Atlantic 1939-1943*, 144.
[22] Commander, North Atlantic Naval Coastal Frontier War Diary, January 1942.
[23] Bruhn, *Wooden Ships and Iron Men: The U.S. Navy's Coastal and Motor Minesweepers, 1941-1953*, 27-28.
[24] Ibid.
[25] Ibid, 29.
[26] Commander, North Atlantic Naval Coastal Frontier War Diary, January 1942.
[27] "M/T *Norness*" (http://warsailors.com/singleships/norness.html: accessed 26 April 2021).
[28] Ibid.
[29] Ibid.
[30] Ibid.
[31] "M/T *Norness*"; Commanding Officer, USS *Ellyson*, Ship's History – Forwarding of, 16 December 1945.
[32] Commander, North Atlantic Naval Coastal Frontier War Diary, January 1942.
[33] Commander, North Atlantic Naval Coastal Frontier War Diary, January 1942; "Ships hit by U-boats in WWII" (https://uboat.net/allies/merchants/: accessed 26 April 2021).
[34] Ut supra.
[35] Commander, North Atlantic Naval Coastal Frontier War Diary, January 1942.
[36] Commander, North Atlantic Naval Coastal Frontier War Diary, January 1942; "*Malay*" (https://uboat.net/allies/merchants/ship/1271.html: accessed 26 April 2021).
[37] "*Malay*"
[38] "*Malay*"; Admiralty War Diary, 19 January 1942.
[39] "*Malay*"; Commander, North Atlantic Naval Coastal Frontier War Diary, January 1942.
[40] "Merchant Marine Heroes: Citations for Distinguished Service Medal
Awarded for 'Heroism Beyond the Call of Duty' during World War II" (http://www.usmm.org/heroes.html: accessed 26 April 2021).

CHAPTER 4 NOTES:

[1] ComEastSeaFron War Diary, February 1942
[2] Ibid.
[3] Doenitz, *The Conduct of War at Sea*, 17.
[4] "Ships hit by U-boats in WWII" (https://uboat.net/allies/merchants/: accessed 30 April 2021).
[5] "Type VIIC" (https://uboat.net/types/viic.htm: accessed 1 May 2021).
[6] Ibid.
[7] Ibid.
[8] ComEastSeaFron War Diary, February 1942; "The Milch Cows" (https://uboat.net/types/milkcows.htm: accessed 30 April 2021).
[9] "The Milch Cows."
[10] "*U-459*" (https://uboat.net/boats/u459.htm: accessed 30 April 2021).
[11] "Milk Cows" (http://rmhh.co.uk/files/Slaughter%20of%20the%20Milk%20Cows.pdf: accessed 30 April 2021).
[12] Ibid.
[13] Ibid.
[14] Ibid.
[15] Ibid.
[16] ComEastSeaFron War Diary, February 1942.
[17] Ibid.
[18] Ibid.
[19] Ibid.
[20] Ibid.
[21] Ibid.
[22] Ibid.
[23] Ibid.
[24] Ibid.
[25] Ibid.
[26] Ibid.
[27] Ibid.
[28] Ibid.
[29] Ibid.
[30] Ibid.
[31] Ibid.
[32] Ibid.
[33] Ibid.
[34] Ibid.
[35] Ibid.
[36] Ibid.
[37] Ibid.
[38] ComEastSeaFron War Diary, "*R.P. Resor*" (https://uboat.net/allies/merchants/ship/1384.html: accessed 2 May 2021).
[39] ComEastSeaFron War Diary, February 1942.
[40] Ibid.

[41] Ibid.
[42] Ibid.
[43] Ibid.
[44] Ibid.
[45] "Casualties: U.S. Navy and Coast Guard Vessels Sunk or Damaged Beyond Repair during World War II, 7 December 1941-1 October 1945" (https://www.history.navy.mil/research/histories/ship-histories/casualties-navy-and-coast-guard-ships.html); "Ships hit by U-boats in WWII" (https://uboat.net/allies/merchants/): accessed 2 May 2021.

CHAPTER 5 NOTES:

[1] Michael Thwaites, *Atlantic Odyssey* (Oxford, U.K., 1999).
[2] COM 6 War Diary, March 1942.
[3] "U.S. Naval Activities World War II by State" (https://www.ibiblio.org/hyperwar/USN/ref/USN-Act/NY.html: accessed 9 June 2021).
[4] Commandant, Third Naval District War Diary, March 1942.
[5] Thwaites, *Atlantic Odyssey*, 49.
[6] Thwaites, *Atlantic Odyssey*, 49-50.
[7] "Lake Class" (https://uboat.net/allies/warships/class/336.html: accessed 17 June 2021).
[8] ComEastSeaFron War Diary, March 1942.
[9] Ibid.
[10] Ibid.
[11] Ibid.
[12] Ibid.
[13] Ibid.
[14] Ibid.
[15] Ibid.
[16] Ibid.
[17] COM 5 Inshore Patrol War Diary, March 1942; Ambrose Section Inshore Patrol Section War Diary, 25-31 March 1942.
[18] Thwaites, *Atlantic Odyssey*, 87, 91.
[19] Ibid, 95-96.
[20] Ibid, 98.
[21] Ibid.
[22] Ibid.
[23] Ibid, 55-56.
[24] Michael Maton, *Honour The Navies – Honours & Awards to the British & Dominion Navies During WWII* (Honiton, UK: Token Publishing Ltd, 2007).
[25] Thwaites, *Atlantic Odyssey*, 56.
[26] Thwaites, *Atlantic Odyssey*, 56; "Charles Carlson's Final Voyage" (http://www.carlson.eclipse.co.uk/charles-voyage/charles-voyage.html: accessed 18 June 2021).
[27] "*Tritonia* LT188 G. Jones Telegraph Obituary" (https://www.shipsnostalgia.com/threads/tritonia-lt188-g-jones-telegraph-

obituary.41996/: accessed 18 June 2021); Nicho Poland, *The Torpedomen – HMS Vernon's Story 1872-1986* (Westbourne, UK: Kenneth Mason Publications Ltd, 1993), 154.
[28] Thwaites, *Atlantic Odyssey*, 56; "*Tritonia* LT188 G. Jones Telegraph Obituary."
[29] Thwaites, *Atlantic Odyssey*, 56; "*Tritonia* LT188 G. Jones Telegraph Obituary"; Maton, *Honour The Navies – Honours & Awards to the British & Dominion Navies During WWII.*
[30] April 1943 and October 1943 Navy Lists, and July 1945 Navy List.
[31] Tim Parker, *Signalman Jones: Based on the Recollections of Geoffrey Holder-Jones* (Woodbridge, UK: Seafarer Books, 2010).
[32] "March 1942" (https://uboat.net/allies/merchants/losses_year.html?qdate=1942-03: accessed 19 June 2021).

CHAPTER 6 NOTES:

[1] ComEastSeaFron War Diary, October 1943.
[2] Ibid.
[3] Ibid.
[4] ComEastSeaFron War Diary, October 1943; "USS *Atik* (AK 101)" (https://uboat.net/allies/merchants/ship/1476.html: accessed 5 June 2021).
[5] ComEastSeaFron War Diary, October 1943.
[6] Ibid.
[7] Ibid.
[8] Ibid.
[9] Ibid.
[10] Ibid.
[11] Ibid.
[12] ComEastSeaFron War Diary, October 1943; "*Captor* (PYc 40)" (http://www.navsource.org/archives/12/1440.htm); "*Atik* (AK 101)" (http://www.navsource.org/archives/12/171608.htm): accessed 15 June 2021.
[13] ComEastSeaFron War Diary, October 1943.
[14] Ibid.
[15] Ibid.
[16] Ibid.
[17] "*Atik* (AK-101) 1942" (https://www.history.navy.mil/research/histories/ship-histories/danfs/a/atik.html: accessed 16 June 2021).
[18] Ibid.
[19] Ibid.
[20] Ibid.
[21] ComEastSeaFron War Diary, October 1943.
[22] Ibid.
[23] ComEastSeaFron War Diary, October 1943; "USS *Big Horn* (IX-207)" (http://www.navsource.org/archives/09/19/19045.htm); "USS *Irene Forsyte*

(IX-93)" (http://www.navsource.org/archives/09/46/46093.htm): assessed 17 June 2021.

CHAPTER 7 NOTES:

[1] ComEastSeaFron War Diary, April 1942.
[2] Ibid.
[3] Ibid.
[4] Ibid.
[5] Ibid.
[6] Ibid.
[7] Ibid.
[8] Ibid.
[9] Ibid.
[10] Ibid.
[11] Ibid.
[12] Ibid.
[13] Ibid.
[14] Commandant, Sixth Naval District War Diary, April 1942; "William Machar" (https://www.findagrave.com/memorial/131939452/william-machar); "The *Hebe*" (http://maritimediver.blogspot.com/2011/05/hebe.html); "HMS *St. Cathan* (FY 234)" (https://uboat.net/allies/warships/ship/6461.html): accessed 1 July 2021.
[15] Commandant, Sixth Naval District War Diary, April 1942; "*William Machar*"; "The *Hebe*"; *Beryl*, *DANFS*.
[16] "Memorial" (http://www.rnpsa.co.uk/cms//memorial/memorial.htm: accessed 1 July 2021).
[17] "The *St Cathan* by Lawrie Burns" (https://www.youtube.com/watch?v=8NBdldr_RNg: accessed 29 June 2021).
[18] ComEastSeaFron War Diary, April 1942.
[19] ComEastSeaFron War Diary, April 1942; "History and Disposition of the *U-85*" by Joe Hoyt (https://nmssanctuaries.blob.core.windows.net/sanctuaries-prod/media/archive/missions/battleoftheatlantic/pdfs/u85_history.pdf: accessed 1 July 2021).
[20] Ibid.
[21] Ibid.
[22] Ibid.
[23] Ibid.
[24] Ibid.
[25] ComEastSeaFron War Diary, "History and Disposition of the *U-85*" by Joe Hoyt.
[26] Commander, Inshore Patrol Fifth Naval District War Diary, April 1942; "History and Disposition of the *U-85*" by Joe Hoyt.
[27] Commander, Inshore Patrol Fifth Naval District War Diary, April 1942.

[28] Ibid.
[29] "History and Disposition of the *U-85*" by Joe Hoyt.
[30] "April 1942"
(https://uboat.net/allies/merchants/losses_year.html?qdate=1942-04: accessed 3 July 2021).
[31] ComEastSeaFron War Diary, April 1942.

CHAPTER 8 NOTES:

[1] ComEastSeaFron War Diary, May 1942.
[2] Ibid.
[3] Ibid.
[4] "May 1942"
(https://uboat.net/allies/merchants/losses_year.html?qdate=1942-05: accessed 6 July 2021).
[5] Ibid.
[6] ComEastSeaFron War Diary, May 1942.
[7] Ibid.
[8] Ibid.
[9] Ibid.
[10] Ibid.
[11] ComEastSeaFron War Diary, May 1942; Morison, *The Battle of the Atlantic 1939-1943*, 205, 218.
[12] ComEastSeaFron War Diary, May 1942.
[13] Ibid.
[14] ComEastSeaFron War Diary, May 1942; USS *Broome* War Diary, May 1942.
[15] ComEastSeaFron War Diary, May 1942.
[16] ComEastSeaFron War Diary, May 1942; Commandant, Sixth Naval District War Diary, May 1942.
[17] USS *Broome* War Diary, May 1942.
[18] Ibid.
[19] ComEastSeaFron War Diary, May 1942.
[20] Ibid.
[21] Ibid.
[22] Ibid.
[23] Ibid.
[24] Ibid.
[25] U.S. Government Printing Office, *Post Mortems on Enemy Submarines Division of Naval Intelligence, Final Report of Interrogation of Survivors from U-352 Sunk by U.S.C.G. Icarus on May 9, 1942, in Approximate Position Latitude 34.12.05 N., Longitude 76.35 W.* (Washington, D.C.: Office of the Chief of Naval Operations, 1942).
[26] ComEastSeaFron War Diary, May 1942.
[27] Ibid.
[28] ComEastSeaFron War Diary, May 1942; "*U-352*"
(https://uboat.net/boats/u352.htm: accessed 8 July 2021).

[29] *Post Mortems on Enemy Submarines Division of Naval Intelligence, Final Report of Interrogation of Survivors from U-352 Sunk by U.S.C.G. Icarus on May 9, 1942.*
[30] ComEastSeaFron War Diary, May 1942.
[31] "Maurice David Jester" (http://arlingtoncemetery.net/mdjester.htm); "The Surfman Register" (https://uscg44363.files.wordpress.com/2019/03/2019mar-surfman-register.pdf): accessed 8 July 2021.
[32] ComEastSeaFron War Diary, May 1942.
[33] Ibid.
[34] Ibid.
[35] Ibid.
[36] *Post Mortems on Enemy Submarines Division of Naval Intelligence, Final Report of Interrogation of Survivors from U-352 Sunk by U.S.C.G. Icarus on May 9, 1942.*
[37] Ibid.
[38] *Post Mortems on Enemy Submarines Division of Naval Intelligence, Final Report of Interrogation of Survivors from U-352 Sunk by U.S.C.G. Icarus on May 9, 1942*; ComEastSeaFron War Diary, May 1942.
[39] *Post Mortems on Enemy Submarines Division of Naval Intelligence, Final Report of Interrogation of Survivors from U-352 Sunk by U.S.C.G. Icarus on May 9, 1942.*
[40] Ibid.
[41] Ibid.
[42] Ibid.
[43] Bureau of Naval Personnel Information Bulletin No. 304 (July 1942); "Maurice David Jester" (https://valor.militarytimes.com/hero/5625: accessed 8 July 2021).
[44] "Maurice David Jester" (https://www.findagrave.com/memorial/36611447/maurice-david-jester: accessed 9 July 2021).
[45] Bruhn, *Battle Stars for the "Cactus Navy": America's Fishing Vessels and Yachts in World War II*, 156
[46] Ibid.
[47] Ibid.
[48] Ibid.
[49] Ibid, 157.
[50] Ibid.
[51] Ibid.
[52] Ibid, 157-158.
[53] Ibid, 158.
[54] Ibid.
[55] Ibid.
[56] Commandant, Sixth Naval District War Diary, May 1942.
[57] Commandant, Sixth Naval District, Commander, Inshore Patrol, Fifth Naval District War Diary, May 1942.
[58] USS *Semmes* War History.
[59] *Semmes*, DANFS.
[60] USS *Semmes* War History.

[61] ComEastSeaFron War Diary, May 1942.
[62] Ibid.

CHAPTER 9 NOTES

[1] ComEastSeaFron War Diary, June 1942.
[2] Ibid.
[3] Virginia Beach Lifesaving Museum (https://scholarship.richmond.edu/cgi/viewcontent.cgi?article=2182&context=masters-theses: accessed 9 July 2021).
[4] ComEastSeaFron War Diary, USS *Decatur* War Diary, June 1942; *Saturn II* (AK-49), *DANFS*.
[5] USS *Decatur* War Diary, June 1942.
[6] ComEastSeaFron War Diary, June 1942.
[7] Ibid.
[8] Ibid.
[9] ComEastSeaFron, USS *Decatur* War Diary, June 1942.
[10] ComEastSeaFron War Diary, June 1942.
[11] ComEastSeaFron War Diary, June 1942; "*Esso Augusta*" (https://uboat.net/allies/merchants/ship/1814.html: accessed 10 July 2021).
[12] USS *Decatur* War Diary, June 1942.
[13] USS *Bainbridge* War Diary, June 1942.
[14] ComEastSeaFron, USS *Decatur*, and Commandant, Fifth Naval District War Diaries, June 1942.
[15] Virginia Beach Lifesaving Museum; "Casualty Lists of the Royal Navy and Dominion Navies, World War 2" (https://www.naval-history.net/xDKCas1942-06JUN.htm: accessed 11 July 2021).
[16] "*U-701*" (https://uboat.net/boats/u701.htm: accessed 11 July 2021).
[17] Brett Leo Holland, *The Tidewater confronts the storm: antisubmarine warfare off the capes of Virginia during the first six months of 1942 (Master's Thesis)* (Richmond, VA: University of Richmond, 1994); Lott, *Most Dangerous Sea*, 41.
[18] Lott, *Most Dangerous Sea*, 48-52.
[19] Office of the Chief of Naval Operations, *Post Mortems on Enemy Submarines Division of Naval Intelligence, Report of Interrogation of Survivors of U-701 Sunk by U.S. Army Attack Bomber No. 9-29-322, Unit 296 B.S. on July 7, 1942* (Washington, D.C.: U.S. Government Printing Office, 1942).
[20] Ibid.
[21] Ibid.
[22] Holland, *The Tidewater confronts the storm: antisubmarine warfare off the capes of Virginia during the first six months of 1942 (Master's Thesis)*; Office of the Chief of Naval Operations, *Post Mortems on Enemy Submarines Division of Naval Intelligence, Report of Interrogation of Survivors of U-701 Sunk by U.S. Army Attack Bomber No. 9-29-322, Unit 296 B.S. on July 7, 1942.*
[23] Office of the Chief of Naval Operations, *Post Mortems on Enemy Submarines Division of Naval Intelligence, Report of Interrogation of Survivors of U-701 Sunk by U.S. Army Attack Bomber No. 9-29-322, Unit 296 B.S. on July 7, 1942.*

[24] Holland, *The Tidewater confronts the storm: antisubmarine warfare off the capes of Virginia during the first six months of 1942 (Master's Thesis).*
[25] Ibid.
[26] Ibid.
[27] Ibid.
[28] Ibid.
[29] Ibid.
[30] Bruhn, *Battle Stars for the "Cactus Navy": America's Fishing Vessels and Yachts in World War II*, 145-146.
[31] Ibid, 146.
[32] Ibid, 146-147.
[33] Ibid, 147-148.
[34] Ibid, 148.
[35] Ibid.
[36] Ibid.
[37] Ibid, 148-149.
[38] Ibid, 149.
[39] Ibid.
[40] Ibid, 149-150.
[41] Ibid, 150.
[42] Ibid.
[43] Ibid.
[44] Ibid, 151
[45] Ibid.
[46] Ibid.
[47] Ibid.
[48] Ibid, 151-152.
[49] Ibid, 152.
[50] Ibid, 303; "*USS YP-389*" (https://uboat.net/allies/merchants/crews/ship1832.html: accessed 12 July 2021).
[51] Bruhn, *Battle Stars for the "Cactus Navy": America's Fishing Vessels and Yachts in World War II*, 303.
[52] Ibid, 152.
[53] Ibid.
[54] "June 1942" (https://uboat.net/allies/merchants/losses_year.html?qdate=1942-06: accessed 12 July 2021).
[55] ComEastSeaFron War Diary, June 1942.
[56] Ibid.

CHAPTER 10 NOTES:

[1] "July 1942" (https://uboat.net/allies/merchants/losses_year.html?qdate=1942-07: accessed 12 July 2021.
[2] ComEastSeaFron War Diary, July 1942.

[3] "U-boat Losses during 1942" (https://uboat.net/fates/losses/1942.htm: accessed 10 May 2021).
[4] ComEastSeaFron War Diary, July 1942; "*Alexander Macomb*" (https://uboat.net/allies/merchants/ship/1883.html); "Convoy BX.27" (http://convoyweb.org.uk/ports/convoy2.php?suffix=BX.27&prefix=BX): accessed 10 May 2021.
[5] ComEastSeaFron War Diary, July 1942; "*Alexander Macomb*."
[6] ComEastSeaFron War Diary, July 1942.
[7] Ibid.
[8] "*Alexander Macomb*."
[9] "*U-215*" (https://uboat.net/boats/u215.htm: accessed 10 May 2021).
[10] "First-ever U-boat found off Canadian coast" (https://www.cbc.ca/news/canada/first-ever-U-boat-found-off-canadian-coast-1.478017: accessed 10 May 2021).
[11] "Type VII U-boat" (http://www.uboataces.com/uboat-type-vii.shtml: accessed 29 April 2021).
[12] "Type VII U-boat"; "Germany Mines" (http://www.navweaps.com/Weapons/WAMGER_Mines.php: accessed 14 May 2021).
[13] "Type VII U-boat."
[14] Navy Lists of December 1942 and October 1943; "Allied Warship Commanders" (https://uboat.net/allies/commanders/: accessed 14 May 2021).
[15] Ut supra.

CHAPTER 11 NOTES:

[1] "Adolphus Andrews 7 October 1879 - 19 June 1948" (https://www.history.navy.mil/research/library/research-guides/modern-biographical-files-ndl/modern-bios-a/andrews-adolphus.html: accessed 13 July 2021).
[2] Ibid.
[3] Ibid.
[4] Ibid.
[5] ComEastSeaFron War Diary, July 1942.
[6] Ibid.

CHAPTER 12 NOTES:

[1] "The Royal Canadian Navy and the Battle of the Atlantic, 1939-1945" by Roger Sarty (https://www.warmuseum.ca/learn/dispatches/the-royal-canadian-navy-and-the-battle-of-the-atlantic-1939-1945/#tabs: accessed 3 May 2021).
[2] ComEastSeaFron War Diary, January 1943.
[3] Ibid.
[4] George Duddy correspondence of 9 May 2021.
[5] ComEastSeaFron War Diary, January 1943.
[6] Morison, *The Battle of the Atlantic 1939-1943*, 348

[7] "Chapter IV Coastal Convoys: Atlantic Seaboard, Gulf, Caribbean and Brazil" (https://www.ibiblio.org/hyperwar/USN/Admin-Hist/011-Convoy/011-Convoy-4.html: accessed 3 May 2021).
[8] Summary of Principal Convoys arriving in Calendar Year 1942" (https://www.ibiblio.org/hyperwar/USN/Admin-Hist/011-Convoy/011-Convoy-F.html: accessed 2 May 2021).
[9] Morison, *The Battle of the Atlantic 1939-1943*, 347-348.
[10] "The Storming of *U-94* – How Two Allied Sailors Took on the Crew of a U-boat in the Caribbean" (https://militaryhistorynow.com/2020/10/14/the-storming-of-u-94-how-two-allied-sailors-took-on-the-crew-of-a-U-boat-in-the-caribbean/: accessed 3 May 2021).
[11] USS *Lea* War Diary, February 1942.
[12] USS *Lea* War Diary, February 1942; "The Storming of *U-94* – How Two Allied Sailors Took on the Crew of a U-boat in the Caribbean."
[13] USS *Lea* War Diary, February 1942.
[14] Ibid.
[15] "The Storming of *U-94* – How Two Allied Sailors Took on the Crew of a U-boat in the Caribbean."
[16] Post Mortems on Enemy Submarines Serial No. 5: *U-94* sunk by USN PBY Plane and HMCS *Oakville* 8-27-42 (https://www.history.navy.mil/content/history/nhhc/research/library/online-reading-room/title-list-alphabetically/u/u94-sunk-usn-pby-plane-hmcs-oakville-8-27-42.html: accessed 3 May 2021).
[17] Ibid.
[18] Ibid.
[19] Ibid.
[20] Post Mortems on Enemy Submarines Serial No. 5: *U-94* sunk by USN PBY Plane and HMCS *Oakville* 8-27-42; Patrol Squadron VP-92 War History.
[21] Post Mortems on Enemy Submarines Serial No. 5: *U-94* sunk by USN PBY Plane and HMCS *Oakville* 8-27-42.
[22] USS *Lea* War Diary, August 1942.
[23] Post Mortems on Enemy Submarines Serial No. 5: *U-94* sunk by USN PBY Plane and HMCS *Oakville* 8-27-42.
[24] Ibid.
[25] Ibid.
[26] USS *Lea* War Diary, August 1942.
[27] Ibid.
[28] USS *Lea* War Diary, August 1942; "*Rotterdam*" (https://uboat.net/allies/merchants/ship/2096.html: accessed 3 May 2021).
[29] "*Rotterdam*."
[30] Post Mortems on Enemy Submarines Serial No. 5: *U-94* sunk by USN PBY Plane and HMCS *Oakville* 8-27-42.
[31] Ibid.
[32] Ibid.
[33] Ibid.

[34] Post Mortems on Enemy Submarines Serial No. 5: *U-94* sunk by USN PBY Plane and HMCS *Oakville* 8-27-42.
[35] "Clarence Aubrey King, D.S.O., D.S.C. & Bar, M.I.D." (http://www.forposterityssake.ca/CTB-BIO/MEM002679); "Clarence Aubrey King 1886-1964" (http://www.canadaveteranshallofvalour.com/KingCA.htm): accessed 4 May 2021).
[36] Ut supra.
[37] "Clarence Aubrey King, D.S.O., D.S.C. & Bar, M.I.D"; "*Merope* in action with a U Boat (*Merope/Merops*, Q-ship)" (https://collections.rmg.co.uk/collections/objects/125302.html: accessed 4 May 2021).
[38] Edward Keble Chatterton, *Q-Ships and Their Story* (London: Sidgwick and Jackson, Ltd, 1922), 77, 190.
[39] "Clarence Aubrey King, D.S.O., D.S.C. & Bar, M.I.D"; "King, Clarence Aubrey" (https://www.blatherwick.net/documents/Royal%20Canadian%20Navy%20Citations/K%20-%20RCN%20-%20WW2.pdf: 3 May 2021); "Clarence Aubrey King 1886-1964."
[40] "Clarence Aubrey King 1886-1964."
[41] "Clarence Aubrey King, D.S.O., D.S.C. & Bar, M.I.D"; "Clarence Aubrey King 1886-1964."
[42] Ibid.
[43] "King, Clarence Aubrey."
[44] "*U-845*" (https://uboat.net/boats/u845.htm: accessed 4 May 2021).
[45] "*U-448*" (https://uboat.net/boats/u448.htm); "*U-247*" (https://uboat.net/boats/u247.htm): accessed 4 May 2021.
[46] "Clarence Aubrey King, D.S.O., D.S.C. & Bar, M.I.D."
[47] "Clarence Aubrey King 1886-1964."

CHAPTER 13 NOTES:

[1] "Good Hunting: German Submarine Offensives and South African Countermeasures off the South African Coast during the Second World War, 1942-1945" by Evert Kleynhans, *Scientia Militaria* vol 44, no 1, 2016, 168-189.
[2] Ibid.
[3] "*U-110*" (https://uboat.net/boats/u110.htm); "*U-571*, World War II German Submarine" (https://www.history.navy.mil/content/history/nhhc/research/library/online-reading-room/title-list-alphabetically/u/u571-wwii-german-submarine.html): accessed 13 May 2021).
[4] "Good Hunting: German Submarine Offensives and South African Countermeasures off the South African Coast during the Second World War, 1942-1945" by Evert Kleynhans.
[5] H.R. Gordon-Cumming, *Official History of the South African Naval Forces during the Second World War (1939-1945)* (Simon's Town: The Naval Heritage Trust, 2008), 77.

[6] Gordon-Cumming, *Official History of the South African Naval Forces during the Second World War (1939-1945)*, 75-76.
[7] "Arnold Hague Convoy Database" (http://www.convoyweb.org.uk/hague/index.html: accessed 13 May 2021).
[8] "Ships hit by U-boats in WWII" (https://uboat.net/allies/merchants/: accessed 13 May 2021).
[9] "Good Hunting: German Submarine Offensives and South African Countermeasures off the South African Coast during the Second World War, 1942-1945" by Evert Kleynhans.
[10] Ibid.
[11] "All U-boats of WWII" (https://uboat.net/boats/listing.html: accessed 13 May 2021).
[12] "*Laconia*" (https://uboat.net/allies/merchants/ship/2157.html: accessed 14 May 2021).
[13] Ibid.
[14] Ibid
[15] Ibid.
[16] Ibid.
[17] "Good Hunting: German Submarine Offensives and South African Countermeasures off the South African Coast during the Second World War, 1942-1945" by Evert Kleynhans.
[18] Gordon-Cumming, *Official History of the South African Naval Forces during the Second World War (1939-1945)*, 79.
[19] Ibid, 79-80.
[20] Gordon-Cumming, *Official History of the South African Naval Forces during the Second World War (1939-1945)*, 79.
[21] Kleynhans, *The Axis and Allied Maritime Operations around Southern Africa, 1939-1945*, 65.
[22] Ibid, 65-66.
[23] Gordon-Cumming, *Official History of the South African Naval Forces during the Second World War (1939-1945)*, 76-77.
[24] Ibid.
[25] Ibid.
[26] Ibid.
[27] Kleynhans, *The Axis and Allied Maritime Operations around Southern Africa, 1939-1945*, 39.
[28] Gordon-Cumming, *Official History of the South African Naval Forces during the Second World War (1939-1945)*, 79.
[29] Ibid.
[30] Ibid, 66-67.
[31] Ibid, 111-112.
[32] "*U-179*" (https://uboat.net/boats/u179.htm: accessed 17 May 2021).
[33] Ibid.
[34] Kleynhans, *The Axis and Allied Maritime Operations around Southern Africa, 1939-1945*, 111-112.

[35] "All U-boats of WWII" (https://uboat.net/boats/listing.html: accessed 17 May 2021).
[36] "Regia Marina Italiana Boats" by Attilio Duilio Ranieri (http://www.regiamarina.net/detail_text_with_list.asp?nid=84&lid=1&cid=12: accessed 17 May 2021).
[37] Ibid.
[38] "Regia Marina Italiana Boats" by Attilio Duilio Ranieri; Kleynhans, *The Axis and Allied Maritime Operations around Southern Africa, 1939-1945*, 111-112.
[39] "Sarthe" (https://uboat.net/allies/merchants/ship/2245.html: accessed 11 May 2021).
[40] Ibid.
[41] Allan du Toit, *South Africa's Fighting Ships Past and Present* (Garden City, NY: Ashanti, 1992), 122-123.
[42] Ibid.
[43] Ibid.
[44] L. C. F. Turner, H. R. Gordon-Cumming, and J. E. Betzler, *War in the Southern Oceans* (Cape Town: Oxford University Press, 1961), 204; Gordon-Cumming, *Official History of the South African Naval Forces during the Second World War (1939-1945)*, 85.
[45] Turner, Gordon-Cumming, and Betzler, *War in the Southern Oceans*, 204.
[46] Turner, Gordon-Cumming, and Betzler, *War in the Southern Oceans*, 204-205.
[47] Turner, Gordon-Cumming, and Betzler, *War in the Southern Oceans*, 204-205; Gordon-Cumming, *Official History of the South African Naval Forces during the Second World War (1939-1945)*, 85.
[48] Gordon-Cumming, *Official History of the South African Naval Forces during the Second World War (1939-1945)*, 85.
[49] Gordon-Cumming, *Official History of the South African Naval Forces during the Second World War (1939-1945)*, 85.

CHAPTER 14 NOTES:

[1] "Trawlers go to War" (http://www.harry-tates.org.uk/tgtw.html: accessed 10 May 2021).
[2] Commandant, Fifth Naval District War Diary, October 1942.
[3] West Africa Command, Freetown War Diary, April to December 1942 (https://www.naval-history.net/xDKWD-WAfrica1942.htm: accessed 6 May 2021).
[4] "Takoradi" (https://www.navalhistoryarchive.org/index.php/Takoradi#:~:text=Takoradi%20was%20a%20naval%20base,Navy%20administered%20its%20worldwide%20responsibilities: accessed 7 May 2021).
[5] West Africa Command, Freetown War Diary, April to December 1942
[6] Ibid.
[7] Ibid.

[8] "South Atlantic Station" (https://www.navalhistoryarchive.org/index.php/South_Atlantic_Station: accessed 7 May 2021).
[9] Du Toit dissertation, 62.
[10] "South Atlantic Station."
[11] Ibid.
[12] "West Africa Station" (https://www.navalhistoryarchive.org/index.php/West_Africa_Station); "Organisation of the Royal Navy 1939-1945" by Graham Watson (https://www.naval-history.net/xGW-RNOrganisation1939-45.htm): accessed 7 May 2021.
[13] Du Toit dissertation, 73-74; "The Axis and Allied Maritime Operations around Southern Africa 1939 1945 – War on Southern Africa Sea" (http://www.sixtant.net/2011/artigos.php?cat=the-axis-and-allied-maritime-operations-around-southern-africa-1939-1945&sub=war-on-southern-africa-sea&tag=19)saaf-coastal-defence-sys: accessed 23 May 2021).
[14] "The Axis and Allied Maritime Operations around Southern Africa 1939 1945 – War on Southern Africa Sea."
[15] Ibid.
[16] Ibid.
[17] Du Toit dissertation, 76.
[18] Ibid, 71, 76.
[19] Ibid, 76.
[20] Turner, Gordon-Cumming, and Betzler, *War in the Southern Oceans*, 204.
[21] Gordon-Cumming, *Official History of the South African Naval Forces during the Second World War (1939-1945)*, 85.
[22] Ibid, 206.
[23] Ibid.
[24] "China's Next Move: A Naval Base in the South Atlantic?" by Robert C. O'Brien (https://www.realcleardefense.com/articles/2015/03/25/chinas_next_move_a_naval_base_in_the_south_atlantic_107803.html: accessed 8 May 2021).
[25] Gordon-Cumming, *Official History of the South African Naval Forces during the Second World War (1939-1945)*, 206.
[26] Ibid, 206-207.
[27] Turner, Gordon-Cumming, and Betzler, *War in the Southern Oceans*, 202; Gordon-Cumming, *Official History of the South African Naval Forces during the Second World War (1939-1945)*, 207.

CHAPTER 15 NOTES:

[1] Kleynhans, *The Axis and Allied Maritime Operations around Southern Africa, 1939-1945*, 114.
[2] Ibid.
[3] "The U-boat bases" (https://uboat.net/flotillas/bases/: accessed 24 May 2021).
[4] "Good Hunting: German Submarine Offensives and South African

Countermeasures off the South African Coast during the Second World War, 1942-1945" by Evert Kleynhans.
[5] Admiralty War Diaries of World War 2 West Africa Command, Freetown - April to December 1942 (https://www.naval-history.net/xDKWD-WAfrica1942.htm: accessed 6 May 2021); West Africa Command, Freetown - January to April 1943 (https://www.naval-history.net/xDKWD-WAfrica1943a.htm: accessed 7 May 2021).
[6] Admiralty War Diaries of World War 2 West Africa Command, Freetown - April to December 1942; West Africa Command, Freetown - January to April 1943.
[7] U.S. Naval Operating Base, Trinidad War Diary, February 1943.
[8] Commandant, U.S. Naval Operating Base, War Diary Trinidad Section Group 92.7 – February 1-28, 1943, 5 March 1943.
[9] West Africa Command, Freetown - January to April 1943; "Blue Star's S.S. Celtic Star 1" (https://www.bluestarline.org/celtic1.html): accessed 25 May 2021.
[10] West Africa Command, Freetown - January to April 1943; "Blue Star's S.S. Celtic Star 1"; "Regia Marina Italiana Boats" by Cristiano D'Adamo (http://www.regiamarina.net/detail_text_with_list.asp?nid=84&lid=1&cid=21: accessed 25 May 2021).
[11] West Africa Command, Freetown - January to April 1943.
[12] Kleynhans, *The Axis and Allied Maritime Operations around Southern Africa, 1939-1945*, 115.
[13] Turner, Gordon-Cumming, and Betzler, *War in the Southern Oceans*, 206.
[14] Turner, Gordon-Cumming, and Betzler, *War in the Southern Oceans*, 206; "*Queen Anne*" (https://uboat.net/allies/merchants/ship/2646.html: accessed 11 May 2021).
[15] Kleynhans, *The Axis and Allied Maritime Operations around Southern Africa, 1939-1945*, 115.
[16] "Ships hit by U-boats in WWII" (https://uboat.net/allies/merchants/: accessed 25 May 2021).
[17] "Convoy DN 21" (https://de.zxc.wiki/wiki/Geleitzug_DN_21: accessed 25 May 2021).
[18] Gordon Smith, Don Kindell, Donald A. Bertke, *World War II Sea War, Vol 9: Wolfpacks Muzzled* (Dayton, OH: Bertke Publications, 2016), 74-75; "Convoy DN.21" (http://www.convoyweb.org.uk/misc/index.html: accessed 25 May 2021).
[19] Turner, Gordon-Cumming, and Betzler, *War in the Southern Oceans*, 211.
[20] Turner, Gordon-Cumming, and Betzler, *War in the Southern Oceans*, 211; "*Harvey W. Scott*" (https://uboat.net/allies/merchants/ship/2709.html: accessed 24 May 2021).
[21] Turner, Gordon-Cumming, and Betzler, *War in the Southern Oceans*, 211.
[22] Turner, Gordon-Cumming, and Betzler, *War in the Southern Oceans*, 211; "*Empire Mahseer*" (https://uboat.net/allies/merchants/ship/2712.html: accessed 24 May 2021).
[23] Ibid.

[24] "*Sheaf Crown*" (https://uboat.net/allies/merchants/ship/2711.html: accessed 24 May 2021).
[25] Turner, Gordon-Cumming, and Betzler, *War in the Southern Oceans*, 212.
[26] Gordon-Cumming, *Official History of the South African Naval Forces during the Second World War (1939-1945)*, 82; "*Aloe*" (https://uboat.net/allies/merchants/ship/2846.html); "*U-182*" (https://uboat.net/boats/u182.htm): accessed 26 May 2021.
[27] "Trawlers go to War" (http://www.harry-tates.org.uk/tgtw.html: accessed 10 May 2021).
[28] Ibid.
[29] "Trawlers go to War"; *City of Baroda*" (https://uboat.net/allies/merchants/ship/2840.html: accessed 10 May 2021).
[30] Ut supra.
[31] "Trawlers go to War."
[32] Ibid.
[33] Ibid.
[34] "Georg Lassen" (https://uboat.net/men/lassen.htm: accessed 26 May 2021).

CHAPTER 16 NOTES:

[1] Doenitz, *The Conduct of the War at Sea*, 20.
[2] "Type IX U-boat" (http://www.uboataces.com/uboat-type-ix.shtml: accessed 28 May 2021).
[3] Kleynhans, *The Axis and Allied Maritime Operations around Southern Africa, 1939-1945*, 117.
[4] "H-033-1: Yanagi Missions and Submarine Atrocities" (https://www.history.navy.mil/content/history/nhhc/about-us/leadership/director/directors-corner/h-grams/h-gram-033/h-033-1.html: accessed 28 May 2021).
[5] Ibid.
[6] "H-033-1: Yanagi Missions and Submarine Atrocities"; Kleynhans, *The Axis and Allied Maritime Operations around Southern Africa, 1939-1945*, 17-118.
[7] "H-033-1: Yanagi Missions and Submarine Atrocities."
[8] Kleynhans, *The Axis and Allied Maritime Operations around Southern Africa, 1939-1945*, 116; "Leonardo da Vinci Submarine: Terror of the Atlantic" (https://comandosupremo.com/leonardo-da-vinci-submarine/: accessed 28 May 2021).
[9] "*Leonardo da Vinci* Submarine: Terror of the Atlantic"; "The *Leonardo da Vinci* wreaks havoc off South Africa's coastline" (https://samilhistory.com/tag/leonardo-da-vinci/: accessed 28 May 2021).
[10] "*Leonardo da Vinci* Submarine: Terror of the Atlantic."
[11] Ibid.
[12] Kleynhans, *The Axis and Allied Maritime Operations around Southern Africa, 1939-1945*, 116; "HMS *Active* (H 14)" (https://uboat.net/allies/warships/ship/4343.html: accessed 28 May 2021).

[13] "Allied Ships Attacked by the Italian Submarine *Leonardo da Vinci*" (https://merchantships2.tripod.com/charlie/veerhavendavinci.html); "Regia Marina Italiana Boats" by di Cristiano D'Adamo (http://www.regiamarina.net/detail_text_with_list.asp?nid=84&lid=1&cid=16): accessed 28 May 2021).
[14] "The *Leonardo da Vinci* wreaks havoc off South Africa's coastline"
[15] Ibid.
[16] "The *Leonardo da Vinci* wreaks havoc off South Africa's coastline"; "Regia Marina Italiana Boats" by di Cristiano D'Adamo; "*Lulworth Hill*" (http://www.sixtant.net/2011/artigos.php?cat=ships-hit-britain-237-*&sub=j-k-l&tag=16)lulworth-hill-(it-sub-da-vinci)-): accessed 28 May 2021.
[17] "The *Leonardo da Vinci* wreaks havoc off South Africa's coastline"; "Regia Marina Italiana Boats" by di Cristiano D'Adamo; "Allied Ships Attacked by the Italian Submarine Leonardo da Vinci."
[18] "Merchant Marine members found danger, but no glory" by Gary Warth, *The San Diego Union-Tribune*, 17 April 2005.
[19] Ibid.
[20] "Regia Marina Italiana Boats" by di Cristiano D'Adamo.
[21] Ibid.
[22] "The *Leonardo da Vinci* wreaks havoc off South Africa's coastline"; "Regia Marina Italiana Boats" by di Cristiano D'Adamo.
[23] Doenitz, *The Conduct of the War at Sea*, 19.
[24] "*Northmoor*" (https://uboat.net/allies/merchants/ship/2928.html: accessed 29 May 2021).
[25] "*William King*" (https://uboat.net/allies/merchants/ship/2947.html: accessed 29 May 2021).
[26] "William King"; "U-boat Commander Takes Master of SS *William King* as Prisoner of War" (http://www.usmm.org/wsa/williamking.html: accessed 3 June 2021).
[27] "*William King*."
[28] "Arnold Hague Convoy Database" (http://www.convoyweb.org.uk/hague/index.html: accessed 13 May 2021).
[29] "*Agwimonte*" (https://uboat.net/allies/merchants/ship/2938.html: 29 May 2021).
[30] "*Agwimonte*"; "*Storaas*" (https://uboat.net/allies/merchants/ship/2939.html: accessed 29 May 2021).
[31] "*Salabangka*" (https://uboat.net/allies/merchants/ship/2942.html: accessed 30 May 2021).
[32] Ibid.
[33] Gordon-Cumming, *Official History of the South African Naval Forces during the Second World War (1939-1945)*, 87.
[34] Ibid.
[35] "*U-177*" (https://uboat.net/boats/u177.htm: accessed 31 May 2021).
[36] "Report on the Interrogation of Survivors from *U-177* sunk 6 February 1944, Final Report - G/Serial 34" (http://www.uboatarchive.net/U-177A/U-177INT.htm: accessed 31 May 2021).

[37] Ibid.
[38] Ibid.
[39] Ibid.
[40] Ibid.
[41] "H-033-1: Yanagi Missions and Submarine Atrocities"; "*U-511*" (https://uboat.net/boats/u511.htm: accessed 31 May 2021).
[42] "Monsun boats, U-boats in the Indian Ocean and the Far East" by Marcin Jedrzejewski (https://uboat.net/ops/monsun.htm: accessed 31 May 2021).
[43] "The Voyage to the Far East" (http://dubm.de/en/the-voyage-to-the-far-east/: accessed 31 May 2021).
[44] "The Voyage to the Far East."
[45] Gordon-Cumming, *Official History of the South African Naval Forces during the Second World War (1939-1945)*, 88.
[46] Ibid.
[47] Ibid, 185.
[48] Ibid, 89.
[49] Ibid.
[50] Ibid.
[51] Ibid.
[52] Ibid, 88-89.
[53] Ibid, 89.
[54] Ibid, 90-91.
[55] Ibid, 90.
[56] Ibid.
[57] Ibid.
[58] Ibid, 91.
[59] Ibid.
[60] Ibid.
[61] Ibid, 92.
[62] Ibid.
[63] Ibid, 92-93.
[64] Ibid, 187.
[65] Ibid, 89.
[66] Ibid.
[67] Ibid.

POSTSCRIPT NOTES:

[1] Doenitz, *The Conduct of the War at Sea*, 23.
[2 "Forgotten history of Grimsby's heroic Second World War trawlermen unveiled in new documentary" (https://www.grimsbytelegraph.co.uk/news/grimsby-news/forgotten-history-grimsbys-heroic-second-1839508: accessed 2 June 2021).

APPENDIX A. NOTE:

[1] Eastern Sea Frontier War Diary, January 1943; "Allied Warships in World War Two" (https://uboat.net/allies/warships/: accessed 16 April 2021); National Register of Historic Places Register Form, Table 1 (https://nmsmonitor.blob.core.windows.net/monitor-prod/media/archive/shipwrecks/bedfordshire_nrn.pdf: accessed 17 April 2021).

APPENDIX E. NOTE:

[1] "Appendix I: Principal Civilian Officials And Naval Officers In Command 7 December 1941 -- 2 September 1945" (https://www.ibiblio.org/hyperwar/USN/USN-Chron/USN-Chron-I.html: accessed 13 July 1942).

Index

About the Author

Rob Hoole joined the Royal Navy as a 'seaman officer' (later termed 'warfare officer') in 1971. He qualified as a Ships' Diving Officer in 1975 and as a Minewarfare & Clearance Diving Officer in 1976. In 1991, he co-founded the Royal Naval Minewarfare & Clearance Diving Officers' Association (MCDOA) of which he is Vice Chairman. Rob acquired an MBA from Oxford Brooks University in 2000 and left the Royal Navy in late 2002 after serving 32 years in all manner of operational and training roles at sea and ashore including Command of diving teams and mine countermeasures vessels. Rob lives near Portsmouth in Hampshire with his wife Linda. They have three grown children and three grandchildren.

Aside from his family, his passions include country pubs & real ale, reading and maritime history, particularly the development of naval mine warfare, service diving, and explosive ordnance disposal (EOD) otherwise known as bomb & mine disposal. He has contributed to many books, journals and other publications covering different aspects of his favourite subjects and was the editor of the book *Last of the Wooden Walls – An Illustrated History of the TON Class Minesweepers & Minehunters*. Last but not least, he was a fierce champion of the Vernon Mine Warfare & Diving Monument, unveiled in March 2020 at Gunwharf Quays in Portsmouth, previously the site of his *alma mater*, HMS Vernon.

About the Author

Commander David D. Bruhn, U.S. Navy (Retired) served twenty-two years on active duty and two in the Naval Reserve, as both an enlisted man and as an officer, between 1977 and 2001.

Following completion of basic training, he served as a sonar technician aboard USS *Miller* (FF 1091) and USS *Leftwich* (DD 984). He was commissioned in 1983 following graduation from California State University at Chico. His initial assignment was to USS *Excel* (MSO 439), serving as supply officer, damage control assistant, and chief engineer. He then served in USS *Thach* (FFG 43) as chief engineer and Destroyer Squadron Thirteen as material officer.

After graduation from the Naval Postgraduate School, Commander Bruhn was assigned to Secretary of the Navy and Chief of Naval Operation staffs as a budget analyst and resources planner before attending the Naval War College in 1996, following which he commanded the mine countermeasures ships USS *Gladiator* (MCM 11) and USS *Dextrous* (MCM 13) in the Persian Gulf.

Commander Bruhn's final assignment was executive assistant to a senior (SES 4) government service executive at the Ballistic Missile Defense Organization in Washington, D.C.

Following military service, he was a high school teacher and track coach for ten years, and is now a USA Track & Field official. He lives in northern California with his wife Nancy and has two sons, David and Michael.

Milton Keynes UK
Ingram Content Group UK Ltd.
UKHW020741010424
440421UK00014B/931

9 780788 440809